Michael Mandle

TRANSACTIONS OF THE
ROYAL HISTORICAL SOCIETY

FIFTH SERIES

VOLUME 26

LONDON

OFFICES OF THE ROYAL HISTORICAL SOCIETY

UNIVERSITY COLLEGE LONDON, GOWER ST., WCIE 6BT

1976

ISBN 0 901050 28 8

Made and Printed in Great Britain by Butler & Tanner Ltd, Frome and London

CONTENTS

ILLUSTRATION

FRANCOIS CHABOT AND HIS PLOT

By Professor N. Hampson, M.A., D.del'Univ., F.R.Hist.S.

READ 7 FEBRUARY 1975

EARLY on the morning of 14 November 1793 the Montagnard deputy, Chabot, woke up Robespierre and denounced a plot to destroy the Convention by corrupting some of its members and slandering those who could not be bought. He produced as evidence 100,000 livres in assignats which he said had been given to him to buy the signature of Fabre d'Eglantine to a fraudulent decree concerning the liquidation of the East India Company.

If Chabot's story was true, several prominent Montagnards were associates of the Baron de Batz, an avowed royalist. Historians of the French Revolution have naturally been reluctant to believe anything so improbable but they have not been quite sure what to make of it. Mathiez, when he published his account of the East India Company scandal, concluded that Chabot had diverted the revolutionary government from a genuine financial scandal into a wild goose chase after a mythical plot.[1] Four years later, he changed his mind: 'l'affaire d'agiotage se doublait d'une intrigue royaliste.'[2] For the rest of his life he continued to refer to a *conspiration de l'étranger*—for behind the royalists loomed their paymaster, Pitt—for which Chabot provided almost all the evidence. More recently, M de Lestapis concluded that Mathiez had originally fallen into the trap set by the revolutionary government, intent on covering up a plot whose exposure would discredit the Montagnards and perhaps provoke a head-on collision with the Paris Commune.[3] His research has done something to restore the credibility of earlier historians whose accounts of a royalist plot had not been taken very seriously.[4] Even if Chabot's royalist plot *was* a deliberate fabrication,

[1] A. Mathiez, *Un procès de corruption sous la Terreur: l'affaire de la Compagnie des Indes* (Paris, 1920), p. 143.

[2] *La Révolution Française* (Paris, 1924), iii, p. 104.

[3] A. de Lestapis, *La 'conspiration de Batz'* (Paris, 1969), pp. 7–8.

[4] G. Lenotre, *Le baron de Batz* (Paris, 1896), de Bonald, *François Chabot* (Paris, 1908), and de Batz, *Les conspirations et la fin de Jean, baron de Batz* (Paris, 1911).

the question of how far he talked the revolutionary government into believing it deserves investigation in its own right.

It is difficult to think of a more unreliable witness than Chabot. Expelled from the Committee of General Security in September 1793, on suspicion of corruption, when the Girondin leaders were tried in the following month he had shown himself to be a virtuoso in the exposure of plots. When he went to see Robespierre he had just been fiercely denounced by Hébert and Dufourny, in the Jacobin Club and it may not have been pure republican *vertu* that led him to proclaim them royalist agents. Whatever he says requires corroboration, but it cannot be dismissed out of hand, especially if the government seems to have believed it.

The first obstacle to the investigation of Chabot's charges is the disappearance of much of the evidence, such as the account of his interrogation, which has not been seen since 1795.[5] The vicissitudes of revolutionary politics sooner or later gave the survivors a chance to get rid of what was better out of the way and the wonder is that one or two incriminating fragments have survived.[6] A second problem is to distinguish between genuine counter-revolutionary activity and the swaggering fantasies of violent men. Dupin, the secretary of the Paris Department, was present at a dinner party with Jourdan, Vincent and Brichet, in September 1793. 'Insensiblement les reproches contre la Convention nationale devinrent plus amers. On murmuroit de ce qu'elle n'organisoit point le Conseil Exécutif suivant la constitution. On dit qu'on savoit bien l'y contraindre avec l'armée révolutionnaire, qu'il falloit une nouvelle journée de 31 mai; qu'on couperoit le cou à tous les traîtres qui existoient parmi la Convention nationale; on ajouta qu'il n'y avoit que 12 ou 15 députés patriotes.'[7] At the time, Dupin disregarded this as drunken nonsense, but when Vincent found himself before the revolutionary tribunal, Dupin thought it wiser to retail it all to Fouquier-Tinville. Purging the Convention might suit both royalists and revolutionaries in a hurry. In such matters the historian's detachment is a luxury denied to revolutionary governments, which had to save the Republic rather than to write its history.

Robespierre left his own brief account of Chabot's visit.[8] He quoted Chabot as pretending to have participated in a financial

---

[5] A. Mathiez, *La conspiration de l'étranger* (Paris, 1918), pp. 57–58.

[6] *E.g.* a letter from Whitehall to the banker, Perregaux, purporting to give instructions for the payment of British agents who posed as extremists in the Jacobin Club. Archives Nationales, AF II 49, printed in Mathiez, *La conspiration de l'étranger*, pp. 131–32. This letter seems to have been part of a regular correspondence.   [7] Archives Nationale, AF II 49.

[8] *Pièces trouvées dans les papiers de Robespierre et complices* (Paris, an III), pp. 59–71.

intrigue in order to expose the men behind it; the latter 'croient que je ne devine pas le reste de leur projet; mais ils vont à la contre-révolution ouverte.' Robespierre advised Chabot to reveal all he knew to the Committee of General Security and, when Chabot seemed apprehensive about this, authorized him to tell the Committee of Public Safety as well. Chabot's own version is rather more informative.[9] He was reluctant to follow Robespierre's advice since the conspirators had told him that they had their agents in the Committee of General Security. Robespierre then advised him to tell his story to the members he trusted and promised him a safe-conduct from the Committee of Public Safety if that of General Security refused him one.[10] Robespierre also *dit de ménager les patriotes*, an expression that Chabot watered down to *m'a recommandé la prudence*. In a letter written to Robespierre from gaol on 15 December, Chabot repeated that it was 'd'après ton conseil que je crus devoir taire quelques faits dans ma déclaration.'[11] One of these 'facts' was that when the Baron de Batz had been denounced for offering bribes to secure the escape of Marie Antoinette, he had thrown the blame on to his accuser and had him arrested.[12] There is no means of knowing what else Robespierre wanted suppressed and one can only guess that the *patriotes* who were to be *ménagés* included Danton and Hébert.

Chabot went to the Committee of General Security, where he chose Jagot as his confident, explaining that he wished to avoid David and Lavicomterie—whom he suspected of links with Batz—and Panis, *par délicatesse*, since Panis was the personal enemy of the men he was accusing. Jagot promptly told all three of them. Chabot made no attempt to exclude anyone else though he was to claim later that he knew Amar had been associated with Delaunay in blackmailing the East India Company. Amar at once showed his hostility when Chabot maintained that Fabre d'Eglantine had been involved in financial speculations of his own.[13] Amar denied him his safe-conduct and, when giving him a written acknowledgment of his denunciation, refused to mention the political side of Chabot's plot.

[9] The fullest version is in *François Chabot à ses concitoyens*, Archives Nationales, F7 4637, fos. 50–51.
[10] This is presumably true, since Chabot maintained, in the *Testament* written before an unsuccessful attempt at suicide (Archives Nationales, W 342) that he had entrusted his memoir to Robespierre.
[11] *Pièces trouvées*, p. 33.
[12] There is no obvious reason why Robespierre should have wanted this information suppressed, but Fouquier-Tinville was equally concerned to leave this particular stone unturned (de Lestapis, *op. cit.* p. 246, n. 28).
[13] *François Chabot à ses concitoyens*. He repeated this in a letter to Robespierre (*Pièces trouvées*, p. 54).

Chabot then went home to write out his denunciation. Like most of his literary efforts, this is a rambling affair, combining specific charges and vague insinuations.[14] He began by saying that he had been surprised to find Batz at a dinner the previous August to which he had been invited by Delaunay and Julien de Toulouse. Soon afterwards, when he attacked corrupt financial interests, in the Convention, he was himself denounced by Hébert, of the Paris Commune, and Dufourny and Lulier of the Department. When Delaunay afterwards approached him with the suggestion that they should co-operate in holding bankers to ransom, 'Je compris qu'il se formoit une faction de corrupteurs et de corrompus. Je crus que l'intérêt de la République exigeoit que je parusse en être.' Delaunay then initiated him into a plan to make money out of the East India Company, telling him that his fellow-deputies, Cambon, Ramel, Danton, Delacroix and Fabre, were all speculating in different ways. 'Je soupçonnoi dès ce moment, plus fort que jamais, que le système étoit de corrompre les plus chauds patriotes, et de les calomnier, quand on ne pouvoit les corrompre.'

Chabot presented the expulsion of Basire, Julien and himself from the Committee of General Security, on 14 September, as a victory for the *diffamateurs*, whom he described elsewhere as *Jacobins révolutionnaires*. Delaunay and Benoît then told him that they had heard from their friend David that the Committee of General Security intended to denounce its three former members. Chabot, suitably frightened, decided to withdraw from the incriminating financial intrigue but recovered his nerve when the danger seemed to have blown over.

Delaunay then told him that Fabre had spoiled their game by an amendment to Delaunay's motion to wind up the East India Company on terms that favoured the company. Chabot was instructed to buy Fabre's complicity in the publication of an unauthorized decree along the lines of the original version. He said that he made no attempt to bribe Fabre and he seemed unaware that the decree had, in fact, been published in a form favourable to the Company. When Chabot raised difficulties about taking his share of the money, Benoît and Delaunay tried to frighten him by revealing their knowledge of a plot to induce the Convention to decimate itself by a succession of purges that would eventually include Chabot himself. This is the only incident for which he provided a date: 8 November. On the next day the Convention ordered the trial of a deputy, Osselin, without giving him a hearing in the House. This alarmed Chabot who persuaded his colleagues to vote on the 10th that all deputies should henceforth be allowed to defend

[14] Archives Nationales, W 342, printed in *Pièces trouvées*, pp. 3–16.

themselves in the Convention. He was violently attacked in the Jacobins, especially by Dufourny and, on the 12th, the Convention reversed its previous vote. Thoroughly alarmed, denied a hearing by the hostile Jacobins, suspicious of the integrity of the Committee of General Security and aware that his apparent participation in the 'plot' made him highly vulnerable, he went to Robespierre on the 14th.

Interwoven with this tale were vague references to the plot's *branche diffamatrice*, which involved David and Hébert's wife. A kind of coda included the charge that the 'ci-devant duchesse de Roche-chouard [sic] m'a dit qu'Hébert, son ami, avoit demandé à la commune la translation d'Antoinette, de la Conciergerie au Temple, par un intérêt qu'il lui portoit.' Chabot also claimed to know that Batz had been involved in a plan for the queen's escape and that Benoît and Delaunay had tried to save three of the Girondin leaders. He quoted Benoît as claiming that Danton, Panis, Robert and Delacroix had formerly worked with Batz and his friends but had now left them.

Chabot's disciple, Basire, followed him to the Committee with a denunciation of his own.[15] This was entirely concerned with financial speculation and made no mention of counter-revolutionary activities. Basire did, however, make it clear that he and Chabot knew they were going to meet Batz at the dinner-party in August. He added that the guests included the Marquise de Jeanson, who was suspected of having participated in the plans to rescue the queen.

Chabot elaborated on his original denunciation in the numerous letters that he wrote from gaol, to Robespierre, Danton and the Committee of Public Safety, of which three dozen have survived.[16] On various occasions he hinted that he knew a good deal more than he was prepared to put on paper, but without explaining why. In the course of his letters he extended the range of his accusations. He wrote to Danton that Delaunay claimed Hébert was *une puissance un peu à sa disposition* and that men from the War Office and the Paris Commune were involved in the plot.[17] In a letter to Robespierre he

---

[15] Archives Nationales, W 342. See Mathiez, *Procès de corruption*, pp. 94–106 for the two versions of Basire's declaration, from one of which the references to Danton's links with Delaunay have been removed. It is this version that is printed in *Pièces trouvées*, pp. 16–24.

[16] Sixteen of these letters, including twelve to Robespierre, are printed in *Pièces trouvées*. Most of the remainder are to be found in Archives Nationales, F7 4434, F7 4637 and W 342. Mathiez, in *Procès de corruption*, reprints 29 of them, including one in his personal collection.

[17] Letters of 28 November (Archives Nationales, F7 4434) and 21 December (*Pièces trouvées*, pp. 46–52).

asserted that Delaunay had claimed to be in league with Amar, and said that Jagot, Moise Bayle and Voulland seemed to want to conceal his original denunciation from Amar.[18] Two months later, he asserted that Amar had been involved in the early stages of the blackmailing of the East India Company.[19] In his long memoir, *François Chabot à ses concitoyens*, written towards the end of January, he maintained that Hébert was working with Batz and Lulier in the *branche diffamatrice*, that Delaunay claimed influence over Panis, Amar, David and other members of the Committee of General Security and that there were British agents in the Commune, the War Office and the revolutionary army.[20]

On the whole, Chabot's various 'revelations' were as consistent as one might reasonably expect from a man writing from prison over a period of several months. To this, however, there are two major exceptions, the first of which concerns the guilt of Fabre. Chabot at first proclaimed his innocence, briefly reversed his attitude after Fabre's arrest on 12 January and then, in his *Testament* of 17 March, again insisted that Fabre was not involved in the East India Company business, although 'On a quelque raison de taire ses autres crimes parce que les membres des deux comités pourroient être impliqués.'[21] Chabot's second inconsistency concerned the time when he realized that the financial intrigue was no more than one part of a primarily political conspiracy. In some of his letters he said this was in early September; elsewhere he put it as late as 8–9 November.[22]

Whatever one makes of his scenario, Chabot does seem to have exposed a real financial scandal of which the government was unaware. The falsification of the decree for the liquidation of the East India Company is a fact and the different versions of the text can still be seen in the Archives Nationales.[23] Chabot may not have known of Fabre's participation, which would go some way towards explaining the first of his inconsistencies. It also looks as though he was right in saying that Amar was involved. The Company's directors, in a memoir written in 1795 when they had no further need of political protectors, denounced Amar, Fabre, Julien and Delaunay as the men who had held them to ransom in 1793.[24] Chabot must have known that his denunciation would antagonize

[18] Letter of 16 December (*Pièces trouvées*, pp. 33–37).

[19] Letter of 17 February (*Pièces trouvées*, pp. 55–57).

[20] Archives Nationales, F⁷ 4637; *François Chabot à ses concitoyens*, fos. 42, 45, 49.

[21] Archives Nationales, W 342.

[22] *François Chabot à ses concitoyens*, fol. 42; Archives Nationales W 342.

[23] Archives Nationales, F⁷ 4434 and W 342; see Mathiez, *Procès de corruption*, pp. 27–75 for the fullest account.

[24] Mathiez, *Procès de corruption*, pp. 30, 379–80.

Amar but he may not have appreciated that he was incriminating Fabre as well and that the two men might join forces to destroy him. What is much more difficult to substantiate is the existence of Chabot's *branche diffamatrice*, the counter-revolutionary plot linking Hébert and extremists in the War Office, the Commune and the revolutionary army with Batz and with the ubiquitous Pitt. His vagueness on this score contrasts with his specific financial accusations and he may have invented the whole business in order to get rid of people who were persecuting him. Even if this were true, he still had to concoct a plausible story and he might have uncovered more than he suspected. If the political plot was a complete fiction it could still acquire a kind of reality if the government acted on the assumption that it was true. There is a good deal here that calls for investigation, even if the surviving evidence permits of only the most tentative conclusions.

The Baron de Batz had certainly shown extraordinary courage and resourcefulness in trying to save both Louis XVI and Marie Antoinette.[25] Chabot's assertion that he was behind the financial scandals is plausible enough in the light of his earlier activities. He had also built up an impressive network of agents and seems to have infiltrated the Paris Commune.[26] The question is whether, in the winter of 1793–94, he was still conducting his royalist campaign, or whether he was mainly concerned with his personal survival. He maintained the latter in 1795 but told a very different story after the Restoration, although in terms too vague to carry much conviction.[27] His own evidence is no more reliable than Chabot's and for the moment there is very little else.

Hébert seems at first sight a most unlikely royalist and all the 'evidence' linking him with Batz seems to lead back to Chabot. In Fouquier-Tinville's notes for Chabot's trial there is something that looks like independent corroboration.[28] Henrion, a business associate of the war-contractor, d'Espagnac, testified that Hébert was to have given Chabot part of the ransom paid by the East India Company. De Lestapis has shown, however, that the original source for this story, which reached Henrion by a roundabout route, was Chabot himself.[29] Chabot apparently intended to invite both Hébert and Batz to a meeting at his house, where they were to be arrested by agents of the Committee of General Security. If this was the only

[25] See the biographies by Lenotre and the Baron de Batz and the writings of de Lestapis: *La 'conspiration de Batz'*, 'Batz et la liquidation de la créance Guichen', 'Autour de l'attentat d'Admiral' and 'Admiral et l'attentat manqué' in *Annales historiques de la Révolution française*, xxiv (1952), xxix (1957) and xxxi (1959).

[26] Batz, *La conjuration de Batz, ou la journée des soixante* (Paris, an III), quoted in Lenotre, *op. cit.*, pp. 304–05.   [27] Lenotre, *op. cit.*, pp. 304–07.

[28] Archives Nationales, W 173.   [29] *La 'conspiration de Batz'*, pp. 174–76.

link between the two men and they had received separate invitations, it proves nothing at all.

This does not mean that Hébert's activities were always what might have been expected from the Père Duchesne. Desmoulins took up Chabot's story that Mme de Rouchechouart persuaded Hébert to have the queen transferred back from the Conciergerie to the Temple.[30] Hébert admitted to have seen the *vieille pécadille* but claimed that he sent her packing.[31] This would be more convincing if he had not, in fact, made the decidedly odd proposal to put the queen back in the Temple, at a meeting of the Jacobins on 27 September. Although there is no proof that Hébert was personally involved, the bureaux of the Commune—of which he was an important official—provided the Duc du Châtelet with a false certificate of non-emigration. Chabot and Basire knew of this, although neither mentioned it in his denunciation.[32] Hébert was also mentioned by Drake, the British consul at Genoa, in a letter to Grenville of 9 November: 'I have since learned that Baldwyn arrived in Paris on the 17th of October and that he had a conference with Hérault de Séchelles, Hébert and Forgues, but I am not yet informed of the result.'[33] Deforgues was Foreign Minister and Hérault a member of the Committee of Public Safety concerned with foreign policy, but the reason for Hébert's presence is not obvious, though it may have been innocent. Drake wrote again in February that '*sans l'aveu du Comité de Salut Public et malgré Robespierre*', the Commune had secured the release of Baldwyn, who had been arrested.[34] None of this proves anything but it suggests that Hébert kept rather surprising company and might have preferred some of his activities not to be widely publicized. The unfortunate Chabot may have been more successful than he realized: he had managed to incriminate a member of the governing committees, Amar, and leaders of both wings of the opposition, Fabre and Hébert.

If there was no more to it than that, one could give Hébert the benefit of the doubt, disregard Batz and write off Chabot as an incorrigible liar. The reactions of the revolutionary government, however, suggest that matters were rather more complicated.

[30] *Le Vieux Cordelier* (ed. H. Calvet, Paris, 1936), pp. 155, 160. Desmoulins presumably got the story from Danton, who had been given a copy of Chabot's denunciation. Archives Nationales, W 173.

[31] *J. R. Hébert, auteur du Père Duchesne, à Camille Desmoulins et compagnie* (Paris, an II), p. 8. (Bibliothèque Nationale Lb41 3615).

[32] A. de Lestapis, 'Un grand corrupteur, le duc du Châtelet', *Annales historiques de la Révolution française*, xxv (1953), pp. 316–28, xxvii (1955), pp. 5–26.

[33] Historical Manuscripts Commission, *The Manuscripts of J. B. Fortesque* ii (London, 1894), p. 456.

[34] *Id.*, p. 510.

Robespierre seems to have accepted Chabot's denunciation more or less at its face value. In the notes for a speech he never made, probably compiled in late November or early December, he repeated Chabot's story of a double plot headed by Batz.[35] Three days after Chabot visited him, he told the Convention that Pitt was behind a double plot involving corruption and calumny.[36] This was, of course, Chabot's trademark. On 12 December Robespierre seemed to hint at possible differences within the government, concerning the 'factions': 'il est du devoir du Comité de Salut Public de vous les dévoiler et de vous proposer les mesures nécessaires pour les étouffer; il le remplira sans doute.'[37] It was not until the last of his unpublished speeches, probably drafted in late January 1794, that he began to describe the factions as moderates and extremists, rather than as *corrupteurs* and *défamateurs*, which may indicate that he was beginning to have second thoughts about Chabot's story.

The Committee of General Security proved curiously reluctant to act on Chabot's information. He eventually told them that if they took no action, he would denounce his plot on the floor of the Convention, which brought a sharp reply from Jagot. Chabot had asked for twenty-four hours, so that he could arrange to be arrested with the ringleaders. A joint meeting of the two governing committees, at three in the morning of 18 November, gave orders for the immediate arrest of Chabot, Basire, Delaunay, Julien, Batz, Benoît, Proly, Dubuisson and three bankers. Desmoulins, when he learned this at his and Chabot's trial, thought the Committee of General Security had rejected Chabot's proposal in order to protect the men Chabot hoped to catch.[38] If one can believe the anonymous pamphlet, *La Tête à la Queue*, Robespierre 'refusa d'abord et obstinément de signer le mandat d'arrêt lancé contre Delaunay d'Angers, Basire et Chabot. Barère le lui arracha, malgré sa frayeur.'[39] What, if anything, this means, is anyone's guess. Of the eleven men named by the committees, only three—Chabot, Basire and Delaunay— were actually caught. The revolutionary government was not usually so incompetent and Robespierre implied that its behaviour could have been deliberate: 'Nous avons été jusqu'ici plus sévères envers les accusateurs qu'envers les accusés.'[40] Ozanne, one of the policemen

---

[35] *Pièces trouvées*, pp. 59–71; printed in *Oeuvres de Maximilien Robespierre* (ed. M. Bouloiseau et A. Soboul) x (Paris, 1967), pp. 397–407. For the reasons why the editors are probably mistaken in ascribing this draft to the spring of 1794, see N. Hampson, *The life and opinions of Maximilien Robespierre* (London, 1974), p. 237.
[36] *Oeuvres*, x, p. 182.   [37] *Id.*, p. 228.
[38] *Le Vieux Cordelier*, p. 293.
[39] Bibliothèque Nationale Lb[41] 1351, p. 8, n. 1.
[40] *Pièces trouvées*, p. 70.

who arrested Chabot, arranged to accompany the man who had been ordered to seize Julien who was on mission outside Paris. Before setting out, he met Julien's former protégé, d'Espagnac, and after arresting Julien, allowed him to escape.[41] When tried for this by the revolutionary tribunal, he was acquitted of counter-revolutionary intent and given a two-year sentence for negligence. In June, however, he was executed with the alleged accomplices of Batz. All of this could be explained by an accumulation of coincidences, but it takes rather a lot of them.

When Amar, as spokesman for the Committee of General Security, asked the Convention to raise the immunity of the three arrested deputies, he seems to have mentioned only the financial side of the plot and to have said nothing of Batz. Put in charge of the interrogation of the prisoners, he enlisted the help of Fabre, although Fabre was not a member of the committee. Fabre in turn tried to twist the evidence to suit his own requirements. In his *Précis et reléve des matériaux sur la conspiration dénoncée par Chabot et Basire*, tuned to Robespierre's ear, he understandably pushed the East India Company side of the business into the background.[42] He added dechristianization to the themes of the plot and emphasized the roles of the revolutionary army, the Commune and its *procureur*, Chaumette. He made only one reference to Hébert and tried to concentrate suspicion on Chaumette, whom Chabot and Basire had never mentioned at all. The two deputies were presented as frightened conspirators rather than as double agents. Since Robespierre still trusted Fabre, this may have helped to turn him against Chabot and Basire.

The unhappy Chabot complained that when the interrogation of the prisoners at last began, it was arranged so as to benefit Delaunay at Chabot's expense. He protested to Robespierre that Amar noted only what suited his own purposes. When he complained to the Convention that Amar's report on the arrest of Fabre (whose involvement with the East India Company had now come to light) was *un tissu de perfidies pour me perdre*, his letter was referred back to the committee, in other words, to Amar. 'Lorsque Jagot (who had replaced Fabre as Amar's fellow-investigator) vouloit donner suite à cette déclaration et découvrir la vérité, Amar n'a pas jugé l'instruction ultérieure nécessaire.' When Chabot accused Amar of being involved in the East India Company Affair himself, 'Jagot vouloit donner sa démission; Amar ne fut pas de cet avis et je fus obligé de

[41] De Lestapis, *La 'conspiration de Batz'*, pp. 20–24.
[42] Archives Nationales AF II 49, printed in Mathiez, *Procès de corruption*, pp. 145–66.

leur demander excuse pour des vivacités qui ne tournoient que contre moi.'[43]

Amar had originally asked the Convention's permission to keep Chabot and Basire under arrest for a few days, *sans rien préjuger sur leur compte*. Fourteen weeks later they were still in gaol, when Amar's colleagues presented him with an ultimatum, rather delicately referring to *des moyens qui contrarieroient notre amitié pour toi* if he did not make an immediate report.[44] He waited for another fortnight and it may have been just another coincidence that his report was eventually delivered on the day after Hébert's arrest. Amar described Chabot, Basire, Delaunay and Julien as the main conspirators, with Batz and Benoît playing minor parts.[45] His speech was sharply criticized by both Billaud-Varenne and Robespierre on the ground that it dealt only with corruption and not with the *branche diffamatrice*. They had the report referred back to the Committee of Public Safety, but when it re-emerged on 19 March as an *acte d'accusation*, it still said very little about politics and the names of Batz and Benoît had disappeared altogether!

When Hébert and his associates were brought to trial on 21 March, the dutiful Fouquier-Tinville declared that no plot had ever been 'plus atroce dans son objet, plus vaste, plus immense dans ses rapports et ses détails.' The accused were charged with every crime in the revolutionary calendar: trying to starve Paris, to massacre the Convention and replace it by a Grand Judge, all at the behest of their British and Austrian paymasters. This makes it rather hard to accept de Lestapis's argument that, to have thrown in the Batz plot for good measure would have dishonoured both Hébert and the Montagnards.[46] What he has shown is Fouquier's determination to keep Batz out of the proceedings.[47] Henrion, as we have seen, was ready to testify to rumours linking Batz with Hébert, but he was not called as a witness. When Westermann repeated the same story, he apparently substituted the name of Hébert's mother-in-law (who died before the Revolution) for that of Batz, and even this was

---

[43] *Pièces trouvées*, p. 56. These assertions were presumably true, since Robespierre could easily check them by consulting Jagot.

[44] Mathiez, *Procès de corruption*, p. 313.

[45] De Bonald and Lenotre both claim that the identity of Batz and Benoît was concealed by mis-spelling: *le baron de Beauce* and *Benoîte*, and that Saint-Just's report on the faction of Fabre was so badly printed that Batz's name was illegible. This seems rather far-fetched.

[46] *La 'conspiration de Batz'*, p. 260.

[47] Topino-Lebrun, who witnessed the trial, commented on Fouquier's reluctance to follow up the evidence linking Hébert and Chaumette with the men who tried to save the queen. *Notes de Topino-Lebrun sur le procès de Danton* (Paris, 1875), p. 28.

omitted from the account published in the *Journal du tribunal révolutionnaire*.[48] On the evening after Westermann's evidence, Ozanne secured an interview with Fouquier and told him that he had met a man in prison who was willing to testify that the baron claimed to be '*fort lié* avec Hébert et qu'il faisoit tout ce qu'il vouloit avec lui.'[49] This was the first time anyone other than Chabot had linked Hébert and Batz. Fouquier disregarded Ozanne's offer— and he was scarcely the man to have scruples about using suspect evidence.

The trial of Chabot himself might reasonably have been expected to reveal *something* but everything was thrown into confusion by the last-minute decision to add Danton, Desmoulins, Delacroix and Philippeaux to the accused.[50] Fouquier, who had no time to prepare any sort of case, was more concerned to keep men like Danton quiet than to maintain even the fiction of a trial. Only one witness was called and everything was rushed through as quickly as possible. Chabot did contrive to bring in both Benoît and Batz: 'J'ai offert de les faire saisir chez moi, mais on les a avertis et on les a fait sauver. On n'a connu qu'une partie de la conspiration, mais ces débats-ci la dévoileront.'[51] Chabot was always an optimist. When Lulier, whom Chabot had accused of complicity with Batz, was called as a witness, Fouquier suddenly broke the apparent tabu, put Lulier in the dock and accused him of being the agent of Benoît and Batz.[52] He was the only one of the accused to be acquitted.

So far, the evidence suggests that the revolutionary government either disbelieved the charges against Batz or had its own reasons for ignoring them. Some of the baron's agents had received such favourable treatment as to suggest that they enjoyed some kind of protection.[53] On 22 April the Committee of General Security suddenly reversed either its opinion or its policy. It wrote to Fouquier: 'Le comité t'enjoint de redoubler d'efforts pour découvrir l'infâme Batz. Souviens-toi dans tes interrogations que ses relations s'étendent partout et jusque dans les maisons d'arrêt, que ce Catiline a été constamment l'âme de tous les complots contre la Liberté et la Représentation nationale.'[54] This time they seem to have been in earnest, although they did not try the agents of Batz whom they were holding in gaol, for another couple of months. When they did so, the Committee of Public Safety offered a free pardon to Batz's

[48] *La 'conspiration de Batz'*, pp. 174–76, 228–30.
[49] *Id.*, pp. 241–43.
[50] On this issue, see N. Hampson, *op. cit.*, pp. 252–59.
[51] *Notes de Topino-Lebrun*, p. 16.
[52] Archives Nationales, W 342.
[53] Lenotre, *op. cit.*, pp. 104–5, 166–68; Archives Nationales, F[7] 4758.
[54] Archives Nationales, W 389.

secretary, Devaux, if he would tell them where to find the baron.[55] When Lacoste, of the Committee of General Security, revealed this latest plot to the Convention, Batz had become what Chabot had always said he was, Public Enemy No. 1. 'Nous allons vous conduire à la source impure de toutes les conjurations . . . Les factions de Chabot et de Julien, d'Hébert et de Ronsin, de Danton et de Delacroix, de Chaumette et de Gobel sont autant de branches de celle dont nous venons vous dévoiler les forfaits.' 'Tous ces leviers destinés à renverser la République étoient mus par un seul homme qui faisait agir tous les tyrans coalisés.'[56] Chabot could not have put it better—and when he had said it all before, no one had wanted to listen. Lacoste pretended that the committees had first heard of the activities of Batz as a result on a denunciation made on April 9.[57] This was, of course, quite untrue, since Chabot had told them all about Batz in November and whatever the nature of the unknown denunciation of 9 April, it looks like a breach of his copyright.

The full story of what is known about the 'Batz plot' is much more complicated than can be suggested in a brief summary of this kind, but enough has been said to show that a great deal remains to be explained. Such conclusions as can be drawn are very tentative indeed and liable to correction if further evidence comes to light. Chabot's vast double plot was probably largely fictitious, even though the revolutionary government, after going to great lengths to conceal it, suddenly made it official orthodoxy in June 1794. Chabot was, however, aware of the existence of a good deal of corrupt speculation, though its ramifications went further than he imagined.

It is difficult to resist the conclusion that some members of the revolutionary government were protecting Batz, whatever their reasons. Some may have feared the exposure of their own speculation, others, like Robespierre, been anxious to 'sauver l'honneur de la Convention et de la Montagne' by preventing too much dirty linen from being washed in public.[58] There was more to Chabot's denunciation than Mathiez at first believed, but the argument of de Lestapis that he exposed Hébert, and perhaps other extremists, as secret royalists, needs more confirmation than it has yet received. He had certainly opened Pandora's box and the subsequent confusion and equivocation of the government may have been due to

[55] Id.
[56] Speech of 14 June 1794.
[57] This is presumably not the denunciation, dated prairial (20 May–18 June) summarized in the Charavay catalogue of 1862 (Bibliothèque Nationale Δ 40153).
[58] A note in Robespierre's private diary, written shortly before 6 December 1793 and printed in A. Mathiez, Etudes sur Robespierre (Paris, 1958), p. 232.

its fear of what men like Hébert and Fabre could reveal if pushed too far and given a chance to speak in public. When the government reversed its policy and put Batz's agents on trial, the law of 22 *prairial* allowed Fouquier to get his victims condemned before they could say anything inconvenient and most of those whom they might have incriminated were now dead.

All such speculations reopen the question of who was trying to conceal what. One thing at least seems clear: Chabot did expose *something*, even if he did not know what it was, and his 'revelations' played an important part in determining the mysterious policies of the Terror, even if not quite in the way that he intended.

University of York.

CATHOLICS AND THE POOR
IN EARLY MODERN EUROPE

By Professor Brian Pullan, M.A., Ph.D., F.R.Hist.S.

INTENDED TO BE READ 7 MARCH 1975*

A quiet revolution has occurred of late in the history of poor people and poor relief in early modern Europe. Shapeless, decentralized and infinite, like the story of most everyday things, it has depended for progress on the laborious accumulation of local examples, garnered from patchy, weedy and erratically surviving evidence; and for vitality on cerebration which outstrips research, on hypotheses which demand to be tested in a hundred detailed trials. Time was when sociologists and students of social legislation encouraged historians to believe that with the Reformation there developed fundamental differences in the ways in which the old and the new faiths treated their poor—variances which sprang essentially from the abandonment in the wake of Luther of the ancient belief that 'good works' (almsgiving included) offered to those who performed them a direct means of securing salvation. To compress is often to parody. But it can perhaps be said that the coming of Protestantism, in all its forms, was believed to have emancipated poor-relief from the control of a too-indulgent Church, which encouraged the almsgiver to think only of the benefit to his own immortal soul. In so doing the Church had allegedly destroyed all incentive to contrive a rational philanthropy—to build systems which would benefit the receiver of alms, which would serve the common weal, which would in general be directed at procuring good order and reducing physical want and suffering. Hence the Church was credited with a very low capacity for organization and even accused of breeding the very poor whom it relieved, by depriving them of all incentive to find employment and attain self-support. Where advances were achieved in Catholic societies, they were said to have been made in spite of the Church and not by its agency, put into effect by the repressive, regulative state which came forward, as it were, to rectify the errors of ecclesiastical sentimentality, and to discipline the tough professional beggar. By contrast, Protestantism was held to have consigned the relief of the poor firmly to a secular sphere. Within its compass there would be far less reason to keep in existence a corpus

* Professor Pullan was unable through illness to read his paper.

of poor that the rich might practise meritorious works upon them,
and in such a context the relief of the poor might even become a
social duty enjoined by the public authorities. It might (perhaps it
must) cease to be an expression of the Christian virtues of charity
and mercy, whose essence lay in their spontaneity. In the Protestant
state, it was believed, the possibilities of collective action by the
community for the relief of the poor would inevitably prove much
greater, and the prospect of outlining a consistent welfare policy
much more immediate.[1]

Needless to say, an effect of much recent historical writing has
been to blur these contrasts to the point at which they are virtually
invisible. Historians now tell us that officially Catholic and officially
Protestant communities, civic or even national, came very close to
following precisely the same principles, though with differences of
stress and timing. Few will now be surprised to hear that Catholics
and Protestants discriminated in a broadly similar way between
different categories of poor, prescribed in much the same manner
a variety of treatments for them, sought in distributing relief to
place them on like ladders of preference. Catholics and Protestants
joined in making the well-worn distinction between the able-bodied
and the helpless poor, in preferring the native to the stranger. True,
clerical voices were sometimes raised in Catholic Europe to protest
against interference with the free and natural movement of migrants
from the poor and barren countryside to the richer cities.[2] And
Vincent de Paul reminded the authorities of Paris in 1655 that the
capital was a sponge which soaked up the wealth of all France and
was not therefore morally entitled to reject its poor: specifically, it
must not repel refugees from the stricken and devastated provinces
of Champagne and Picardie.[3] But such outcries often went unheeded,
Vincent de Paul chose to obey the magistrate, and a hard-pressed

---

[1] For references to these arguments, see B. Tierney, *Medieval Poor Law: a Sketch
of Canonical Theory and its Application in England* (Berkeley and Los Angeles, 1959),
p. 46 *et seq.*, N. Z. Davis, 'Assistance, humanisme et hérésie: le cas de Lyon',
Études sur l'histoire de la pauvreté (Moyen Âge—XVIe siècle), sous la direction de
Michel Mollat. ii (Paris, 1974), pp. 762–64 (originally published as 'Poor Relief,
Humanism and Heresy: the Case of Lyon', *Studies in Medieval and Renaissance
History*, v, 1968—I have referred to the French version because the references have
been brought up to date); B. S. Pullan, *Rich and Poor in Renaissance Venice: the
Social Institutions of a Catholic State, to 1620* (Oxford, 1971), pp. 11–12, 197–98.

[2] *E.g.* those of the four Mendicant Orders in Ypres, 1530: see doc. viii printed in
J. Nolf, *La réforme de la bienfaisance à Ypres au XVIe siècle* (Ghent, 1915), pp. 63–64;
and that of D. Soto, *Deliberacion en la causa de los pobres* (Salamanca, 1545), fos.
8v.–11.

[3] P. Coste, *Le grand saint du grand siècle: Monsieur Vincent*, ii (Paris, 1932), pp.
502–03; *cf.* also p. 612.

community such as Amiens could dump even maimed and helpless strangers outside its walls with little ceremony or compunction.[4] There seems now to be little question that the Catholic and Protestant community showed an almost equally strong tendency to transform the wandering penniless stranger into the fearful and repulsive figure of the vagrant. And his condemnation by Catholics was not founded purely on utilitarian arguments appropriate to policemen and innocent of religious terms. He was not merely a threat to public order, a presumptive criminal, a masterless man untouched by the family's control, a breaker of children's limbs to increase their profitable pathos, a burden on rates and stocks of food, or one who defied inclusion in a stable hierarchy and tidy confinement within administrative boundaries.[5] Far more than that, he was (or became in the Italy of Borromeo and Sixtus V, in France a century later) a blasphemer, a heathen, a disturber of churches, contemptuous of the sacraments of marriage and baptism: indeed, a rebel against God, and one who transgressed the solemn command-ment 'Thou shalt eat thy bread in the sweat of thy brow' and shrugged off his share in the penalties of original sin.[6] A potential robber of the man of property, he was an actual robber of Christ's own poor, because he stole their alms—and some city authorities, like those of Ypres, expressly traced this maxim back to the canon law.[7] It may of course be true that Catholic opinion, both official and popular, was less inclined to eliminate certain categories of

[4] In 1644: see P. Deyon, *Étude sur la société urbaine au XVIIe siècle: Amiens, capitale provinciale* (Paris and The Hague, 1967), pp. 350–51.

[5] Compare, for example, J. P. Gutton, *La société et les pauvres: l'exemple de la géneralité de Lyon, 1534–1789* (Paris, 1971), pp. 11–13, B. Geremek, 'Criminalité, vagabondage, paupérisme: la marginalité à l'aube des temps modernes', *Revue d'histoire moderne et contemporaine*, xxi (1974), p. 345 *et seq.* and J. Depauw, 'Pauvres, pauvres mendiants, mendiants valides ou vagabonds? Les hésitations de la législation royale', *ibid.*, pp. 402–07, with P. Clark, 'The Migrant in Kentish Towns, 1580–1640', in *Crisis and Order in English Towns, 1500–1700: Essays in Urban History*, ed. P. Clark and P. Slack (London, 1972), p. 138 *et seq.*, P. Slack, 'Poverty and Politics in Salisbury, 1597–1666', *ibid.*, pp. 165–69; P. Slack, 'Vagrants and Vagrancy in England, 1598–1664', *Economic History Review*, second series, xxvii (1974), pp. 360–79, and A. L. Beier, 'Vagrants and the Social Order in Eliza-bethan England', *Past and Present*, no. 64 (August 1974), pp. 3–29.

[6] See P. Tacchi Venturi, *Storia della Compagnia di Gesù in Italia*, I i (Rome, 1938), pp. 202–12; Sixtus V's Bull 'Quamvis infirma' of 11th May 1587, *Bullarium diplo-matum et privilegiorum sanctorum Romanorum pontificum* (Aosta, 1857–72), viii, pp. 847–53; J. Delumeau, *Vie économique et sociale de Rome dans la seconde moitié du XVIème siècle*, i (Paris, 1957), pp. 404–05; Pullan, *Rich and Poor*, p. 365; M. Foucault, *Folie et déraison: histoire de la folie à l'âge classique* (Paris, 1961), p. 86 *et seq.*; Coste, M. Vincent, ii, p. 483; Deyon, *Amiens*, p. 352; Gutton, *La société et les pauvres*, p. 271.

[7] See William Marshall's translation (1535) of the Ypres scheme of poor relief, reprinted in F. R. Salter, *Some Early Tracts on Poor Relief* (London, 1926), pp. 50–51.

persons who begged or wandered on pretext of religion. For, as the burghers of Ypres were constrained to admit, 'no man is to be letted to folowe that way that maye help to his salvatyon: for it might so happen that the ryche man all thinges set at nought either beggynge or travelynge might highly please god by wyllynge sufferance of mekenesse of labour and of shame fastnesse.'[8] Catholic communities had their dubious friars and shady mass-priests, but respect for them was not to be taken for granted, and an irritable commission of magistrates in Venice could threaten maverick Mendicants with mutilated noses or service at the galley's oar if they dared to beg again in the streets of the city.[9] There was perhaps some justification for the misgivings of those friars in the Low Countries who protested that the city poor-laws would imperil their livelihood and their titles to respect, in addition to starving the poor laymen they were bound to defend.[10] A century later Vincent de Paul, who plainly felt more at home when justifying the working orders than in defending the Mendicants,[11] proved willing to accept an intake of priestly vagabonds to the house of correction for madmen, wastrels and genteel debauchees inherited when he took over the Priory of St Lazare outside Paris.[12] Pilgrims, admittedly, remained an accepted part of the Catholic scene, as they did not in Protestant Europe. Luther's message had been, 'let every man stay in his own parish; there he will find more than in all the shrines even if they were all rolled into one', and the coming of Lutheranism could in practice deflate magnetic and crowd-catching cults with remarkable speed.[13] But in France even the people and authorities of Lyons, that pioneer in the internment of beggars, persisted in showing a marked indulgence to pilgrims who sought to cure their epilepsy in the church of St John, or their bladders at Valfleury, or body and soul together by taking off for Loretto.[14]

All in all, however, it seems pretty doubtful whether the survival of the pilgrim and the loose-footed clerk were enough in themselves

---

[8] F. R. Salter, *Some Early Tracts on Poor Relief*, p. 44.

[9] Pullan, *Rich and Poor*, pp. 303–04. *Cf.* Gutton, *La société et les pauvres*, pp. 187–89, 239–40.

[10] Nolf, *Bienfaisance à Ypres*, doc. viii, pp. 40–76.

[11] See his 'conference' on the Christian duty of work, 28 November 1649, in *Conferences of St Vincent de Paul to the Sisters of Charity*, transl. J. Leonard, ii (London, 1938), p. 117.

[12] R. Allier, *La Cabale des Dévots, 1627–1666* (Paris, 1902), pp. 135–36; Coste, *M. Vincent*, ii, p. 516.

[13] 'To the Christian Nobility of the German Nation', *Luther's Works*, xliv, ed. J. T. Atkinson (Philadelphia, 1966), p. 187; B. Moeller, *Imperial Cities and the Reformation: Three Essays* (Philadelphia, 1972), pp. 58–59.

[14] Gutton, *La société et les pauvres*, pp. 191–92, 238–39, 286, 372–73.

to differentiate Catholic attitudes to the traveller and the vagrant very starkly from those which prevailed in Protestant communities. And when it came to the correction of the homeless poor by means of internment, hard labour, corporal punishment and compulsory piety, there can have been few English bridewells to compare in scope or scale with the motley complex of barrack-like hospitals and dungeons controlled by the governors of the Hôpital Général in seventeenth-century Paris. Puritanism may or may not have administered a 'new medicine for poverty' to English unfortunates in that century; but it certainly represented a form of godly rigour which transcended religious frontiers, and permeated the works of the Compagnie du Saint Sacrement as much as it informed the writings of Baxter and Perkins.[15]

Can we defend the simple associations whereby Catholic poor relief is the charity of the Church, and the Protestant poor are the pensioners of the laity and the state? These, too, have begun to seem dubious. In northern and central Italy the great flagellant movement which flared up in 1260 deposited a lasting sediment in the form of hundreds of lay religious fraternities, many of which turned in effect from flagellation to philanthropy, and some of which (as in late medieval and Renaissance Venice) were strictly under lay management and supervised by formidable, watchful organs of state. Priests were their chaplains and not their masters.[16] Likewise, in the cities of the Low Countries, Germany and Switzerland the magistrates often appear to have taken over some portion of local hospitals and charities as part of a general process of assuming responsibility for the moral life of the citizens, for the externals and the material shell of the local church: a movement which can be seen in retrospect as an essential preliminary for the magisterial Reformation and not as a consequence of it.[17] We can even find hints

---

[15] Cf. Allier, La Cabale, passim; Foucault, Folie et déraison, p. 57 et seq.; E. Chill, 'Religion and Mendicity in Seventeenth-Century France', International Review of Social History, vii (1962), pp. 400–25; Gutton, La société et les pauvres, p. 298 et seq.; Depauw, 'Pauvres, pauvres mendiants', passim.

[16] For the fullest discussions of the flagellant movements of 1260 and of the fraternities which they founded, see Il movimento dei Disciplinati nel settimo centenario dal suo inizio (Perugia—1260), Appendice 9 to Bollettino della Deputazione di Storia Patria per l'Umbria (Spoleto, 1962); also the wide-ranging but not entirely accurate survey by G. M. Monti, Le confraternite medievali dell' alta e media Italia (2 vols., Venice, 1927). On Venetian lay fraternities, see Pullan, Rich and Poor, pp. 33–193, and R. C. Mueller, 'Charitable Institutions, the Jewish Community, and Venetian Society', Studi veneziani, xiv (1972), p. 41 et seq.

[17] Cf. P. Bonenfant, 'Les origines et le caractère de la réforme de la bienfaisance publique aux Pays-Bas sous le règne de Charles-Quint', Revue belge de philologie et d'histoire, v (1926), p. 898 et seq., and vi (1927), p. 207 et seq.; Moeller, Imperial

that the coming of religious revolution actually brought attempts to deflect the process whereby the relief of the poor was taken out of the hands of the Church and became a function of the magistrate— although it could be checked only by according a much more positive and active role to the laity within the Church. This is undoubtedly true of certain Calvinist communities and of Geneva itself, whose most ardent reformers strove to 'consecrate' poor relief by insisting that the local hospital commissioners be regarded as deacons of the Church.[18] In Scotland the parliament might be the body which issued poor-laws, but for a century and a half after Knox's time the efficient unit for the care of the poor seems to have been the kirk assembly. Here the state had no machinery of its own to enforce the policies it recommended.[19] And where the position of the Calvinists was that of a beleaguered minority, as in seventeenth-century France, the Reformed Church could be driven of necessity to maintain its own charitable arrangements independently of the public hospitals and almonries: only by such means could it guarantee relief to its faithful and save them from attempts to convert them by the withholding of alms from non-attenders at the Mass.[20] Where confessional conflict raged, poor relief was inevitably a weapon in the armoury of churches, and its dispensation was frequently tinged by religious motives: in Catholic France these seem to have been more strongly avowed with the advance of the century, and especially after 1640.[21] In Catholic communities, too, the old fraternities survived, were multiplied, were modified, and some of them were certainly tied more securely into the administrative structure of the Church, pegged to the parish and the diocese

---

Cities, p. 45 *et seq.*; M. U. Chrisman, *Strasbourg and the Reform* (New Haven and London, 1967), pp. 35, 42–44, 275 *et seq.*; R. C. Walton, *Zwingli's Theocracy* (Toronto, 1967), p. 4 *et seq.*; R. M. Kingdon, 'Social Welfare in Calvin's Geneva', *American Historical Review*, lxxvi (1971), pp. 53–55.

[18] *Cf.* A. Biéler, *La pensée économique et sociale de Calvin* (Geneva, 1959), pp. 153–56, 365–68; R. W. Henderson, 'Sixteenth-Century Community Benevolence: an Attempt to Resacralize the Secular', *Church History*, xxxviii (1969), pp. 421–28; Kingdon, 'Social Welfare', pp. 59–65. P. Bonenfant, 'Un aspect du régime calviniste à Bruxelles au XVIème siècle: la question de la bienfaisance', *Bulletin de la Commission Royale d'Histoire*, lxxxix (1925), discusses at pp. 266–68, 270 *et seq.* the role of deacons in the care of the poor in the Netherlands.

[19] See R. Mitchison, 'The Making of the Old Scottish Poor Law', *Past and Present*, no. 63 (May 1974), p. 62 *et seq.*

[20] For clear examples of this, see W. J. Pugh, 'Social Welfare and the Edict of Nantes: Lyon and Nîmes', *French Historical Studies*, viii (1973–74), pp. 360–66. For the decision of Parisian parish fraternities to deny assistance to Protestants and to Catholics who accepted charity from Protestants, see Allier, *La Cabale*, p. 102.

[21] In the judgment of Gutton, *La société et les pauvres*, pp. 324–26.

instead of being left to float freely and conceivably pass under public surveillance.[22]

When, therefore, we speak of the secularization of poor relief on either side of the confessional frontier, we are often really referring to an increase of skill on the part of the Christian churches—that is, to their greater capacity for enlisting the laity in the enterprise of caring for the souls and bodies of their faithful in an orderly, disciplined and systematic manner. We are not describing a wholesale abdication of responsibility on the part of the individual or of the Church, or its surrender to the state or civic authority. Public initiative in England, on the part of such effective pressure groups as the puritan burgesses of Salisbury in the 1630s, should certainly not be despised even if its bolder experiments failed to endure.[23] But it needed at all times to find a complement in the generous action of private persons, and the role of the individual philanthropist was, if anything, more conspicuous in England than in either France or Italy.[24] New doctrines of good works had by no means erased the religious incentive to the individual to care for the poor. There is at least a superficial resemblance between Calvin's suggestion that the chosen should forward their wealth to heaven like advance baggage by way of the poor, and the confident remark of Sister Jeanne Dalmaigne (a disciple of Vincent de Paul) that she was 'just investing' the money she gave to the poor and would be paid it back a hundredfold.[25] We cannot make the simple equation of Catholicism with individual action springing from a religious motive, of Protestantism with collective action inspired by worldly reasoning. Here again the old sharp contrasts blur and fail.

Furthermore, to dismiss the care of the poor in Catholic countries as essentially casual, ineffective and haphazard is to fly in the face of evidence which suggests a high level of ingenuity and inventiveness on the part of some of them. Umbria, Tuscany and Lombardy were the first to build a new species of credit institution, the Monte di Pietà. This was designed to give the poor some means of

[22] Cf. J. Bossy, 'The Counter-Reformation and the People of Catholic Europe', Past and Present, no. 47 (May 1970), pp. 59–60.

[23] See Slack, 'Poverty and Politics', pp. 180–91. Cf. also Poor Relief in Elizabethan Ipswich, ed. J. Webb, Suffolk Records Society Publications, ix (1966), for effective interaction between public and private relief institutions in an English provincial town.

[24] As has been so amply demonstrated by W. K. Jordan, in Philanthropy in England, 1480–1660 (London, 1959); The Charities of London, 1480–1660 (London, 1960); The Charities of Rural England, 1480–1660 (London, 1961).

[25] Calvin, Institutes of the Christian Religion, III, xviii, 6 (7th American edn, Philadelphia, 1936, ii, pp. 68–69); Conferences of St Vincent de Paul, i. p. 172, 15 January 1645.

borrowing cheaply and turning their scanty assets into cash: it was calculated, not to further business enterprise at any level, but to tide them over the spells of penury which often set in as a result of sickness, stoppages of work or bad harvests. Funded at first essentially by the donations of the faithful, these publicly administered banks in cities and townships broadened out in the sixteenth century to take on the functions of savings banks attracting deposits, and their accumulated reserves could sometimes be used to finance measures of relief in times of general disaster.[26] One might of course suggest that the Monti di Pietà did not spring from any streak of inspiration latent in Catholicism. Can they not rather be traced to some peculiarly italianate genius for administration and sophisticated economic technique—and can this not account for the relative slowness of, say, Flanders or France to adopt these pawnshops and make them work effectively? Possibly; but the promulgators of Monti di Pietà were not laymen but Observant Franciscan preachers, and they were undoubtedly exercising their traditional function of defending the poor against real or supposed oppressors—in this case usurers, and more especially the Jewish moneylenders licensed by the cities. Like impulses pressed the Observants to advocate, in Lombard cities, the fusion of small and scattered hospitals into a single large and comprehensive organ under central direction: a measure designed to cut administrative costs, to keep the foundations under constant surveillance, and perhaps to root out dubious paupers souping up benefits from more than one mouldering charity.[27] And schemes for the fusion of hospitals were not to be confined to Italy, for they touched Aragon and Castile in the sixteenth century and spread widely through the France of Louis XIV.[28] Though less comprehensive, these Italian moves towards rationalization anticipated by some seventy years the many attempts in Germany, France and the Low Countries in the 1520s and '30s to pool resources in a common chest or all-embracing almonry.

Moreover, the Catholic revival in seventeenth-century France bred, among much else, the organizing genius of Vincent de Paul—

[26] For the origins of Monti di Pietà, see H. Holzapfel, *Die Anfänge der Montes Pietatis (1462–1515)* (Munich, 1903), and the monograph by S. Majarelli and U. Nicolini, *Il Monte dei Poveri di Perugia: periodo delle origini (1462–74)* (Perugia, 1962). For their subsequent development, see the miscellaneous essays in *Archivi storici delle aziende di credito* (2 vols., Rome, 1956); M. Martelli, *Storia del Monte di Pietà in Lugo di Romagna (1546–1968)* (Florence, 1969); Pullan, *Rich and Poor*, pp. 524–26, 579–625.
[27] See Pullan, *Rich and Poor*, pp. 203–05, with references.
[28] See the excellent Ph.D. thesis of L. M. Martz, 'Poverty and Welfare in Habsburg Spain: the Example of Toledo', University of London, 1974, p. 43 *et seq.*, p. 84 *et seq.*; Coste, *M. Vincent*, ii, p. 496 *et seq.*; Foucault, *Folie et déraison*, p. 58 *et seq.*

the obscure priest from the diocese of Dax in Gascony who rose to be almoner and tutor to the family of Gondi, and initially from that vantage point launched systematic assaults on the problem of ignorance and poverty in the countryside. It was he who made the most determined attempts to enlist the poor in the service of the poor, and who (by recruiting tough and strong-armed peasant girls into the ranks of his order of the Filles de la Charité) strove to eliminate some of the condescension and patronage implied in the relationship between the giver and the receiver of care. His girls were to be servants, not mistresses, of the sick and dying poor.[29] And in the days of the Fronde and the Thirty Years War Vincent de Paul and his highborn Dames de la Charité succeeded in at least delineating something like a national philanthropy: that is, one in which the relief of the poor in disaster areas would no longer depend entirely on locally levied contributions, but rather on making all France aware of the distress of devastated provinces and on soliciting large donations for their benefit from court and capital.[30] And in general, one conspicuous feature of Catholic philanthropy in early modern Europe was its use of standardized, exportable institutions, whose rules and statutes could be transplanted with very little adaptation from one city, parish or village to another. They offered the means whereby a travelling preacher could organize and inspire the local laity through a short, intensive spell of missionary work, inducing them to establish quickly available (though not always adequately funded) institutions for the poor, and leave them to struggle for survival. Monti di Pietà, brotherhoods of charity, houses for 'whores repenting', even general hospitals could all be established by this means[31]—though one could hardly pretend that they were all equally successful. Partly for this reason we tend to think much less of great donors in the field of Catholic philanthropy and not to seek out equivalents for Thomas Sutton, or Tooley of Ipswich, or Edward Alleyn, although they could sometimes in fact be found.[32] The dominant figures in the crowd are the great

[29] Cf. Conferences of St Vincent de Paul, i, pp. 13, 56–57, 80–82, 184–85, 279; Coste, M. Vincent, i. p. 260 et seq., 391–92, 428–30.

[30] Coste, M. Vincent, ii, pp. 581–723.

[31] For French examples see Allier, La Cabale, p. 233 et seq., Coste, M. Vincent, i, pp. 184, 312–13, 334–35; Gutton, La société et les pauvres, pp. 373–76, 394–97. For Italian, Holzapfel, Die Anfänge, passim, and Tacchi Venturi, Storia della Compagnia di Gesù, I i, p. 385, II ii, p. 174.

[32] E.g. in Bartolomeo Bontempelli, a Brescian mercer of Rialto, who gave 36,000 ducats to the construction of the beggars' hospital in Venice in his lifetime, and 100,000 ducats to the same foundation by the will he made in 1613—see Capitoli della veneranda congregatione dell' Hospitale di Santo Lazaro et Mendicanti della città di Venetia (Venice, 1619), pp. 7–8.

organizers, and it is their names that are commemorated in the titles of institutions—Antonino, Archbishop of Florence, as a founder of societies to care for the shamefaced poor and decayed gentry;[33] Carlo Borromeo, Archbishop of Milan, famous even in France as the inspirer of campaigns for the elimination of begging.[34]

Charting and exploring the common ground between confessions, historians have, both rightly and effectively, spoken of the common heritage of Catholicism and Protestantism, of the role of humanism in shaping shared attitudes. It took the romance out of poverty by extolling the middle state and praising the rich man's virtue of generosity; it was an enemy of disorder and a friend to education; it came to extol the consistent and deliberate practice of the Christian virtue of charity above all mechanical ritual, and to uphold the service of the living above the service of the dead. The beggar on the streets and the chaotic distribution of alms alike offended its sense of reason and beauty.[35] For other writers economic forces take first place—or rather those non-economic cataclysms of famine, war and pestilence, by which early modern economies were so easily wounded and crippled and which respected no religious frontiers. There was, after all, nothing like plague or typhus for depriving the poor wanderers believed to carry them of any veneer of holiness they might once have possessed. The infective stench of syphilis could easily drown the odour of sanctity.[36] There was nothing like a subsistence crisis for forcing the most open-handed and traditionally minded of Catholic towns to adopt an order of priority in the distribution of relief.[37] Beneath the flail of crisis few societies could resist the urge to impose taxation in order to save the poor from death.[38] Nearly two centuries before the Reformation the grim

[33] See R. Morçay, *Saint Antonin, Archêveque de Florence (1389–1459)* (Paris, 1914), pp. 86–88; Tacchi Venturi, *Storia della Compagnia di Gesù*, I i, pp. 401–04.

[34] For the decrees of Borromeo's provincial synods on begging, 1565–79, see *Acta Ecclesiae Mediolanensis* (Milan, 1583), fos 21v., 29v., 87v., 88, 129v. For the spread of fraternities or hospitals dedicated to St Charles Borromée in France, see Coste, *M. Vincent*, i, pp. 132–33; Deyon, *Amiens*, p. 352; Gutton, *La société et les pauvres*, pp. 394–95.

[35] See Davis, 'Assistance', *passim*; Gutton, *La société et les pauvres*, pp. 234–37.

[36] See Pullan, *Rich and Poor*, pp. 219–23, 235–36, 245 *et seq.*, 315–23; Gutton, *La société et les pauvres*, pp. 225 *et seq.*, 264–65, 266–69, 271; Deyon, *Amiens*, pp. 353–54; and, in general, J. N. Biraben, 'Les pauvres et la peste', in Mollat, *Études*, ii, pp. 505–18.

[37] For examples see H. Hauser. 'Une famine il y a 400 ans: organization communale de la défense contre la disette', in his *Travailleurs et marchands dans l'ancienne France* (Paris, 1920), pp. 114–29; R. Gascon, *Grand commerce et vie urbaine au XVIème siècle: Lyon et ses marchands*, ii (Paris, 1971), pp. 774–75; Gutton, *La société et les pauvres*, pp. 261–62; Pullan, *Rich and Poor*, p. 240 *et seq.*, 355 *et seq.*

[38] For French examples see M. Fosseyeux, 'La taxe des pauvres au XVIème siècle', *Revue d'histoire de l'Église de France*, xx (1934), pp. 407–32.

association of poverty with disease and crime had begun to breed a second official attitude to the poor, coexisting uneasily with the ancient but still hardy belief that the poor were the representatives of Christ upon earth and that poverty was the condition that Christ had chosen and sanctified. Perhaps it foreshadowed that blunt distinction between the poor of Christ and the poor of the Devil which became current, at least in England and France, before the close of the seventeenth century.[39] And if the ubiquity of disease, crime and crisis helped to iron out distinctions, there was also a good deal of straightforward competition between Catholics and Protestants, especially in cities where they lived at close quarters, and congregations might well be urged by their preachers to emulate the methods of their religious rivals, or at least to match their generosity without misapplying it.[40] In Brussels in the 1580s and later in Nîmes the public almonries and hospitals themselves became contested citadels, the competing faiths struggling for possession of them.[41] Where perhaps 15 or 20 per cent of the population were liable to be plunged below the poverty line by subsistence or other crises, and where some 5 per cent might be constantly on relief,[42] almsgiving became a form of social control which could easily be turned towards ensuring religious conformity or even winning converts. To neglect the opposition's techniques for dealing with the poor might well appear at best improvident and at worst suicidal.

But it is still worth putting the question: was there then nothing distinctive in the practice of poor relief in Catholic countries? In our anxiety to refute traditional arguments and dispose of unrefined contrasts, have we not lost sight of certain very pronounced characteristics of Catholic theory and practice which, taken together,

[39] Cf. B. Geremek, 'La lutte contre le vagabondage à Paris aux XIVème et XVème siècles', Ricerche storiche ed economiche in memoria di Corrado Barbagallo, ii (Naples, 1970), pp. 213–36; B. Geremek, 'Renfermement des pauvres en Italie (XIVème–XVIème siècle): remarques préliminaires', Histoire économique du monde méditerranéen, 1450–1650: mélanges en l'honneur de Fernand Braudel, i (Toulouse, 1973), pp. 206–07; Geremek, 'Criminalité, vagabondage, paupérisme', p. 339 et seq.; J. Misraki, 'Criminalité et pauvreté en France à l'époque de la Guerre de Cent Ans', in Mollat, Études, ii, pp. 535–46; R. Favreau, 'Pauvreté en Poitou et en Anjou à la fin du Moyen Âge', ibid., ii, p. 604 et seq.; Gutton, La société et les pauvres, pp. 211–18, 343–45, 364, 369; Foucault, Folie et déraison, pp. 74–75; Slack, 'Poverty and Politics', p. 165.

[40] Cf. Pugh, 'Social Welfare', p. 375, and Jordan, Philanthropy in England, pp. 230–32.

[41] See Bonenfant, 'Un aspect du regime calviniste', p. 270 et seq.; Pugh, 'Social Welfare', pp. 362–66.

[42] Estimates for Lyons, in Davis, 'Assistance', pp. 800, 819–20, and in Gascon, Grand commerce, i, pp. 403–04; also R. Gascon, 'Économie et pauvreté aux XVIème et XVIIème siècles: Lyon, ville exemplaire et prophétique', in Mollat, Études, ii, pp. 755–56.

find no real parallel in Protestantism? Is there no real possibility of discerning, in the historical dimension, a specifically Catholic theory and practice of charity? There are of course formidable obstacles blocking any such view. Not least of these are the facts that Catholics did not always think or act in the same way, that there was a spectrum of opinion in the Church rather than a core of agreed and accepted precept, and that the proper organization of poor relief more than once became a subject of vigorous public controversy. Representatives of different religious orders displayed very different preoccupations, even where they were not openly arguing about such matters as the propriety of charging interest on loans to the poor from Monti di Pietà,[43] or the justification for interfering with the fundamental human right of begging and travelling.[44] And Catholicism was not, any more than the varieties of Protestantism, an abstract and static principle which could flourish *in vacuo*: to influence the course of history it must grow in local soils and take on some of their colour. The conclusions of every local study are clouded by the suspicion that its people were acting, not as Catholics, but as Parisians, or Lyonnais, or Venetians. There is the sensible reservation that a prominent determinant of philanthropy in any particular place may well have been the magistrate's concern with law and order, and not the preoccupations of religion. In general, the arrangements of any particular Catholic society were liable to be determined by a very complex interplay of forces—by the various religious orders represented within it, by lay fraternities old and new, by circles of devout persons exerting pressure on the public authorities, by the personal attitudes of the magistrates and by their knowledge of what was being done elsewhere. And in Catholic societies patterns are complicated by the hardy survival of medieval institutions beside the *nouvelle vague* philanthropy of Catholic reform and the Counter Reformation.[45]

Impressionism, though, is sometimes a good counter to feelings of defeat. Let us ask whether Protestant societies knew any exact equivalent to what we can perhaps define as the most prominent

---

[43] See M. Ciardini, *I banchieri ebrei in Firenze nel secolo XV e il Monte di Pietà fondato da Girolamo Savonarola* (Borgo San Lorenzo, 1907), doc. xvi, pp. lii–liii, 63–67 J. T. Noonan, Jr., *The Scholastic Analysis of Usury* (Cambridge, Mass., 1957), p. 294 *et seq.*

[44] Nolf, *Bienfaisance à Ypres*, doc. viii, pp. 40–76. Soto's *Deliberacion*, already cited; stands opposed to the work of a Benedictine, Juan Medina, *De la orden que en algunos pueblos de Espana se ha puesto en la limosna: para rimedio de los verdaderos pobres* (Salamanca, 1545). For some interesting new points about the Soto-Medina controversy, see Martz, *Poverty and Welfare*, p. 29 *et seq.*

[45] *Cf.* Gutton, *La société et les pauvres*, pp. 410–11; Pullan, *Rich and Poor*, Parts I and II.

features of the charity and mercy systematically practised by the standardized institutions of the Counter Reformation. Let us, to begin with, hark back to one of the traditional contrasts between Catholicism and Protestantism: the hoary question of whether Catholic doctrine really encourages the almsgiver to think only of self-advantage and to treat the poor with a total absence of discrimination. For this belief there is, or seems to be, ample authority in the famous treatise of Charles V's chaplain, Domiñgo Soto. The core of it lies in his declaration that almsgiving is an expression of the Christian virtue of mercy, which gives eternal life to its practitioners, and that as mercy is a thing distinct from justice it can actually be more meritorious to give alms to the unjust than to the righteous man.[46] Now, one cannot deny that some such motif continued to exist in Catholic social theory, or refuse to acknowledge that the desire for self-sanctification through acts of mercy did in fact constitute a very powerful and openly avowed incentive to action among devout Catholics in, let us say, sixteenth-century Italy or seventeenth-century France. The fault lies, not in reporting Soto, but in repeating his sentiments as if they were those of the whole Church. It lies also in making the assumption that a desire for self-sanctification will automatically cancel out regard for the condition of other people. The two could be fused together in the manner of the Italian Jesuit Benedetto Palmio, when addressing two congregations of Christian workers in Venice in 1588: for he then proclaimed that the highest form of merit lay in the conquest of the souls of others and in snatching them from the jaws of the prowling Demon of sin.[47] Exhaustive treatment of the more practical theologians being impossible, let us jump almost at random over another fifty years. Let us cross the frontier into Bavaria to look at the writings of another Jesuit, the court preacher Jerome Drexel, whose treatise on almsgiving, *Gazophylacium Christi*, earned translation from the original Latin into Flemish and may have had some international circulation. Some Soto-like opinions certainly survive in Drexel, and he is undoubtedly more concerned with the almsgiver's state of mind than with the effect of the donation. ' "Give in the best way, with the highest intentions", otherwise you will lose your bread, your money *and* your merit'.[48] Alms, he says, do not lose

[46] Soto, *Deliberacion*, fos 21v., 26–27.

[47] See B. Palmio, 'Alle congregationi delli magnifici Signori Governatori et delle magnifice Signore Governatrici della Casa delle Cittelle di Venetia nella Zuecca', in *Constitutioni et regole della Casa delle Cittelle di Venetia* (Venice, 1701), pp. 7–8. *Cf.* Pugh, 'Social Welfare', p. 358 *et seq.*

[48] J. Drexel, *Gazophylacium Christi; sive, De Eleemosyna*, Pars II, *caput* v, in his *Opera omnia*, iii (Lyons, 1647), p. 178. For a biographical note on Drexel,

their merit by finding their way into unworthy hands, and he adopts a view of mercy which is rather similar to Soto's. 'Charity embraces the goodness of man, mercy his misery: the merciful man is like God to the wretch whom he assists, and in this respect charity is inferior to mercy and yields place to it'.[49] He declares that moral judgments should be excluded almost entirely from acts of mercy and thinks it unlikely that the giving of alms could ever corrupt their recipient. But if he rejects moral judgments on the poor, he does not intend to eliminate economic judgments or reject attempts to discriminate between the *miser* and the *miserior*, where funds will not suffice for both.[50] And he is quite prepared to recommend an order of priority, somewhat coloured by the preoccupations of the order to which he belongs. 'The poor are not, as we shall see, to be subjected to too much prying curiosity. Nonetheless one must consider where the benefit can best be bestowed and where the need presses with greatest weight. Ill-considered and totally blind giving is not to be commended. Therefore let some choice be exercised, after this fashion. We ought to give, above all others, to the aged and to the sick, and then to youthful scholars who go in want. Some account may be taken of age, and let us give preference to old men who, although they do not fly from labour, still cannot easily earn their bread. . . .'[51] Discrimination and self-regard on the part of the almsgiver were not mutually exclusive, and the clearly established presence of discriminating measures in Catholic societies should not cause us to deduce that the quest in them for merit and self-sanctification had altogether ceased. On the contrary it permeates the sermons of such active people as Palmio or Drexel or Vincent de Paul, and is clearly evident in the spirit which informed the fraternities that they created.

In effect, the regard of the merciful man was being deliberately focused so that it turned, not only inwards upon himself, but at the same time outwards upon his fellow-men, who were not to be treated merely as physical beings suffering material want and hardship, but chiefly as endangered souls. The practice of mercy was not simply to be a method of notching up merit points by blind and undirected gifts. Subtler and richer than that, it was to become a means of imitating and obeying God, and of achieving contact with

---

1581–1638, C. Sommervogel, *Bibliothèque de la Compagnie de Jésus* (Brussels–Paris, 1890–1909), iii, col. 181. The *Gazophylacium* was published in Latin at Munich in 1637 and subsequently also at Antwerp; a Flemish edition appeared at Antwerp in 1641.

[49] J. Drexel, *Gazophylacium*, Pars III, *caput* vi, p. 204.

[50] *Ibid.*, Pars II, *caput* v, p. 177; Pars III, *caput* vi, p. 210.

[51] *Ibid.*, Pars II, *caput* ii, p. 167.

him through his members, the true and patient poor of Christ.[52] An essential part of it was the compassion which could only come from personal contact with the poor—a thing which must not be destroyed either by haphazard almsgiving (the coin or loaf tossed fastidiously out of window to a crowd below)[53] or by any internment of the poor that might become necessary in the interests of moral or medical hygiene. Such personal contact, and the regular service of the poor, were a kind of asceticism which entailed, not only loss of self, but mortification of the senses by immediate proximity to dirt, disease and stench.[54] Furthermore, beyond physical ministration to the body of the poor lay spiritual ministration to the soul, and it was in this that the mercy and charity of the Counter Reformation found their highest goal and purpose. In principle physical relief was frankly subordinated to this higher end. Quite simply, the Counter Reformation was a campaign for the conquest of souls, and in many places the most immediate enemies of the soul were, not heresy or infidelity, but ignorance and sin. Poverty and vagrancy were their allies, and could be attacked by extending relief even to the wicked, but at the same time using it in such a way as to effect in them a total moral transformation. If the grand strategic aim was the conquest of souls, corporal relief was a tactic aimed towards it, and had always to be completed by the extension of spiritual physic—whether in the form of very basic Christian doctrine, or in that of the sacraments: especially that of the general confession to a competent priest, which would atone for the inadequacies of previous confessions and might well save a soul from perdition.[55] When the duty ladies of Vincent de Paul's Dames de la Charité advanced gallantly into the squalor of the Hôtel-Dieu in Paris, the soups and dainties they carried to the sick poor were frankly intended to secure a receptive audience for their exhortations to make a general confession.[56] To rescue a poor child from the threat of being sold into prostitution was, to certain ladies and gentlemen of Venice, to save her from the capital sins of adultery and fornication.[57] The beggar was a lost soul because he died on the streets without benefit of the sacraments, the vagrant in danger of hell for his idle body and his blasphemous tongue.[58] Such ills could and should be remedied. Perhaps no theme was more consistently

[52] *Ibid.*, Pars II, *caput* v, p. 178; Pars III, *caput* v, p. 199; *Conferences of St Vincent de Paul*, i, pp. 56–59, 16 March 1642; Coste, *M. Vincent*, i, pp. 95–96, 106–07, 317–19.

[53] Drexel, *Gazophylacium*, generally, and especially at Pars II, *caput* iv, p. 173.

[54] *Cf.* Pullan, *Rich and Poor*, pp. 265–67; *Conferences of St Vincent de Paul*, i, pp. 19–20, 19 July 1640, p. 168, 10 January 1645.

[55] Coste, *M. Vincent*, i, pp. 88–90.   [56] *Ibid.*, i, pp. 281, 325–28.

[57] Pullan, *Rich and Poor*, p. 386 *et seq.*   [58] See above, n. 6.

stressed by the religious leaders of Catholic Europe than the superiority of spiritual to merely corporeal charity.[59] One finds the surprisingly optimistic assumption in the pronouncements of Vincent de Paul and the Compagnie du Saint Sacrament that a sufficiency of physical charity can virtually be taken for granted. What one needs to do is to ensure its extension to the soul.[60] Can we find the same emphasis in, say, a community dominated by the faith of Calvin—the same accent on the saving of souls by merciful human action with the aid of the divine mysteries? We are talking of the actual saving of souls, and not merely of enforcing outward conformity to an official religious creed.

Another distinguishing feature of Catholic acts of mercy is the importance of action, not by the individual and not by the religious community as a whole, but by the confraternities which proliferate within it. They are, in effect, societies which seek a special degree of merit through the following of a man-made Rule, and whose members do in common things believed to contribute to salvation. They are friendly societies where premiums are paid in good works and the rewards mature in eternal life. Through them the community of Catholics becomes fragmented and many-celled in a way in which the Protestant community is not.[61] For religious fraternities, as they were in the early sixteenth century, stood for certain principles and attitudes which excited Luther's deep disapproval. It was not merely that he objected puritanically to their beeriness and bonhomie. He disliked them on the much more serious grounds that they existed only for mutual aid and congratulation, and 'by means of these many external brotherhoods devoted to works they oppose and destroy the one, inner, spiritual, essential brotherhood common to all saints'.[62] But even as Luther wrote the concept of the brotherhood was changing, in Italy if not in Germany; the Societies for the Poveri Vergognosi and the Companies or Oratories of Divine Love were far more outward-looking than their predecessors. They, and their later descendants in the Jesuit societies, the Compagnie du Saint Sacrement and the organizations of Vincent de Paul, adopted

[59] Cf. e.g. Gutton, La société et les pauvres, pp. 324–26; Conferences of St Vincent de Paul, i, pp. 4, 17–18, 31 July 1634, 19 July 1640: Pullan, Rich and Poor, pp. 402–03.

[60] Conferences of St Vincent de Paul, iii, p. 293, 11 November 1657; cf. Coste, M. Vincent, ii, pp. 484–85.

[61] Cf. N. Z. Davis, 'Some Tasks and Themes in the Study of Popular Religion', in The Pursuit of Holiness in Late Medieval and Renaissance Religion: Papers from the University of Michigan Conference, ed. C. Trinkaus and H. A. Oberman (Leiden, 1974), pp. 316–18.

[62] 'The Blessed Sacrament of the Holy and True Body of Christ and the Brotherhoods (1519)', Luther's Works, xxxv, ed. E. T. Bachmann (Philadelphia, 1960), pp. 67–73.

the dual aims of sanctification for themselves by the practice of mutual love, and salvation for outsiders by the practice of acts of mercy which would redeem the soul through the care of the body.[63] This led to a renewal of concern with the uprooted and unrespectable, with the kind of person who was not merely slack in his devotions but did not even know what they were, and who might find in the gaol or the galley little opportunity to practise them. In its more attractive phases it led, also, to a determination to imitate that side of Christ which had made him go down among the lost people, to rub shoulders with the harlot, the leper and the possessed.[64] These new fraternities might, as did the Compagnie del Divino Amore, begin by concentrating on a narrowly defined sphere of action, such as the care of 'incurable' (i.e. pox-ridden) patients, the new lepers of the sixteenth century, and later broaden out their interests into a much more general concern for the poor. The dual aim of the confraternities was well expressed by Vincent de Paul when he said in two of his weekly 'conferences': 'God has also another design, my dear sisters; that of your own perfection; for, my daughters, what will it profit you to gain all souls for God, if you lose your own?' And, fifteen years later, 'the Daughters of the Hôtel-Dieu have as their end first their own perfection and then the relief of the sick. . . .'[65]

There were many fraternities which closely reflected the more advanced trends in Catholic devotion, and especially the new enthusiasm for frequent communion and confession. As the attacks of iconoclastic reformers multiplied, these repeatable sacraments had become triumphant insignia of the Catholic faith.[66] They began, incidentally, to impart a peculiar flavour to Catholic charity, with which they were associated through statutes which enjoined their

[63] On the Compagnie del Divino Amore, see P. Paschini, 'Le Compagnie del Divino Amore e la beneficenza pubblica nei primi decenni del Cinquecento', in his *Tre Ricerche sulla storia della Chiesa nel Cinquecento* (Rome, 1945), and S. Tramontin, 'Lo spirito, le attività, gli sviluppi dell' Oratorio del Divino Amore nella Venezia del Cinquecento', *Studi Veneziani*, xiv (1972), pp. 111–36. For the statutes of the early Compagnie, see Tacchi Venturi, *Storia della Compagnia di Gesù*, I ii, pp. 25–38, and A. Cistellini, *Figure della riforma pretridentina* (Brescia, 1948), pp. 273–77. On the Compagnie du Saint Sacrement, see Allier, *La Cabale, passim*; Chill, 'Religion and Mendicity', *passim*; Gutton, *La société et les pauvres*, p. 377 *et seq.*; Pugh, 'Social Welfare', pp. 371–74.

[64] Palmio, 'Alle congregationi', pp. 18–19; Coste, *M. Vincent*, ii, p. 516; Foucault, *Folie et déraison*, pp. 191–92.

[65] *Conferences of St Vincent de Paul*, i, p. 19, 19 July 1640; iii, p. 98, 29 September 1655.

[66] See Tacchi Venturi, *Storia della Compagnia*, I i, pp. 217–90; H. O. Evennett, *The Spirit of the Counter Reformation* (Cambridge, 1968), pp. 37–39; Bossy, 'The Counter Reformation', pp. 62–64.

regular use upon brothers and sisters.[67] From one standpoint the sacraments were simply the greatest gift the charitable person could bestow upon the unfortunate. From another, communion (or the adoration of the sacrament) offered to the servant of the poor not merely a reminder but an actual experience of the charity of Christ to mankind, and a means as it were of impregnating oneself anew with the divine love—which was then expressed outwardly in charity or mercy towards the poor. Alternatively, the taking of the sacrament and the works of corporal mercy were complementary means of establishing contact with Christ—who, as the Gospel made plain, would count as done to himself every merciful act done to the poor. Often the poor themselves were urged to the frequent use of the sacraments, even as the three hundred paupers of Mâcon identified by the new fraternity of St Charles Borromée in 1621 were assembled every Sunday in the church of Saint-Nizier, and there exhorted to go to confession once a month and at the same time to take communion if their confessors would allow it.[68]

Confraternities of the devout showed a natural enough desire to induce the poor to follow a regime which rather resembled their own. Determination to reshape the poor person's life on earth in the interests of his soul could, in Italy or France, result in his internment within the walls of an institution closely resembling a penal monastery. Catholic and Protestant communities were about equally likely to establish houses of correction and hospitals designed to eliminate practically all begging; but they may have attained their positions via rather different routes. Where Protestant cities and states would sometimes transform their monasteries and convents into hospitals or schools, or switch their revenues to educational and charitable uses,[69] their Catholic counterparts extended monasticism and imposed it on the poor. One gets the impression that the line between a monastic and a charitable institution was often rather finely drawn: both, in Venice at least, were comprised under the same term, 'luoco pio', and sixteenth-century institutions designed to combat prostitution were avowedly cast in the form of religious houses.[70] The so-called 'hospitals' for Tertiaries offered refuges to

[67] See Pullan, *Rich and Poor*, pp. 232–33, 262, 276–77, 328–29, 388, 404; *cf.* Allier, *La Cabale*, pp. 18–20, and Coste, *M. Vincent*, i, pp. 120–21, 325–26.

[68] Coste, *M. Vincent*, i, p. 135.

[69] For examples, see F. L. Carsten, *Princes and Parliaments in Germany from the fifteenth to the seventeenth century* (Oxford, 1959), pp. 39, 40, 160–61, 206–11; Chrisman, *Strasbourg*, pp. 236–38; Walton, *Zwingli's Theocracy*, pp. 177–78; R. A. Dorwart, *The Prussian Welfare State before 1740* (Cambridge, Mass., 1971), pp. 147–148; Webb, ed., *Poor Relief in Ipswich*, p. 12.

[70] *Cf.* Delumeau, *Vie de Rome*, i, pp. 429–31; Pullan, *Rich and Poor*, pp. 376–94; Gutton, *La société et les pauvres*, pp. 389–92; Deyon, *Amiens*, pp. 354–55.

spinsters who might otherwise have sunk into poverty or been forced into immorality.[71] In France and Italy we find by the seventeenth century what are in effect civic religious houses inhabited by the involuntary and the allegedly wilful poor, where internment by administrative decree has taken the place of claustration and where the regime alternates between more or less painful and back-breaking labour and an endless round of sacred readings and devotional activity.[72] Let it be said at once that there were in the process other things beside the element of 'imposed monasticism'. Segregation did not proceed only from a desire to protect the poor or contrive for them the conditions most favourable to salvation: it sprang also from the anxiety to produce in the city an order in which the grosser sins—together with such infidelities as adherence to the Jewish faith—could be physically as well as morally isolated, and through such isolation resisted and condemned. And more basically it could be said that decent conditions of public worship could never be obtained unless beggars and harlots were forcibly pre-vented from plying their trade in churches: and the religious im-pulse to get rid of begging, the concomitant of blasphemy, had become at least as strong as the magistrate's desire to put down vagrancy, the ally of crime, contagion, and possibly even civil disturbance.

I would not suggest that these features of Catholic mercy and charity are necessarily the dominant ones in every (or indeed any) Catholic society, or that the religious motive towards the relief of the poor outweighs of necessity the economic or administrative. I stress it chiefly because there is a danger of its being unduly obscured by our current and fashionable preoccupations with economic crisis and with problems of law and order in early modern Europe. These can sometimes trap us into forgetting the professedly transcendental aims of much charitable action. No-one can reason-ably fail to recognize, in these matters and in these centuries, much common ground between the overlapping territories of Catholicism and Protestantism. I have made a tentative effort to isolate a few distinguishing marks of the theory and practice of poor relief among Catholics, to focus on what is arguably peculiar, to offer what is (if regarded uncharitably) the blindingly obvious statement that certain fundamental and deliberately emphasized characteristics

---

[71] Pullan, *Rich and Poor*, pp. 208, 426.

[72] Delumeau, *Vie de Rome*, i, p. 412 *et seq.*; Pullan, *Rich and Poor*, pp. 362–70; P. Prodi, *Il Cardinale Gabriele Paleotti (1522–1597)*, ii (Rome, 1967), pp. 192–93; Foucault, *Folie et déraison*, p. 57 *et seq.*; Gutton, *La société et les pauvres*, p. 295 *et seq.*; Chill, 'Religion and Mendicity', p. 403 *et seq.*; Depauw, 'Pauvres, pauvres men-diants', p. 402 *et seq.*

of Catholic belief, devotion and organization were carried over into Catholic treatment of the poor. To concentrate on the doctrine of good works alone is not so much incorrect as unduly narrow. Let me in the end retreat, not into drawing conclusions, but into putting questions. Can we find in Protestant Europe—and before the days of General Booth—a situation in which the practice of mercy becomes a tactic at once in a personal quest for Christ and a war against sin, a campaign for the conquest of souls conducted by lay brotherhoods and sisterhoods, clerically inspired and bent on self-sanctification through the salvation of others in the greatest possible numbers? Can we find there these platoons of men and women who both observe and impose an ascetic discipline in accordance with explicit man-made Rules, whose magical weapons are the sacraments, and who attack poverty in so far as it becomes, not a way to salvation, but a peril to the soul?

University of Manchester.

IMPERIAL FACADE:
SOME CONSTRAINTS UPON AND CONTRADICTIONS IN THE BRITISH POSITION IN INDIA, 1919-35

By Judith M. Brown, M.A., Ph.D., F.R.Hist.S.

READ 9 MAY 1975

THE Raj still has a peculiar fascination for the British public, judging by the stream of popular books, radio and television programmes whose constant themes are the panoply of empire and the life-style of imperial rulers. Among English-speaking historians, however, approaches to Britain's Indian empire have changed markedly in the last twenty years. By the 1950s 'Imperial history' was a thing of the past. Gone was its admiring concentration on the men who ruled India and their measures as a way of understanding political change in the subcontinent. Attention shifted to indigenous initiatives and growth points. At first the emphasis was on India's western educated as organizers and spokesmen of a new kind of overtly nationalist politics. In the late 1960s the focus altered to whole localities within the subcontinent as it became clear that the western educated were not elites divorced from local, more traditional societies, but were still subject to its pressures, influenced by its perceptions and involved in its webs of patronage and alliance. In such an environment apparently nationalist politics were shot through with conflicts and contradictions: they were only one aspect of diverse manoeuvres for influence in society and the state structure. In the present decade the wheel has almost come full circle. Imperial overlords again receive attention: not now as architects and guardians, but as elements essential in the analysis of the changing style and content of Indian politics to the extent to which they created the framework of political life, defined its categories, means and ends. Indians' political behaviour is seen as explicable only in the context of responses to the perceptions and expectations of their rulers.

Although the British are the object of renewed scholarly interest they emerge as faceless, passionless parts of the analysis. Emphasis is on the parameters they imposed on Indian political development, rarely on the forces constraining them. There are studies of Indian politicians struggling with the constraints imposed on them by their

35

society and their rulers, but not of Viceroys and civil servants racking their brains in the early hours. This trend is confirmed by the memoirs of former administrators which tend to stress the 'hunting, shooting and fishing' aspects of expatriate life, rarely giving insights into the pressures to which their authors were exposed. In stark contrast Wavell's journal displays the dilemmas of the head of a rickety administration caught between war, famine, Indian political aspirations in conflict with each other and the attitudes of their rulers, and unsympathetic governments in London.[1] Nevertheless beforeWavell wasViceroy and the Raj's dissolution imminent there were considerable if less dramatic constraints upon British administrators in India and contradictions in their imperial position.

This paper discusses the years when India was governed under the 1919 Montagu–Chelmsford constitution—years when the Indian National Congress, the premier Indian political organization, oscillated between grudging constitutional cooperation and outright hostility to the Raj demonstrated in varieties of non-cooperation. It is not a survey of British policy;[2] but an enquiry into some of the pressures on those who helped to make and had to execute policy. It suggests that the complexities of Indian politics are revealed by seeing the British as politicians making as difficult choices as their Indian counterparts. Like Indian politicians they had to weigh a multiplicity of conflicting considerations, what was desirable against what was practicable. In a difficult climate, at times in lonely positions, this task often resulted in overwork, sometimes in illness or total collapse. One Chief Commissioner disappeared from the turbulent North-West Frontier with a nervous breakdown. A Governor of Bombay went home on leave in 1931 with an ulcer reactivated by what he called two and a half years of 'unremitting strain and anxiety'.[3] The empire, however, still seemed a formidable edifice. India had contributed munificently to the Great War: in the 1920s the British built themselves a new capital outside the old city of Delhi. But this was the façade of an increasingly vulnerable structure. Pressures were forcing men recruited as administrators to transform themselves into politicians, while their political options were seriously curtailed. To demonstrate this the paper sketches the structure of the Raj, indicating some inbuilt contradictions and weaknesses, and then illustrates the theme with particular examples.

[1] *Wavell. The Viceroy's Journal*, ed. P. Moon (London, 1973).
[2] For an analysis of British policy towards India's constitutional status, with particular emphasis on the role of British politics see R. J. Moore, *The Crisis of Indian Unity 1917–1940* (Oxford, 1974).
[3] F. Sykes, *From many Angles. An Autobiography* (London, 1942), pp. 413–14.

The Indian empire was a complex governmental structure in which the British were not a monolithic group with a coherent ideology and clear chain of command. This fact contributed greatly to the Raj's internal strains. Responsibility lay in three main centres—London, where the Secretary of State for India was answerable to Cabinet and Parliament; Delhi, where the Viceroy ruled with an appointed council and an elected legislative assembly; and the provincial capitals, where governors had their counterparts of the Delhi machinery with the difference that Indian ministers responsible to the provincial legislature controlled certain aspects of government. Although Parliament was the ultimate authority and questions were frequently asked on Indian affairs, most policy decisions were not the outcome of parliamentary debates but pragmatic compromises between men administering India from these three centres, whose perceptions and priorities varied as they faced different situations, experienced different pressures and had to defend their decisions before very different audiences.

The Secretary of State had to balance advice from the Viceroy and from his own council which was often heavily weighted with 'Old India Hands'. More constricting was his need to sanction only policies acceptable to the Cabinet in the context of British public opinion and party politics. This constraint was particularly tight when an election was imminent or the government had a weak or divided parliamentary base. In 1922 the Secretary of State in the Lloyd George coalition reported to the Viceroy how Liberal weakness and growing Conservative antipathy were straining the government, and that if they were to avoid a reversal of their reform policy for India, which he thought 'would mean the end of the Indian empire,' they 'must try and avoid, until things get brighter, presenting to the Government or Parliament proposals that they would reject.'[4] In 1929 his successor expressed relief that the Viceroy had decided against a fresh cotton excise which would have alienated Lancashire voters: 'you have provided me with a useful store of merit on which I can draw in the Cabinet if any criticism is made upon the Government of India.'[5] The appearance of Labour M.P.s and their electoral supporters posed new problems for any government which supported tough measures in India against trade unions or apparently popular movements: the Labour Government was particularly embarrassed at having to sanction means of combating civil disobedience in 1930. On the other hand the persistence

[4] Montagu to Reading, 23 February 1922, India Office Library (IOL), Reading Papers, MS. EUR.E.238 (4).
[5] Peel to Irwin, 14 February 1929, IOL, Halifax Papers, MS. EUR.C.152 (5).

of 'die-hard' attitudes towards India in vocal British circles constrained Secretaries of State who believed that constitutional reform
was the only foundation for imperial stability. Sam Hoare, representing the National Government in the early 1930s, experienced this
pressure most savagely as Churchill worked up an attack on the
proposed reforms, backed by the *Morning Post* and the *Daily Mail*.[6]

The Viceroy, often an aristocrat with little previous knowledge of
India, depended heavily on the advice of Government of India
bureaucrats, particularly in his Home Department. He also had to
consider the needs and fears of his military and financial advisors,
and to support his governors, while ensuring that provincial
decisions did not conflict with what was desirable from an all-India
view-point. Moreover under the 1919 constitution he had to woo his
Legislative Assembly, although he could resort to his reserve powers
and certify legislation in emergency and his council was not responsible to the legislature. Far from being a decorative figurehead
as the sovereign's representative, the Viceroy had to exercise considerable political skill not only in weighing these often conflicting
considerations but in presenting them to Whitehall. His position was
particularly difficult when the party which had appointed him had
fallen from power in Britain. Reading pointed this out in a formidable telegram to Olivier, the Labour Secretary of State, in 1924.[7]
Within months he protested at Olivier's condemnation in the Lords
of the 'narrow and unfortunate' attitude of some I.C.S. men towards
Indian politicians when the new incumbent of the India Office had
felt it necessary to dispel what he called 'the fiction rather prevalent
in England that the Government of India and its whole civil service
is an organization of infallible and impeccable supermen, entirely
impartial and free from political prejudice.'[8]

Clashes between Delhi and London were generally smoothed
over; but occasionally resignations threatened. Willingdon resented the National Government's failure, because of the need for
speed, to inform him before giving orders to his own currency
officials on the status of the rupee when Britain left the gold standard
in September 1931. Within days another crisis threatened his relations with London, and he appeared likely to resign when the
Cabinet refused his proposed cuts in I.C.S. pay. At the turn of the
year he again had to bend to Whitehall over the composition of his

[6] Hoare to Willingdon, 25 February, 3, 17 and 31 March, 19 May 1933, IOL,
Templewood Papers, MS. EUR.E.240 (3).
[7] Viceroy to Secretary of State, telegram, 4 March 1924, IOL, MS. EUR.E.238
(13).
[8] Olivier to Reading, 26 June 1924, Reading to Olivier, 17 July 1924, IOL,
MS. EUR.E.238 (7).

council. He requested freedom to appoint more Indians and demonstrate that the British were in earnest about granting Indians more responsibility despite the simultaneous suppression of civil disobedience. Whitehall refused, partly because of the reaction it anticipated from European businessmen and officials. The government's main reason was Conservative opposition to such an idea: for it needed to conciliate them as it was manoeuvring through Parliament plans for an all-India federation in which the sting of responsible government would be drawn by the presence of India's Princes in the governmental structure.[9]

Meanwhile provincial governors argued from their particular local situations. They had to work the constitution yet maintain the prestige, morale and efficiency of their officials. Forces liable to precipitate local unrest demanded constant attention, not merely political aspiration but communal conflict and economic distress. Such constraints sometimes compelled governors to take action which embarrassed Viceroys looking to the all-India scene and London. Delhi's strictures on Bengal for its reluctance to release political prisoners provoked this outburst from the governor:

> We seem now to have got into the very position in which you have repeatedly assured me that you had no intention of placing us, namely, the position of receiving orders from the Government of India to take action which will very gravely imperil the safety of this province and which we can neither justify nor explain.[10]

There was considerable potential for conflict in an imperial structure whose centres of authority were so divided by situation and therefore by priority. The speed of communications intensified this potential. No longer were different sectors of government able to go their own ways in the knowledge that the Viceroy was far off by road or that London was some weeks journey away by sea. As telephones linked Viceroy and governors, as telegrams passed in hours between India and Britain, press messages flashed inconveniently between continents and air travel increased, so the varying needs of the different echelons of imperial authority were exposed and thrust into conflict.

The priorities of administrators in India stemmed from the Raj's particular point of vulnerability, the fact which constrained all their decisions and determined the viability of any policy. This was the size and composition of the civil bureaucracy. The British ruled a

[9] Templewood, *Nine Troubled Years* (London, 1954), pp. 77–79; correspondence between Hoare and Willingdon on the composition of the Viceroy's council, December 1931–February 1932, IOL, MS. EUR.E.240 (1), (5).
[10] Lytton to Irwin, 25 February 1927, IOL, MS. EUR.C.152 (21).

subcontinent the size of Europe without Russia whose population was about one-fifth of the world's total, of whom 247 million lived in British rather than Princely India, directly under imperial administration. To do this they employed the I.C.S.—just over 1000 men—and under 3000 supporting all-India officials in such fields as education, medicine and forestry. In the 1920s Indianization increased in these services which had been predominantly British. Lower rank officials were almost all Indians: they were so numerous that the Statutory Commission did not even attempt to count them in 1930.[11] British taxpayers contributed not a penny to the Raj. It was financed from Indian revenues which dropped sharply during the world-wide slump of the 1930s.

India therefore posed for the British problems common to many governments but in acute form—how to recruit and control their servants. Expatriate recruitment to the all-India services was a constant difficulty in this period; and Indianization became a practical as well as political necessity. Control at I.C.S. level was generally effective, although on occasion district officers embarrassed superiors by their actions. The I.C.S. was, however, badly strained by demands made on it as a result of the 1919 constitution and growing Indian expectations of official support for educational and economic development. One governor commented, 'For long, it seems to me, we have been carrying on in a sort of hand-to-mouth struggle to meet our daily obligations, without the reserve necessary to adapt our administration to new problems and new requirements in a way which would command the confidence and respect of the public . . . [any] additional call on the available higher staff, is sufficient to dislocate the machine and to paralyse all progress.' Moreover as Indians entered the ranks of the 'Heaven-born' so the sensitivity of the service to political and social pressure in times of conflict between rulers and subjects increased.[12] In the lower levels of the administration and the police such dangers were multiplied. Government never lacked Indian recruits for such posts

[11] *Report of the Indian Statutory Commission Volume I—Survey* (London, 1930), Cmd. 3568, pp. 263–80.
[12] For problems of recruitment see Reading to Peel, 20 July 1922, IOL, MS. EUR.E.238 (5); *Report of the Royal Commission on the Superior Civil Services in India* (London, 1924), Cmd. 2128; D. C. Potter, 'Manpower Shortage and the End of Colonialism. The Case of the Indian Civil Service', *Modern Asian Studies*, 7, 1 (1973), pp. 47–73. An example of local action embarrassing superiors was the arrest of Vallabhbhai Patel in March 1930 by a Gujarat district magistrate without previous approval of Bombay government; Viceroy to Secretary of State, telegram, 10 March 1930, National Archives of India, Home Political Department (NAI, Home Poll.), 1930, File No. 247/II. For the strain on the administration see Sir Frederick Sykes, Governor of Bombay, to Irwin, 21 May 1930, IOL, Sykes Papers, MS. EUR.F.150 (2).

as government service was traditionally prized and there were few other openings for those whose caste forbade manual labour. But the problems of securing the loyalty of these poorly paid allies and controlling their actions were never solved.[13]

Because the administration was thinly spread and dependent on Indian co-operation the Raj was extremely vulnerable—not to isolated riots or rebellious movements, which could be dealt with by emergency powers and the army, with military assistance from Britain if necessary.[14] The real danger was widespread collapse of Indian acquiescence and co-operation, in the form of resistance to law or refusal to pay the taxes which financed the Raj, particularly if combined with disaffection among Indian officials. Consequently the British needed assistance from individuals and groups besides those whom they employed, to secure the loyalty of the vast majority, to provide channels of information, to man the infrastructure of public life and to finance the imperial edifice. Imperialists on a budget and few in number, the British only survived in India—as they had entered it—by eliciting collaboration from Indians in a multiplicity of ways. In the 1920s, however, this political aspect of their governmental task was complicated by developments within and outside India.

In India social and economic change generated demands from desirable allies which the British found difficult to concede without endangering what they considered their essential interests. For example, Indian businessmen clamoured for Delhi's release from London's domination in financial matters to prevent the subordination of Indian interests to those of British manufacturers and investors. By the 1920s Delhi effectively controlled tariff policies; but the rupee's exchange rate remained a source of acrid controversy, and as a symbol of India's inability to protect her interests was partly responsible for the business funds which financed civil disobedience.[15] More unmanageable were escalating political demands. By the 1920s even so-called Moderates demanded a constitution akin to Dominion Status; while a section for whom Jawaharlal Nehru spoke called for complete independence. The latter demand

[13] For an example of problems of control caused by injudicious recruiting and weak discipline in the Bombay Presidency police see Bombay Inspector-General of Police to Bombay Home Secretary, 29 May 1930, NAI, Home Poll., 1930, File No. 257/V and K.-W.; Irwin to Wedgwood Benn, 6 December 1930, IOL, MS. EUR.C.152 (6).

[14] For an assessment of British strength in India see Viceroy to Secretary of State, telegrams, 7 January and 5 February 1922, IOL, MS. EUR.E.238 (11).

[15] Sir Frederick Sykes, Governor of Bombay, to Irwin, 25 March 1931, IOL, MS. EUR.C.152 (26); L. Naranji to M. R. Jayakar, 27 January 1932, National Archives of India, M. R. Jayakar Papers, File No. 456.

was clearly incompatible with British interests: even the former met fierce resistance in Parliament. Yet neither could be ignored if the Raj was to retain an effective substructure of alliances.

As disruptive of imperial stability were changes in the relative status and influence of potential allies of government, and the clash of interests between Indian groups which complicated British choices and endangered the peace. The clearest example of economic change undermining a former imperial buttress was the case of India's great landholders. In this century their status and actions provoked unrest among their tenants and alienated many of the educated whose co-operation the Raj now needed, whereas immediately after the Mutiny a landlord alliance had seemed the empire's best security. Similarly British businessmen in India, stalwart supporters of empire, increasingly became a liability to administrators trying to conciliate those Indian businessmen whose frustrations impelled them towards Congress politicians. Conflict among Indians, particularly growing communal tension, also threatened the country's tranquillity. British devolution of power to secure Indian assistance in the imperial enterprise and the categories their perceptions of Indian society imposed on the constitutional parameters of politics exacerbated communal hostility. To welcome and use such divisions to retain control was also a natural response by some local administrators pushed into tight corners by Congressmen's actions. That arch-Tory Secretary of State, Birkenhead, explicitly approved of this approach.[16] However it was denounced by his successors and other holders of high office in the Raj as contrary to British intentions of training their subjects for self-government, and liable to provoke serious disorder.[17] Nonetheless in controlling opposition the government had to support and reward its current friends, a political necessity which narrowed its options, disturbed its conscience and ultimately made the creation and operation of a new constitution more difficult.

Developments in India were not isolated from world events. Improving communications further complicated the business of governing India; and the constraints on the British increased as India was integrated into a world political and economic community. One tiny indication of this was the Viceroy's concern in 1927 that one province intended to combine for a year the posts of

[16] Birkenhead to Reading, 22 January and 5 March 1925, IOL, MS. EUR.E.238 (8).
[17] Wedgwood Benn to Irwin, 20 March 1930, IOL, MS. EUR.C.152 (6); Sir Montagu Butler, Governor of Central Provinces, to Irwin, 8 April 1929, Sir Geoffrey de Montmorency, Governor of Punjab, to Irwin, 24 November 1929, IOL, MS. EUR.C.152 (23).

Director of Public Health and Inspector-General of Prisons. He feared the impression this would create outside India when the League of Nations Health Organization was arranging an exchange of Health Officers and planned to send a Malaria Commission to India.[18]

More significantly news of external events impinged on the Raj's relations with important groups of its subjects. The post-war fate of the defeated Turkish Sultan, head of the world Islamic community, temporarily alienated many Indian Muslims from the British whom they saw as despoilers of Islam. Their consequent participation in Gandhi's non-cooperation campaign of 1920–22 gave that movement much of its thrust. In the 1920s treatment of Indians in Kenya and South Africa hurt even the most moderate Indian politicians, and generated suspicion that they would never be equal partners in the empire.[19] Administrators handling delicate political situations in India were further hampered by rapid reporting in the Indian press of intemperate and ill-phrased statements in Britain about India. A Prime-Ministerial speech in 1922 caused a political furore in India because its description of the British core of the I.C.S. as the steel frame of the imperial structure, essential for India's stability, proved to many Indian politicians that British promises of reform were insincere or at best miserly.[20] When Birkenhead left the India Office Irwin breathed a viceregal sigh of relief: 'His person and personality have become too great a standing cause of sub-conscious offence to the political Indian.'[21] His troubles from reports of opinion in Britain were not ended by Birkenhead's departure. His attempts to secure Congress co-operation in the Round Table Conferences of 1930 and 1931 were, for example, jeopardized by Tory outbursts in Parliament.

Further external factors affected India during Irwin's viceroyalty. Among them was communist infiltration into India. More damaging than any political influence was the catastrophic impact of the

[18] Irwin to H. Marten, Acting Governor of Central Provinces, 29 September 1927, IOL, MS. EUR.C.152 (21).

[19] Reading to Peel, 30 August, 13 September 1923, IOL, MS. EUR.E.238 (6); Reading to Birkenhead, 24 December 1925, IOL, MS. EUR.E.238 (8). For the Khilafat movement and the thrust it gave to non-cooperation see J. M. Brown, *Gandhi's Rise to Power. Indian Politics 1915–1922* (Cambridge, 1972), chs. 6, 8 and 9.

[20] Secretary of State to Viceroy, telegram, 3 August 1922, Viceroy to Secretary of State, telegram, 10 August 1922, IOL, MS. EUR.E.238 (16). Olivier complained to Reading, 31 July 1924, of the reaction of British public opinion, dominated by 'Old India Hands', on moderate Indian politicians' willingness to believe that British promises were sincere; IOL, MS. EUR.E.238 (7).

[21] Irwin to Sir Malcolm Hailey, Governor of United Provinces, 19 October 1928, IOL, MS. EUR.C.152 (22).

economic depression. As prices plummeted and trade declined the Government of India faced rural unrest, urban turmoil in the once prosperous port of Bombay, and a slump in revenue just as expenditure on police and jails rose to deal with civil disobedience which fed on economic hardship. India's incorporation into a world community increased the constraints on her rulers and underlined the contradictions in their position.

One area where the realities behind the imperial façade were particularly plain was the operation of the 1919 constitution, itself an attempt to solve some of the British dilemmas. It was designed to safeguard British interests and shore up the Raj by channelling Indian political aspirations and providing a means for the peaceful adjustment of interests between Indians and the British and between Indians themselves. In two important respects it merely increased imperial dilemmas.

It put the British in a semi-parliamentary situation, an uncomfortable half-way house between autocracy and parliamentary government. Neither Viceroy nor governors now had official majorities in their respective legislatures which were enlarged and given more power. Consequently they were exposed to the danger either of concerted Indian opposition or of non-cooperation (whether in council or by refusal to stand and vote in elections) which would make nonsense of the whole experiment. As a safeguard against deadlock between a hostile legislature and an irremoveable executive the Viceroy and governor retained emergency powers; but their use was guaranteed to generate further hostility and convince potential Indian legislators that seats in the assemblies were not worth having.[22]

Moreover the British had little of the political equipment essential to securely based governments in politics where debate and consent are deemed important. They had no political party either in the country to rouse electoral support or in the assemblies to secure the passage of legislation. Nor did they feel they could remedy this situation, because official electioneering would have undermined their stated commitment to allowing free choice and meant abandoning their proclaimed impartiality by pandering to particular interests in order to attract support. However odd this seemed to people who expected governments to do all in their power to secure their supporters' success only informal influence was deemed possible. This was widely exerted. An ex-Governor of the Punjab testified to this, pointing as evidence to sixteen volumes recording interviews he

[22] Viceroy to Secretary of State, 18 February 1922, telegram, IOL, MS. EUR.E.238 (11).

gave and the state of his digestion after numerous meals in the homes of Punjabi landholders.[23] The honours system was a way of rewarding government adherents:[24] but it never produced a firm political grouping.

Official propaganda techniques were also weak, just when increasing literacy and the growth of the vernacular press made them more necessary. Although the Parliamentary Joint Committee on the 1919 constitution had recommended that government should be more in touch with the people little progress was made and provincial practice varied. Most provincial publicity departments survived only a couple of years. In 1924 the Bombay legislature threw out the department's grant, for example; and later to minimize opposition the governor linked the Directorates of Information and Labour in one post. The Punjab had one of the best propaganda bureaux. Its Director liaised with the press, issued communiqués and ghosted letters and articles which appeared in the press as from private individuals.[25] Not until the 1930 civil disobedience movement did propaganda become more professionalized. The Government of India then established a central publicity advisory committee: local governments issued bulletins and leaflets and organized meetings and loyalty leagues. The United Provinces government dropped leaflets from 'planes and used peripatetic cinemas. Bengal, too, used touring cinemas and publicity vans carrying material from the Departments of Agriculture, Industry, Veterinary and Public Health; it even ran to radio time.[26]

As British administrators tried to transform themselves into effective politicians in the 1920s they relied for support in the constitutional arena on men who stood for special seats (for landholders, Europeans, commerce, Universities and minorities) and on Moderates who did not join Congress in boycotting the 1920 and 1930 elections or in obstructing the legislatures' business. But such

[23] Willingdon to Hoare, 3 September 1934, IOL, MS. EUR.E.240 (7); Sir Malcolm Hailey, Governor of United Provinces, former Governor of Punjab, to Irwin, 10 September 1928, IOL, MS. EUR.C.152 (22); Sir William Marris, Governor of United Provinces, to Irwin, 1 June 1926, IOL, MS. EUR.C. 152 (20).
[24] For the reasoning behind grants of honours see, for example, Memorandum on King's Birthday Honours, 1922, enclosed in Reading to Peel, 20 April 1922, IOL, MS. EUR.E.238 (5).
[25] Sir Frederick Sykes, Governor of Bombay, to Irwin, 22 May 1929, IOL, MS. EUR.F.150 (1); Sir Geoffrey de Montmorency, Governor of Punjab, to Irwin, 7 April 1929, IOL, MS. EUR.C.152 (23).
[26] For propaganda during civil disobedience see NAI, Home Poll., 1931, File Nos. 35/28 and 152; Punjab Chief Secretary to Bengal Chief Secretary, 17 May 1930, NAI, Home Poll., 1930, File No. 307; *Report on the Administration of Bengal 1932-33* (Calcutta, 1934), pp. xxxi–xxxii; *Report on the Administration of Bengal 1933-34* (Calcutta, 1935), pp. xix–xx.

alliances were pragmatic and unreliable. At elections which Congressmen did contest Moderates were by contrast disorganized and dull.[27] Once in the legislatures they often proved feeble allies, easily alienated by such factors as Lloyd George's 'steel frame' speech or the position of Indians in Kenya, often pushed into greater political demands by the need to prove themselves as patriotic as their obstructive compatriots. The British realized the difficulty of the Moderate position. Despite constant bemoaning among themselves what Reading called 'the curious instability of mental attitude displayed by many of the moderates',[28] they did their best to bolster these constitutional collaborators. In 1924, for example, when Congressmen in the central assembly called for complete self-government the Government of India appointed a committee to investigate the working of the constitution as a device to detach Moderates from those who wished to precipitate a constitutional breakdown.[29] As a result of such expedients and Indian disunity the constitution was made to work—after a fashion. Only in two provinces did obstruction force governors to suspend it; and the Government of India managed the central assembly with a judicious combination of organization and the Viceroy's powers.[30]

The 1919 constitution added to the contradictions of the British position in a second way. It committed them to a structure which they could not change quickly because that needed Parliamentary sanction, with all the pitfalls debates involved. Meanwhile in India its operation generated increasing pressure for change. Only eighteen months after the first elections under it the Viceroy underlined his government's predicament of trying to reconcile the British wish for dominance with Indian demands for more responsibility.

We are always in this dilemma that whilst we give a generous meed of praise to those in the legislatures and outside them who take part in public affairs with Government as an encouragement to others to join and do likewise, we are every day stimulating them to consider themselves fully capable of managing and governing their own country, and the more we praise them the more impatient the many become for the great experiment. . . .[31]

[27] Reading to Olivier, 7 and 21 February 1924, IOL, MS. EUR.E.238 (7).
[28] Reading to Montagu, 9 February 1922, IOL, MS. EUR.E.238 (4). For the problems of relying on the Moderates see also Montagu to Reading, 1 March 1922, *ibid.*; Viceroy to Secretary of State, telegram, 10 August 1922, IOL, MS. EUR.E. 238 (16); Reading to Peel, 20 September 1923, IOL, MS. EUR.E.238 (6).
[29] Viceroy to Secretary of State, telegrams, 26 January 1924, IOL, MS. EUR.E.238 (18), 15 February and 23 May 1924, IOL, MS. EUR.E.238 (13).
[30] Viceroy to Secretary of State, telegram, 27 March 1927, IOL, MS. EUR.C.152 (8).
[31] Reading to Montagu, 5 January 1922, IOL, MS. EUR.E.238 (4).

By 1929 one governor was arguing that it was impossible to maintain the present system. In the previous year administration had been possible only because people were waiting for the Statutory Commission's report on the constitution. He believed that if they reversed the trend towards Indian responsibility there would be an upheaval which they would have to quell with troops—a course the British public might not stand and which would rouse international opinion. The risks in advancing towards self-government were great, but other courses were more dangerous. Tersely he maintained they had no other option: 'Is it not wiser to do something before the machine peters out or blows up [?]'[32] Yet many British administrators felt that such concessions would amount to a dereliction of duty. As they saw it, by handing over more power to high caste Hindus who were the majority of political activists they would be sacrificing the minorities and the masses for whom they were trustees. Contradictions of ideology as well as interest thus restricted their ability to respond to pressures they had helped to create.[33]

Not surprisingly the 1919 constitution never proved an adequate mechanism for the peaceful adjustment of interests. Extraconstitutional conflicts erupted between Indians, and between subjects and rulers. The predicaments of British officials in dealing with these demonstrated the contradictions in their position and the limited options open to them.

In 1928, for example, Gandhi and Vallabhbhai Patel led a Gujarati farmers' campaign of refusal to pay an increased land revenue demand in Bardoli *taluka* in, Bombay Presidency. Sir Leslie Wilson, the Governor, determined to deal with it firmly lest he should have to give in wherever reassessment raised the revenue demand.[34] In practice he found this impossible. In the first place the campaign aroused widespread sympathy and threatened to have repercussions in his province which he could not countenance. His legislature was about to decide whether to co-operate with the Statutory Commission and he knew that the vote would probably be hostile if a compromise was not reached over Bardoli. Gujarati legislators and representatives of Bombay merchants had already threatened resignation on the issue, and Wilson feared he might lose all his Hindu ministers and possibly his Hindu legislators if he took action against Gandhi and Patel. Moreover Bardoli coincided with a strike in Bombay's cotton mills and the impending arrival of a new

[32] Goschen to Irwin, 26 February 1929, IOL, MS. EUR.C.152 (23).
[33] Sykes, *From Many Angles*, p. 335; Sir William Marris, 'India: the Political Problem', Cust Foundation Lecture, 16 May 1930, Manchester University Library.
[34] Wilson to Irwin, 14 March 1928, IOL, MS. EUR.C.152 (22).

governor whom Wilson wished to protect from a conflict-ridden start to office. He was also hampered by the actions of his local officials, not least by the questionable accuracy and fairness of the reassessement which was the bone of contention.

Local considerations were not the only factors constraining Wilson. The Viceroy intervened when Bardoli attracted India-wide attention. His doubts about the political nous of the Bombay government and the competence of its revenue officials convinced him that it would be impolitic to support Wilson in a conflict which would sour the Raj's political relationships throughout the subcontinent. 'I have been cudgelling my brains,' he wrote, 'to suggest ways to Leslie Wilson by which . . . he might extricate us all from a very threatening position.'[35] As a result of Delhi's pressure Wilson agreed to a committee of enquiry as a means of compromise. As Governor and Viceroy wrestled with conflicting pressures within India they received exhortations from Birkenhead who was insensitive to forces constraining men on the spot and was more perturbed at criticisms of the government in London from his own party for an apparently supine response to an insolent challenge. On such a local matter his diatribes had little effect for Irwin parried them successfully. Wilson admitted to Irwin that Bardoli had made him quite ill with worry and that he lost 12 lbs in weight![36] The conflict demonstrated more than the physical and mental strains of an imperial administrator's position. These stemmed from the very structure of British rule—the divided authority and different priorities within the administration, the frailties of the administrative machinery, and the need to conciliate Indian legislators while dealing with an extra-constitutional movement which appeared to threaten the government's position.

These pressures were even clearer in 1930 when Irwin had to co-ordinate policy towards civil disobedience—a campaign to break selected laws and undermine the loyalty of the Raj's Indian officials which Congress launched after refusing to attend the Round Table Conference to discuss a new constitution because Dominion Status was not its assured outcome. Yet Irwin's government could not attempt simply to suppress it as a seditious movement. His council's decisions in consultation with London and the provinces were a finely calculated balance between conflicting pressures.[37]

[35] Irwin to Goschen, 11 July 1928, *ibid*. For details of pressures on Wilson see communications between him, Irwin and Birkenhead, IOL, MS. EUR.C.152 (4), (5), (9), (22), (23).

[36] Wilson to Irwin, 15 August 1928, IOL, MS. EUR.C.152 (22).

[37] For details of Government of India policy towards non-cooperation and civil disobedience see D. A. Low, 'The Government of India and the First Non-

There were cogent arguments against a knock-out blow at Congress. Irwin knew that it was essential ultimately to secure peace with Congress and its co-operation in working any new constitution. Moreover Moderate politicians pressed him to negotiate with Congress leaders because they disliked seeing their compatriots jailed in thousands, revered Gandhi who led civil disobedience though they disagreed with him politically, and recognized that the movement had attracted wide support. Men such as Sir T. B. Sapru were vital to the success of the Round Table Conference, and Irwin strove to conciliate them before and during the London meeting. Consequently he was always open to possible contacts with Congress leaders, even those in jail, in order to procure their abandonment of civil disobedience, provided contacts did not look like negotiations. He was also consistently reluctant to sanction really firm measures of suppression.[38] A further disincentive to all-out repression was Irwin's awareness of the delicate position of Wedgwood Benn, Labour Secretary of State, who feared the effects of tough action on Labour voters and world opinion, particularly in America. 'It is a fact,' he told Irwin, 'that while . . . the Government backs you when you think it necessary to take action, we are all profoundly grateful when you can produce an atmosphere which makes action unnecessary.'[39]

However other considerations suggested that a hard line was essential. To combat the movement as far as possible under ordinary law, by steady pressure rather than wholesale arrests, forfeiture of funds and property, imposed immense and prolonged strain on local governments. Police and village officials were the weakest links in the administrative chain; and they were forced into conflict with their neighbours and compatriots and exposed to severe social pressure to resign. Governors urged this consideration on Irwin, the most vocal being Sykes, now Governor of Bombay, the storm centre of the movement. He argued for a comprehensive emergency powers ordinance similar to Britain's war-time DORA, to enable local governments to act swiftly and vigorously and thus save already stretched administrations from further strain. Military men and

---

Cooperation Movement—1920-22', *Journal of Asian Studies*, XXV, 2 (1966), pp. 241–59; ' "Civil Martial Law": The Government of India and the Civil Disobedience Movements 1930–34', *Congress and the Raj*, ed. D. A. Low (forthcoming).

[38] Irwin to Sir Frederick Sykes, Governor of Bombay, 12 and 26 September 1930, IOL, MS. EUR.C.152 (25); Irwin to Wedgwood Benn, 3 November 1930, IOL, MS. EUR.C.152 (6).

[39] Wedgwood Benn to Irwin, 27 February 1930 (also 15 and 22 May 1930), *ibid.*

Europeans in India also demanded tough action.[40] Such views underlined fears within the Government of India that by apparent weakness and willingness to parley with Congressmen the Raj was in danger of undermining those who stood by it and thus of losing their support—whether they were Muslims, Moderates, Europeans, Indian soldiers or civil servants. Irwin's dilemmas of juggling actual and potential allies, of bolstering the administration and squaring British and world opinion as he tried to control subversion while the Secretary of State steered a constitutional conference, demonstrated some of the contradictions behind the imperial façade.

Gandhi's leadership of civil disobedience further complicated the calculations of Irwin and his successor, Willingdon, when the campaign was resumed in 1932–34. Here was a leader of immense repute in India where many accorded him almost religious veneration, and abroad where some thought he brought spiritual values into public life. He professed non-violence yet he was a skilled practitioner of non-cooperation, the very technique to which the Raj was most vulnerable. This combination proved peculiarly difficult to deal with. If the administration imprisoned Gandhi and refused to talk with him it provoked demonstrations throughout India and alienated not only his followers but the wide circle of sympathizers who never participated in seditious struggles but were essential to the British for the successful operation of the constitution. However, government supporters and outright Congress opponents looked on British treatment of Gandhi as a barometer of official intentions and a sign whether they were to be sacrificed for a settlement with Congress. Irwin's inclination was to use Gandhi as far as possible to control Congressmen and to bring them into constitutional co-operation. This lay behind his reluctance to arrest him in 1930, his permission for Gandhi to meet fellow leaders in jail (even to the extent of providing a special train to take the two Nehrus between jails in Allahabad and Bombay), and ultimately his personal negotiations with Gandhi early in 1931 which resulted in a truce. Willingdon however refused even to see Gandhi when he was on the brink of renewing civil disobedience, and declined to have dealings with him in jail. The difference between the two viceregal approaches lay partly in personality; but also in the fact that by late 1931 many non-Congressmen and Indian Princes supported the National Government's constitutional proposals, as did Britain's Tory leaders.

[40] Sykes, *From Many Angles*, pp. 363–4, 402–3; E. Villiers, of Calcutta European Association to Irwin, 20 August 1930, IOL, MS. EUR.C.152 (25); G.O.C., Eastern Command, to Chief of General Staff, 14 June 1930, NAI, Home Poll., 1930, File No. 174; Government of India to Secretary of State, 17 June 1930, NAI, Home Poll., 1930, File No. 257/111.

This consensus Willingdon refused to endanger by parleying with Gandhi.

Gandhi's potential value as an ally in India was not the only calculation Viceroys had to make in their treatment of him. In Britain, too, his fate roused strong and conflicting reactions which had implications for governments' freedom of action on the whole front of Indian policy. Left-wing, anti-colonial and Christian spokesmen, among them the Archbishops of Canterbury and York, voiced unease at Gandhi's incarceration from the beginning of 1932, the terms of his imprisonment and Willingdon's refusal to talk with him. Conservatives however abhorred any suggestion of negotiations with or leniency towards him. Hoare and the National Government were thus caught in an unenviable dilemma. If they maintained a hard line towards Gandhi they risked Liberal and Labour hostility: if they talked with him they would rouse the ire of Conservatives, some of whom were conspiring to wreck the constitutional proposals which the government hoped would resolve some of Britain's Indian dilemmas and ensure co-operation in a new imperial framework. However they moved in relation to Gandhi they jeopardized British support essential to the acceptance of their proposals in Parliament. Hoare's reports of his dilemmas to Willingdon added to the pressures on the Viceroy generated in India.[41]

The problems Willingdon and Irwin experienced in dealing with Gandhi and civil disobedience were symptomatic of some of the constraints on imperial administrators and policy-makers between 1919 and 1935. These stemmed from the very structure of the Raj at a time when developments in India coincided with the subcontinent's integration into a world economic and political community and generated pressures which made the British position in India extremely vulnerable. The administration was stretched to cope with situations for which it was not designed; and a constitution was imposed which far from defusing these tensions increased the contradictions in the British position. Such changes moreover increased the potential for conflict inherent in a governmental structure where different echelons faced such diverse pressures and were answerable to such different audiences.

To appreciate the complexity and richness of Indian politics in a period which lacks the glamour and drama of the ultimate phase of the Raj it is essential to see the British participants in the political process not as guardians who according to an older historical vision

[41] Hoare's letters to Willingdon in 1932–4 were full of the implications of their treatment of Gandhi for British support for the constitutional proposals currently before Parliament. See IOL, MS. EUR.E.240 (2), (3), (11), (12); also Hoare to Stanley (Acting Viceroy), 3 August 1934, IOL, MS. EUR.E.240 (4).

brought their wards into the modern world, nor as faceless bureaucrats significant only for the way their perceptions and structures
forced Indians into new political styles and groupings. They were
men under pressure as much as their Indian counterparts, fumbling
for pragmatic solutions to problems for which there were no precedents. As the ground shifted under them, however, they kept up an
imperial façade which was more appropriate to the realities of
British power at the turn of the century.

University of Manchester.

WHY DID THE DUTCH REVOLT LAST EIGHTY YEARS?

By Geoffrey Parker, M.A., Ph.D., F.R.Hist.S.

READ 20 JUNE 1975

THE Dutch Revolt lasted longer than any other uprising in modern European history—from the iconoclastic fury in August 1566 to the Peace of Munster in January 1648; and it involved more continuous fighting than any other war of modern times—from April 1572 to April 1607 (with only six months' cease-fire in 1577) and from April 1621 to June 1647. Its economic, social, and political costs were enormous.[1] The longevity of the revolt becomes even more remarkable when one remembers that the two combatants were far from equal. The areas in revolt against Spain were small in size, in natural resources, and in population—especially in the first few years. In 1574 only about twenty towns, with a combined population of 75,000, remained faithful to William of Orange; Amsterdam, the largest town in Holland, stayed loyal to the king until 1578.[2] Against the 'rebels' Philip II could draw on the resources of Spain, Spanish America, Spanish Italy and, of course, the Spanish Netherlands. Although by the seventeenth century the odds had narrowed somewhat—by then there were seven 'rebel' provinces with a combined population of over one million—Spain could still call on vastly superior resources of men and money. There were a number of occasions in the course of the war when Spain seemed to stand on the threshold of success. In 1575, for example, the conquest of the islands of Duiveland and Schouwen in South Holland divided the rebel heartland in two and appeared to presage the collapse of the revolt. A decade later, in 1585, Antwerp was re-captured against all predictions, leaving Holland and Zealand dispirited and prepared to discuss surrender. As late as 1625, with the

[1] An effort has been made to quantify these costs at least for the major belligerents: G. Parker, 'War and economic change: the economic costs of the Dutch Revolt', in *War and economic development*, ed. J. M. Winter (Cambridge, 1975), pp. 49–71.

[2] For assessments of the population of Holland (and indeed of the Netherlands as a whole) cf. *The Sources of European economic history, 1500–1800*, ed. G. Parker and C. H. Wilson (to be published London, 1976), chap. 1, and J. de Vries, *The Dutch rural economy in the Golden Age, 1500–1700* (New Haven and London, 1974), pp. 74–101.

reconquest of Breda in Brabant and Bahía in Brazil, Spain's final victory seemed near. But total success never came. Spain never regained the seven northern provinces of the Netherlands and by 1648 Philip IV counted himself lucky to have retained the ten southern ones.

It is not difficult to explain Spain's initial failure to suppress the Dutch Revolt. Rapid victory was ruled out, in effect, by a combination of logistical factors. In the first place the Dutch population may have been small, but it included some who were determined to resist the Spaniards by all means and at all costs. For the Sea Beggars, the Calvinists and the other exiles who returned to Holland and Zealand in 1572 there could be no surrender: they, like the Prince of Orange, had decided to make Holland and Zealand their tomb, either in victory or defeat.[3] The Anabaptists too, who had a powerful following in most of the northern provinces, had everything to gain by renouncing their obedience to Philip II: they had been the victims of ruthless persecution in the Habsburg Netherlands.[4] More surprisingly, perhaps, and more important, Orange had the support of the Catholic majority of Holland and Zealand. Although their first reaction was, understandably, to avoid a commitment to either side for as long as possible, the Catholics were soon forced into Orange's camp by the brutal behaviour of the government forces. In a conscious attempt to expedite the end of the Revolt, the duke of Alva pursued a policy of 'beastliness' towards certain rebellious towns. In October 1572 he allowed his troops to sack the city of Mechelen, which surrendered unconditionally, in the expectation that such an example would encourage the other Orangist towns in the south to make their peace with him. It did.

---

[3] G. Groen van Prinsterer, *Archives ou correspondance inédite de la maison d'Orange-Nassau*, 1st series, iv (Leiden, 1837), pp. 2–6: a despairing letter from William of Orange to his brother, Count John of Nassau, written at Zwolle on 18 October 1572, announced that the prince was sailing forthwith to the only province remaining loyal to his cause, Holland, 'pour maintenir les affaires par delà tant que possible sera, ayant deliberé de faire illecq ma sépulture.'

[4] Of the 880 Netherlands Protestants recorded in the various 'Books of Martyrs' as having perished in the course of the sixteenth century, 617 (or 70 per cent) were Anabaptists; their total losses through Habsburg persecution must have numbered many thousands. Not surprisingly, as early as July 1572, the Anabaptists declared their support for Orange and provided money for his army. (G. Brandt, *The History of the Reformation and other ecclesiastical transactions in and about the Low Countries from the beginning of the 8th century down to the famous Synod of Dort, inclusive*, i (London, 1720), p. 295.) This was, of course, a bribe. In the 1560s Orange, like most other princes, had persecuted and even executed Anabaptists. For some of the reasons which underlay this intolerance, *cf.* W. Kirchner, 'State and Anabaptists in the sixteenth century: an economic approach', *Journal of Modern History*, xlvi (1974), pp. 1–25.

In November the duke inflicted the same fate on Zutphen, which brought about the capitulation of all strongholds in the north-east. In December, the Spanish army proceeded to massacre the entire population of Naarden, a small Orangist town in Holland: 'Not a mother's son escaped' Alva reported smugly to the king, and he passed on to Amsterdam to await the surrender of the rest of the province.[5] But the massacre of Naarden did not have the desired effect. Catholics and Calvinists alike became terrified of admitting the brutal Spanish troops, and their fear was reinforced in July 1573 when the citizens of Haarlem surrendered on condition their lives would be spared. Alva nevertheless ordered the execution of a score or so of them, together with most of the garrison. Haarlem was the last town in Holland to negotiate a settlement. Leiden in 1574 preferred starvation to surrender; the burghers of Oudewater in 1575 set their town on fire rather than see it fall intact to the Spaniards.

There was, of course, more to the resistance of Holland and Zealand than desperate courage. The physical and military geography of the north-west Netherlands was also of crucial importance. The area was, in the words of an English traveller writing in 1652, 'The great Bog of *Europe*. There is not such another Marsh in the World, that's flat. They are an universall Quag-mire. . . . Indeed, it is the buttock of the World, full of veines and bloud, but no bones in't.'[6]

It was certainly hard for the Spaniards to regain Zealand and South Holland, since the islands captured by the Sea Beggars in 1572 were separated from the mainland by deep channels (although with courage and resolution all things were possible, as the relief of Ter Goes in 1572 and the invasion of Schouwen in 1575-6 demonstrated). It was almost as hard for the Spanish army to operate in North Holland because of the great lakes, rivers and dikes which covered the country, much of which was below sea-level. In 1573 at the siege of Alkmaar and in 1574 at the siege of Leiden, dikes were

[5] *Epistolario del III duque de Alba*, ed. the duke of Alba, (Madrid, 1952), vol. iii, p. 261, Alva to the king, 19 December 1572: 'Degollaron burgueses y soldados sin escaparse hombre nacido'. The policy of 'beastliness' almost worked in Holland too: news of the massacre of Naarden spread fast and three magistrates from Haarlem came to offer the surrender of their town on 3 December, the day after the massacre; the Spanish commander, however, unwisely insisted on unconditional capitulation and this the town refused to do. Other towns also showed a willingness to negotiate but would not throw themselves on the Spaniards' mercy. *Cf.* the eye-witness account of a Catholic living in Amsterdam, the Spanish headquarters at this time: *Dagboek van Broeder Wouter Jacobszoon, prior van Stein*, ed. I. H. van Eeghen, i (Groningen, 1959), p. 90.

[6] Owen Feltham, *A brief character of the Low-Countries under the States. Being three weeks observation of the Vices and Vertues of the Inhabitants* (London, 1652), pp. 1 and 5.

broken in order to flood the fields around the town and thus prevent the formidable Spanish infantry from launching an attack on the walls. But Holland was not only a 'great Bog'; it was also almost an island and the Dutch took care never to lose control of the sea which surrounded them. Between 1572 and 1574, the war fleet of the Brussels government was destroyed in a series of violent engagements. Some of the actions were Spanish successes (like the battles on the Haarlemmermeer during the siege of the city); others were Spanish defeats (like the battle off Enkhuizen in October 1573 and the battle off Bergen-op-Zoom in February 1574). But whatever the result, the Spaniards lost ships which they were incapable of replacing since the principal shipyards (and the naval arsenal at Veere) were in rebel hands and it proved impossible to send new ships from Spain. The Dutch were thus able to keep their own ports open to receive reinforcements and supplies from abroad (especially from the exiled Netherlandish communities in England),[7] and to continue their vital trade with the Baltic (in 1574, almost 1,000 Dutch ships passed through the Danish Sound).[8] Surely, the royalist Owen Feltham speculated in 1652, the Dutch Revolt had succeeded because of:

> their strength in shipping, the open Sea, their many fortified Towns, and the Country by reason of its lowness and plentifull Irriguation becoming unpassable for an army when the winter but approaches. Otherwise it is hardly possible that so small a parcell of Mankind, should brave the most potent Monarch of Christendome who . . . hath now got a command so wide, that out of his Dominions the *Sunne* can neither rise nor set.[9]

Philip II's empire was indeed one on which the sun never set, and to most contemporaries the advantage in the Low Countries' Wars, at least during the reign of the Prudent King, seemed to lie with Spain. After all, only a few Dutch towns, such as Alkmaar or Rammekens, were entirely protected by an effective system of defence, with bastions, in the 1570s, and even they might have been

---

[7] Queen Elizabeth sent perhaps 1,200 men unofficially in the months of April and May 1572, but then withdrew them. The support of the Flemish and Walloon churches in England was smaller but steadier: the correspondence of the churches pullulates with details on the aid in men and money sent over to the Low Countries. *Cf. Ecclesiae Londino-Batavae Archivum*, ed. J. H. Hessels, ii (Cambridge, 1889), *e.g.* nos 112, 115, 123, 129; iii part i (Cambridge, 1897), *e.g.* nos 195, 197, 257, 367, 380. The Scottish government also sent substantial aid.

[8] F. Snapper, *Oorlogsinvloeden op de overzeese handel van Holland, 1551–1719* (Amsterdam, 1959): 989 Dutch ships passed out of the Sound in 1574, but only 840 in 1575 and 763 in 1576—clear evidence of the growing impact of the war.

[9] Feltham, *op. cit.*, pp. 83–85.

starved out in time.[10] Antwerp, Ghent and Brussels, three of the best-fortified towns in Europe, capitulated after a year's siege in 1584-85 and Antwerp (at least) possessed all the natural advantages of the Holland towns. It was near the sea, it was surrounded by low-lying land which could be (and was) flooded, and its population was predominantly Protestant.[11] Yet in spite of stout hearts, naval superiority and superb defences, Antwerp fell; and there is every reason to suppose that, given time, the towns of Holland and Zealand would have succumbed too. Time, however, was what the Spanish government lacked; time and money. The total cost of the Spanish army in the Netherlands between 1572 and 1576, a force of over 80,000 men at times (at least on paper), was estimated at 1.2 million florins every month. Spain simply could not provide such a sum. 'There would not be time or money enough in the world to reduce by force the 24 towns which have rebelled in Holland, if we are to spend as long in reducing each one of them as we have taken over similar ones so far', wrote the Spanish commander-in-chief, Don Luis de Requesens, in October 1574. 'No treasury in the world would be equal to the cost of this war', he echoed in November.[12] The siege of Mons in 1572 took six months; the siege of Haarlem in 1572-73 took eight months; the siege of Zierikzee in 1575-76 took nine months. Admittedly all three blockades were eventually successful, but while the Spanish field army was occupied in the sieges, the 'rebels' were free to attack and capture other strongholds in other areas. Moreover this siege warfare, with the winter months spent in frozen trenches three years running, was unpleasant for the troops; and the unpleasantness was exacerbated by the inability of the government to pay its soldiers for their heroic service. Inevitably it produced discontent in the Spanish army and both desertion and disobedience grew to alarming proportions. Whole companies broke away from the army and fled to France; whole regiments defied their officers and mutinied, and it might take

[10] The new bastions of Alkmaar appear clearly in the drawing of the siege of 1573 by Thomas Morgan, an eye-witness: All Souls College, Oxford, MS. 129, published by D. N. Caldecott Baird, 'Een engelse visie op het beleg van Alkmaar', *Alkmaars Jaarboekje*, 1970, pp. 101-07.

[11] A partial census of Antwerp in 1584 revealed 3,248 Protestant and 3,011 Catholic households, out of a total of 10,176 households covered by the census (perhaps 60 per cent of the city's population). *Cf.* the interesting and important article of A. van Roey, 'De correlatie tussen het sociale-beroepsmilieu en de godsdienstkeuze te Antwerpen op het einde der XVIe eeuw', in *Sources de l'Histoire religieuse de la Belgique* (Louvaine, 1968), pp. 239-58.

[12] *Nueva Colección de Documentos Inéditos para la historia de España*, v (Madrid, 1894), p. 368, Requesens to the king, 6 October 1574; Archivo General de Simancas, *Estado* 560 fo 33, Requesens to the king, 7 November 1574.

weeks, even months, and millions of florins, before they could be brought back into service. The deliverance of Alkmaar (1573), Leiden (1574) and Zierikzee (1576) from the grip of the king's forces can be confidently ascribed to the Spanish mutinies.[13]

To some extent, however, the Spanish troops in the Low Countries were actors on a wider stage. The punctual payment of their wages lay at the mercy of political decisions taken elsewhere. Philip II had other problems to resolve besides the Netherlands. He had to maintain Spanish influence in the Caribbean in the face of English and French competition: the French Huguenots attempted to plant colonies in Florida in 1563, 1564–65, 1568 and 1577–80; the English tried their hands at colonization too after 1560, but then found piracy at Spain's expense more rewarding.[14] Within Europe Philip II was concerned to keep both France and England as weak as possible, sending military aid to the French Catholics in 1563, 1567 and 1569, promising military aid to the English Catholics in 1570–71. It all cost money. Above all the King of Spain had to defend the Western Mediterranean against the Ottoman Sultan and for most of the 1570s this was a major concern which tied down men, money and material resources in large quantities. In order to defeat the Turkish fleet at Lepanto in 1571 and capture Tunis in 1573, and even more in order to defend Spain and Italy against the Sultan's counter-attacks, Philip II had to maintain and man a permanent fleet of 150 galleys in the Mediterranean. Several times between 1572 and 1576 the king's advisers had to decide whether to allocate resources to the Mediterranean or to the Netherlands; almost always they decided in favour of the former.[15] Although it is possible that Philip II's revenues in the 1570s were not equal to the cost of the Army of Flanders in any case, Spain's commitment to the defence

---

[13] On mutiny and desertion *cf.* G. Parker, *The Army of Flanders and the Spanish Road: the logistics of Spanish victory and defeat in the Low Countries' Wars, 1567–1659* (2nd edn, Cambridge, 1975), chaps. 8 and 9; and 'Mutiny and discontent in the Spanish Army of Flanders, 1572–1607', *Past and Present*, lviii (1973), pp. 38–52.

[14] D. B. Quinn, 'Some Spanish reactions to Elizabethan colonial enterprises', *Transactions of the Royal Historical Society*, 5th series, i (1951), pp. 1–23. On the cost of all this to Spain—the defence of Florida against the French cost 180,000 ducats in 1565–66 alone—*cf.* P. E. Hoffman, 'A study of Florida defense costs, 1565–85: a quantification of Florida history', *Florida Historical Quarterly*, li (1973), pp. 401–22; and K. R. Andrews, *Elizabethan privateering: English privateering during the Spanish war, 1585–1604* (Cambridge, 1964).

[15] For a few examples among many: Archivo General de Simancas *Estado* 550 fos 115–16, 'Parescer' (opinion) of secretary of war Juan Delgado, 1574, 'Flanders' or the Mediterranean; *Estado* 554 fo 89, king to duke of Alva, 18 March 1573; Institute de Valencia de Don Juan (Madrid), *envio* 109 fo 59, secretary of state Gabriel de Zayas to Don Luis de Requesens, 8 May 1575 (a copy of the same letter is at *Estado* 565 fo 79).

of the Mediterranean certainly accelerated the State Bankruptcy of 1575 and the military collapse in the Netherlands which followed in 1576.

Taken together, these logistical factors—the determination of the defenders and their strength by sea; the defensibility of the north-western provinces; and the diversion of Spanish resources to other theatres—explain Spain's failure to win an early victory over the Dutch revolt. The collapse of Spanish power in the autumn of 1576 permitted the rebellion to spread to most of the other provinces of the Netherlands. In the south and east strong Calvinist cells were established and new fortifications were built, complicating Spain's subsequent attempts to regain the areas in revolt. Virtually no progress was made by force of arms between 1577 and 1582, while Philip II disengaged his forces from the Mediterranean and absorbed the Portuguese empire, but from 1583 until 1587 Spain's entire energies were channelled into the Netherlands offensive and superior resources soon began to tell. One town after another fell into Spanish hands; all the south and east was recaptured, leaving only Holland, Zealand and parts of Friesland, Utrecht and Gelderland to continue the struggle. Even William of Orange, a crucial figure in the Republic, was assassinated in 1584. The outlook for the 'rebels' seemed bleak indeed.

Orange, however, had always known that the Dutch alone could not hope to withstand the might of Spain for long. Ever since 1566 he had endeavoured to involve foreign powers in the struggle, either as mediators to deflect the wrath of Philip II, or as allies to divert his resources. In 1566–68 Orange and his associates had pinned their hopes on the Emperor and the German princes.[16] In 1572, 'all our hopes lay with France'—only to be shattered by the Massacre of St Bartholomew.[17] Thereafter England, France, the German princes and any other power not allied with Spain was importuned: in 1574 Orange even exchanged envoys with the Ottoman Sultan in

[16] As early as January 1566 Orange made enquiries about raising troops in Germany (Groen van Prinsterer, *Archives*, ii, pp. 23–25; letter to Count Louis of Nassau, 25 January 1566); in August, Count Louis signed a contract with a German military enterpriser to raise 1,000 horse for service against the king in the Netherlands (*op. cit.*, pp. 257–58, 'Accord' of 30 August); and in February 1567 he actually came to the camp of the Imperial army at Gotha in Saxony and tried to recruit soldiers (M. Koch, *Quellen zur Geschichte des Kaisers Maximilian II*, ii (Leipzig, 1861), pp. 36–37, letter to the Emperor dated 19 February 1567). On Orange's efforts to persuade the Emperor and princes to intervene in the Netherlands troubles in 1566–67, *cf.* Groen, *op. cit.*, ii, pp. 27–30, 178–80 and 299–302, and iii, pp. 1–6, 9–10, 26–40 and so on.

[17] Orange wrote to his brother John: 'il a ainsy pleu à Dieu pour nous oster toute espérance que pouvions avoir assise sur les hommes' (Groen van Prinsterer, *Archives*, iii, pp. 501–10 and iv, p. cii, letter of 21 September 1572).

order to co-ordinate his attacks on Spain.[18] However, none of these overtures succeeded in creating an alliance which would permanently divert Spain's attentions from the Netherlands.

Only in 1585 did a sovereign prince enter into formal alliance with the Dutch and offer permanent and substantial military aid. The Treaty of Nonsuch, signed by Queen Elizabeth of England in August 1585, may not have prevented the Spanish army from recapturing Grave in 1586 and Sluis in 1587, but it did provoke Philip II to transfer his resources from the reconquest of the Netherlands to the invasion of England. The decision to send the 'Invincible Armada' against England in 1588, followed by the resolution to intervene on the Catholic side in the French Religious Wars after 1589, proved a godsend to the Dutch. The two unsuccessful enterprises siphoned off most of Philip II's resources, causing new mutinies and defeats for the 'Army of Flanders' and enabling the Dutch to regain the north-east provinces and establish their frontier along the Maas and Rhine in the 1590s. The principal towns were now fortified according to the latest designs with bastions, ramparts and ravelins, and a sort of 'Hadrian's Wall' of connected forts and blockhouses was built in 1605–06 along the River Ijssel from the Zuider Zee to Nijmegen and from there westwards along the Maas to Tiel. These 'lines' of the Dutch Republic, although for the sake of economy built of earth and wood rather than of stone, effectively held back the powerful Spanish offensives of 1605 and 1606.[19]

It had clearly become impossible for Spain to achieve the sort of victory in the Netherlands that would force the Dutch to submit, and many members of the Spanish government came to the conclusion that failure was more or less a foregone conclusion. The pessimism of Don Luis de Requesens, Philip II's commander-in-chief in 1574, has already been noted. It was entirely shared by the king himself and by his principal advisers. On 31 May 1574 (after only two years of war) Philip II wrote to his secretary that he believed 'the loss of the Netherlands and the rest [of his Monarchy],

<hr/>

[18] G. Parker, 'Spain, her enemies and the revolt of the Netherlands 1559–1648', *Past and Present*, xlix (1970), pp. 72–95, at p. 83; A. C. Hess, 'The Moriscos: an Ottoman Fifth Column in sixteenth-century Spain', *American Historical Review*, lxxiv (1968), pp. 1–25, at pp. 19–21; G. Parker, 'The Dutch Revolt and the polarization of international politics', *Tijdschrift voor Geschiedenis*, lxxxviii (1976), no. 4.
[19] The new fortifications, the 'houten redoubten', and the campaign plans of 1605–06 are described and illustrated by the eye-witness P. Giustiniano, *Delle Guerre di Fiandra, libri VI* (Antwerp, 1609), pp. 228–29 and figs. 14 and 25. There is some correspondence about their construction in Algemeen Rijksarchief, the Hague, *Staten-Generaal* 4748. The classic account of how to construct fortifications in the cheapest way possible was by the mathematician Samuel Marolois, *Fortification ou Architecture militaire* (Amsterdam, 1615). Marolois was military adviser to the States 1612–19.

to be as certain as, in this situation, anything can be. . . . It is a terrible situation and it is getting worse every day'.[20] The same refrain was heard again several times in the course of that year and in the years to come. In 1589 the Council of State warned that to speak of 'conquering [the rebellious provinces] by force is to speak of a war without end', and in 1591 Philip's faithful secretary Mateo Vázquez pointed out that the king's expensive policies in France, the Netherlands and the Mediterranean had depopulated Castile so that 'We may fear that everything here will collapse at a stroke'. 'If God wished Your Majesty to attend to the remedy of all the troubles of the World,' he added, 'He would have given Your Majesty the money and the strength to do it'.[21] Yet despite the widely-held and persistent belief at the Spanish Court that the war could not be won, Spain kept on fighting continuously from 1577 to 1607 and from 1621 to 1647.

There were several reasons for this curious reluctance to accept failure. Most important was an unwillingness to accept the conditions put forward by the Dutch for ending their rebellion. As early as February 1573 William of Orange enunciated two demands which he regarded as the indispensable preconditions to peace: 'I see nothing else to propose,' he informed his brothers, who were trying to negotiate a settlement, 'but that the practice of the reformed religion according to the Word of God be permitted, and that this whole country and state return to its ancient privileges and liberty'. These twin demands for religious toleration and 'constitutional guarantees' were fundamental to the Dutch cause and they were repeated at every round of negotiations between Spain and the Dutch.[22] And every time they were rejected: these were precisely the points on which Philip II would admit of no compromise. In

[20] Instituto de Valencia de Don Juan, *envio* 51 fo 31, Mateo Vázquez to the king with holograph royal reply, 31 May 1574 (this document is cited, with others, in an unacceptable translation by A. W. Lovett, 'Some Spanish attitudes to the revolt of the Netherlands', *Tijdschrift voor Geschiedenis*, lxxxv (1973), pp. 17–30, at pp. 24–25.

[21] Archivo General de Simancas, *Estado* 2855, unfol., 'Sumario de los 4 papeles principales que dio el presidente Richardot'; Instituto de Valencia de Don Juan, *envio* 51 fo 1, Mateo Vázquez to the king with holograph royal reply, 8 February 1591.

[22] Orange to Counts Louis and John, 5 February 1573 (Groen van Prinsterer, *Archives*, iv, pp. 49–51). *Cf.* also Orange to Marnix, 28 November 1573 (L. P. Gachard, *Correspondence de Guillaume le Taciturne*, iii (Brussels, 1851), pp. 88–93). Precisely the same two demands were made at the peace negotiations at Breda in 1575 (*cf.* E. H. Kossman and A. F. Mellink, *Texts concerning the revolt of the Netherlands* (Cambridge, 1975), pp. 124–26); at St Geertruidenberg in 1577 (G. Griffiths, *Representative government in western Europe in the sixteenth century* (Oxford, 1968), pp. 454–62); and at Cologne in 1579 (Kossman and Mellink, *op. cit.*, pp. 183–87).

1574 an English agent in the Netherlands observed that: 'The pride of the Spanish government and the cause of religion' constituted 'the chief hindrance to a good accord'. It was perfectly true. In August 1574 Philip II gave his lieutenant in the Netherlands permission to open talks with the Dutch, but forbad him to make any concession which would affect the exclusive position of the Roman Catholic Church or prejudice his sovereign power: 'On these two points,' he ordered, 'on no account are you to give in or shift an inch.'[23] The same reluctance to concede toleration and constitutional guarantees sabotaged the peace arranged in 1577 (the Perpetual Edict) and prevented the conclusion of a settlement in 1594.[24] As late as 1628, the count-duke of Olivares was able to summarize Spain's reasons for fighting the Dutch in much the same way as Philip II: 'The matter may be reduced to two points', Olivares informed the king: 'religion and reputation'.[25] This remarkable consistency of outlook, which lasted from the 1570s until at least the 1630s, is explained by the prevailing concepts of statecraft at the Court of Spain. 'Reputation', or prestige, was recognized to have a tangible influence in politics and diplomacy, and Spain feared that acknowledgment of weakness in the Netherlands would decrease her stature (*'reputación'*) as a world power. The view was expressed that if the Dutch Revolt were allowed to succeed, heresy and rebellion would immediately follow in other parts of the Spanish Monarchy.[26] Even the need to preserve the Catholic religion in the Netherlands could be justified in terms of honour and reputation. It was, admittedly, a course of action by which 'Your Majesty will have done his duty to God', but the ability to protect Catholicism was also a touchstone of Spanish power. 'We should consider the issue of religion not only as a matter of piety and spiritual obligation, but also as a temporal one involving

[23] Kervijn de Lettenhove, *Relations politiques des Pays-Bas et de l'Angleterre sous le règne de Philippe II*, vii (Brussels, 1889), p. 397, Dr Thomas Wilson to Walsingham, 27 December 1574; Archivo General de Simancas, *Estado* 561 fo 95, the king to Don Luis de Requesens, 9 August 1574.

[24] W. J. M. van Eysinga, *De wording van het Twaalfjarige Bestand van 9 april 1609* (Amsterdam, 1963), chap. 1; J. den Tex, *Oldenbarnevelt*, i (Cambridge, 1973), pp. 199–201.

[25] Archivo Histórico Nacional (Madrid) *Estado* 3285, unfol., *voto* of the Count-Duke of Olivares, 1 September 1628.

[26] *Cf.* the opinions of various Spanish ministers printed by G. Parker, *The Army of Flanders* (2nd edition), p. xiv and pp. 127–34. There was also an 'ideological floodgates' theory, which argued that if heresy were allowed to prevail in northern Europe all heretics would attack the possessions of Philip II. 'Much . . . will be risked in allowing the heretics to prevail' the king wrote in 1562: 'For if they do, we may be certain that all their endeavours will be directed against me and my states'. (Quoted by H. G. Koenigsberger, 'The statecraft of Philip II', *European Studies Review*, i (1971), pp. 1–21, at p. 13.

reputation', Olivares told the king in 1628. He went on to say that 'He did not consider it possible to conclude a truce with honour, even if the Dutch expressly conceded us sovereign power, unless there is some improvement in the religious position.'[27]

By 1628, however, another reason had emerged to strengthen Spain's determination to carry on the struggle: she was also fighting to preserve her overseas commerce. In the 1580s, Dutch ships began to trade directly with the Spanish and Portuguese empires in America and Africa, both now controlled by Philip II. At first this trade was intended to supplement the goods freely available in the Iberian peninsula (for with only a few interruptions—1585, 1596, 1599 and 1601–02—Dutch ships came and went to all Iberian ports relatively easily throughout the Eighty Years War).[28] In the 1590s, however, an element of economic warfare crept in: Dutch vessels, like the English, sought to injure Habsburg commercial interests as well as maximizing their own profits.[29] Between 1598 and 1605, on average 25 ships sailed to West Africa, 20 to Brazil, 10 to the Far East and 150 to the Caribbean every year. Sovereign colonies were founded at Amboina in 1605 and Ternate in 1607; factories and trading posts were established around the Indian Ocean, near the mouth of the Amazon and (in 1609) in Japan.[30] By the time of the truce talks in 1607–09 the Dutch investment in these overseas trades was already so great that they were not prepared to forgo them. Spain had encountered exactly the same problem in settling the peace with England in 1603–04. The talks almost broke down over the freedom of navigation to the East and West Indies, ('the point of most moment and difficulty' according to the chief Spanish negotiator), and the issue had to be resolved by an ambiguous silence—the final treaty made no specific mention of overseas trade. Oldenbarnevelt made full use of this precedent and, in the end, the same solution had to be adopted in the Netherlands.[31] In February

[27] Archivo Histórico Nacional, *Estado* 3285, *ubi supra*.

[28] P. J. Blok, 'De handel op Spanje en het begin der groote vaart', *Bijdragen voor Vaderlandsche Geschiedenis en Oudheidkunde* 5th series i (1913), pp. 102–20; J. H. Kernkamp, *De handal op den Vijand 1572–1609*, 2 vols (Utrecht, 1931), gives the definitive account of Dutch trade with the Iberian peninsula during the war period.

[29] On English policy and profits, *cf.* K. R. Andrews, *Elizabethan privateering: English privateering during the Spanish War 1585–1603* (Cambridge, 1964), *passim*.

[30] C. C. Goslinga, *The Dutch in the Caribbean and on the Wild Coast, 1580–1680* (Assen, 1971); E. Sluiter, 'Dutch maritime power and the colonial status quo, 1585–1641', *Pacific Historical Review*, xi (1942), pp. 29–41.

[31] K. R. Andrews. 'Caribbean rivalry and the Anglo-Spanish peace of 1604', *History*, lix (1974), pp. 1–17; R. D. Hussey, 'America in European diplomacy, 1597–1604', *Revista de Historia de América*, xli (1956), pp. 1–30—*cf.* pp. 24 and 29–30 in particular; J. Den Tex, *Oldenbarnevelt* (Cambridge, 1973), ii, p. 386.

1608 the States-General 'roundly' informed the Spanish delegation
to the peace talks, 'that they intended to continue their trade with
the East and the West Indies by means of a general peace, truce or
war, each on its own merits.'[32] It was this attitude which determined
that there would be a truce and not a peace in the Low Countries'
War in 1609: Spain was not prepared to abandon for ever her monopoly status in the New World, but neither was she prepared to continue fighting in the Netherlands for the sake of the Portuguese
Indies (the Dutch had been chased out of the Caribbean—albeit
temporarily—by a Spanish fleet in 1605). The Twelve Years Truce,
therefore, made no mention of areas outside European waters, and
warfare did indeed continue there intensively. In the Far East the
Dutch conquered Jakarta (renamed Batavia) in 1619; in Guinea
they established their first trading post (Fort Mouree) in 1612; in
North America, they appeared to trade along the Hudson River in
1614 and founded 'Fort Orange' near the site of present day Albany
(New York). The Dutch also planted more colonies on the 'Wild
Coast' near the mouths of the Amazon, opened political and commercial contacts with the Indians of Chile, and began to make war
on Spanish shipping and settlements on the Pacific coast.[33] Side by
side with this geographical extension of Dutch trade, there was also
a quantitative increase. The number of East Indiamen rose from an
average of 10 in the 1600s to 17 in 1619 and 23 in 1620; the number
of ships going to Guinea doubled (to 40); and the Dutch gained
over half of the carrying trade between Brazil and Europe (there
were 29 sugar refineries in the Northern Netherlands by 1622 as
against 3 in 1595).[34] In the discussions at the Spanish Court in
1619–20 over the possibility of renewing the Truce (due to expire
April 1621), the strongest and perhaps the decisive argument
against prolonging the existing arrangement was the damage which
the Dutch were doing to the Indies and American trade. In the end
Philip III (at death's door but for once determined on a specific

[32] *Resolutiën der Staten Generaal van 1576 tot 1609. xiv: 1607–1609*, ed. H. H. P.
Rijperman (The Hague, 1970), pp. 377–79.

[33] P. Gerhard, *Pirates on the West Coast of New Spain, 1575–1742* (Glendale, 1960),
pp. 101–34. The first Dutch attack on the Spanish Pacific was the 'trading
mission' of Joris van Spilsbergen, sent by the States-General in 1615. The journal
of the expedition refers to the Spaniards throughout as 'the enemy'! (An English
translation appeared as *The East and West Indian Mirror*, ed. J. A. J. Villiers (Hack-
luyt Society, London, 1906), pp. 11–160.)

[34] For a general survey of the expansion of Dutch trade, *cf.* C. R. Boxer, *The
Dutch seaborne empire 1600–1800* (London, 1965). For the expansion of the East
India trade, *cf.* Algemeen Rijksarchief (The Hague), *Kolonialische Archief* 4389
'Schepen voor de Generale Vereenigde Nederlandsche Geoctroyeerde Oostin-
dische Compagnie nae d'Oostindies uytgevoeren'.

policy) insisted on the reopening of the Scheldt and Dutch withdrawal from the Indies as the two inflexible conditions for the conclusion of any new truce; the questions of religion and royal authority
were shelved.[35] The Dutch, however, were not prepared to give up
either of these economic advantages and in June 1621, three months
after the expiration of the truce, a Dutch West India Company was
formed to promote trade and war in Latin America. In 1624–25 the
Dutch occupied Bahía, the capital of Brazil; in 1628 they seized
a Spanish treasure fleet worth 20 million florins, in Matanzas Bay,
Cuba; and in 1630 the province of Pernambuco in northern Brazil,
the centre of the colony's sugar production, was captured by a Dutch
expeditionary force of 67 sail and 7000 men. Before long three
hundred miles of the coast and hinterland of north-east Brazil was in
Dutch hands and sugar production began to rise again—this time
to the advantage of the United Netherlands.[36]

The following years brought more Dutch victories abroad—the
seizure of parts of Guinea and Ceylon in 1637–38; the defeat of one
Spanish navy in the English Channel in 1639 and another off Brazil
in 1640; the capture of Malacca in South-East Asia, the Maranhão
in South America and Luanda in Southern Africa in 1641—but by
far the most important success was the conquest of Brazil. It immediately transformed the issues at stake in the Low Countries Wars.
Brazil and its sugar were the mainstay of the Portuguese economy
and without them Portugal's union with Spain rapidly became less
popular. There was discontent in Lisbon, there were riots in Evora;
and the Spanish government became fearful of the consequences
should they fail to drive out the invaders. A perceptive Venetian
observer noted in October 1638 that Brazil in Dutch hands was
'more damaging than the continuance of the Low Countries wars.'[37]

[35] Archives Générales du Royaume (Brussels), Secrétairerie d'Etat et de Guerre 185,
fo 24, King Philip III to the Archduke Albert, 4 February 1621. Later on, the
Count-Duke of Olivares was to claim that the Truce had not been renewed by
Spain 'solely for the cause of religion': this appears to be false. (Cf. the voto of 1628
referred to in note 25 above.) On the expiry of the Truce cf. the admirable study
of J. J. Poelhekke, 't Uytgaen van den Treves. Spanje en de Nederlanden in 1621 (Groningen, 1960). It is interesting to note that at exactly the same time Spain's solicitude
for the fate of the English Catholics diminished: A. J. Loomie, 'Olivares, the
English Catholics, and the peace of 1630', Revue belge de philologie et d'histoire,
xlvii (1969), pp. 1154–66.
[36] The basic study on Dutch Brazil is by C. R. Boxer, The Dutch in Brazil, 1624–
1654 (Oxford, 1957). Pernambuco contained about 50 per cent of the population
of the entire colony and produced about 60 per cent of its sugar.
[37] Archivio di Stato, Venice, Senato: dispacci Spagna 74, unfol., T. Contarini to
the Doge and Senate, 2 October 1638. On the gains and losses accruing to Portugal from the Union with Spain, cf. S. B. Schwarz, 'Luso-Spanish relations in Habsburg Brazil, 1580–1640', The Americas, xxv (1968), pp. 33–48. The English

Olivares offered 3, 4 even 5 million crowns to the Dutch if only they would restore Brazil.[38] By 1640, according to Olivares, 'The item which seems to be indispensable [in any settlement with the Dutch] is the restitution of Brazil'; 'The restoration of Brazil is inexcusable' Philip IV echoed in May and he declared his readiness to bargain away everything else in order to regain it.[39]

And yet in the end Spain made peace without regaining Brazil, without retaining the monopoly of the East Indies Trade, without reopening the Scheldt, without securing any official toleration for the Dutch Catholics and without persuading the Republic to recognize Spanish suzerainty in any way. After struggling for so long, Spain eventually gave in on all points.

This collapse came about for a number of reasons. First there was the deteriorating condition of Spain. The run of poor harvests, the falling tax returns and the decline of the American trade with its silver remittances in the 1620s and 1630s were serious.[40] Far worse, however, was the spate of rebellions in the 1640s: the revolts of Catalonia and Portugal in 1640, the 'Huelga de los grandes' of Castile in 1642–43, the 'Green Banner' revolts in the main towns of Andalusia and the contemporaneous risings in Sicily and Naples in 1647–48.[41] All these problems encouraged the Madrid government

discerned somewhat earlier, in the 1590s, that Brazil was a weak but lush part of the empire of the Spanish Habsburgs. *Cf.* K. R. Andrews, *Elizabethan privateering*, pp. 133 and 201–13.

[38] In 1636 the Dutch wanted 5 million crowns but Spain would only offer 2 million; in 1638 Spain did offer 5 million but by then it was not enough. A. Waddington, *La République des Provinces-Unies, la France et les Pays-Bas espagnols de 1630 à 1650*, i (Paris, 1895), pp. 343–46; A. Leman, *Richelieu et Olivares: leur négociations secrètes de 1636 à 1642 pour le rétablissement de la paix* (Lille, 1938), p. 55.

[39] A. Leman, *op. cit.*, p. 126; J. J. Poelhekke, *De vrede van Munster* (The Hague, 1948), p. 65. As early as 1632–33 Brazil had been almost the only point at issue in the peace talks then underway: *cf.* L. P. Gachard, *Actes des Etats-Généraux de 1632*, i (Brussels, 1853), pp. 96, 108, 124, 159; ii (Brussels, 1866), pp. 665–68, 677–78, 680–81.

[40] On the falling Indies receipts *cf.* A. Domínguez Ortiz, 'Los caudales de Indias y la política exterior de Felipe IV', *Anuario de Estudios Americanos*, xiii (1956), pp. 311–89. There is a growing volume of evidence, as yet unsynthesized, that the critical period for the collapse of the Spanish economy was 1625–30. *Cf.* G. Anes Alvarez and J.-P. le Flem, 'Las crisis del siglo XVII: producción agricola, precios e ingresos en tierras de Segovia', *Moneda y crédito*, xciii (1965), pp. 3–55; C. J. Jago, 'Aristocracy, war and finance in Castile, 1621–65: the titled nobility and the house of Béjar during the reign of Philip IV' (Cambridge University Ph.D. thesis, 1969), chaps. 4 and 7; M. Weisser, 'Les marchands de Tolède dans l'économie castillane, 1565–1635', *Mélanges de la Casa de Velásquez*, vii (1971), pp. 223–36; F. Ruiz Martín, 'Un testimonio literario sobre las manufacturas de paños en Segovia por 1625', in *Homenaje al profesor Alarcos*, ii (Valladolid, 1967), pp. 1–21.

[41] On the main revolts there is a clear and concise exposition (with bibliography) by J. H. Elliott, 'Revolts in the Spanish Monarchy', in *Preconditions of revolution in*

to seek peace on all external fronts in order to concentrate its resources on quelling the unrest within the empire. Gradually the
flow of Spanish treasure to the Netherlands dried up: the Army of
Flanders received an average of almost 4 million crowns a year from
1635–41, 3.3 million in 1642, but only 1.5 million in 1643.[42] On
19 May 1643 the Spanish army was decisively defeated by the French
at Rocroi. It was, according to Philip IV's chief minister Don Luis de
Haro, 'Something which can never be called to mind without great
sorrow'. It was 'a defeat which is giving rise in all parts to the consequences which we always feared': the French took Thionville and
Sierck in August and their navy defeated Spain's principal Mediterranean fleet off Cartagena in September.[43]

It would not be true to say that serious negotiations for a settlement to the Low Countries wars only began after these disasters, for
there had been so many other rounds of fruitless talks.[44] However
after 1640 a new urgency and a new desperation entered Spain's
overtures for peace. 'A truce or a peace is necessary and unavoidable
whatever the cost and whatever the price,' wrote one minister in
1645. Spain's leaders were prepared to 'give in on every point which
might lead to the conclusion of a settlement'. Philip IV, according
to one (admittedly hostile) observer, was so desperate for peace that
'If necessary he would crucify Christ again in order to achieve it'.[45]

---

early modern Europe, ed. R. Forster and J. P. Greene (Baltimore and London, 1970),
pp. 109–30. The 'Green Banner' revolts, with which Professor Elliott does not deal,
are covered by A. Domínguez Ortiz, Alteraciones andaluzas (Madrid, 1974).

[42] Figures from G. Parker, The Army of Flanders, p. 295, based on the audited
accounts of the army paymaster. Slightly lower figures were put forward by the
vanquished Spanish commander as an explanation for his defeat: Bibliothèque
royale (Brussels), MS. 12428–29 fo 328, 'Memorial . . . sobre materia de hacienda'
(30 September 1644) gives a receipt of 4.7 million crowns in 1640, 4·5 million in
1641, 3·4 million in 1642 and only 1·3 million in 1643.

[43] Bibliothèque publique et universitaire (Geneva), MS. Favre 39 fos 88–89,
Don Luis de Haro to the Marques of Velada, 17 November 1643. So few of Haro's
letters have survived that this one, giving vent to his personal views, is particularly
important.

[44] Talks between Spain and the Dutch went on almost continuously at an
informal level, but formal negotiations took place in 1621–22, 1627–29, 1632–33,
1635, 1638–39, 1640–41 and (of course) 1644–48. They are all mentioned in the
first chapter of J. J. Poelhekke, De vrede van Munster (The Hague, 1948). There were
also semi-continuous talks about peace between France and Spain from 1636
until 1659.

[45] Colección de Documentos Inéditos para la Historia de España lxxxii (Madrid, 1884),
pp. 138–39, Count of Fuensaldaña to the king, 17 September 1645; Archivo
General de Simancas, Estado 2065, unfol., apostil of Philip IV to a report by the
'junta de estado', 3 January 1646; Correspondência diplomática de Francisco de Sousa
Coutinho durante a sua embaixanda em Holanda, 1643–1650, ed. E. Prestage and P. de
Azevedo, ii (Coimbra, 1926), p. 256.

The king's broken spirit sank even lower after the death of his son and heir, Don Balthasar Carlos, in October 1646. He lamented: I have lost my only son, whose presence alone comforted me in my sorrows. . . . It has broken my heart.'[46]

Fortunately for the depressed Philip IV, by 1646 the Dutch had also come to appreciate the advantages of a settlement even if they could not obtain everything they wanted. There were several reasons for this change of heart. First there was the unwillingness of the Holland oligarchs (who paid almost two-thirds of the Republic's budget) to finance the war indefinitely: they had long resented the heavy cost of the army (in 1628 and 1630, when the Spaniards did not campaign, Holland refused to pay for more than defensive operations) and in 1645 and 1646 the province reduced its military outlay to a bare minimum, directing its resources instead to intervene in the war between Sweden and Denmark which threatened its Baltic interests.[47]

The prince of Orange also had his reasons for desiring an end to the war. In the first place, his son and heir was married to the daughter of Charles I of England and he earnestly desired a peace with Spain which would leave him free to help his Stuart relatives in the civil war. However at the battle of Sherborne in October 1645 the Parliamentary army captured a number of highly compromising letters concerning the aid offered to Charles by the prince of Orange behind the backs of the States-General. Early in 1646 these papers were printed in English and Dutch and they totally discredited the ageing prince. After Naseby, in any case, Frederick Henry realized that further attempts to save the Stuarts were futile.[48] Nevertheless the House of Orange continued to favour peace on other grounds, the chief of which was financial. A settlement with Spain would bring the restoration of the extensive Nassau lands in the South Netherlands (confiscated from Frederick Henry's father, William of Orange, in 1568) and it would bring immediate cash rewards from the king of Spain. The total gain was estimated at £350,000 per annum. Peace would be, in the phrase of Frederick Henry's wife, 'nostre avantasche'. [49]

In the end, however, it was not the prince and princess of Orange,

[46] Quoted by M. A. S. Hume in *Cambridge Modern History*, iv (Cambridge, 1906), p. 659.

[47] On Holland's objections to the cost of the war in 1646–47, *cf*. the documents cited by Poelhekke, *Vrede van Munster*, pp. 307 ff.

[48] *The Lord George Digby's Cabinet* (London, 1648: 68 pages of documents and commentary) and *Eenighe extracten uyt verscheyde missiven gevonden in de Lord Digby's Cabinet* (also London, 1646). These are discussed by P. Geyl, *The history of the Low Countries: Episodes and Problems* (London, 1965), pp. 75 and 246.

[49] The policy of the Prince of Orange and his family is discussed by P. Geyl,

but the delegates of the seven United Provinces, or rather of the 2,000 oligarchs who elected them, whose decision in favour of peace proved critical. Bribery played its part here too—Spanish gold undoubtedly eased a few consciences towards accepting the peace— but the States-General had two sound reasons of state for desiring a settlement with Spain. In the first place there was the growing power of France. Until 1640, France had seemed unable to get the upper hand in the war against the Habsburgs—peasant revolts, court intrigues and military defeats seemed to dog every French effort. Although Catalonia and Artois were overrun in 1640–41, a considerable Spanish victory at Honnecourt in May 1642 kept the French at bay, followed by the death of Richelieu (4 December 1642) and Louis XIII (14 May 1643). But five days after the king's death the French victory at Rocroi effaced the memory of all previous defeats and it became the springboard for further successes. In 1645 alone, 10 major towns in Spanish Flanders fell to the French

The Dutch were not concerned by these encroachments on the southern border of the Spanish Netherlands; on the contrary they made use of the French presence to extend their own territory by capturing Sas van Gent in 1644 and Hulst in 1645, and they cheerfully renewed their 1635 treaty with France to partition the Habsburg Low Countries should they be entirely overrun (1 March 1644). Unknown to the Dutch, however, France and Spain were negotiating for a settlement. In the winter of 1645–46 Spain proposed a marriage between Louis XIV and Maria Theresa, Philip IV's eldest daughter, giving her part of the Spanish Netherlands as a dowry. News of this projected arrangement reached the United Provinces in February 1646. Immediately there was a major political storm: there were anti-French riots in the Hague; moves were made to expel all the French residents from the Republic; and consternation broke out in the States-General. The States of Holland passed a formal resolution declaring: 'That France, enlarged by possession of the Spanish Netherlands, will be a dangerous neighbour for our country.'[50] Fear of a separate Franco-Spanish deal provoked the first spurt of negotiations between Spain and the Dutch at Munster in March and April 1646. Undismayed by the mistrust of her allies, the French advance continued: Kortrijk fell in June 1646; Dunkirk, the only serviceable port of the Spanish Netherlands, in October. This increased the concern of the Republic's leaders that, unless Spain's forces on the Dutch frontier were

---

Orange and Stuart, 1641–1672 (London, 1969), chap. 1, and by J. J. Poelhekke, *De vrede van Munster*, chap. 5.

[50] *Cf.* Poelhekke, *op. cit.*, chap. 7 (quotation from p. 256).

released, the South Netherlands would be totally overrun, especially when the peace concluding the Thirty Years War in Germany was signed, releasing France's armies in Alsace for operations in the Netherlands. A cease-fire between Spain and the Dutch was therefore agreed at length in June 1647. There were further delays before this preliminary agreement could be made permanent. French entreaties and French gold, liberally applied, kept in being a small but devoted party dedicated to sabotaging the peace, while French diplomats created 'an artificial labyrinth, constructed in such a way that those who allow themselves to be led into it can never find the exit', in order to place further delays in the way of all decisions. The system of government in the United Provinces which required unanimity in all major policy resolutions, naturally favoured the *status quo* at all times: continuing war during wartime, avoiding war when at peace. However in the mid-1640s the province which had resolutely and consistently opposed a settlement with Spain— Zealand—was forced to change its mind by some unforeseen and unfavourable developments in the Iberian world.

As early as January 1634, just after the failure of another round of peace talks, the French agent at the Hague, Charnacé, noted that if Dutch Brazil were reconquered the States-General would be driven to negotiate an immediate settlement with Spain.[51] A decade later, that is precisely what happened, even though on the eve of the disaster the Dutch position in South America appeared to be stronger than ever. In 1637 the Dutch West India Company sent out Count John Maurice of Nassau, great-nephew of William the Silent, to govern Brazil. Almost at once the new governor captured another province (Ceará) and sent an expedition to Africa which captured São Jorge da Minha in West Africa, gateway to the Ashanti goldfields. In 1641 one more province was added in Brazil (Maranhão) extending Dutch control over 1,000 miles of the Brazilian coastal plain between the São Francisco and the Amazon rivers, and an expedition sent from Recife to West Africa captured Luanda in Angola, key to the supply of slave labour upon which Brazilian sugar production depended. In the midst of these successes, in December 1640, Portugal successfully threw off its allegiance to Spain and a local grandee, the Duke of Bragança, became King John IV. There was no longer any risk of Spanish forces being sent to win back Brazil and in 1641–42 a truce was concluded between

---

[51] Charnacé to Richelieu, 2 January 1634, quoted Waddington, *La république des Province-Unies*, I, p. 221. The influence of Charnacé and the French was critical in aborting the peace-talks of 1632–33 between Spain and the Dutch: cf. M. G. de Boer, *Die Friedensunterhandlungen zwischen Spanien und den Niederlanden in der Jahren 1632 und 1633* (Groningen, 1898).

the new Portuguese régime and the Dutch. The States-General even sent an expeditionary force to Lisbon in August 1641 to bolster Portuguese resistance to Spain.[52]

So healthy did the Dutch position appear in 1643–44 that the Directors of the West India Company decided to economize by reducing their military establishment (which cost some 1·4 million florins annually) and John Maurice, together with many of his soldiers, was recalled. It was a fatal mistake. The Portuguese planters of Pernambuco had never accepted their new Calvinist masters whole-heartedly and they resented the high interest charged by Dutch moneylenders on the loans provided to re-stock the sugar plantations after the fighting of the 1630s. In June 1645 there was a major uprising of the Portuguese settlers against the Dutch. In August a battle was fought at Tobocas, outside Recife, which the settlers won. This minor engagement, fought 6,000 miles from the Netherlands and involving under 1,000 men on each side, was one of the most important 'actions' of the Eighty Years' War. It destroyed Dutch power in Brazil (only four toeholds on the coast, Recife the chief among them, remained). The great profits from the sugar trade were gone. The West India Company based on Zealand was therefore desperate to recover its lost empire and looked urgently at the means available. The short term remedy was to send immediate relief to the beleaguered defenders in Recife and other places, and this was done in Spring 1646: 20 ships with 2,000 men set sail. However the rebellious settlers were in receipt of aid both from Bahía, the capital of Portuguese Brazil, and from Portugal herself, and it was clear that a far larger expedition would be required to restore Dutch power fully.

There were thus two problems: the first was to mount a major expedition from the Netherlands to reconquer Brazil; the second was to end the assistance from Portugal. In former years, the West India Company had vehemently opposed any settlement with Philip IV on the grounds that it would free Spanish resources to defend the Portuguese Indies. After the rebellion of Portugal in 1640, however, this was no longer the case. On the contrary, a settlement with Spain might now be of benefit to the West India Company since Philip IV would be free to use some of his resources on the reconquest of Portugal, which would in turn prevent Portugal from sending reinforcements to Brazil. By itself, of course,

[52] Cf. M. de Jong, 'Holland en de Portuguese restauratie van 1640', Tijdschrift voor Geschiedenis, lv (1940), pp. 225–53; C. van der Haar, De diplomatieke betrekkingen tussen de Republiek en Portugal, 1640–1661 (Groningen, 1961); and J. Pérez de Tudela, Sobre la defensa hispana de Brasil contra los Holandeses, 1624–1650 (Madrid, 1974).

peace with Spain would not be enough to regain Brazil: for that, the great fleet was still required. Throughout 1646–47, therefore, hard bargaining took place between the states of Holland and Zealand, on these two connected problems. In the end, Holland offered to pay for a major expedition to save Brazil if Zealand would sign the peace with Spain. In August 1647, despite the efforts of the Portuguese and the French to sabotage the settlement, Holland and Zealand reached agreement on the terms for the reconquest of Brazil: a force of 41 ships and 6,000 men would be assembled ready to sail in October 1647; then the peace with Spain would be signed. Inevitably there were more delays, and the fleet did not sail for Brazil until 26 December 1647, but this did not affect the other half of the bargain: Zealand instructed her representative at Munster to sign the peace with Spain in any case, which he did in a solemn ceremony on 30 January 1648, bringing the Eighty Years' War to its formal close.[53]

For Owen Feltham, writing four years later, the Dutch were supermen. 'They are' he wrote, 'in some sorte Gods. . . . They are a *Gideons* Army upon the march again. They are the Indian *Rat*, knawing the Bowels of the *Spanish Crocodile*. . . . They are the little sword-fish pricking the bellies of the Whale. They are the wane of that Empire, which increas'd in [the time of] Isabella and in [the time of] Charles the 5th was at full'.[54] The Dutch Revolt, which began among a few thousand refugees in north-western Europe, had spread until it affected the lives of millions of people and brought about the collapse of the greatest world empire ever seen. In the 1640s there was fighting in Ceylon, Japan and Indonesia, in southern and western Africa, on the Indian, Pacific and Atlantic Oceans, and of course in Brazil and the Low Countries. It all stemmed from the revolt of the Netherlands. The struggle had become, so to say, the First World War, and it is only when one surveys the global scale of the conflict and the complexity of the alliances and coalitions of the participants that one can satisfactorily explain why the Dutch Revolt lasted eighty years.

[53] In fact Zealand was cheated: the great fleet was badly delayed by storms and arrived late at Recife with many of its soldiers dead and the rest mutinous for lack of pay. On 19 April 1648 and again on 19 February 1649 the surviving Dutch troops were routed by the Portuguese on the heights of Guararapes outside Recife. These defeats sealed the fate of Dutch Brazil, and that in turn led to the loss of Dutch Angola. *Cf.* C. Moreira Bento, *As batalhas dos Guararapes* (Recife, 1971), text and maps; W. J. van Hoboken, 'De West-indische Compagnie en de Vrede van Munster', *Tijdschrift voor Geschiedenis*, lxx (1957), pp. 359–68; W. J. van Hoboken, 'Een troepentransport naar Brazilië in 1647', *Tijdschrift voor Geschiedenis*, lxii (1949), pp. 100–09.
[54] Feltham, *op. cit.*, pp. 91–92.

St Salvator's College, University of St Andrews.

RENAISSANCE INFLUENCES
IN ENGLISH COLONIZATION

The Prothero Lecture

By Professor D.B. Quinn, M.A., Ph.D., D.Lit., D.Litt.,
M.R.I.A., F.R.Hist.S.

READ AT THE SOCIETY'S CONFERENCE
18 SEPTEMBER 1975

Every Country left to it selfe, and not much molested with famine, or devoured by warres, will at length grow too populous, unable to sustaine its owne weight, and relieve its owne Inhabitants. Whence it hath bin a policy practised by most Kings & States in such cases, to make forraine expeditions, and send forth Colonies into other Countryes lesse peopled, to disburden their owne of such encombrances; as we see the Kings of Spaine to have sent many into the West Indies; and we at this day discharge many Idlers into Virginia and the Barmudas.

(Nathanael Carpenter, *Geographie delineated*, London, 1625, bk. ii, p. 137)

THE New World of the sixteenth century grew directly out of the Old not merely in a physical but in an intellectual sense. The men of the late fifteenth and early sixteenth centuries, who found the new lands overseas, were educated in a humanistic tradition which made the classical past, especially the Roman past, alive and relevant to them. Consequently, there is an element of continuity in the thinking about the discoveries and the problems they presented on the basis of older intellectual concepts, which continues to influence much of the thought of the sixteenth century about cosmography, natural history and about the planting of colonies in lands unknown to the ancients. It is astonishing how Ptolemy remained the standard-bearer of the new discoveries: maps of the New World and other novel areas, added to his *Geography* for the first time in 1513, continued to proliferate in edition after edition until by the later sixteenth century the original maps and text had been so overlaid with new matter that they bore even less relationship to the original than the first issue of Gray's *Anatomy* has to the current edition. It was much the same with Pliny: the *Natural History* remained the starting point for New World and Asiatic botany and zoology throughout the sixteenth century. Oviedo in 1526 paid his respects to the master before suggesting that genuine novelties could now be added

73

to his text: well before the end of the century Pliny too had been swamped in new material, though his text was also retained intact.

So far as colonies were concerned many commentators proved to be willing to compare what was being done in the Americas with what had been done long before by the Romans and to seek inspiration from the narratives of Livy, Sallust, Caesar and the rest. Moreover, classical writings, when they suited the particular axes they had to grind, were being used by political commentators in Italy as guides to action. The most notable of these was, of course, Machiavelli, whose advocacy of colonization on Roman models pervaded his writings. To men brought up on Livy the narratives of the historian and the commentaries of the *Discorsi* became almost indistinguishable; both were guides to action not merely subjects for reflection.

There was an English reaction to the first generation of novel, oceanic voyages which took place between 1487 and 1522, but it was, so far as we can tell at present, a muted one. John Cabot certainly represented an Italian Renaissance view of the earth, originating, it is thought, in Florence and with Toscanelli, that the ocean between Europe and Asia might be crossed by westward voyaging. There is no evidence so far that Cabot had any direct impact on English humanists, unless we class Henry VII as one, or had any positive influence on concepts of colonization, even though in 1498 he proposed to bring convicts with him to lay foundations for a halfway house on the route to Asia. The voyages he initiated petered out in the prosaic fishery off Newfoundland.[1] At the same time it may not be wholly without significance that the first Latin translation from the Greek of one classical text on cosmography was made by an Englishman, Thomas Linacre, Proclus's *De sphaera*, appearing at Vienna in 1499 and being thereafter frequently reprinted.[2] This was one of the very few early works which proclaimed that the whole surface of the globe was habitable. Linacre had apparently been in contact with Thomas More at Oxford and became his friend in London. He may perhaps, have been influential in introducing him to the new as well as the old cosmography.[3]

---

[1] See especially J. A. Williamson, *The Cabot Voyages and Bristol Exploration*, Cambridge (1962), and the not uncontroversial account in D. B. Quinn, *England and the Discovery of America* (London, 1974).

[2] Proclus, Diadochus, *De sphaera* (Vienna, 1499, Leipzig [1500], Vienna, 1511, London c. 1522, Paris 1534); translated into English as *The description of the sphere or frame of the worlde*, by William Salysburye (London, 1550).

[3] More commented favourably on 21 October 1515 on Linacre's work in translating part of Aristotle's *Meteorologica* and a commentary on it, though neither of these works were published (Elizabeth F. Rogers, *St Thomas More: Selected Letters*,

Certainly More seems to have soaked himself in the reports of the new discoveries overseas, though there is little evidence that he did so before he visited the Netherlands in 1515. Antwerp, above all, was a centre for the dissemination of knowledge of the new lands in northern Europe (at least five printings of American tracts had taken place there between 1493 and the time of More's visit), and it was there he picked up much of his information. While the setting of *Utopia* (published at Louvain in 1516) was in the New World, he never uses the name America which was only slowly taking hold from 1507 onwards. He may also have learnt there something of the great debate which was already taking place in Spain on the treatment of the Amerindians and on the legitimacy of both colonization and enslavement. What is striking in *Utopia* for our purpose, is his emphasis on the legitimacy of colonization. He poses the question[4] whether it is right for the Utopians to send their people out to form colonies in other lands which are insufficiently occupied even though the inhabitants may resist. He concludes that 'wherever the natives have much unoccupied and uncultivated land, they found a colony under their own laws (*coloniam suis ipsorum legibus propagant*). . . . The inhabitants who refuse to live according to their laws, they drive from the territory which they carve out for themselves. If they resist they wage war against them. They consider it a most just cause for war when a people does not use its soil but keeps it idle and waste nevertheless forbids the use and possession of it to others who by the rule of nature ought to be maintained by it.'[5] More appeared to identify himself with this somewhat rigid view of natural rights, but it nonetheless represents a considered view and, since More appears to be the first Englishman to use the word *colonia* in a Roman meaning, he provides an essential starting point for this study. His hint is clear; to colonize can be legitimate, even good.[6]

It is highly probable that it was under More's influence that his brother-in-law John Rastell took up the study of the new lands and especially of colonizing prospects there.[7] He aimed to be the first

---

New Haven, 1961, pp. 52–53). More made further reference to the discovery of new lands in his 'Confutacion' (1532), in *The workes* (London, 1557), p. 428.

[4] *Utopia*, edited by E. L. Surtz and J. H. Hexter (Yale edition of the Works of St Thomas More, iv, New Haven, 1965), p. 136.

[5] *Ibid.*, p. 137, and see pp. 415–46.

[6] New English settlements in Ireland had already been suggested about 1515, but we have no evidence that More had Ireland in mind (see *State Papers, Henry VIII*, ii (1834), p. 25; 'to send one man oute of every paryshe of England, Cornwale, and Wales, into this lande, to inhabit').

[7] John Clement (in 1515) and Thomas Lupset (1518) were drawn to More's work on *Utopia*, and so involved, if only peripherally, in New World literature (Rogers, *Selected Letters*, pp. 73, 110).

English colonizer of the new continent which lay between England and Asia. He had read Waldseemüller's *Cosmographiae introductio*, in its 1507[8] or a later edition, which had named America (after Americus Vespuccius) as the southernmost of two novel continents. Indeed, he is amongst the first to carry the name to North America as well as South. He planned a colony there and set out to establish it in 1517, though his men refused to sail off into the ocean beyond Ireland to the west and he lost his substantial investment. His *Interlude of the four elements*,[9] which appeared several years later, showed he had not lost his belief in the value of colonial experiments across the Atlantic. His words are well known, but significant:

> O what a thing had been then
> if that they that be Englishmen
> might have been the first of all
> that there should have taken possession
> and made first building and habitation
> a memory perpetual.

Rastell was, however, a lone voice crying in the wilderness; he was not heard or at least not regarded, even if he seems to have encouraged his son William to go on a prospecting voyage to the Strait of Belle Isle in 1536, though this voyage too was failure.

The appearance in the works of Machiavelli of fairly frequent references to the need to imitate the Romans and send out colonies to increase the power of the state or the ruler[10] was directed mainly, of course, to Italian city states which might thereby extend the range of their power into the territories surrounding them. This might be applied by easy extension to the Irish lordship of the king of England as well as, by a further extension, to the new lands across the Atlantic. It is still not clear that, before the reign of Queen Elizabeth, Machiavelli was indeed being cited in support of such enterprises, but the use of Roman precedents can be found, and where they were in question Machiavelli's hand, in the *Discorsi* at least, may not have been far behind.

If colonization is not heard of again in England in connexion with America for a generation, it crops up from time to time from 1521 onwards in relation to Ireland, though when an English administration was installed in Dublin in 1534 the proposals to resettle

[8] Published at St Dié, Lorraine, see J. Fischer and F. von Weiser, *Die älteste Karte mit dem Namen Amerika aus dem Jahre 1507* (Innsbruck, 1903).

[9] *A new interlude and a mery of the nature of the iiij. elementes* [London, c. 1525] sig. Clv.

[10] *Principe*, chap. 3; *Discorsi*, bk. i, chap. 1, bk. ii, chap. 6, bk. iii, chap. 19; *Istorie*, bk. ii, chap. 1. See J. H. Whitfield, 'Machiavelli's Use of Livy', in *Livy*, edited by T. A. Dorey (London, 1971), pp. 73–96.

Ireland with more Englishmen were submerged for some years by a tide of conciliation. They were to re-emerge at the opening of the reign of Edward VI in a context of military necessity. Two great forts, Governor and Protector (later Philipstown and Maryborough), were established on the western border of the settled English area, the Pale, to defend it against Irish incursions, and these forts grew into towns which gradually spread their influence and their settlers over the surrounding country, very much as a Roman colony would have done. Sir Thomas Smith, one of the most academic of English statesmen of the period, later looked back to the achievements of Sir Edward Bellingham, the rather obscure lord-deputy of the years 1547–48, as beginning a new era of colonization in Ireland, and may already have been struck by the Roman analogy. As secretary of state, 1548–49, he was partly responsible for the policies which brought women to join soldiers in the forts and encouraged cultivation outside them, while the lord deputy, Sir James Croft, moved on in 1551 to plan settlements over a considerable area. In 1552 Edward Walshe, an educated Waterford man, gave us the first clear indication that Roman precedents were being invoked when he put forward the example of 'the politic Romans' as an argument for keeping holdings small and making settlement intensive.[11] Clearly colonization was developing in Ireland though the terms used were 'inhabiting' and 'planting' rather than 'settling colonies'. The plantation of Leix and Offaly went on with repeated setbacks until it finally took hold in the 1560s. What we still cannot determine is at precisely what point settlement in Ireland and colonization in America came to be considered in parallel and equivalent terms.

It was in the 1550s that colonization in America came to be discussed openly in England, even though the word 'colony' had been slow to appear; indeed Ralph Robinson avoided using it when translating *Utopia* into English in 1551.[12] When Richard Eden published *A treatise of the newe India* in 1553 he drew attention to the riches which Englishmen, like Spaniards, might draw from empire-building overseas, but refrained from using the word 'colony' and

[11] See D. B. Quinn, 'Edward Walshe's "Conjectures" Concerning the State of Ireland [1552]', *Irish Historical Studies*, v (1947), pp. 302–22. Walshe (who saw service at Boulogne in 1544) showed in his pamphlet, *The office and duety in fightyng for our countrey* (London, 1545), dedicated to Sir Anthony Saintleger, that he was well acquainted with Livy and other classical histories. (I am indebted to Dr Dean White for suggesting that this pamphlet would be worth examination.)

[12] 'Then they chewse out of euery citie certeyn cytezins and buylde vp a towne vnder their own lawes in the next land. . . .' *A fruteful and pleasaunt worke of the beste state of a publyque weale and of the newe yle called Vtopia* (London, 1551), fo 15v., and in 2nd edn (London, 1556), fo 15v.

from direct advocacy of overseas colonization by the English. By
1555, when his *The Decades of the newe World* appeared, he was less
reticent. He translated a dialogue between two Italians who considered that modern peoples ought to emulate Alexander and
Caesar 'by assigning colonies to inhabit divers places of that continent (America).' He told also how, in his opinion, the Spaniards
in their settlements improved the conditions, and religion, of the
Indians, while enriching themselves in the process. He was the first
to describe in English the North American expeditions by Cartier
and Coronado and to ask 'Oh what did Christian princes mean that
in such lands discovered they do not assign certain colonies to
inhabit the same?'[13] This was the first clear call since Rastell for
English colonization in North America, though it may have been
caution which suggested that settlements be made well to the north
of the empire of King Philip. Here classical precedents simply
provide an excuse for raising the question of colonization in an
English context. At the same time the question was very slow to
emerge as a topic for debate. Even when, in 1563, a half-hearted
attempt was being made to prepare a colonizing expedition to
occupy a deserted French fort in Florida, the publisher of a translation of a French tract advocating the advantages of the southeast
coast of North America for settlement could do no more than point
to the pleasure and profit of overseas voyaging, 'as well for the en-
larging of the Christian faith as the enriching of kingdoms'.[14] It was
not, indeed, until the late 1570s that Englishmen began talking in
earnest about American colonization, though when at last they had
begun to do so, they surpassed all other European nations of the
time in the amount of discussion of objectives, ways and means, and
so on, which took place. Indeed, between 1578 and 1630 talking and
writing about colonies was rather more frequent in England than
attempts to establish them and may even have paved the way for
success in the longer run in the difficult process of planting really
viable colonies in temperate latitudes in North America.

By the time such discussion began, however, many Englishmen
were familiar with at least some of the problems of colonization
because they heard enough about the subject in an Irish context
and had become aware of experiments made there. In this process
Sir Henry Sidney, during his lord-deputyship of Ireland, 1565–
1571, and Sir Thomas Smith in England, between 1565 and 1577,
played outstanding parts, while the young captain, Humphrey

13 In *The First Three English Books on America*, ed. E. Arber (Birmingham, 1885)
pp. 49–60, 285–8.
14 Jean Ribault, *The whole and true discouerye of Terra Florida* (London, 1563),
sig. *2v.

Gilbert, from 1566 onwards, focused his mind on techniques of exploiting Irish lands through English settlers which he was afterwards, in the late 1570s, to translate into an American context.[15] There was, in this period, both discussion and experiment Roman precedent, with possibly the indirect influence of Machiavelli's writings, came to play some part in shaping both ideology and concrete plans for settlements.

Smith, it would appear, was already under the influence of the Roman historians as well as Machiavelli when he revived with William Cecil the possibilities of large scale colonies in Ireland in 1565,[16] for the following year showed that his library at Hill Hall[17] contained not only an array of Greek and Roman historians but Richard Eden's *Decades* (Smith had been his tutor at Cambridge) and Machiavelli's *History of Florence*, his *Discorsi* and *The Prince*, all three works, of course, expressing the view that a ruler who wished to extend and enforce his rule should not merely conquer but colonize. In the *Discorsi*, in particular, he had stressed that the Romans had sent out compact bodies of men not only to hold down conquered territories, but to bring Roman law and custom to the occupied areas, and provide a loyal nucleus of inhabitants, an argument which fitted in very well with Smith's views on Ireland and indeed with the whole situation which was emerging there.

We can see Sidney steadily advocating colonization here and there in the island, largely under private auspices though with government supervision,[18] and using classical terminology such as 'that there might be induced there some colony',[19] and also being answered in a royal letter by a reference to 'deducing some colonels of people out of our realm to inhabit the same.'[20] This was in 1560–69, though we cannot link Sidney directly with Machiavelli's injunctions. Smith, however, after his admission to the privy council in March 1571 and especially when he became secretary of

---

[15] See D. B. Quinn, *The Voyages and Colonising Enterprises of Sir Humphrey Gilbert* 2 vols., (London, 1940), I, 9–12, II, 490–97.

[16] Smith to Cecil, 6 June and 7 November 1565, P.R.O., State Papers, Foreign SP 70/78, 1007 and 1302; Smith to Sidney, May 1565, State Papers, Ireland, SP63/13, 51, see Mary Dewar, *Sir Thomas Smith* (London, 1964), pp. 156–57.

[17] John Strype, *The Life of the Learned Sir Thomas Smith* (Oxford, 1820), pp. 276–77. *See* Christopher Morris, 'Machiavelli's Reputation in Tudor England' *Il Pensiero Politico*, II (1969), no. 3, p. 90. (I am indebted for this reference to Dr Cecil Clough.)

[18] Nicholas Canny, *The Elizabethan Conquest of Ireland. A Pattern Established 1565–1576* (Hassocks, 1976).

[19] Sidney to the Queen, 12 November 1568. P.R.O. State Papers Ireland, SP63/26, 18.

[20] Queen to Sidney, 6 June 1569. T. ÓLaidhin, *Sidney Papers, 1565–70* (Dublin, 1962), p. 108.

state in 1572 and so took on, under the Queen, responsibility for directing Irish policy, became obsessed with Roman-style colonization as the model for Ireland. Moreover, he proposed to engage himself in the creation of a model 'Roman' colony, equipping his illegitimate son, Thomas, with a patent and some corporate backing to found the city of 'Elizabetha' in the Ards in Ulster, and issuing a printed pamphlet, a prospectus and a map to draw in men and money. Curiously, he avoided in this printed publicity any mention of Rome and even of the word 'colony' and spoke only of 'inhabiting' the Ards, but in his correspondence he reiterated time after time for some four years the classical jargon about colonies which had become for him a living directive to action.[21] His didactic letters spoke of his son as 'a leader forth of men, who in ancient time were *deductores coloniarum* and the action was called *deducere coloniam*'.[22] 'The truth is', he said several years later, 'that I and my deputies be indeed *Coloniae deductores*, the distributors of land to English men in a foreign country.'[23] Smith was talking nonsense of course, since Ireland was a kingdom under the English crown and the very land involved in his grant had been part of the earldom of Ulster which Edward IV had inherited in 1461. A young scholar[24] put it to me recently that Smith seemed throughout to be thinking in terms of an independent entity where English laws (or Smith's laws perhaps) would run, not those of the royal administration in Dublin, so that the inhabitants would be carrying English law, like Roman colonists, into a new environment. It does indeed appear that he thought in some such terms with emphasis on the city. This was to be a strong town, as a magazine of victuals, a retreat in time of danger, and a safe place for the merchants. 'Mark Rome', he said, 'Carthage, Venice, and all other where any notable beginning hath been.'[25] After his son had been killed, he sent a further expedition to erect the city which he described in detail, together with an elaborate plan for its govern-

[21] See D. B. Quinn, 'Sir Thomas Smith (1513–1577) and the Beginnings of English Colonial Theory', *Proceedings of the American Philosophical Society*, lxxxix (1945), 343–60; Dewar, *Sir Thomas Smith*, pp. 156–70; N. Canny 'The Ideology of English Colonization: Ireland to America', *William and Mary Quarterly*, 3rd ser. xxx (1973), 575–98.

[22] Smith to Sir William Fitzwilliam, 17 July 1572. Bodleian Library, Carte MS 57, fo 38.

[23] Smith to Fitzwilliam, 31 July 1574, Carte MS 56, fo 218. In the same letter he designated *de facto* leaders of the colony 'Colonel, and *coloniae ductor* and *agrorum divisor*.'

[24] Mr Barry Langston.

[25] Smith to his son Thomas, May 1572, *Calendar of State Papers, Foreign 1583, and Addenda*, pp. 491, and see 467–68, 492. John R. Hale, 'To Fortify or not to Fortify', *Essays in Honor of John Humphreys Whitfield*, ed. H. C. Davis, D. G. Rees, J. M. Hartwell and G. W. Slowey (London, 1975), p. 110, shows that Machiavelli

ment,[26] which was that of a virtually independent principality. But his fantasy was finally revealed for what it was when this expedition too collapsed. He must have become something of a laughing stock before he died in 1577, but his words about Roman colonies and the means by which they might be brought to life again went widely round official circles in England. After Smith, few officials can have had any doubts about the supposed nature or at least the terminology of Roman colonization, though they may have had many doubts about its relevance to Irish conditions.

It was between 1576 and 1578 that the notion of planting American colonies took hold in England. The debate on their nature and function was really opened in 1577 by the elder Richard Hakluyt and was later taken up by his younger and better known cousin of the same name. Sir Humphrey Gilbert, Edward Hayes, a Liverpool man, Christopher Carleill, Sir George Peckham and Thomas Harriot were the other main protagonists during the following decade. [27] This discussion was almost wholly empirical and pragmatic, based on what America was like or was thought to be like, and not to any appreciable extent on long-term historical precedent or the Machiavellian precept. The discussion turned on the possibility of creating in North America such amenities as mining camps, military garrisons, trading posts, great aristocratic estates, communities of village size which would operate small holdings, and large-scale company plantations. There was strong English nationalist sentiment behind it as hostility to Spain developed from piracy to open war. There was a missionary impulse, too, but it was tentative and perhaps, hypocritical. The discussion was based also, to some extent, on practical experiments, Frobisher's unsuccessful mining camp on Baffin Island,[28] Gilbert's aborted territorial colony in 1583 in the later New England,[29] the moderately successful garrison-colony on Roanoke Island in 1585–86, and the village community which John White planted in 1587 and which was never

---

stressed both the importance of fortifying conquered territories and of colonizing them, but he did not put the two themes together. Smith, rather than Justus Lipsius, *Politicorum Libri sex* (1589), in *Omnia opera*, iv, (Wesel, 1675), 73–74, who is cited by Hale, appears to be the earliest, or at least one of the earliest, to do so.

[26] See Dewar, *Sir Thomas Smith*, pp. 164–68 and review by D. B. Quinn *Irish Historical Studies*, viv (1964–65), 285–87. The emphasis is again on the city: 'The chief strength to fortify a colony is to have a city or town of strength well walled and defended.'

[27] Listed in *Appendix*, pp. 92–93 below.

[28] See V. Stefansson, *The Three Voyages of Martin Frobisher*, 2 vols. (London 1938).

[29] See Quinn, *Gilbert*. 2 vols. (London, 1940), and *England and the Discovery of America* (London, 1974).

seen again,[30] experiments which were in the shorter run failures but which provided in turn the material for further discussions.

The younger Richard Hakluyt impressed on Queen Elizabeth in 1584 the need for her to assert her personal authority across the Atlantic to enhance her majesty no less than her territory,[31] but he did so without reference either to Roman precedent or to Machiavelli, though he found scripture useful, as a clergyman could, to reinforce his arguments. Laudonnière, the French historian of French Florida ventures in the 1560s, used Roman precedents to justify French actions, but Hakluyt translated and published his words without comment.[32] Sir George Peckham used scriptural precedents too, but the only references to the Romans in his tract were in prefatory poems by John Ashley and John Hawkins. The naval hero lollops along in good style, reducing the Roman analogy to its lowest common denominator:

> The Romans when the number of their people grew so great
> As neither wars could waste nor Rome suffice them for a state
> They led them forth by swarming troops to foreign lands amain
> And founded divers colonies unto the Roman reign.

We must, however, analyse the underlying assumptions and conclusions in social and economic terms and not in those of Roman influence. In summary we can say that they revolved round three main considerations and a number of minor ones, the complementary economy, the supplementary economy and the emigration thesis.

The first of these, the idea that the colonies must exist mainly to supplement English production, was of primary importance. Settlers established along the North American coast from about latitude 30° to 60° N. could produce almost all the products which England would normally obtain from European trade and a certain number of sub-tropical exotics as well. The English economy would thus become virtually independent of imports from all but tropical lands. This programme could well have been deduced from Spanish and Portuguese precedents in dealing with their overseas empires, but in the English discussions it was developed coherently and in detail, in a way which became stereotyped only in the following century.[33]

[30] See D. B. Quinn, *The Roanoke Voyages, 1584–90*, 2 vols. (Cambridge, 1955).

[31] 'A particuler discourse', the so-called 'Discourse of Western Planting', in E. G. R. Taylor, *The Original Writings and Correspondence of the Two Richard Hakluyts*, 2 vols. (London, 1935), ii, 211–326.

[32] R. Laudonnière, *A notable historie containing foure voyages made by certayne French captaynes vnto Florida* (London, 1587), sig. A1–A1v.

[33] G. L. Beer, *The Origins of the English Colonial System, 1578–1660* (New York, 1908), is still the fullest account, though his interpretations have been modified

The second of these, the idea of a supplementary economy, arose from the realization that North America could produce many of the products which England herself produced but in greater quantities. The English share in European and Newfoundland fisheries, if boosted into domination of all North American fisheries, could create a profitable monopoly in the international fishery which at that time was booming. Timber was clearly another complementary product. Not only could Baltic timber be done without, but English timber would be supplemented and conserved by bringing in masts and yards, barrel staves and clapboards, building ships on the spot, and above all substituting American timber for English in expensive timber-using heavy industry—iron-smelting, glass-making, potash manufacture—as well as by providing tar and resin. The vision of an infinite resource in timber, especially oak, was attractive. Then, too the cultivation of English grains and other food plants would enable the colonists to adjust their diet to that to which they were accustomed and obviate the need for food exports to them. This was an original idea. It did not take into account the possibility (which developed with New England in the next century) that certain colonies might produce *only* products of a comple-mentary nature and could only produce an unmarketable surplus or else become direct competitors with England, nor did it stress the great mercantilist plank of the next century that the colonies would offer a major closed market for English manufactures.

The last major consideration was the presumed need for the export of English men and women. The tendency for population to increase after the mid-century, together with endemic unemploy-ment associated with the decline of certain branches of the cloth trade, impressed—over-impressed—almost all those who thought about it with the idea that there was a surplus population which ought to be exported. Those who read Machiavelli seem to have turned their thoughts especially to Ireland as a home for surplus English people, and they had some influence, but 'the Americans', as we may call the group of projectors with whom we are here concerned, thought America was more suitable. Here there would be a free hand to experiment. And in the social blueprints for colonies there was wide agreement that attempts should be made to re-create something very like ideal English communities, whether they were the great feudal lordships of Gilbert's dream or the com-pact and democratic village communities envisaged by the Lost Colonists of 1587 and created at last in 1620 by the Pilgrims.

and developed in books such as Ralph Davis, *The Rise of the Atlantic Economies* (London, 1973) and K. G. Davies, *The North Atlantic World in the Seventeenth Century* (Minneapolis, 1974).

Linked with the desire to plan newer Englands in North America, was the incentive of upward social mobility. It is constantly stressed that persons going to America could expect to move at least one or two steps, if not more, up the steeply graded ladder of Elizabethan social hierarchy. Moreover, groups who sat uneasily at home, penally-taxed Catholic gentry, or Puritans of one denomination or another, might there be able to carry with them ideological idiosyncrasies which might not be so easily tolerated at home.

There were other incentives less original. There was the hope of selling to Amerindians vast quantities of woollen cloth or receiving rich furs and other products in exchange for worthless trinkets. Gold, silver and jewels were powerful incentives but they were muted in propaganda appeals after Frobisher's fiasco in finding worthless and not golden metals on Baffin Island. There was, too, the possibility of converting the heathen. Very often this appeared as a competitive necessity, since the Spaniards were attempting it, rather than as a moral imperative, or else it was thought of as a precondition for setting the Amerindians to work for the settlers, though too much optimism was not expressed after early reports had reached England on the attitudes of native peoples to European servitude.

Over the whole picture the idea of creating in North America another England or Englands, on a larger scale, with more generous opportunities (in theory at least) for all settlers though retaining essentially English social gradations, was dominant in this thinking. How far it went back to *Utopia* or Utopianism, how far it was influenced by a humanistic education, how far simply by self-interest is difficult to say. We may suggest that the total picture represents the practical approach of the Northern Renaissance, moulding its dreams and projections into specific, possibly attainable, social and economic objectives. New and improved Englands in North America, and an England improved by its American colonies, took shape on paper at this time.

It was in Ireland that the first large English colonial settlement was achieved. The plantation of Munster was developed between 1585 and 1594, wrecked in an Irish rising in 1598 and slowly reconstituted after 1603.[34] It was there, after the initial pangs of settlement, that the holders of some great Irish seignories began to think in terms of Roman models and Machiavellian warnings. Sir William Herbert, Richard Beacon and Edmund Spenser were all prepared to quote classical precedents and the works of the more recent

---

[34] R. Dunlop, 'The Plantation of Munster', *E.H.R.*, iii (1888), 250–69; D. B. Quinn, 'The Munster Plantation: Problems and Opportunities', *Journal of the Cork Historical and Archaeological Society*, lxxxi (1966), 19–40.

political master, Machiavelli, to justify what had been done in Munster and to commend its extension over the rest of Ireland. Sir Walter Ralegh, largest planter of all, may well have been in their company but has left no written record.[35] The reason may have been only personal idiosyncrasy or an intellectual game worked out in their Irish semi-exile. Yet Machiavelli's talk about colonies being instruments of strong government and a means of reforming and consolidating an existing regime had in some degree a special application to Irish conditions. Herbert, a scion of the Mont-gomeryshire family, was the most articulate. In 1588–89 he wrote a Latin treatise, entitled *Croftus, sive De Hibernia liber*, in honour of the lord-deputy of the 1550s, which was probably intended for publication as a learned excursus on English policy in Ireland, though it did not find its way into print until the late nineteenth century.[36] Herbert was concerned to explain why the conquest begun by Henry II had failed and how the reconquest of Ireland could be made fully effective. He was full of classical analogies and terminology and made several bows in the direction of 'that per-ceptive Italian', Machiavelli.[37] Briefly, the earlier conquest failed because, as he said, 'the transplanting of the colonies was without towns, castles or sufficiently satisfactory regulations': such colonies degenerate 'when colonists imitate and accept the morals, customs and laws of the native peoples.' Machiavelli had stressed the need for giving wide powers to regional officials (men no doubt like him-self who held wide seignories) and he was said also to endorse the wiping out of the native inhabitants if they remained, in the last resort, irreconcilable. The objectives of the regime Herbert favoured in Munster and wished to extend to the rest of Ireland were 'the building of cities, the planting of colonies, the defending of the power-less against the harshness and oppressions of the rulers, the periodic calling up and levying of soldiers from among the more vigorous inhabitants, and finally the educating of the flower of the youth in English academies.'[38] It is interesting to compare the emphasis here, a contrast with what was being discussed regarding America.

Richard Beacon's treatise, *Solon his follie, a politique discourse, touching the reformation of commonweales*, was published at Oxford in 1594. Ostensibly it was about the relations of two hypothetical

---

[35] P. Lefranc, *Sir Walter Ralegh écrivain* (Paris, 1968), pp. 237–40, 633–35.

[36] Edited by W. E. Buckley (Roxburghe Club, 1887). For Sir William Herbert of St Julians, Monmouthshire, see biography by A. H. Dodd in *Dictionary of Welsh Biography* (London 1959), p. 355, and *Herbert Correspondence*, edited by W. J. Smith (Cardiff and Dublin, 1963), pp. 4, 8, 61–64.

[37] Pp. 35, 41.

[38] P. 54, see also pp. 26, 35–8. I am indebted to Dr Cecil Clough for translations.

states, 'Athens' and 'Salamina', but in fact about Anglo-Irish relations. Beacon generalized from his experiences in Munster.[39] In
Ireland England should do as the Romans had done. He said:
'the Romans in all countries by them conquered did labour nothing
more than to protect and defend the feeble and weak, and to deliver
the people from oppression'. Earlier colonies had failed since,
'instead of planting of colonies, we placed garrisons.' Saturation
settlement was desirable, therefore 'let us lose no opportunity of
deducting colonies': such 'a reformation of a declined common-
weal is an happy restitution unto his perfection'.[40] The whole tract
is informed by reading amongst Italian and French writers, though
acknowledgments are seldom specific Beacon is very eloquent if at
times obscure, but an able exponent of this theme. Spenser in his
View of the state of Ireland, published only in 1633, found justification
for plantation in the defects of the Irish as well as in the achievements of the Romans. He cited Machiavelli, 'where he commendeth
the manner of the Romans' government, in giving absolute power
to all their consuls and governors, which, if they abused, they
should afterwards clearly answer.'[41]

A third writer of this period, who comes chronologically between
Herbert and Beacon, was Matthew Sutcliffe, who afterwards, as
Dean of Exeter, was prominently associated with the Plymouth
Company, the northern branch of the Virginia Company. His substantial work, *The practice, proceedings, and lawes of armes* (1593),
criticized Machiavelli as an amateur soldier who wrote about wars
he did not understand, but was content to use the *Discorsi* to help
out his plentiful citations from the Roman historians. He cited with
approval Vegetius' maxim 'The Romans did subdue the world by
the exercise of arms.' Moreover, he saw Roman colonization, by its
soldiers after conquest in the field, as an example to be followed in
subjecting conquered territories in his own time. Such colonies were
also economical: 'To maintaine a force therefore without great
charge, the meane is to send Colonies of the English nations into
the country conquered.' Such a programme had, he felt, a special
relevance to Ireland, saying 'And if Colonies had now of late bene

[39] For Richard Beacon, fellow of St John's College, Cambridge, Queen's
Attorney in Munster, 1586–91, grantee of 6,000 acres in Munster, 1591, see
Joseph Foster, *Alumni Oxonienses*, i (London, 1891), 94, and, for the grant of 1591,
Calendar of Patent and Close Rolls of Ireland, 18–45 Elizabeth, edited by James Morrin
(Dublin, 1862), p. 266.

[40] Pp. 81, 108, 114. I am indebted for information on *Solon* to Dr Sydney Anglo
who is making a study of the text.

[41] *A View of the State of Ireland*, ed. W. L. Renwick (Oxford, 1970), pp. 98–100,
125, 169; *Prose Works* (Variorum Spenser, ix), edited by R. Gottfried (Baltimore,
1949), pp. 229, 279, 286, 304, 397, 429.

sent into Ireland, not as now scattering and disunited, and few in number, but in good strength and united by lawes, and dwelling in townes as the Romans did, I doubt not, but the countrey would bee better assured, and the charge farre lesser then now it is.' Nor should there be any compunction about dispossessing the native inhabitants in such a case: 'If any man say, that it is hard to dispossesse the ancient inhabitants of the countrey out of their dwellings: he considereth not that rebels, and enemies are so to be used; and that if they be placed other where, it is of mercie rather then desert.' Sutcliffe, indeed, sums up very neatly the application of Roman and Machiavellian military-colonial precedent to contemporary Irish affairs.[41a]

Both Beacon and Spenser had a narrow, almost purely Irish perspective, but Sir Thomas Smith's Roman city could well have been envisaged in an American setting. Sutcliffe's also was narrow, set inside a purely military perspective, and applicable primarily to Ireland though capable of more general extension once external conquest was embarked on. Herbert's viewpoint lay somewhere in between: he was concerned with ancient history and the analogies it could supply both to point to political and military reforms and also to advocate a new beginning in dealing with the whole problem of intruded colonial settlement, which might in certain respects have been appropriate to America as well as to Ireland. These Irish instances, especially those applied to Munster, bring out clearly that Machiavelli was concerned with colonies as instruments of government in territories adjacent to or degenerated from the rule of the parent power. In Ireland colonization was primarily one means of solving the problem of government; colonies are associated with power rather than with the expansion of peoples into new areas. In America the problems seemed initially almost wholly concerned with establishing a secure social and economic base, while those presented by the native inhabitants and by the government of the colonies appeared to be of secondary significance.

Once expeditions with colonizing objectives had begun to be despatched to America a main element in published promotion material was narrative—accounts of what had actually occurred on particular expeditions—which could be analysed and compared with the experience of the French, Spanish and Portuguese at an earlier stage in other parts of the Americas. When colonies had actually been set up in America, from 1607 onwards, the achievements of the colonists, in however discreetly censored a form, in turn became the main ingredient in colonial promotional literature.

[41a] Sig. B4r., pp. 205–06.

The Virginia Company, throughout its career from 1606 to 1624, tried its best, and with some considerable success, to control the material which was published on its American colony. Consequently, much published colonization material is promotion matter in a narrower sense than that of the earlier phase. There was not, consequently, much need to look back into the Roman, or indeed any other past, and the main influences were more likely to be men with colonial experience rather than theorists like Machiavelli. None-the-less, especially when things were going wrong in the colony, some appeal to the past was still part of a continuing tradition.

The habit of reference to the Roman past continued in Ireland during the growing pains of the great Ulster plantation, which was to surpass Munster and Virginia alike as a new colony in the period before 1630. Thomas Blenerhasset in 1610 thought James I should preen himself like a Roman emperor on the strength of his colonizing achievements in Ulster,[42] while Sir John Davies,[43] making still another review of the mistakes of the initial Norman conquest, before going on to praise the Ulster plantation, could not refrain from pointing out how the Romans would have done much better than Henry II and the rest. In the Virginia Company literature, Roman example comes up also from time to time. Robert Gray, in *A good speed for Virginia* (1609), maintained that for the Romans colonization was the chosen means for dealing with a population surplus and should be for England also.[44] Robert Johnson in 1609 and 1612 also glanced at Roman precedents.[45] It was really only when there were serious problems arising in Virginia, and a closer look at the longer perspective was needed, that serious consideration was given to historical precedent. The learned writer of *A true declaration of the estate of the colonie in Virginia* (1610), was one who thought in this way. The Virginia Company's settlement of 1607 in Virginia, though reinforced twice in 1608, had singularly failed to root itself firmly at Jamestown. The first large reinforcement in 1609 had been no more successful; so many died and food had run so short that a further relief expedition in 1610 had barely arrived in time to prevent the colonists leaving Virginia. Much of this was blamed on the incapacity of the colonists to rule themselves. *A true declaration,* therefore, was intended to explain failures and to recommend

[42] Dedication to *A direction for the plantation in Ulster* (London, 1610).

[43] *A discouerie of the true causes why Ireland was neuer entirely subdued, nor brought vnder obedience of the crowne of England, vntill the beginning of his maiesties happpie reigne* (London, 1612), pp. 77, 124–25, 156, 164.

[44] Sig. B4.

[45] *Nova Britannia* (London, 1609), sig. C2, E2v., and *The new life of Virginia* (London, 1612), sig. F1, G4.

reforms which would create a successful colony. The author had a long excursus on the prevalence of colonization throughout the ages, ending with the Romans, who 'deduced 53 colonies out of the city of Rome into the womb of Italy'. The chief lesson to be learnt was the need for order and discipline in the colonizing process: 'how easily might ambitious discord tear in pieces an infant colony,' he said, 'where no eminent and respected magistrates had authority to punish presumptuous dissentience.' He worked up into a fine rhetorical passage: 'Tacitus hath observed that when Nero sent his old trained soldiers to Tarantum and Autium, but without their captains and centurions, that they rather made a number than a colony. Every soldier secretly glided into some neighbouring province, and forsook their appointed places, which hatched this consequent mischief. When therefore license, sedition and fury are the fruits of a heady daring and unruly multitude, it is no wonder, that so many in our colony perished. . . . A colony is heretofore denominated because they should be *coloni*, the tillers of the soil and stewards of fertility. Our mutinous loiterers would not sow with providence, and therefore they reaped the fruits of too dear-bought repentance.'[46]

In this case the Roman analogy was not merely academic but the headline of a new policy, namely a plan to place the colony under a firm administration in a legal strait-waistcoat, in which the settlers would be compelled to obey orders, to work, to build, to grow crops and to behave as they were told to do. The legal code developed in 1610–11 and imposed on the colony was as draconic as any which could have been derived from classical authorities. William Strachey, who wrote the introduction to *For the colony in Virginea Britannia. Lawes divine, morall and martiall*, published in 1612, presented the code as 'a transcript of the Toparchia or state of those duties by which their colony stands regulated and commanded, that such may receive due check who maliciously and desperately heretofore have censured of it.'[47] In his own work, 'The history of travell to Virginia Britania', which he wrote about the same time, but did not publish, Strachey maintained that had the Romans not conquered and civilized the Britons, England would be savage yet. Perhaps this may be the last case where Roman law and precedent regarding colonies was called in to justify a particular line of policy.[48] And indeed, whether the Roman influence was effective or not, the

[46] In Peter Force, *Tracts . . . Relating Principally to the Origin . . . of The Colonies in North America*, III (Gloucester, Mass. 1963), no. 1, pp. 4, 15.

[47] Sig. A2v.

[48] *The Historie of Travell into Virginia Britania (1612)*, ed. L. B. Wright and V. Freund (London, 1953), p. 24.

colony did survive and begin to grow under its hard taskmaster, the code of 1611, until it could be gradually relaxed after 1616.

There were a few traditional echoes still to come. The clergy in particular liked to show off their learning by citing Roman as well as biblical precedents for colonization. The Reverend William Symonds in his *Sermon* (1609) asked rhetorically, when insufficient colonists were coming forward for Virginia—'Is only now the ancient planting of colonies, so highly praised among the Romans and all other nations, so vile and odious among us that what is and hath been a virtue is all others must be sin in us?'[49] But he did not provide an answer to his own question. The Reverend Richard Eburne compiled, in *A plaine path-way to plantations* (1624), the fullest compendium of all on why England should establish colonies in America, especially in Newfoundland. Among his many reasons was that plantations were 'both usual and ancient . . . above all to the Roman state, which from their very first years, *ab urbe condita*, after that Rome itself was builded, fell apace to that practice and had ever on hand one or other colony.'[50] We need not conclude, however, that he placed Roman precedent high on his list of incentives. We may take the Reverend John White of Dorchester a little more seriously. *The planters plea. Or the grounds of plantations examined, and usuall objections answered* (1630), was the last of the early classical treatises, by an eminent pioneer who sent many settlers to New England. The argument throughout is a mixture of religious and economic incentives and imperatives. There are side glances at Roman colonizing precedents. The bringing in of religion was the main thing to be hoped for, religion for colonists and the Indians alike, but, obliquely, the Romans are brought into it too. 'I make no question,' he said, 'but God used the same way to other barbarous nations, which he held with us, whom he first civilized by the Roman conquests and mixture of their colonies with us, that he might bring in religion afterwards, seeing no man can imagine how religion should prevail upon those who are not subdued to the rule of nature and religion:'[51]—a statement which contained the germ of a programme for settlers and Amerindians alike in the new Commonwealth of Massachusetts Bay, which was then just forming.

We can see that in most respects Roman analogies and precedents and the reading in Machiavelli which may well have lain behind many of them, had only marginal and occasional practical importance in the later development of colonial planning in early seven-

[49] Sig. C4.

[50] *A plaine path-way to plantations* (London, 1624), p. 17, and *A Plain Pathway to Plantations*, ed. Louis B. Wright (Ithaca, N.Y., 1962), p. 41.

[51] P. 11, other references to Roman colonies are on pp. 37, 43–44.

teenth century England. The broad considerations of economic and social policy, sketched before 1600, were in the main followed during the period when theorizing was turned into effective, if risky, experiments in colonization. They were inevitably modified in their application as practical lessons were learnt. The real America proved in many ways different from the America which appeared in the early debates and projects. It had its own distinctive climate and its own faunal and floral characteristics which made some of the early plans for economic exploitation fruitless. Its natives were not the simple, obedient savages whom some theorists hoped for, but they were not wholly intractable barbarians either: a sophisticated native policy was called for. Ideas on the organization of particular types of settlement had to be worked out by trial and error. A chartered company, for example, proved excellent for raising capital if it had high-level government sponsorship, as had the Virginia Company for most of its existence: it proved unsatisfactory for developing a colonial community. It led, on the other hand, by a process of trial and error, to the production of a viable cash crop, tobacco, which made Virginia self-supporting in the end. Similar organizations failed in Newfoundland partly because of undue optimism about the climate, but principally because its main harvest, that of the sea, could best be handled by unco-ordinated seasonal fishing voyages from Europe. In New England hard experience revealed that a small village-type community could indeed make a living for itself within a span of about four years, but it needed outside help if it was to do more than survive its early growing pains and prosper. In 1629–30 the Massachusetts Bay Company was to begin to demonstrate that capital, if put up by the settlers themselves and used to feed the colony through its early years, together with a process of adapting company organization to the task of internal self-government,[52] could work wonders in enabling a New England in the end to be created.

Did any of these later developments owe anything substantial to earlier discussions which involved looking back to Rome or to Machiavelli or other Renaissance theorists? It is hard to give any precise answer. Renaissance learning certainly contributed to the spread of Europe overseas in all sorts of ways, many of them indirect, rather than direct, but it was gradually subsumed as an immediately

[52] General guides to the early development of colonies in North America are J. E. Pomfret, and F. M. Shumway, *Founding the American Colonies* (New York, 1970), W. F. Craven, *The Southern Colonies in the Seventeenth Century* (Baton Rouge, 1949); C. M. Andrews, *The Colonial Period of American History* (New Haven, 1934), i, and D. B. Quinn, 'North America from First Discovery to Early Settlements' (forthcoming).

effective force. In the case of England, it was clearly only one among a wide spectrum of influences. We may consider that Roman precedent, however imperfectly understood, directed Englishmen's attention to certain incentives to colonization, perhaps the issue of presumed pressures of population and that of intensive forward planning for the government of both settlers and natives. Other means and other channels would have probably brought them to very similar positions, though perhaps by longer routes. While in a few cases some concrete effects can be deduced from theoretical reliance on Rome or Machiavelli for guidance, it is hard to regard either as decisive over a very wide area of discourse or experiment. Perhaps the main significance of their appearance at all is that they indicate that the new colonial situation created by the overseas discoveries was being envisaged very much inside a historical context.

University of Liverpool.

Appendix

English Discussions of Colonization in North America, 1576–160

In the following list individual colonizing projects are dated as closely a possible, but they are placed in sequence under date of publication if they appeared before the end of Queen Elizabeth's reign. Later publication is referred to in a few instances.

(i) Sir Humphrey Gilbert, *A discourse of a discouerie for a new passage to Cataia* (London, 1576);

(ii) Richard Hakluyt, the elder, 'Notes framed by a Gentleman', [1578]; in Richard Hakluyt, the younger, *Diuers voyages touching the discouerie of America* (London, 1582);

(iii) Christopher Carleill, *A breef and sommarie discourse vpon the entended voyage to the hethermoste partes of America* (London, 1583, 2 edns);

(iv) Sir George Peckham, *A true reporte, of the late discoueries, and possession taken in the right of Englande, of the New-found Landes* (London, 1583), 2 issues;

(v) Richard Hakluyt, the younger, 'A particuler discourse' (Discourse of Western Planting, 1584), in E. G. R. Taylor, *The Original Writings and Correspondence of the Two Richard Hakluyts*, vol. ii (London, 1935), pp. 211–326;

(vi) Richard Hakluyt, the elder, 'Inducements to the lykinge of the voyadge intended to that parte of America which lyethe betwene 34. and 36. degree of Septentrionall Latytude', [1584–85], in *Ibid.*, ii, 339–43;

(vii) Edward Hayes, 'Discourse of the Newfounde lande,' 1586, Brit. Lib., Lansdowne MS 100, fols 83–94;

(viii) Thomas Harriot, *A briefe and true report of the new found land of Virginia* (London, 1588);

(ix) Edward Hayes, 'A report of the voyage and success thereof, attempted in the yeere of our Lord 1583, by Sir Humphrey Gilbert knight', in Richard Hakluyt, *Principall nauigations* (London, 1589), pp. 679–97;

(x) Edward Hayes, 'A discourse conserning a voyage intended for the planting of chrystyan religion and people in the Northwest regions of America' [1592], C.U.L. MS Dd. 3. 85, No. 4;

(xi) Anon., 'Plantacion in America' [c. 1595–1600], P.R.O., State Papers, Colonial, C.O. 1/1, 9;

(xii) Charles Leigh, 'A brieffe platforme For a voyadge with three ships vnto the Iland of Ramea in Canada', 1597, Brit. Lib., Additional MS 12505– fols. 77ʳ–77ᵛ;

(xiii) Edward Hayes, 'A treatise' [c. 1592–3], in John Brereton, *A briefe and true relation of the discouerie of the north part of Virginia* (London, 1602), both edns, sig. B4–C4;

(xiv) Richard Hakluyt, the elder, 'Inducements to the liking of the voyage, intended towards Virginia,' 1585, in *Ibid.*, 2nd edn, sig. D1–E2V.

SCANDINAVIAN SETTLEMENT IN THE NORTH AND WEST OF THE BRITISH ISLES— AN ARCHAEOLOGICAL POINT-OF-VIEW

By Professor David M. Wilson, M.A., F.S.A., F.R.Hist.S.

READ AT THE SOCIETY'S CONFERENCE 18 SEPTEMBER 1975

THE Scandinavians came to Britain first as raiders, then as settlers. The length of the periods of raiding, the form of raids, the character and duration of settlement and the speed with which Scandinavian influence was lost, varied considerably in the different regions. In simple terms the Viking Age lasted from 790 to 1070, but within and beyond these dates is infinite variety. In England the first settlements are not recorded before 876, eighty years or more after the first raids; in Scotland, however, there is fairly firm evidence of settlement in the first half of the ninth century, while in some parts of Scotland settlement may not even have been preceded by raids. It is clear too that Guthrum's conquests are of an entirely different character to those of Knut the Great. Guthrum was a petty chief. Knut a great ruler, was accepted as such by his royal contemporaries and his power achieved imperial proportions. In Ireland, where they settled in very limited areas, the Scandinavians lost most of their political power in the late tenth century. Their commercial importance there, however, grew by leaps and bounds, but even in this role they lost all semblance of influence after the Norman conquest of Ireland of 1169. Norse power was broken in western Scotland after the battle of Largs in 1263 (although Norse earls held sway in the Isles until 1331). The Isle of Man was transferred to the Scottish crown in 1266, while Orkney and Shetland remained Norwegian until the impignorations of 1468 and 1469.

This paper outlines the archaeological evidence for the Scandinavian settlement of the British Isles during the period from 700 to 1100. While based on archaeological methods, it takes into account material and evidence from other closely-related disciplines—history, place-names and philology. It largely ignores the settlement of the Danelaw and eastern England to concentrate on the settlement of Scotland and the Irish Sea region, for here the archaeologist provides most of the evidence—more at least than in the lowland zone of eastern England.[1] Here is no discussion of the administrative and tenurial system of the Danelaw, nor of Germanic systems of *Königsfreie* or *agrarii milites* which lead back into dim—and perhaps irrelevant—comparison with subjects such as Langobardic colonization or the *laeti* of the late Roman Empire. The Scandinavians in the late ninth century brought administrative sense to the newly conquered lands of eastern England. They adopted local systems of organization and tenure (and probably introduced one or two of their own ideas). Extending Christopher Morris's work,[2] it is clear that the passing of many estates from church control into the hands of the new overlords released much land for redistribution. The consequent reorganization of the agricultural and tenurial systems must have resulted in the foundation of many secondary settlements, represented on the ground today by place-names. What seems clear, both in the historical and archaeological material, is that the Scandinavians, with their usual eclectic good sense, adapted much of the material culture and even the administrative machinery of the English on whom they imposed themselves. Archaeology tells us little of the Scandinavian situation in the Midlands and East Anglia—the occasional grave or piece of sculpture is all that remains. The region is reasonably well documented in the historical sources and the archaeologist, for the moment, can contribute little.

Northern England

In the north of England the historical background can be simply outlined. York was captured in 867 and Yorkshire was settled under the leadership of Halfdan in the years after 876; the north-west was presumably settled in the period after 900 probably from Norway and Ireland. There was much internicene warfare between the Norwegians and Danes in the north of England, particularly after 919, when the Norwegians took York. The English, however, gradually regained political control of the north under such formidable leaders as Æthelflæd, the lady of the Mercians, while the battle in Brunanburh in 937 led to the collapse of Danish power in the north, the gradual decline of the Norse kingdom of York and the final expulsion of Eric Bloodaxe in 954.

The settlement pattern is well demonstrated by Scandinavian place-names which abound in the north. These seem to tell (as most people now believe) of a considerable and enduring settlement

[1] D. M. Wilson, 'Archaeological evidence for the Viking settlements and raids in England', *Frühmittelalterliche Studien*, ii (1968), pp. 293 ff.

[2] Lecture given at the conference of the Society of Antiquaries of Scotland, 1975.

by the Scandinavians.[3] The tenurial situation reflects a similar tale. Linguistically things are more difficult, but the problems raised by language have been dealt with, *inter alia*, by Eilert Ekwall,[4] Raymond Page[5] and Dietrich Hoffman.[6] Perhaps the clearest statement concerning language is that of the late Hugh Smith in his consideration in 1962 of the place-names of the West Riding of Yorkshire:

> . . . the Vikings, whilst retaining many elements of their vocabulary and features of their pronunciation, soon adopted Old English as their basic language . . . and would appear to have spoken their English with a Norse accent. The formation of an early English dialect so rich in Scandinavian elements . . . and so poor in the structural features of Old Scandinavian points to the almost complete and early integration of the Old English and Viking folk in the West Riding.[7]

The archaeological evidence—though sparse—would seem to support the picture of a complete and early integration of Anglo-Saxon and Scandinavian in the north of England in the settlement period. Scandinavian traits are rare in the archaeological record; no houses, no temples, no churches of Scandinavian type are known. A handful of burials are accompanied by grave goods in the normal non-Christian European fashion—swords, brooches and other objects of adornment or daily use. But there are few of them; there are, for example, more Scandinavian graves (and more richly furnished) in the Isle of Man (fig. 1).[8] The very paucity of this evidence seems to indicate that the Scandinavian incomers accepted Christianity quickly, and this supposition is heightened by the large number of sculptured funerary monuments of Christian character raised in English churchyards.[9] These are Christian crosses of English

---

[3] But see P. H. Sawyer, *The Age of the Vikings* (2nd edn, London, 1971), pp. 169 ff.

[4] E. Ekwall, 'How long did the Scandinavian language survive in England', *A grammatical miscellany offered to Otto Jespersen* . . . (London and Copenhagen, 1939), pp. 17–30.

[5] R. I. Page, 'How long did the Scandinavian language survive in England. The epigraphical evidence', *England before the Conquest*, (eds. P. Clemoes and K. Hughes (Cambridge, 1971), pp. 165–82.

[6] D. Hoffmann, *Nordisch-englische Lehnbeziehungen der Wikingerzeit* (Copenhagen, 1955).

[7] A. H. Smith, *The place-names of the West Riding of Yorkshire*, vii (Cambridge, 1962), p. 63.

[8] Listed D M. Wilson, *The Viking Age in the Isle of Man* (Odense, 1974), pp. 44–45.

[9] Best gathered together in W. G. Collingwood, *Northumbrian Crosses* (London, 1927).

inspiration but decorated with Scandinavian ornament. The new religion used an old art, as well as a material—stone—familiar enough to the Anglo-Saxons but barely used before as a medium for decoration by the Scandinavians in their homelands.[10]

Coin-hoards may also provide evidence of various kinds. The hoard material is significant in size and variety. The work of Christopher Blunt, Michael Dolley and their colleagues over the last twenty years has opened up areas of study which stretch far beyond the normal boundaries of numismatic endeavour. In the period between 900 and 930, for example, hoards found in northern England hint at the commercial activity of the Scandinavians;[11] of contact with the Baltic, and beyond, whence came the Arabic coins which only occur in this period in Britain. More importantly, they tell of contact between York and the Irish Sea, a contact based on both political and commercial interests, which presumably was based on a route which passed through Chester and Meols and perhaps up the Ribble. The hoards also hint at a route to the Viking homelands by way of the Scottish islands. At this period hoards provide the only real evidence for Scandinavian trade to and within the British Isles.

The Scandinavians, who came from a homeland without a monetary economy, quickly adapted to the more sophisticated English standards and about 895 were producing their own coins in York.[12]

Excavation in York, the great commercial centre of Scandinavian England, has produced little archaeological evidence of Scandinavian oriented trade. Nevertheless, York apparently developed considerably in the Danish period;[13] the Roman walls seem to have been strengthened and the Roman fort possibly served as a refuge for the merchants and craftsmen who were developing the extramural settlement around present-day Ousegate. There are no specifically Scandinavian traits among the buildings so far discovered, the town is apparently as English or as European as any major town of this character in the tenth century. Here once again the Scandinavians showed their eclecticism.

---

[10] I have developed this thesis in D. M. Wilson and O. Klindt-Jensen, *Viking Art* (London, 1966), p. 104 *et passim*.

[11] *Cf.* D. M. Wilson, 'An Irish mounting in the National Museum, Copenhagen', *Acta Archaeologica*, xxvi (1955), fig. 8.

[12] *Cf.* R. H. M. Dolley, *The Hiberno-Norse coins in the British Museum* (London, 1966).

[13] Recent excavations in York are reported quarterly in *Interim, Bulletin of the York Archaeological Trust*. See also J. Radley, 'Economic aspects of Anglo-Danish York', *Medieval Archaeology* xv (1971), pp. 37–57.

Scotland

In Scotland, there is little contemporary literary evidence of a Scandinavian presence. Early raids are recorded in the *Annals of Ulster* (which *inter alia* enshrine a lost Iona chronicle) whilst casual mentions of some reliability are found in other Irish sources. Norse sources are late, but using them critically it is possible to glean certain facts, particularly from *Orkneyinga Saga*. We depend in our study of Scandinavian Scotland almost entirely on archaeology, largely interpreted in the light of later written sources; fortunately this archaeological evidence is significant. There is, however no material trace of any raid, but plenty of evidence of settlement. Scattered along the western coastline of Scotland (mainly in the islands), the northernmost counties and in Orkney and Shetland are a good number of graves (fig. 1), including a handful of cemeteries (particularly Westness and Pierowall in Orkney and Kiloran Bay on Colonsay).[14] The graves are accompanied by grave-goods in a pagan fashion long outmoded in Christian Scotland. The objects found in these graves are similar in almost every respect to those found in any other Scandinavian Atlantic area. They show no particular relationship, as has sometimes been suggested, to any specific area of Norway. The graves are not particularly rich, in comparison for example with some of the western Norwegian examples, but one of the Westness graves did produce a fine jewelled pin of insular origin,[15] and other graves are rich in weapons and tools.

Women's graves are common and this fact is important. Oval brooches found in a number of Scottish graves, are a distinctive and integral part of Scandinavian folk dress. The brooches were not worn by local women; they represent Scandinavians, wives and daughters who moved to Scotland with their Scandinavian menfolk as settlers. One such brooch is even found on the remote island of St Kilda.[16] The Scottish graves, like those in England, represent settlers not raiders. Interestingly, there is little trace of a phenomenon remarked in England and Man, namely the burial of Scandinavians in a pagan manner in pre-existing Christian cemetaries, but this may be because we have little record of such finds.

[14] For Westness see S. H. Hanssen Kaland, 'Westnessutgravningene på Rousay Orknøyene', *Viking*, xxxvii (1973), 77–102. For other graves in Scotland see H. Shetelig, *Viking Antiquities in Great Britain and Ireland*, ii (Oslo, 1940), *passim*.

[15] R. B. K. Stevenson, 'The brooch from Westness, Orkney', *The Fifth Viking, Congress* (Tórshavn, 1968), pp. 25–31.

[16] A. B. Taylor, 'The Norsemen in St Kilda', *Saga Book of the Viking Society for Northern Research*, xvii (1967–8), pl. II.

It is not easy to date the graves closely. Ninth- and early tenth-century objects are reasonably common, and some burials—like that found by Anna Ritchie at Buckquoy in Orkney[17] (which included a silver penny of the English king Edmund who died in 946)—almost certainly date from the second half of the tenth century. There seem to be no eleventh-century graves. Very few, if any, graves of a later date are found elsewhere in the British Isles. Perhaps these late graves indicate that the areas of Scotland settled by the Scandinavians relapsed into paganism, from which they only emerged with the conversion of Norway.

A fair number of graves found in Norway contain insular material, and most of them were catalogued by Shetelig and his colleagues in the 'twenties and 'thirties, when it was only possible to distinguish English and Irish material.[18] It is now clear that some of the objects catalogued then (certain penannular brooches,[19] for example) were of Pictish or Scottish origin. Some of these objects undoubtedly represent the products of Viking raids (mounts from shrines and books, for example, taken home as booty) but some may be gifts or purchases.

Although many of these objects may date from the eighth century, they do not necessarily indicate contact between Scotland and Scandinavia much before 800. Consider, for example, the eighth-century shrine which was found in the north of Norway now in the National Museum in Copenhagen.[20] This object, which may well be of Scottish origin (it could of course be Irish), has a Norse runic inscription on the base which reads in translation, 'Ranvaig owns this casket'. The inscription is itself probably of tenth-century date, and one might suspect that the lady—Ranvaig—had used it as a trinket-box. The box, however, was probably never secularized for it still contains relics, some wrapped in medieval silks and labelled with the names of saints. It may well be that the shrine was brought to Norway in the tenth or eleventh century (at the time of the conversion of that country) and that Ranvaig or one of her descendants presented the casket to her own church in Norway. It was almost certainly never buried, and presumably languished in a church cupboard until it was re-discovered in the early nineteenth century. This is an extreme case, but eighth-century insular objects found in Norwegian graves almost certainly did not get to Norway before 800.

[17] A. Ritchie, 'Pict and Norsemen in northern Scotland', *Scottish Archaeological Forum*, vi (1974), p. 30.

[18] Shetelig, *op. cit.*, v.

[19] For example, *ibid.*, fig. 58. This identification was made in A. Small, C. Thomas and D. M. Wilson, *St Ninian's Isle and its treasure*, i, (Oxford, 1973), pp. 81 ff.

[20] Shetelig, *op. cit.*, v, fig. 89. See also *Antikvarisk tidskrift*, 1843–45, p. 220.

The graves tell us, then, of settlements—a story easily inferred from literary sources. A similar story is told by the hoards, the distribution of which is roughly the same as that of the graves. Some hoards—St Ninian's Isle, Rogart and Croy particularly[21]—were perhaps laid down by their Pictish owners in the early ninth century in the face of Scandinavian attack, and if so, provide a slender indication of the period of the raids. The hoards[22] of the tenth century which contain silver coins and objects in a Scandinavian taste tell (as do the English hoards) their individual story of an unstable political situation and of economic activity, of contact with Norway and the Baltic and of contact with England and Ireland.

Unlike England, Scotland provides a fair amount of evidence concerning the settlement sites and the economy of the incomers. Settlement sites have been excavated, or are being excavated, in Shetland (at Jarlshof[23] and Underhoull[24]), in Orkney (at Buckquoy,[25] Skaill-by-Deerness,[26] at Birsay,[27] Westness[28] and Gurness[29]), on the mainland at Freswick[30] and in North Uist at the Udal.[31] With the exception of Birsay, which at certain periods at least was the site of an earl's house and a bishop's palace, all these settlements are farm complexes—some, like Underhoull, being comparatively simple; some, like Jarlshof, being reasonably wealthy. Nucleated settlements—villages and towns—were apparently a rarity in Viking Age Scotland. The economy of the previous inhabitants seems to have continued with the coming of the Scandinavians, as most of the sites listed have a more or less continuous history from before the Viking Age into the full medieval period. The historical geographers have produced a reasonable model for a Scottish Scandinavian settlement,[32] and (with a little more work in the Western

[21] These hoards are discussed in Small, Thomas and Wilson, *passim.*

[22] These hoards are shortly to be published by my colleague, James Graham-Campbell.

[23] R. J. C. Hamilton, *Excavations at Jarlshof, Shetland* (Edinburgh, 1956).

[24] A. Small, 'Underhoull, Unst, Shetland', *Proceedings of the Society of Antiquaries of Scotland*, xcviii (1964–66), pp. 225–48.

[25] Ritchie, *op. cit.*   [26] Unpublished.

[27] New excavations by Christopher Morris are now in train on this site. The old excavations are summarized most recently in S. Cruden, 'Excavations at Birsay, Orkney', *The Fourth Viking Congress*, ed. A. Small (Aberdeen, 1965), pp. 22–31.

[28] Unpublished.

[29] Unpublished save for Dept. of Environment site guide.

[30] A. O. Curle, 'A Viking settlement at Freswick, Caithness', *Proceedings of the Society of Antiquaries of Scotland*, lxxiii (1938–39), pp. 71–110.

[31] I. A. Crawford, 'Scot, Norseman and Gael', *Scottish Archaeological Forum*, vi (1974), 1–16; and J. Graham-Campbell, 'A preliminary note on certain small-finds of Viking-Age date from the Udal excavations, North Uist', *ibid.*, pp. 17–22.

[32] A. Small, 'The Viking highlands—a geographical view', *The Dark Ages in the Highlands* (Inverness, 1971), pp. 69–88.

Isles) it will soon be possible to generalize concerning the basic economy, although field systems must be investigated. It is not without interest that there was apparently little need for elaborate fortification round the settlements of this period; all that was needed was a stake fence or stone wall. Attacks on individual sites when they came would usually only represent the crew of a single ship and would be in proportions manageable by the total population of a farm. Indeed, even in their homelands it was not until the tenth and eleventh centuries that the Scandinavians began to be interested in fortification and then only in regard to major settlements— towns, trading stations and the like. In Scotland the first Norse fortifications were the castles of the mid-twelfth century,[33] well outside our period.

In England and the Isle of Man one of the most important traces of the Scandinavian presence is funerary sculpture. In Scotland, on the other hand, sculpture in the Scandinavian taste is rare. In England such monuments first appeared within, say, a generation of Halfdan's settlement. In the Isle of Man they appeared in the middle of the tenth century, some generations after the initial settlement of the island. A tenth-century stone slab from Kilbar on Barra,[34] however, is obviously derived from a Manx prototype: the ornament below the arms of the cross being a degenerate version of ornament found in Man. The apparent lack in Scotland of tenth-century stone funerary monuments—specifically Christian objects—may be due to the late conversion of the Norse in this area: a not unreasonable suggestion in view of the undoubted presence of pagan-type graves in at least the third quarter of the tenth century.

In common with northern England and Man, Scotland has practically no eleventh-century sculpture in the Viking taste, although the Hebridean stone from Dòid Mhàiri has Ringerike scrollwork.[35] From the vastly muddled site of Iona comes an eleventh or twelfth century recumbent slab, which bears a corase interlaced cross and a fragmentary runic inscription:

kaul × aulus × sunr × laþi × stan × þinsi ×
ubir :fukl × bruþr ×
(Kali son of Aulus laid this stone over [his] brother Fugl).[36]

---

[33] S. Cruden, *The Scottish Castle* (Edinburgh, 1963).

[34] Shetelig, *op. cit.*, vi (1954), fig. 40.

[35] R. B. K. Stevenson, 'The Inchyra stone and some other unpublished Early Christian monuments', *Proceedings of the Society of Antiquaries of Scotland*, xcii (1958–59), pp. 33–55.

[36] I am grateful to Aslak Liestøl for this reading.

This is one of the most interesting of the handful of runic inscriptions found in Scotland. Other runic inscriptions include that on the back of the famous Hunterston brooch[37] (where a person with a Celtic name, Melbride is recorded in presumably tenth-century Norse characters as owning a very early eighth-century brooch), and the long and complicated inscription inside the megalithic tomb of Maeshowe on the mainland of Orkney.[38]

The actual evidence provided by archaeology for the Scandinavian presence in Scotland, outlined above, adds some flesh to the bare bones of the literary material—Anglo-Saxon, Irish and Norse—from which the brief description of the Viking Age in Scotland is normally assembled. Place-name research emphasizes the pattern. Nicolaisen's[39] maps of the Norse place-name elements in Scotland—in the Hebrides in Orkney and Shetland, and on the west coast—shows that their distribution coincides exactly with that of the graves, of the hoards and even of the settlement sites. If we are to place Viking Age Scotland within its Atlantic context and within the polity of the Scandinavian world much previous work must be re-examined, the work of the place-name specialist not excluded. Who dares nowadays to place so firm a date on a place-name element as Nicolaisen did less than ten years ago? We must also take into account other disciplines which have been little regarded: personal names, for example. Iain Crawford has made an interesting excursion into this area.[40] He suggests that 'a very precise regional pattern' of personal name forms emerges. Such Norse names as MacLeod, MacAulay and MacAskill are found within a political frontier of at latest twelfth-century origin, coinciding with the distribution of Norse loan words. This frontier might have some meaning in an earlier period. This is but one of many groups of evidence which must be investigated before we can write the history of Viking Age Scotland.

The Isle of Man

By its position in the centre of the Irish Sea the Isle of Man had a strategic importance in any power struggle concerned with that area, as is illustrated by the suggestion that after 902 the Norse

[37] R. B. K. Stevenson, 'The Hunterston brooch and its significance', *Medieval Archaeology*, xviii (1974), pp. 16–42.

[38] The literature on this inscription is enormous. The latest work is A. Liestøl, 'The Maeshowe runes, some new interpretations', *The Fifth Viking Congress* (Tórshavn, 1965), pp. 55–61.

[39] W. F. H. Nicolaisen, 'Norse settlement in the Northern and Western Isles', *The Scottish Historical Review*, xviii (1969), pp. 6–17.

[40] Crawford, *op. cit.*, pp. 2 ff.

and Irish followers of Ingemund fled to Man, before mounting an attack on the Wirral. It is proper to assume that Man, like other parts of the British Isles suffered from a period of Scandinavian raids, but of this period we have no archaeological or literary remains. Indeed, any coherent historical account of the island is lacking before 1066, when the events recorded in *Chronicon Manniae et Insularum* lend some shadowy reality to this important Norse kingdom. Place-names tell of the density of Scandinavian settlement,[41] whilst the political institutions of the island reflect to this day the Scandinavian background. The representative assembly (Tynwald), the land divisions, the administrative divisions and the name of the bishopric are all of Scandinavian origin.[42]

The archaeological evidence for the Scandinavian presence on the island is important and reasonably plentiful. Nineteen sites have produced pagan Scandinavian graves (some more than one), and there is a distinct possibility that another six finds also represent graves.[43] In general the graves date from the ninth century and it would be difficult to point to any object in the graves which could be dated as late as the mid-tenth century, by which period the incomers had apparently turned to Christianity. This is shown by the richest body of material of Scandinavian character—the corpus of sculpture. This consists of slabs cut out of the soft Manx slate and carved with Christian crosses and Norse ornament.[44] Some of these even depict scenes from Norse legends, whilst some bear runic inscriptions, which record the name of men and women with Norse names. Occasionally a person with a Celtic name is mentioned in the inscriptions, indicating at least some intermarriage with the native population. The slabs, which copy a native Christian tradition, were mostly carved in the tenth and early eleventh centuries (say 930–1030).

It is in the same period that we find the first coin hoards. Thirteen such hoards have now been recognized and Michael Dolley has added two further finds to this number as possible hoards of the Viking Age.[45] Three of the hoards, at least, contain objects other

[41] M. Gelling, 'The place-names of the Isle of Man', *The Journal of the Manx Museum*, vii (1970), pp. 30–39.
[42] B. R. S. and E. M. Megaw, 'The Norse heritage in the Isle of Man', *The early cultures of north-west Europe*, ed. C. Fox and B. Dickins, (Cambridge, 1950), pp. 141–70.
[43] D. M. Wilson, *The Viking Age in the Isle of Man, the archaeological evidence* (Odense, 1974), pp. 44 ff.
[44] D. M. Wilson, 'Manx memorial stones of the Viking period', *Saga Book of the Viking Society for Northern Research*, xviii (1970–71), 1–18.
[45] R. H. M. Dolley, 'The pattern of Viking Age coin-hoards from the Isle of Man', *Seaby's Coin and Medal Bulletin*, 1975, pp. 296–302, 337–40.

than coins and one of them—that from Ballaquayle—even has a gold armlet. The confidently identified hoards date from between the 960s and the 1070s, although Dolley has postulated at least one earlier example. These dates reflect the rise in the economic importance of Dublin after the fall of York, and it seems clear that the Isle of Man's fortunes were in this period at least linked with those of the Dublin Vikings.

Norse settlement is also represented by two or three inland habitation sites,[46] but, if it is right that the quarterland farms of the middle ages were lived in by the Scandinavians, then they are unavailable to archaeologists as their sites are still occupied by farm buildings. There is some evidence of continuity from the pre-Scandinavian period at the Braaid, where a Celtic round-house occurs alongside a Scandinavian building. An extraordinary phenomenon derived from the pre-Viking age are the promontory forts. There are fifteen of these, each of which consists of a house on a precipitous headland cut off from the mainland by a deep ditch and a bank. Similar fortifications occur elsewhere in the Celtic lands,[47] but only in the Isle of Man have they been shown by excavation to have been used by Scandinavians as well as by their predecessors and successors.

Ireland

The first recorded Scandinavian contacts with Ireland were sporadic. The first raid (on Lambay Island) took place in 795 and, apart from a possible incursion to Roscommon (in 807), the raids were carried out from the sea by small forces of highly mobile fighters who were only occasionally defeated by the native inhabitants. The burning of monasteries had long been a feature of Irish life and the shocked tones of the Irish writers are only more noticeable in the Viking Age because such raids were carried out by foreigners. As elsewhere in the British Isles there is no archaeological trace of such attacks, either Scandinavian or Irish.

By the middle of the ninth century, however, the first attempts at settlement were being made by the Scandinavians in Ireland. These settlements were near the coast, and were often merely defended fortresses—initially centres for raids on Irish and Scottish objectives. Dublin was the most important of these, but groups of Scandinavians are recorded at Waterford, Cork, Wexford, Limerick and St Mullins: all places later consolidated as 'towns' by the

---

[46] Wilson, *Viking Age in the Isle of Man*, pp. 12ff.

[47] *Cf.*, for example, E. R. Norman and J. K. St Joseph, *The early development of Irish society* (Cambridge, 1969), pp. 78 ff.

Scandinavians. The earliest remains of the Scandinavians in Ireland are the graves, but apart from the Dublin cemeteries, only some ten or eleven graves are known from Ireland and practically all these are on the coast (fig. 1).[48] The Dublin cemeteries (particularly Islandbridge, Kilmainham) are rich and contain more men's than women's graves. They probably cannot be said to represent raiders, rather the first settlers in the towns. The graves largely date from the ninth century and James Graham-Campbell has suggested that Islandbridge was the cemetery of the first Scandinavian settlers of Dublin.[49] Dublin was apparently deserted for twelve years after the defeat of the Scandinavians in 902 and the cemetery could well be dated before then.

It is clear from the grave finds and from the pattern of later settlement that the Scandinavians never attempted to settle much of Ireland. Archaeology only emphasizes what is well known to historians, that the immediate hinterland of the coastal ports was all that was ever controlled by the Scandinavians. The most widespread archaeological remains of the Vikings are their hoards—there are 73 of them—but even these indicate no significant inland concentration.[50] The hoards do, however, demonstrate the tenth and eleventh century wealth of Ireland: the hoard from Hare Island alone consisted of ten arm-rings, which together weighed some five kilos of gold; this is the richest surviving gold hoard from any Viking Age context in Europe.[51]

Dublin is the only major site of which there is archaeological evidence. Excavations during the last ten years have revealed much of the medieval life of this great city.[52] There is a great deal of evidence of Scandinavian activity in the town, although there is as yet little evidence of the initial settlement of the ninth century. There is, however, no reason to suggest that the site of the town was shifted in the early tenth century. The wealth of Dublin and its function as an international market is well demonstrated amongst the rich finds of the late tenth–twelfth centuries. Its enormous economic growth in the late tenth century and beyond is symbolized by the first minting of coins in Ireland in 997,[53] an indication of the growth

[48] J. A. Graham-Campbell, 'The Viking Age silver hoards of Ireland', *The Eighth Viking Congress*, ed. D. Greene (Dublin, 1976), forthcoming.

[49] *Ibid.*   [50] *Ibid.*

[51] J. A. Graham-Campbell, 'A Viking-Age gold hoard from Ireland', *The Antiquaries Journal*, liv (1974), pp. 269–72.

[52] B. Ó. Ríordáin, 'Excavations at High Street and Winetavern Street, Dublin', *Medieval Archaeology*, xv (1971), pp. 73–85.

[53] R. H. M. Dolley, 'The Forms of the Proper Names Appearing on the Earliest Coins Struck in Ireland', *Otium et Negotium*, ed. F. Sandgren (Stockholm, 1973), p. 49.

of trade with countries with a monetary economy. These first coins were modelled on those produced in south-western English mints, some being more or less faithful copies of pennies of Æthelred II.

A remarkable element in the archaeological material of Dublin is the large number of bone trial-pieces used by craftsmen to sketch patterns later produced in metal. Many of the motifs which appear on these objects are in the Scandinavian taste,[54] and some of them are found on the finest ecclesiastical metalwork of the eleventh and twelfth century, on objects produced for the Irish themselves— the shrine of the Cathach of St Columba, for example.[55] Many of these ecclesiastical objects may well have been produced in Dublin itself; but in the twelfth century Scandinavian artistic taste reached further afield. Such art is found in sculpture in Cashel, on the so called 'Cormac's sarcophagus',[56] and on stone crosses as far away as County Clare.[57] It is clear from this material, as it is clear from the documentary sources, that the Scandinavians played an impor- tant—but not dominant—role in the life of Ireland. Only in their mercantile activity did they achieve any real dominance.

The Irish, though competent seamen, were not particularly interested in international trade. Giraldus Cambrensis' words con- cerning the Scandinavians in Ireland, although written many years after the event, contain a kernel of truth:

> For since by fault of their native indolence the Irish nation . . . would not traverse the seas, or apply themselves to any extent to merchandise, it seemed advisable . . . that some nation should be admitted in some districts of the realm, in order that by their efforts other countries' wares, which this land lacked, might be brought hither.[58]

The Scandinavians brought the idea of organized international trade to Ireland. By their control of the Irish Sea they could control much of the rich Atlantic trade and make inroads into the trade of western Europe. Hence the foundation of trading stations in Ireland.

The economic function of the Scandinavians in the West

In its initial stages the Norse settlement of the northern and western Isles of Scotland was based on a need for land and for access to

---

[54] *E.g.* Ó. Ríordáin, *op. cit.*, fig. 21a and pl. viii A and B.
[55] D. M. Wilson and O. Klindt-Jensen, *Viking Art* (London, 1966), pl. lxvi b.
[56] *Ibid.*, pl. lxxiv b.
[57] *E.g.* F. Henry, *Irish Art in the Romanesque Period 1020–1170 A.D.* (London, 1970), pl. 56 right.
[58] *Topographia Hibernica*, III, 43.

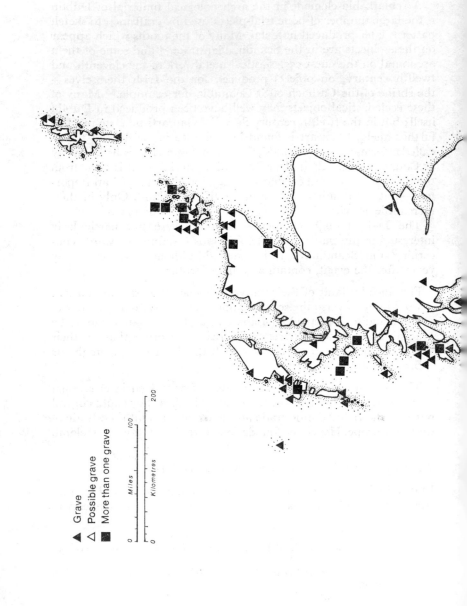

Grave ▲

Possible grave △

More than one grave ■

Miles

0   100   200

Kilometres

0

Fig. 1. The distribution of Scandinavian graves of the Viking Age in the British Isles.

plunder. The first settlements in Ireland demonstrate a similar process; Dublin, for example, was used as a base for expeditions to Scotland and north-west England (even to Iceland) which led to settlement there. In York, by the end of the ninth century, the Danes had set up a trading station which attracted merchants from all quarters until the middle of the tenth century when Eric Blood-axe was finally expelled from his kingdom. The mercantile relationship between Dublin and York until then is illustrated by the distribution of coin hoards in the Irish Sea region in the period, when the Wirral and the Ribble probably functioned as points of entry from the Irish Sea to the rich trading station of York.[59] These routes apparently were little used after 950 and, as York declined in economic power, the Norse re-established themselves in Ireland and the power of Dublin grew. The mystic quality of the battle of Clontarf did not effect the growth of the economic power of the Scandinavians. The Scandinavians remained in Ireland as traders and grew in economic power through their control of the Atlantic trade.

The rise of mercantile Dublin is symbolized by the first striking of Irish coins in 997. In the course of the eleventh century Dublin became pre-eminent as a port. Its merchants opened up a rich trade with England through the Bristol Channel, the trade route being indicated by the distribution of Scandinavian place-name elements (most of them sea-markers) on the south coast of Wales.[60] Further indication of this contact lies in the fact that the first Dublin coins are modelled on coins minted in the west of England. From Dublin merchants also traded to the west of France to Britanny and Bordeaux: hence Scandinavian place-name elements in the English Channel.

To Dublin from the North Atlantic came precious materials, ivory, furs, amber, resins and so on—substances much sought after in the south. From Dublin there were traded to the north, to Iceland and Norway, wines, silver, wool and other goods readily obtainable in the markets of England and the Continent. Dublin was also ideally situated in relation to any trade in slaves in these regions.

The geographical situation of other Scandinavian colonies in the Irish Sea region and in Scotland and the islands now paid off. The settlers on the route northwards were now in a splendid position to control the trade. They could victual the ships, exact tolls from them, or indulge in outright piracy against them. At this period the Isles and Orkney and Shetland arguably became richer

[59] Wilson, *loc. cit.* in note 11.
[60] M. Richards, 'Norse place-names in Wales', *Proceedings of the International Congress of Celtic Studies* (Dublin, 1962), 51–60.

than they were ever to become again. A combination of good land and external revenue from the trade routes brought wealth which is reflected in the splendour of the latest buildings at Birsay and the beginnings of the rise of Kirkwall. In a strange way Scotland was not, as Alan Small once had it,[61] remote from the core of the Viking world, it was central to it. As the lands around the mouths of the great Russian rivers became rich as a result of the Scandinavian trade from the Swedish controlled merchant centres of Novgorod and Kiev, so the Norse settlers in the west and north grew in wealth as a result of the presence of Dublin, which (until the Norman conquest of 1169) was probably the richest port in the west of Britain and one of the richest in western Europe. For this reason the Orkney earldom and the kingdom of Man and the Isles would have been organized to control the route northwards:

'Go south to Dublin', said Brynjólfr in *Egils Saga* 'for that is the most popular route'.

Influences northwards

The influence of Britain on Scandinavia was immeasurable. Britain —together with Germany—provided Scandinavia with Christianity and respectable (and literate) European statehood. With the Church came the culture of the western European nations in one of its most classicizing phases. The powerful, eclectic and rather mysterious culture of the north was swamped by the influence of the vigorous Church of the tenth and eleventh centuries. Britain and Germany may also have encouraged by pressure and example the growth of centralized power in Scandinavian, one expression of which may be seen in Danish fortifications like Trelleborg, thrown up in the late tenth century by a powerful national ruler.

Interestingly, however, it was not until the twelfth century that the formalized and powerful art of the western European Church really took hold in Scandinavia. In the eleventh century the self-sufficient successors of the Vikings were producing art as fine as any in Europe, but the wooden carvings of the early Norwegian stave-churches in no way reflect the Romanesque art of western Europe.

Even at the beginning of the Viking Age, Britain contributed to Scandinavian material culture. From England the Danes, for example, learnt the techniques of the stone sculptor—hitherto unknown to them. From Scotland they learnt other crafts. The incomers adapted certain objects of daily use from the Picts and Scots.

[61] A. Small, 'The Viking Highlands—a geographical view', *The Dark Ages in the Highlands* (Inverness, 1971), p. 69.

The bone pins for example, found on a number of Scandinavian sites in Scotland[62] were almost certainly made in the local taste by Picts in some sort of subservient position to their Scandinavian masters. The same continuity is seen on other settlement sites, Jarlshof and the Udal for example. Ring-headed pins of bronze show a similar continuity.[63] The indigenous population of a conquered region could no longer afford grand works of jewellery and had to make do with the poorer materials. But the incomers also adopted some of their fashions.

There is nothing to be wondered at here. The incoming people being conquerors, would naturally employ the indigenous craftsmen—even if they had first enslaved them. The ring-headed pins and penannular brooches made in Scandinavia in the Viking Age[64] show that these enslaved craftsmen had influence outside the boundaries of their own country. Perhaps there were other elements of technology which came to Scandinavia from Scotland in the Viking Age. The incomers put the local populace to work, ploughing the fields, minding the cattle, weaving cloth and building houses. Perhaps, and only perhaps, in this latter role—as house-builders—we may see certain non-Scandinavian traits adapted to the north Atlantic Viking Age house. That the Scandinavians did indeed use local craftsmen is demonstrated elsewhere. In Russia, for example, there is not a single house built in an undoubted Scandinavian manner in any of the areas controlled at any time by the Scandinavians—houses found in places controlled by the Scandinavians were always built in the Slav fashion. The same is true, as far as we can tell, of the Scandinavian areas of England, the few houses of Viking Age date that have been found are indistinguishable from contemporary English buildings. This is because the houses were built by a subject population for their new masters. It is not surprising, therefore, to see on sites which have continuity from the pre-Viking Age to the Viking Age a certain similarity of detail. The Scandinavians probably introduced the strictly rectangular house to north and western Scotland, but I think it possible that the idea of the lateral stone-built benches was taken from Scotland into the rest of the Atlantic area, for it is clear that such benches occur in pre-Viking Age Scotland and that they do not appear in Scandinavia until the Viking Age, even the late Viking Age.[65]

There is little evidence of direct Scandinavian contact with the British Isles before the Viking Age. There must have been a considerable cultural shock when Christian British and pagan Scan-

---

[62] Ritchie, *op. cit.*, p. 29.   [63] Hamilton, *op. cit.*, p. 29.
[64] J. Petersen, *Vikingetidens Smykker* (Stavanger, 1928), pp. 172 ff.
[65] *E.g.* Ritchie, *op. cit.*, fig. 1.

dinavians met. The efficient ships and warlike qualities of the Scandinavians must have appeared surprising to the rural, possibly rather self-satisfied, people of the British Isles. The Scandinavian effect on the country was gradual, but ultimately devastating. The Scandinavians in the west and north of the British Isles appear to have remained in pagandom for a number of generations—probably until Norway itself turned to Christianity. Western and northern Scotland and the Irish Sea region at the height of the Viking Age were indeed just as Scandinavian as Scandinavia.[66]

University College London.

[66] My thanks are due to much help during the writing of this paper particularly from James Graham-Campbell, but also from Michael Dolley, Raymond Page, Robert Stevenson and many other colleagues who have discussed aspects of their own research with me.

FROM HUMANISM TO THE SCIENCE OF MAN: COLONIALISM IN AFRICA AND THE UNDERSTANDING OF ALIEN SOCIETIES

By Professor T. O. Ranger, M.A., D.Phil., F.R.Hist.S.

READ AT THE SOCIETY'S CONFERENCE
19 SEPTEMBER 1975

Introduction

IN his 'English Contributions to Renaissance Colonisation' Professor Quinn treats one only of the interactions between humanism and overseas expansion. He does not here discuss, as he has done elsewhere, the stimulus to speculation about human history and society which was given by the discovery of new worlds of custom. He concentrates rather upon the ways in which those who advocated, planted and managed colonies were inspired by or appealed to humanist learning, and in particular the example of Rome. In much the same way I am not centrally concerned in this paper to discuss the stimulus given to academic enquiry by the intensified encounter of Europe with the rest of the world during the last hundred years. My main concern is with the ways in which those who advocated, pacified and administered colonies were inspired by or appealed to the new sciences of man.

Of course, many of those who colonized Africa in the nineteenth century were themselves the product of a classical education. They continued to appeal back to the example of Rome, though this time to Imperial Rome rather than to Rome as the progenitor of colonies. His biographers tell us that the favourite saying of Cecil John Rhodes —who carried his copy of Marcus Aurelius about with him and who was flattered to be told that he resembled Imperial Roman busts— was 'remember always that you are a Roman'.[1] Rhodes' ally, Lord Grey, when Administrator in Rhodesia, deplored his predecessor's employment of Matabele policemen with the comment that 'the right principle is that followed by Caesar when he kept England quiet with a legion raised from the Danube and the Danube quiet with a British legion'.[2] And Lord Lugard maintained that Britain stood in a kind of apostolic succession of empire—'as Roman

[1] J. G. Lockhart and C. M. Woodhouse, *Rhodes*, (London, 1963), p. 31.
[2] Cited in T. O. Ranger, *Revolt in Southern Rhodesia, 1896–7* (London, 1967), p. 119.

imperialism . . . led the wild barbarians of these islands along the path of progress, so in Africa today we are re-paying the debt, and bringing to the dark places of the earth . . . the torch of culture and progress'.[3]

But as the main intellectual problem of colonialism changed, the Roman example proved inadequate. Most administrators in late nineteenth century tropical Africa were not primarily concerned with 'colonies' in Professor Quinn's sense of communities of Europeans living together in an overseas 'plantation'. The chief problem of the new colonialism was to understand the indigenous colonized. And here, it was widely felt, the classical precedents were of little help. The Romans might have civilized Britain but they had left all too few accounts of how they had done so, or of the state in which Britons had been at the beginning of the process. It was with this argument that Lord Bryce persuaded the great missionary scholar, Henri Junod, to turn from his study of the fauna and flora of southern Mozambique and to concentrate upon African man. Lord Bryce, writes Junod, 'was trying to stimulate men on the spot to undertake a scientific study of [African] primitive life'. 'How thankful we should be,' he said to Junod, 'we men of the XIXth century, if a Roman had taken the trouble fully to investigate the habits of our Celtic forefathers! This work has not been done, and we shall always remain ignorant of things which would have interested us so much;' 'Since then', remarked Junod of his studies, 'ethnography has more or less supplanted entomology'.[4]

This transition from resort to classical precedent towards the deployment of the new sciences of man was more than a mere shift in intellectual fashion. Some recent writers, indeed, have seen it as marking the very essence of modern colonialism. 'History has known many kinds of colonialism', writes Gerard Leclerc, 'and the special character of modern colonialism does not reside in the fact of a society which thinks itself superior but in the fact of a society which bases that superiority on science, and especially on social science. . . . There has been colonization in all eras but only in our own time have we studied scientifically the people we have colonized—and colonized scientifically. The brief remarks of Caesar on the Gauls or Tacitus on the Germans appear very inadequate. What do they

[3] F. D. Lugard, *The Dual Mandate in British Tropical Africa* (Edinburgh, 1926), p. 618. Lugard is cited by Ali Mazrui in a discussion of the white colonial claim to be the inheritors of the civilization of Greece and Rome and of the African nationalist challenge to that claim. Ali A. Mazrui, *World Culture and the Black Experience* (Seattle, 1974), pp. 42–43. See also Mazrui, 'Ancient Greece in African Political Thought', Inaugural Lecture, Makerere University, Kampala, August, 1966.
[4] H. Junod, *The Life of a South African Tribe* (Neuchatel, 1912), p. 1.

amount to when compared to the new social sciences, to archaeology, ethnography, anthropology?'[5]

Leclerc remarks that the epics of colonialism were more a matter of feats of mind that of feats of arms. This is a novel perspective for historians, who have spent a great deal of time chronicling the conquest and 'pacification' of Africa, but very little time describing the colonial deployment of the science of man. In the first part of this paper I want to see how far it is possible to argue Leclerc's case for Africa particularly and in more concrete terms; to see how the science of man was deployed at successive levels of colonial understanding and action; and to see how far we can argue that its deployment generated the power of colonialism. In the second part of the paper I wish to ask what the significance of all this is to historians. In the first part, as I compile and accumulate arguments for Leclerc's thesis and catalogue the layers of colonial understanding, I shall sometimes cite authorities with whose emphases I shall later disagree. In both parts I shall cite many opinions about anthropology and anthropologists, and often very adverse opinions. But it is no part of my intention either to glorify the power or traduce the motives of anthropologists. I shall write about them because 'Africa remained virtually an academic monopoly of the anthropologists until the [nineteen] fifties'.[6] In Africa, anthropology has to stand for the academic science of man as a whole. In any case, if anthropologists can be validly criticized this does nothing to redeem historians who during this period made no attempt to understand Africa at all.[7]

I

Knowing One's Natives and half-knowing the Science of Man

The first level of colonial understanding of Africans was, of course that of the old hand, the man on the spot. The Nigerian novelist, Chinua Achebe, has characterized this very well. 'To the colonialist mind it was always of the utmost importance to be able to say: *I know my natives*, a claim which implied two things at once: (a) that the native was really quite simple and (b) that understanding him and

[5] G. Leclerc, *Anthropologie et colonialisme* (Paris, 1972), p. 36.

[6] Adam Kuper, *Anthropology and Anthropologists* (London, 1973), p. 135.

[7] As late as 1961 the distinguished anthropologist, Professor E. E. Evans Pritchard was able to remark that the British historians capable of writing a history of the people of Africa—or India or China—could be counted 'on the fingers of both hands if most of them had been amputated'. 'Anthropology and History', *Essays in Social Anthropology*, (London, 1962).

controlling him went hand in hand—understanding being a precondition for control and control constituting adequate proof of
understanding'.[8]

For much of the time and in many parts of Africa this rough and
ready pragmatism often did 'work'. It was based on a handful of
imperial slogans and a working knowledge of the surfaces of African
societies; it provided the ideology of what Tony Hopkins calls the
'art of light administration',[9] administration without too much
expense or too much overt violence. This sort of 'knowing the native'
worked when it did because 'the native' knew equally well what the
rules of the game were; knew equally well what 'a native' was supposed to be and think and do; the concept of 'native', in short, was
somewhere in the space between the European and the African
and manipulated by both.

This kind of 'understanding' struck academic observers as worlds
removed from any dependence on the science of man. It seemed to
them to represent the sort of imperial 'wisdom' that was as old as
Rome. In recent years, indeed, a number of anthropologists have
reacted to the allegation that there has been an intimate relationship between their subject and colonialism by documenting their
frequent clashes with the old colonial hands, the men who 'knew the
native'. 'The colonial officer in British Africa . . . believed that he
knew the relevant facts', writes Adam Kuper in his history of British
anthropology, 'and suspected the anthropologist's commitment to
his own goal of peace and quiet . . . many District Commissioners
believed that they "knew their natives", and that their years of experience made them far more expert than the anthropologists'.[10]
Evans Pritchard remarked that during the fifteen years in which
he worked on 'sociological problems' in the Sudan he 'was never
once asked' for 'advice on any questions at all'.[11] Lucy Mair has
given a graphic account of the suspicion with which she, as a field
anthropologist,was regarded by colonial officials. They told her that
she 'had got it all wrong. I was interpreting in terms of social structure when they preferred to interpret in terms of personalities'. They
feared she had come to dig out scandals; to stir up trouble; to
serve some Communist conspiracy. Reviewing all this she finds it
hard to regard herself or her discipline as 'the handmaid of
imperialism'.[12]

---

[8] Chinua Achebe, *Morning Yet on Creation Day* (London, 1975), p. 5.
[9] A. Hopkins, *An Economic History of West Africa* (London, 1973), p. 189.
[10] Adam Kuper, *Anthropology and Anthropologists*, pp. 139–40.
[11] E. E. Evans Pritchard, 'Applied Anthropology', *Africa*, 1946, p. 97.
[12] Lucy Mair, 'Anthropology and Colonial Policy', *African Affairs*, vol. 74, no.
295, April 1975.

And yet for all this administrative suspicion of anthropologists there were two ways in which the men who 'knew their natives' *were* touched by the influence of the science of man. The French scholar, R. Jaulin, has emphasized that the interaction of colonialism and 'ethnography' was not so much a matter of the work of scholars as a matter of 'the politicization, vulgarization and diffusion' of their conclusions.[13] Many of the 'practical' common-sense attitudes of the administrators were a reflection of precisely this process of 'vulgarization' and 'diffusion' of the tenets of ethnography, though almost always of an ethnography of a much earlier vintage than the assumptions of the anthropologists with whom they quarrelled.

Brian Street in his recent *The Savage in Literature* has shown the interplay of 'popular literature' with 'contemporary science' and 'imperial politics' during the heyday of empire in Africa. The novels which shaped the ideas of thousands of Europeans about Africa and Africans, and which so often featured the Native Commissioner as their hero, made 'wide use of anthropological theory', 'the English popular writers . . . [giving] . . . imaginative life to these theories by presenting them through vivid characters and exciting adventures'.[14] Colonial administrators read this sort of literature and one or two of them wrote it; it helped to shape the self-image of the man on the spot and to confirm his categories of 'knowing his natives'.

Behind pragmatic common-sense lurked some of the wilder ideas of evolutionist and diffusionist ethnography. But there was in addition to this a frequent realization that the 'knowledge' possessed by the old hand was incomplete and provisional. Achebe remarks that he is 'not saying that the picture of Nigeria and Nigerians presented by [such] a conscientious European must be invalid. I think it could be terribly valid just as a picture of the visible tenth of an iceberg is valid'. He adds that many Europeans were 'conscious of this kind of validity' and of its limitations, aware of the submerged nine-tenths.[15] And this was true of many of the Europeans in Africa who found that their 'knowledge' worked for most practical purposes but who were very well aware of its superficiality. The Anglican missionaries in southern Tanganyika constantly wrote of the vast 'secret life' of the surrounding Africans into which they had never been able to penetrate; this did not prevent them from offering practical advice on what Africans thought and how their institutions worked, and from being 'expert' consultants for the

[13] R. Jaulin, *La Paix Blanche* (Paris, 1972), p. 36.
[14] Brian V. Street, *The Savage in Literature* (London, 1975), pp. 2, 47, 80.
[15] Achebe, *Morning Yet on Creation Day*, p. 48.

establishment of Indirect Rule, but it led some of them into a dialogue with the anthropologists in an effort to understand more.[16]

Even those who were perfectly satisfied with the way in which they knew the natives so long as it worked, so long as 'control constituted adequate proof of understanding', were shaken out of this complacency when it no longer suited Africans to play the native and when administration was shaken by revolt. 'In the heyday of colonialism', writes Achebe, 'any serious incident of native unrest, carrying as it did disquieting intimations of slipping control was an occasion not only for pacification by soldiers but also [afterwards] for a royal commission of inquiry', for an attempt to restore self confidence in knowledge by a further exploration of 'native psychology and institutions'.[17]

Rebellion was the surest persuader of practical men to open their minds to the newer discoveries of the science of man. The 1896 risings in Rhodesia called forth from the administrators frank confessions of incapacity. 'This outbreak was got up as a matter of fact so quickly and in opposition to all our native lore', admitted the Acting Chief Native Commissioner, 'that we feel almost unable to venture any further opinion on natives at all, except this—that they are not for one moment to be trusted.' The Resident Magistrate articulated the outrage of a man who had suddenly found out that in acting as 'natives' the Matabele and the Shona had been playing out a role. The uprising, he wrote, was 'the greatest surprise to those who from long residence in the country thought they understood the character of these savages . . . and to none more than the Native Commissioners themselves. . . . With true kaffir deceit they have beguiled us into the idea that they were content with our administration of the country and wanted nothing more than to work for us and trade with us and become civilized'.[18]

In this situation the native commissioners professed their ignorance; they knew too little of history, too little of the science of man. 'In those days', wrote one of them, 'Sir J. Frazer's *Golden Bough* was unknown to me and there was scant means of obtaining books on anthropology'.[19]

---

[16] This expression or its equivalent is constantly repeated in the correspondence of the missionaries of the University Mission to Central Africa in south-eastern Tanganyika; the correspondence is in the archives of the USPG in Tufton Street, Westminster.

[17] Achebe, *Morning Yet on Creation Day*, p. 5.

[18] Cited in Ranger, *Revolt in Southern Rhodesia*, p. 1.

[19] Cited in Ranger, *Revolt*, p. 79.

The Science of Man as a Charter for Colonial Rule

The aftermath of a rebellion, then, is a suitable context in which to introduce a representative figure of a second sort of claim to understanding. This time it is the Maji Maji rising against the Germans in southern Tanganyika in 1905. The rising was suppressed with terrible suffering, but its outbreak had provoked similar confessions of administrative failure to understand, predict or control. On this scene of devastation there appeared in 1906 the quintessential self-confident professor of the science of man—the ethnographer Karl Weule.

Weule was in Tanganyika as a result of 'a vigorous agitation for the application of [German government funds] on a large scale to the systematic investigation of our dependencies. From specialists in all branches of knowledge—geography and geology, anthropology and ethnography, zoology and botany, linguistics, comparative law, and the new science of comparative music—arose the same cry'. The Colonial Congress of 1905 had marked out the 'principal fields of research in each subject'; Weule's expedition was one of those designed 'to realize a long cherished dream of German science'.[20] He arrived in southern Tanganyika full of confidence in the scientific foundations of German enterprise. German 'intellectual pre-eminence', he wrote, 'is everywhere acknowledged'. Moreover, his own science had reached the point where it could make sense of the apparently disparate collection of artefacts and customs which he was assembling in southern Tanganyika. 'At a time when hundreds of students are continually busy investigating and describing the remotest and most forlorn of primitive tribes at present accessible . . . it is strange to think of the earlier and much less fortunate period which had to be content with mere arm-chair theories'.[21]

Weule was enthusiastically ready to put the heritage of Greece and Rome in its proper ethnographic perspective. On the way out to East Africa he travelled through Italy by train and was able from its windows to observe 'the stratification of successive races' and the dominance of the Apennines. 'The Romans were originally started on their career of conquest', he concluded, 'by want of space in their own country'. Returning from East Africa he travelled by sea. 'Tomorrow . . . we shall pass the coast of Greece. I must confess that I am looking forward to a sight of this country, though I do not regard its classic age with the same unbounded and uncritical

---

[20] Karl Weule, *Native Life in East Africa*, translated by Alice Werner (London, 1909), pp. 10–11.
[21] Weule, *Native Life*, pp. 125, 417.

enthusiasm of many of our countrymen, to whom the ancient Greek is the embodiment of all historical and cultural values. One thing only even the blackest envy cannot deny to the Hellenes of old—a courage in colonial enterprise which we should do well to imitate both now and in the future'.[22]

Weule took it for granted that his professorial status would win him instant respect from German administrators and Africans alike. He was given full official support, an escort of *askaris*, a junior administrator as his travelling companion. He moved with his armed porters among those who had fought the Germans and those who had remained loyal to them; he sent his men into the huts of the people to bring out ethnographic specimens; he summoned chiefs to come and give him information; he sent soldiers to bring him from the country of the defeated and ravaged Mwera some of the most ancient informants on their customs, who appeared before him famished and terrified; he photographed everything and recorded the sound of everything, on one occasion placing the head of a Yao minstrel in a vice so that the motions of the old man should not disturb the recording equipment.[23]

Here with a vengeance was the European colonizer as he is seen in the poetry of the Burundi martyr priest, Michael Kayoya:

> 'At home in Europe
> The white man can be seen as a man.
> As soon as he leaves home he is frightful.
> He analyses, spies, classifies, defines, appropriates,
> Conquers and dominates.
> What? Everything:
> Grass which dies and grows again
> Bone:
> Dead Wood, green Wood
> Song Bird
> Flower of the Fields
> Dainty Child
> Woman
> Good Action, short-coming
> Bodies, Hearts, Spirit, Man'.[24]

And so Weule cheerfully set out in a few short weeks to analyse, classify, study the flora and fauna and crafts and residences and religion and politics of the Africans of south-eastern Tanganyika—activities which in his mind too were very closely connected with conquest and domination. 'The native is not without an important

[22] Weule, *Native Life*, pp. 5, 422.   [23] Weule, *Native Life, passim.*
[24] Michael Kayoya, *My Father's footprints* (Nairobi, 1973), pp. 8–9.

bearing on the future of our East African colony. As an ethnographer I am in a better position to form an opinion about him.' He concluded that the African agriculture of south east Tanganyika was the product of 'an evolution extending over a period of incalculable length' and that it 'must certainly have great potentialities for good or all the teachings of racial psychology and history are falsified'. 'Let us be wise enough', he urged, 'to get the full advantages of it ourselves.' The crucial question was 'how shall we, on this basis, make our black fellow-subjects useful to ourselves?' Weule's own answer was that African agriculture should be encouraged and that the Germans should 'go further and, by artificial selection, deliberately raise their co-efficient of multiplication'.[25]

I am very ready to accept the objection that it is grossly unfair to professors and to social scientists to write as though this insensitive grotesque was typical. Yet caricature—and self-caricature—often illuminates. Weule's book does present us with a bundle of attitudes which were of crucial importance. He makes essentially three claims. Ethnography can through its diffusion inform and educate the public about 'our really splendid possessions'; ethnography as a triumph of the mind can liberate us from the classical heritage and establish the right of our own culture to dominate; ethnography can show us how best to 'make our black fellow-subjects useful to ourselves'. I have already discussed the first of these points—the diffusion of ethnographic ideas to a wide public. I wish now to discuss the remaining two and in this section especially the first—the idea of the science of man as a charter for domination.

This proved to be an enormously influential idea and not only for Europeans. Just as Africans enabled the 'knowledge' of the pragmatic man on the spot to work because for much of the time they accepted the role of native, so too this idea of scientific knowledge as giving title to power obtained much of its continued force from African belief in it. The difference was that from the beginning Africans manipulated the role of native, while for a long time they submitted to the claims of scientific knowledge.

In the long run, however, the shift from one strategy of 'understanding' to another by the Europeans led to a shift from one strategy of response to another by the Africans. Some Africans moved out of the game of knowing the native and prepared themselves instead to capture the magic knowledge which underlay colonialism.

Here the most striking symbolic figure is Jomo Kenyatta. In some ways Kenyatta's career makes most sense if we see him in the role of

[25] Karl Weule, *Native Life in East Africa*, pp. 418, 420, 421.

Prometheus—the hero who returns with the fire stolen from the gods. In Bildad Kaggia's recent autobiography, Kenyatta is described on his return to Kenya, carrying the sparks of the divine fire. Kaggia shows Kenyatta addressing a rural audience in 1951 in a speech which endorsed, though from a very different perspective, the assumptions of Karl Weule. 'Education was the most important thing in modern life, he said, and he wanted all children to go to school. The *mzungu* [white man] brought education to Kenya only to give Africans enough education to make them good servants . . . [but] . . . education was the magic through which the *mzungu* managed to rule Africans in Kenya. As soon as the Africans learned this magic, they would be able to rule themselves'.[26]

For their part the whites also believed that Kenyatta in his visit to Europe had somehow managed to steal some of the divine fire, and that this enabled him to manipulate and control men. The fact that he had been an anthropologist and a student of Malinowski was central to their apprehension. 'He has been immersed in politics', warned the missionary Philip; 'has visited Moscow and lived in London for long . . . 'and now he is an anthropologist and writes a book'.[27] Kenyatta's own view was that anthropology helped 'to learn their clever way of talking' and so to acquire 'wisdom (to) safeguard the country'.[28] And the Corfield report on the organization of Mau Mau found that Kenyatta had combined his anthropological understanding of the mentalities of the Kikuyu with 'the technique of revolution undoubtedly learnt while he was in Russia', to summon up almost single-handed this great challenge to white rule.[29]

It hardly seemed to matter to either African intellectuals or the colonial administration that the Mau Mau upheaval was founded in reality upon the agonizing experience of the social and economic transformations of colonialism by thousands of unlearned men, of changes which Kenyatta's anthropological training hardly equipped him to comprehend, let alone to control. After Kenyatta's arrest, young Kenyans went on dreaming about playing Prometheus.[30] As

[26] Bildad Kaggia, *Roots of Freedom*, (Nairobi, 1975), p. 88.

[27] Philip's letter is cited in C. Rosberg and J. Nottingham, *The Myth of Mau Mau*, (London, 1966), p. 134.

[28] Jomo Kenyatta, *My People of Kikuyu* (London, 1942). Jeremy Murray Brown in his biography of Kenyatta remarks that 'in anthropology Kenyatta had found the weapon he needed to answer the philosophy of colonialism'. J. Murray Brown, *Kenyatta* (London, 1972), p. 219.

[29] F. D. Corfield, *Historical Survey of the Origins and Growth of Mau Mau*, Cmd. 1030, 1960, p. 52.

[30] The clearest expression of this is R. Mugo Gatheru, *Child of Two Worlds*, *A Kikuyu's Story*, (London, 1964), pp. 101–03.

for the Europeans they set about once again the business of repairing the rents in the cloak of knowledge. This time African rebellion did not demonstrate inadequate scientific understanding as in 1896; nor did it clear the way for the gathering of further data as in 1905. Mau Mau was seen as the result of a breakdown in the white monopoly of the applied science of man. The European answer was increasingly sophisticated. The Mau Mau emergency was a great time for applied social science; academic experts were not then rejected by practical men. The experts studied the psychology of Mau Mau and devised counter-oathing ceremonies; they offered anthropological analyses of the revolt; they devised and supervised land settlement programmes. And however beside the point of socio-economic grievance was the policy of 'rehabilitation' it certainly succeeded in restoring the prestige of white knowledge.

Thus it came about that even with the acquisition of political independence African recognition of the power of white knowledge continued. Odinga wrote his *Not Yet Uhuru* to demonstrate that formal political independence had done little to change economic realities. Others protested that it had done little to change intellectual realities either.[31]

Writing last year in *Presence Africaine* Mazi Okoro Ojiaku generalized this point from Kenya to the whole of black Africa. 'Knowledge is power and he who has knowledge has power', says Ojiaku. 'Euro-America has such knowledge and such power. To have knowledge is to be in command of both facts and information not only of oneself but also of others and to interpret the facts and information from one's own perspective. Knowledge brings to its possessor two additional benefits: it endows him with greater awareness of himself, just as it enables him to know others on his, rather than their, terms. . . . Consequently he is his own master as well as that of others'.

Since the nineteenth century, writes Ojiaku, 'Africa's knowledge has increasingly ceased to be rooted in Africa's soil . . . [and has] . . . become increasingly foreign because western in origin'. The white man first began to 'discover', enumerate and classify the lakes and rivers and mountains. Then as African humanity proved recalcitrant the European turned to men themselves. After the second world

---

[31] Oginga Odinga, *Not Yet Uhuru* (London, 1967). Odinga has another version of the roots of the Promethean myth in Kenya. He writes of the words of the prophetic elders about the whites: 'We should never, never try to fight them because their weapons were better than ours . . . we should give whatever they requested. But we should study their lives and their minds to know exactly what they wanted. We should never fight them. But we knew that when we had studied them our children would probably be able to get rid of them'. p. 1.

war and with the challenge of nationalism, research on African humanity grew apace, and with the achievement of formal independence by African states there began a veritable research scramble with the launching of academic African Studies. Euro-America 'shifted interest from the geography of mountains, rivers and lakes to the geography of the African man; the contours and contents of his mind, his cosmology, his eschatalogy, his institutions and values, his history, politics, philosophy and ideology'. This 'new form of exploration' was designed to maintain a 'scientific colonialism in which A knows B more than B either knows himself or A, and in which A tells B what he is or ought to be'.[32]

The Science of Man as an instrument for social transformation

Ojiaku is mainly concerned with knowledge as a means of mastery. European knowledge is power—even if, as Ojiaku complains, its 'discoveries' are often things which Africans have 'always known', or else frequently bear little relation to African self-knowledge on its own terms. But there lurks in his essay the additional idea that perhaps European knowledge is so powerful and penetrating that it can be used for social engineering, to transform the people to whom it is applied, And this was certainly Weule's additional assumption. The ethnographer could advise on how best to 'make our black fellow-subjects useful' and he could advise on how best to manipulate population increase or agricultural techniques. The science of man gave not only title to power but also the means of social and economic transformation.

Colonial rule was by no means always a matter of the 'art of light administration'; by no means always a matter of preserving the prestigious monopoly over the magic of knowledge. Some historical accounts of the colonial period in West Africa, it is true, have seen things very much in these terms.[33] But increasingly historians of East, Central and Southern Africa are emphasizing the immensity of the social changes which took place within the framework of colonialism. Thus Clayton and Savage describe the Kenya in which Jomo Kenyatta's Promethean drama was played out as having 'undergone modernization of an almost Stalinist severity'.[34] Other historians have described the far-reaching manipulations which produced a flow of labour, which transformed these labourers into

[32] Mazi Okoro Ojiaku, 'Traditional African Social Thought and Western Scholarship', *Presence Africaine*, 90, 2, 1974, pp. 204–05.

[33] For example, M. Crowder, *West Africa Under Colonial Rule* (London, 1968).

[34] D. Savage and A. Clayton, *Government and Labour in Kenya, 1895–1963*, (London, 1974), p. 459.

workers, which dulled their initial resistance to the transformation and wheedled them into a sort of voluntarism which allowed the system to continue to work without too overt coercion.[35]

All this is very much the theme of the new historiography of under-development. Once upon a time anthropologists and historians vigorously defended the African farmer or worker against the charge of economic irrationality or fecklessness. Today the historians of under-development are seeking to show that the *colonial state* was not economically irrational or content to drift. It is argued that the colonial powers had clearly conceived and persistently pursued aims, the implementation of which led to the systematic under-development of colonial Africa.[36] With such an interpretation it is easy to reconcile the anthropologists' repeated protest that no-one ever asked *them* to engineer social change and easy to reconcile the rural administrator's concern for 'peace and quiet'. The role of the administrator in this historiography was mainly to preserve order and to maintain the appearances; to create the *impression* that in the rural areas things were as they had traditionally been; to foster a false consciousness among Africans which obscured the profundities of transformation. Administrators, it is argued, often did this the more effectively in that they shared in this false consciousness themselves. As for the anthropologists, they are seen not as the main agents of social change but rather as involuntary apologists for it. Bernard Magubane, in a scathing passage, writes that 'the colonial system as a productive system of exploitation had to have scribes and an ideological superstructure built to maintain and justify it. The theorists of migrant labour by accepting white assumptions about African labour did not develop a critical attitude and thus were unable to portray the African as a human type. . . . The alienated conditions of the African due to social degradation was accepted as "normal" to his inferior character. . . . One can detect in the studies of migrant labour a cynical mixture of contempt and tenderness towards the defeated foe. Kneeling awe-stricken before

[35] A striking example is: Charles van Onselin, 'The Randlords and Rotgut, 1886–1903', Institute of Commonwealth Studies seminar, London, May 1975. See also his 'Black Workers in Central African Industry: a critical essay on the historiography and sociology of Rhodesia', *Journal of Southern African Studies*, 1, ii, April 1975, pp. 228–246.

[36] For example: E. A. Brett, *Colonialism and Underdevelopment in East Africa, The Politics of Economic Change, 1919–1939*, (London, 1973); Richard Wolff, *Britain and Kenya, 1870–1930, The Economics of Colonialism*, (Nairobi, 1974), p. xiii. Wolff writes: 'Kenya's economic history as a British colony exhibits both the radical transformation of African society and the consistent application of British colonial development strategy. I will seek to demonstrate that such a strategy made economic sense, did operate and did cause the transformation of Kenya.'

the colonial system, they refused to make any moral judgements on the resulting waste of African labour'.[37]

So the anthropologist is seen as providing the 'ideological super-structure' rather than as acting to engineer change. Yet Magubane is clear that change was not haphazard and accidental; it was planned and brought about coherently, with an almost diabolical skill. The system needed labour but it did not need a self-conscious proletariat—so the first was achieved and the second avoided. Something of the same emphasis emerges from the work of Charles van Onselin on African labour in the mines of Rhodesia and South Africa, or of Anse Tambila on African labour on the sisal planta-tions of the Tanganyika coast. These studies see the lives of workers as programmed by a deliberate arrangement of living quarters and by the manipulation of sex, drink, religion and education.[38]

So in studies such as these there is little hit or miss about the creation of an African work force. We encounter here another 'diffusion' and 'vulgarization' of the science of man. The social engineers are men who work with very effective pragmatic assump-tions derived from the processes of industrialization and urbaniza-tion in other parts of the world—compound managers, township welfare officers, labour recruiters. They are the effective urban and industrial sociologists, while the colonial administrators keep things quiet and academics provide the 'ideological superstructure'.

As this argument is extended to the transformation—or attempted transformation—of the African rural areas in the years especially after the second world war more attention is given to official agen-cies. These attempts to extract more food or more cash crops out of the African areas, to change tenures, to create yeomen peasants, and so on were more directly a concern of the colonial state and less the concern of private enterprise. As a result there arose within colonial service the 'expert'—the agricultural officer, the soil scientist, the agronomist, and others—whose presence was often resented by the administrative officers themselves. The defeat of Mau Mau gave such men an unrivalled opportunity to effect social and economic change, but it was attempted throughout East and Central Africa and justified in terms of a science of rural develop-ment.

In this historiography one reaches an extreme of European

[37] Bernard Magubane, 'Some methodological and ideological problems in the study of social change in Africa as reflected in the studies of migrant labour', University Social Science Conference, Makerere, January 1969; see also his 'Crisis in African Sociology', East Africa Journal, December 1968, pp. 21–40.

[38] Anse Tambila, 'A History of the Tanga Sisal Labour Force, 1936–64', M.A. thesis, University of Dar es Salaam, 1974; Charles van Onselin, 'African mine-labour in Southern Rhodesia, 1900–1933', D.Phil thesis, Oxford, 1974.

dominance. Africans could play the game of 'knowing your native'; they could aspire to and sometimes succeed in snatching the Promethean fire. But in this shrewd process of social engineering Africans were *done to*. Their own attempts to innovate and adapt were patterned by the whites; their own initiatives carried them further into the trap. Here indeed 'A tells B what he is and what he ought to be'.

The Science of Man and the model of traditional African society

Meanwhile in conscious isolation from all this—however significant the unconscious interactions—academic anthropology strove to understand African societies on their own terms. Most anthropologists were very different from Karl Weule; few of them had the same sort of confidence in the power of the knowledge of Europe; few of them were conscious admirers of colonialism. Indeed, some recent commentators have stressed that many anthropologists were writing as critics of European industrial society. And yet even in their 'purest' studies—those loving reconstructions of African traditional societies in all their functioning coherence—there was a further dimension of A telling B what he is.

We have seen that Africans learnt to play the role of native; that they aspired to re-define themselves so as to add to old insights the magic knowledge of the west; that they were exposed to the transforming experiences of westernization and peasantization. But beyond that, even in their retreat back into a sense of what it had meant and could still mean to be African, what it could mean to exist outside the structures of colonialism, many Africans were profoundly influenced by white analysis.

It was not merely a matter of the intellectuals who put together the ideals of negritude from the ideas of anthropologists—and sometimes very odd ones, as Senghor drew on the racist theorizing of Frobenius.[39] In some places the anthropological constructs came to shape traditional senses of identity. Wyatt MacGaffey, writing of the Bakongo, tells us that 'published accounts of Kongo society have become a cultural influence in their own right'. He speaks of 'the ethnographic model of Kongo society which had modified the notion of themselves entertained by the Kongo elite. . . . The anthropologist working today in the Congo is likely to meet the ghosts of his forerunners. . . . The conclusions of previous generations of anthropologists have become part of the situation he seeks to understand. . . . There are times when it is almost his own image that the

[39] J. M .Ita, 'Frobenius, Senghor and the Image of Africa', in Robin Horton and Ruth Finnegan, eds., *Modes of Thought* (London, 1973), pp. 306–36.

anthropologist confronts as in a mirror'. In this way the French ethnographic model of the matriarchate 'has become an essential part of modern Kongo culture . . . an explanatory model that tends to orient the thought and action of Congolese as well as of Europeans'.[40]

It should be added that the rise of African historiography over the last twenty years has had the same sort of effect. A good deal of historical writing has taken the oral evidence offered by people who have a very specific and localized view of the past and processed it so as to produce wide patterns which are not recognizable as part of experience but which have been adopted as a new prestigious history.[41]

Out of all this, then, there emerges a complex picture of the involvement of Europeans and Africans in a variety of different layers of 'understanding'—a pragmatically effective administrative knowledge; an enormously prestigious justifying and validating knowledge; a transforming knowledge underlying social engineering; and an elegant intellectual discipline which recreates what it seeks to comprehend. It would seem that Leclerc is fully justified in quoting the claim of the colonial social scientist: 'We have studied African populations as no conqueror has ever studied or understood the conquered. We know their history, their customs, their needs, their weaknesses, even their prejudices. And on this knowledge we base our policy'.

II

African attempts to understand Europeans during colonialism

Despite all that has gone before I remain uneasy about the image of the multiple triumph of European knowledge. This triumph seems to me to possess an ambivalent character which has not yet been fully brought out. I wish to begin to re-assess the matter from what may initially seem an odd angle.

I want to emphasize that Africans were also engaged in the task of understanding Europeans, not merely at the level of constructing the artefact 'bwana' to go alongside the artefact 'native', and not merely on the level of acquiring the white man's wisdom and comprehending him on his own terms. Africans were also engaged in

[40] Wyatt MacGaffey, *Custom and Government in the Lower Congo* (Los Angeles, 1970), p. 259.
[41] T. O. Ranger, 'Towards a usable African past', in *African Studies since 1945: a tribute to Basil Davidson*, ed. Christopher Fyfe, forthcoming.

applying their own modes of comprehension in an attempt to
fathom the whites. In this enterprise, indeed, they had certain
advantages. It was often crucially important to them to comprehend the new ruler, and he was very much on display before them.
Thus the Congolese Mavumilusa Makanzu contrasts superficial
white knowledge of black men with profound African knowledge of
whites: 'The black continent has been studied in detail, but the
secret of the inner life of the African has not been pierced. . . . Books
have been edited, studies done on Africa and her natural beauties,
the richness of her subsoil, the life of the native, their music and
their dances . . . but the books, the novels and the photos portray
only a weak part of Africa's secrets. The whites can only know a few
things. . . . The whites observe the Africans during the day, but the
life of an African is a nocturnal life. . . . On the contrary, the black
has a thorough knowledge of the white man. He has time to employ
to observe him from morning until evening, in work and at rest.
Employed by the white, the African knows his habits, understands
his language and knows the awkward thoughts of the white man.
The white cannot hide himself from an African for he is obvious'.[42]

There is plenty of evidence of the shrewd persistence with which
Africans set about assessing the whites in the first days of contact
and plenty of evidence—in carvings and stories and the enactment
of white roles in folk drama or possession cults—of the capacity to
drive through to a caricatured truth. But it is far from my purpose
here to make a tit for tat Africanist point, even if on another
occasion it would be very worthwhile to pursue in more detail these
African enquiries and assessments. The point I want to make here is
in fact a very different one. African knowledge of whites was extensive even if it was often not a knowledge of a total European society
but of the bits and pieces fragmented from it into Africa. (Sometimes the bits and pieces were so fragmentary that it was difficult
for Africans to imagine whites as social beings at all: the Africans
of Chishawasha near Salisbury in Rhodesia concluded from their
observations of the conduct of the first whites in their area that
Europeans recognized no rules of social interaction or moral
obligation at all.)[43]

Yet in the context of this paper the main point in looking at
African attempts to understand whites on a 'deeper' level is precisely because in them we can see so clearly the intellectual or
conceptual *failure* of the attempt. Africans applied to the understanding and adaptation of white modes of behaviour and organiza-

[42] Mavumilusa Makanzu, 'The Twentieth Century Missionaries and the Mur-
murs of the Africans', *Apophoreta of African Church History*, 3, (Aberdeen, 1974).
[43] Lawrence Vambe, *An Ill Fated People* (London, 1972), pp. 93–95, 101.

tion a serious and protracted attention. Before missionary schools offered to them a rudimentary white-supplied tool kit for the job, they approached it in ways which drew on traditional modes of thought and of conceptual innovation. Whites were comprehended, for example, at the level of spirit possession, by means of cults which had introduced the idea of intrusion by alien spirits and which in their treatment of the sufferer acted out a drama designed to establish and to satisfy the essential nature of the alien and of his demands. Whites were comprehended at the level of the prophetic vision. Spokesmen of the divinities found new words and symbols to express *their* apprehension of the nature of the whites and advised their people on how best to respond to them.[44] Founders of new Christian independent churches drew for their prophetic vision of whites and for their symbolic innovations upon the texts of the translated Bible.[45] Whites were comprehended at the level of the collective work group or the voluntary association, and in early colonial East and Central Africa numbers of Africans attempted to live together on the basis of a hierarchy and discipline based on European military uniform and drill.[46]

The point about all these attempts is that they were deeply serious; that at many levels they *worked*; and that seen as attempts to produce a complete and convincing model of white society— seen that is by us who believe ourselves to possess a functioning model of that society—they were manifestly incomplete and faulty. One could take as an example some of the Zulu prophets described by Bengt Sundkler in his richly detailed new book. Some of these men siezed upon a cluster of texts relating in one case to blood and the colour red, in another case to stones as the bearers of messages from God to man; out of these texts they constructed a coherent reinterpretation of religious ideas; they innovated new symbols, sometimes directly clashing with and transcending their meaning in traditional thought; for their followers they successfully created

[44] Two among many studies of spirit possession cults are:
Okot p'Bitek, *Religion of the Central Luo*, chapter 6, (Nairobi, 1971); J. Beattie, 'Group Aspects of the Nyoro Spirit Medium Cult', *Rhodes Livingstone Journal*, vol. 30.
On prophetic images of whites see: Roy Willis, 'Oral tradition of a Fipa prophet', *Africa*, XL, 3, July 1970; Roy Willis, *Man and Beast* (London, 1974), pp. 110–112, 123; John Middleton, 'Prophets and Rainmakers', in T. Beidelman, *The Translation of Culture* (London, 1971); M. A. Mabona, 'The interaction and development of different religions in the Eastern Cape', School of Oriental and African Studies, 1974.
[45] Mabona, 'The interaction and development of different religions'; Wyatt MacGaffey and John Janzen, *An Anthology of Kongo Religion* (Kansas, 1974).
[46] T. O. Ranger, 'The Military Mode in Eastern Africa', U.C.L.A. colloquium paper, Spring 1972.

a complete universe of discourse. They were serious and successful users of new knowledge, even if the solutions in this case were so specialized and esoteric that they worked only for small handfuls of the chosen. They were serious and successful—yet a Biblical scholar would be fully justified in saying that the assemblage of a number of unrepresentative texts came nowhere near to conveying the full value of the biblical message or of representing it without profound distortion.[47]

The case of Sundkler's prophets can be extended to be used as a parable for very many of these African attempts. The concentration on the European military mode did not carry people to the heart of what European twentieth century society was about (though it perhaps came closer to the heart of what early colonialism was about), but it *did* provide a useful aid to re-defining conduct in the face of the new demands. The largely symbolic significance ascribed to literacy fell some way short of comprehending how Europeans exploited it, but it *did* allow for a widening and deepening of symbolic thought and its power to innovate.[48] The employment in competitive dance associations of the badges of European rank and power did not bring their members any closer to acquiring that power—nor was it in fact expected to—but it *did* provide a useful means of reasserting desire and capacity to change.[49]

All this seems to me to provide a useful analogy for *European* understanding of *Africans*. It was serious, it worked, but seen from the perspective of those *within* African society it was almost always, and in all its forms, badly skewed, out of perspective, and often plain mistaken. Like African attempts to comprehend European society, European knowledge about Africa worked *despite* its failure to arrive at really balanced, penetrating and accurate analyses of African society.

The Working Misunderstandings of the Science of Man

Susan Broadhead has remarked that the interaction of Europeans and Africans in the kingdom of the Kongo during the sixteenth and seventeenth centuries was based on a 'working misunderstanding'. This seems to me to be true of much of the interaction between Africans and Europeans in twentieth century Africa.[50]

---

[47] Begnt Sundkler, *Black Zion*, forthcoming.
[48] Jack Goody, ed. *Literacy in Traditional Societies*, (Cambridge, 1968); MacGaffey and Janzen, 'Literacy and Truth', *An Anthology of Kongo Religion*, pp. 1–27.
[49] T. O. Ranger, *Dance and Society in Eastern Africa, The Beni Ngoma*, (London, 1975).
[50] Susan Herlin Broadhead, 'The case of the Kongo: Christianity Africanised

We can see this time and again when we turn back to the examples already given. Karl Weule's interpretations of the origins and nature of African culture in south–east Tanganyika are not now taken seriously by anyone, and Africans who were pressed into his service used gleefully to report how they had amused themselves by selling the tallest of tall tales to the German ethnographer.[51] Neither Jomo Kenyatta nor the British administration expected the Mau Mau outbreak, understood its nature, or knew how to deal with it.[52] I find it difficult myself to accept the emphases of Magubane or Van Onselin or Tambila on the calculated skill that went into the processing of the African work force. Fascinating and valuable as their work is, it seems to me that it underrates the shaping force of the processes of industrialization and urbanization in themselves, underrates the incoherence and inconsistency of European managerial activity, and underrates the extent to which Africans were able themselves to put together an urban or compound way of life, often by means of the sort of tentatives which I described above.[53]

The failure of most attempts at direct social engineering in the rural areas is certainly plain enough. This failure arose partly because the administration rarely commanded the sort of forces which were at the disposal of the Kenya colonial government during the Mau Mau emergency, but largely because of the flaws in expert understanding of local soils and environments and agricultural systems.

One very striking example of this sort of failure to comprehend what was involved in rural change has been advanced by Helge Kjekshus. He has pointed out that Europeans in East Africa worked on quite mistaken assumptions not only about African agriculture but also about its physical environment. The British administrators in Tanganyika found a situation in which large areas of the territory were infected with tsetse fly, there was very extensive scrub and bush, and human population was distributed very unevenly. They assumed that this represented an age-old environment and a standing proof of the inadequacy of African methods of agriculture.

and politicised', African Studies Association (Syracuse, October–November 1973), p. 2.

[51] Interview with Canon C. Lamburn, Rondo, August 1975. Canon Lamburn recalls Father Daudi Machina, who is mentioned in Weule's book as an informant, describing the tricks played on the German.

[52] Recent work by Frank Furedi has brought out the complex grass roots organization of Mau Mau. See especially, 'The Social Composition of the Mau Mau movement in the White Highlands', *Journal of Peasant History*, vol. 1, no. 4, July 1974.

[53] Some part of my argument for a degree of creative autonomy by Africans undergoing the process of urbanization is set out in *Dance and Society*, London, 1975.

Administrators and scholars alike both assumed that people who lived in the extensive woodlands possessed an essentially mobile, hunting-gathering culture. In 1956, for example, the anthropologist Crosse-Upcott carried out a study on the Ngindo people of Tanganyika. He found them to be 'essentially forest minded', mobile, without deep attachment to the soil, 'readily transplanted'. He thus reinforced what Kjekshus calls 'the myths of the Ngindo woodsman prevailing among the British administration at that time'. The administration moved |out 40,000 Ngindo to make a Game Reserve.

In fact, so Kjekshus powerfully argues, the facts of the case were very different. The many travellers who criss-crossed nineteenth century Tanganyika had reported herds of cattle grazing in what by the twentieth century had become tsetse fly areas. They reported extensive cultivation in areas which were covered with forest in the twentieth century. Among such reports were those concerning the Ngindo which spoke in terms of rich agriculture and shortage of game. Kjekshus argues that in nineteenth century Tanganyika there existed a successful and balanced agro-pastoral system, which allowed for the control of the environment and which kept the bush, wild animals and tsetse fly at bay. He argues that this successful economy broke down with ecological and human disasters at the end of the nineteenth and the beginning of the twentieth centuries. Human and animal plague, drought, the upheavals of conquest, revolt and the first world war, depopulation—all these allowed the bush and wild animals and tsetse to spread. The Ngindo, like other peoples, suffered 'almost total loss of control of the environment' and were compelled to make 'a mental accommodation to the situation.' The alleged deep-rooted forest-mindedness of the Ngindo is recent and shallow.[54]

Here in one sense was knowledge that worked—the Ngindo were moved and a Game Reserve was created without disorder. It also worked in another way. It has left Tanganyika with the legacy of the belief that the territory has always been a paradise for game animals and with a sense of obligation not to destroy this animal heritage. Kjekshus would argue that the more profound obligation, and one which arises from a fuller grasp of the facts, it to restore the nineteenth-century situation.

Finally, it seems to me that the anthropological reconstructions of functioning traditional societies have something in common with

[54] Helge Kjekshus, 'Wildlife and Ecological Control: a Historical Perspective', seminars, History Department, University of Dar es Salaam, January 1975. More generally see, Helge Kjekshus, 'Ecology Control and Economic Development: A Study in the Economic History of East Africa', forthcoming.

Sundkler's Zulu prophets. The anthropological models often depended upon selecting and high-lighting institutions or customs which did not seem central to the creators of the culture themselves. Often they were based on only a part of what there was to understand. Like the Zulu prophets, the creators of these models were primarily concerned to find in their examination of African societies usable symbols and concepts which related to their own concerns and needs. Just as the followers of the Zulu prophets were seeking for a harmonious, if limited, world into which to withdraw, so many anthropologists constructed an 'image of traditional culture which can be understood entirely as a reaction to the stresses and strains of life in the modern West'.[55]

Like most African formulations about European culture these anthropological constructs achieve utility at the expense of distortion and omission. But while Europeans, self confident in their knowledge of their own society, at once identify the African formulation as incomplete—often with a good deal of mockery, few Americans under colonialism were in a position to feel such a self confidence or to stigmatize European interpretations as imperfect. Indeed, so great was the prestige of European knowledge that many Africans came to accept the anthropologist's new creation as representing the revealed truth. MacGaffey tells us that the Kongolese came to see their culture in terms of the anthropological concept of the matriarchate. He also tells us that this concept bore no relation to past reality.[56]

Thus there is a constant discrepancy between the power and the accuracy of the various manifestations of European understanding of Africa under colonialism. French scholars have emphasized that the fact of power, of dominance, has underlain and distorted this understanding from the beginning. In this respect at least there can be little parallel with African attempts to comprehend Europeans. 'While one can find traces of the premises of ethnology among the Greek and Roman geographers', writes P. Bonte. 'the establishment of ethnology as a specific discipline within the human sciences parallels the "objectification" of societies dominated through colonial conquest and the expansion of commerce'.[57] Jaulin stresses this sort of intellectual triumphalism. Colonizing man produced a model of 'a separate and dehumanised category which must be

[55] Robin Horton, 'Levy-Bruhl, Durkheim and the Scientific Revolution', in *Modes of Thought. Essays on Thinking on Western and non-Western Societies*, eds. R. Horton and Ruth Finnegan (London, 1973), pp. 285–293.

[56] Wyatt MacGaffey, *Custom and Government in the Lower Congo* (Los Angeles, 1968).

[57] P. Bonte, 'From Ethnology to Anthropology: On critical approaches to the Human Sciences', *Critique of Anthropology*, no. 2, Autumn 1974, p. 37.

completely dominated and enslaved and not taken into account in our definition of ourselves: the savages and our past are both relegated to this category'. By means of ethnology colonising man 'fused the savage and our past together', located both 'at the foundations of nature', and celebrated his own passage to culture.[58]

The historian and European understanding of Africa

We are confronted, then, with the situation that we depend for our knowledge of the rest of the world, and of Africa in particular, largely on the social science of colonialism; yet we know that this knowledge is gravely flawed. It seems to me that the historian has three things to do in this situation. The first is to study more deeply the ways in which the knowledge produced by colonial social science has been corrupted by the circumstances in which it developed. The second is to realize that once one has established the falsity of a proposition one cannot just dismiss it from further historical consideration. A good part of the historian's task in reconstructing twentieth century African change is to record and study the multiple misunderstandings that worked. African innovations based on misapprehensions distort past reality but become part of present reality; so too do anthropological constructs. The third task—and obviously the most difficult—is to strive towards a more humane and less flawed knowledge, a truer picture of Africa.

I find that the incipient debate among historians about how best this third task can be achieved links up with a wider debate among social scientists and among African statesmen, writers and prophets. At the moment I detect three broad answers developing.

The first is the idea of a return to African modes of understanding reality. The poet Kayoya contrasts such modes with European enquiry:

Often we do not speak openly to the white man until we have
    discovered his human identity,
We give him whatever satisfies his often tiresome curiosity
Some say such curiosity is inhuman because it wants to analyse man.
My father never wanted us to study man
Enemies study a person to take him by surprise
We don't study man
We try to draw near to communicate.[59]

[58] R. Jaulin, *La Paix Blanche*, Paris, 1970, I do not wish to give the impression that Bonte and Jaulin agree in their interpretation. In fact Bonte is very critical of Jaulin in the second part of his article, 'From Ethnology to Anthropology', *Critique of Anthropology*, no. 3, Spring 1975.
[59] M. Kayoya, *In my father's footprints*, pp. 23–24.

The theologian Walter Hollenweger, in his study of the Pente-
costal churches, tells us that 'hymns, speaking in tongues, dreams,
spontaneous forms of worship are of decisive importance in the third
world. Information and impulses are exchanged by a kind of atmos-
pheric communication. . . . For the African . . . truth and untruth
lies at a more profound level than for the white man. It is not the
correspondence of the words which concerns him, but the interior
correspondence of sentiments'.[60] The anthropologist, Roy Willis
calls for a really alternative anthropology which will break from both
bourgeois and Marxist preconceptions and explore African societies
on their own terms.[61] The Kongolese teacher, Yoswa Kusikila kwa
Kilombo, calls his countrymen back to the roots of their own
science. 'Before the coming of the white man, back in the seed time
of our country, our doctors cured people of various illnesses. . . . The
white man came to suppress these skills and to replace them with the
medicines of his country. . . . In the beginning God granted different
powers to each land. To the people of Africa was distributed a spirit
at one with the roots of Africa so that great harmony and co-ordi-
nation prevailed between the created universe and man. Only those
original roots can help us, like a true friend, when we find ourselves in
pain and suffering. Those who brought civilization to our midst instead of guiding us in the work of developing the methods they found
here, considered it necessary to replace our economy and resources
with theirs. . . . Listen to the voice of our land calling: it is given to
every man to use the created world for good or evil; may the day of
obedience come. . . .'[62] We may well regard these prescriptions with
some reserve. As Hollenweger remarks of his own task, 'How can one
present in a book a movement whose main characteristic is not
verbal agreement but correspondence of sentiments?' Historians
can indeed draw near to communicate, but we might reasonably
think that the activity of academic historiography is bound for good
or ill to be very different from whatever chronicling arises from the
roots of the Congo.

This is precisely the issue confronted by Wyatt MacGaffey in
what I have found to be the most enlightening discussion of this
point. In a talk last year MacGaffey argued that under colonialism
the Kongolese moved between a public domain in which European
rules and assumptions dominated and a private domain of custom.
Each domain was

[60] Walter Hollenweger, *The Pentecostals* (London, 1972), p. xvii.

[61] Roy Willis, 'Towards an Alternative Anthropology', Anthropology seminar,
Manchester, 1975.

[62] Kusikila-kwa-Kilombo, 'A Blighted Society', translated and published in
MacGaffey and Janzen, *An Anthology of Kongo Religion*, pp. 53, 55.

predicated on an entirely different cosmology. . . . Cosmology begins with basic assumptions about space and time. The cosmology of the colonial regime is also the cosmology of social science. . . . [Its] terms presuppose an oriented and linear concept of the movement of time, the assumption of historical progress. . . . The concept is part of the cosmology that gives meaning to European institutions, and thus to social science in the European tradition. In applying it . . . to the study of twentieth century African social movements we adopt the perspective of actors in the European sector of the society studied and tend to ask questions accordingly: is this activity bureaucratic or not, is it modernizing or not, does it represent resistance, or nationalism, or a *prise de conscience* by the proletariat.

MacGaffey says that these questions make sense and are perfectly legitimate. But

'formally speaking, it is equally legitimate to write history from the point of view of the African sectors of these same societies, whose institutions are predicated upon racially different cosmologies.' If one does this a very different view of the colonial state and reaction to it emerges a perspective which often interprets European action in terms of witchcraft. 'It is not a matter of adopting one or the other perspective . . . but of recognising both and carefully distinguishing them. . . . The coexistence of distinct institutional sectors, each with its own ideology, generates two different histories of the same events, as apprehended by the actors in two different temporal and spatial perspectives. Inevitably, each perspective distorts the relations institutionalised in the alternative sector'. The European historian 'will inevitably and rightly prefer to apprehend the structure of events in the terms provided by his own cosmology'. But it is essential that he should be aware of the other categories of interpretation and recognize that if to him the explanations of an African cosmology can at best be metaphors, they are nevertheless 'very apt metaphors, superior on the whole to such non-explanatory mystifications as racial heredity, culture contact, development, and the like'.[63]

[63] Wyatt MacGaffey, 'Marginality and Leadership in a Plural Society', American Historical Association, Chicago, December 1974. See also his 'Kongo and the King of the Americans', *Journal of Modern African Studies*, vi, 2, 1968, pp. 171–181; 'Oral Tradition in Central Africa', *International Journal of African Historical Studies*, 7, 3, 1974. In a rather different way many of these issues are stimulatingly discussed in Martin Channock, 'Law and History in Colonial Central Africa: Nyasaland and North-Eastern Rhodesia, 1890–1930', Institute of Commonwealth Studies, London, 1975.

The second reaction to the dilemma is a very different one. It regards both colonial social science and African cosmologies as incapable of offering real insights into the objective realities of Africa—the first because it has been an instrument of exploitation and the second because it has been an articulator of false consciousness. A sound history of Africa can rest on the same foundations as a sound history of any other part of the world; namely a radical, revolutionary, Marxist historical science aimed at liberation from both colonialism and custom. I describe this reaction briefly not because there is less to be said about it but because so much more has already been said. A great deal of recent historiography and social science has been inspired by it.

Finally there is a third view, best expressed, I think, in a paper by Peter Rigby, currently Professor in the Sociology Department of the University of Dar es Salaam. This view declares war on all orthodoxies, Marxist, liberal and Africanist. It believes that false oppositions have been drawn between the insights of different schools. It believes that Marxist social science has been as much 'a tool of domination, not liberation' as Western sociology, which in turn is seen as now 'in its fragmented state incapable of doing anything but damage'. It believes that many African governments still make use of the social sciences—and of history—not so much because of their 'truth' but because of their validating prestige. 'What social anthropology was frequently alleged to have been for the colonial administrator has often become what sociology is for some African governments'. It believes that the social scientist must declare his independence from functional research. 'Manipulative anthropology/sociology, even if demanded by favoured governments', writes Archie Mafeje in a paper cited by Rigby, 'is to be rejected because it is a harmful perversion of anthropology and a negation of its emancipatory potential.' In short, the options need to be kept open; 'everything must be examined, everything must be shaken up, without exception and without circumspection'.[64]

I am enough of a utopian to be carried away by these different visions of emancipation from the distortions of the colonial science of man; enough of a historian to know that all three will keep us busy sifting through their distortions of the past and busy chronicling the new realities which will arise from their fruitful errors. But let the utopian or visionary note dominate at the end of this often depressing review. I am not sure how it is to be achieved but it is certainly appropriate to end this particular paper with the visionary

[64] Peter Rigby, 'The Sociologist in Decision Making; or the logic of False Dichotomies', Dar es Salaam, 1975; A. Mafeje, The Witchcraft of British Social Anthropology', forthcoming.

analysis and aspiration of the great French anthropologist, Claude Levi-Strauss:

> What we call the Renaissance was a veritable birth for colonialism and for anthropology. Between the two, confronting each other from the time of their common origin, an equivocal dialogue has been pursued for four centuries. If colonialism had not existed, the elaboration of anthropology would have been less belated; but perhaps also anthropology would not have been led to implicate all mankind in each of its particular case-studies. Our science arrived at maturity the day that Western man began to see that he would never understand himself as long as there was a single race of people on the surface of the earth that he treated as an object. Only then could anthropology declare itself in its true colours: as an enterprise reviewing and atoning for the Renaissance, in order to spread humanism to all humanity.[65]

University of Manchester.

[65] C. Levi-Strauss, *The Scope of Anthropology,* 1967, pp. 51–2.

THE FRENCH COLONIALIST MOVEMENT DURING THE THIRD REPUBLIC: THE UNOFFICIAL MIND OF IMPERIALISM

By C. M. Andrew, M.A., Ph.D., F.R.Hist.S.

READ AT THE SOCIETY'S CONFERENCE
19 SEPTEMBER 1975

BRITISH colonial expansion, it has been argued, was governed during the nineteenth century by the workings of the official mind. French colonial expansion was not. The official mind of French imperialism was slow to develop and at best half-formed. The first steps in the creation of the modern French Empire under the July Monarchy and Napoleon III followed no grand design or strategic obsession. Empire-building in Africa, Indo-China and the South Pacific proceeded instead by a series of fits and starts of whose significance successive governments were usually unaware. When the Third Republic embarked on colonial expansion in the 1880s, its policies proved almost as incoherent as those of precedessors. Intervention in Tunisia was swiftly followed by refusal to intervene in Egypt; a forward policy in Indo-China was first accepted, then violently rejected; in West Africa Army officers carved out a private empire on their own initiative. After 1880, however, French expansion at last acquired a clear sense of direction. French imperialism, in its final phase from 1890 to 1920, consciously pursued and substantially achieved a series of imperial grand designs; the unification of France's African Empire in the 1890s; the completion of French North Africa by the Moroccan protectorate in the early twentieth century; the acquisition of a Middle Eastern Empire and German West Africa during the First World War. These grand designs, however, were the product not of the official but of the *un*official mind of French imperialism. That unofficial mind forms the subject of this paper.

It is a commonplace of colonial history throughout the ages that policy at the outposts of empire tends to escape the control of the central government. What is remarkable in the French case, however, is the degree to which colonial policy even at the centre was not decided by central government. During the final phase of French expansion the abdication of government control in Paris was even

more striking than at the periphery. Because the official mind of
French imperialism was so weak, the unofficial mind possessed for
thirty years an influence to which it could not aspire in England.
That unofficial mind was known to contemporaries as *le parti
colonial*, the French colonialist movement.

For most of the nineteenth century France possessed colonialists
but no colonialist movement. During the sixty years which followed
the Algiers expedition separate groups of servicemen, academics,
politicians, businessmen and missionaries emerged from time to
time with an interest in, and an influence on, the course of French
expansion. Both Garnier and Brazza, for example, had influential
groups of supporters in France itself.[1] Not until the early 1890s,
however, did those separate interests which had previously provided
intermittent support for the colonial cause merge into a single
movement dedicated to the expansion and *mise en valeur* of the French
Empire. The French colonialist movement was thus both a consequence and a cause of French expansion. The passions aroused by
the first wave of colonial expansion under the Third Republic
produced the *parti colonial*. The *parti colonial* then produced a further
wave of colonial expansion.

It promoted most of the expeditions which unified France's
African Empire in the 1890s. It led a less successful drive for the
expansion of French Indo-China. Having brought Britain and
France to the brink of war at Fashoda, the leaders of the *parti
colonial* then devised the formula—the barter of Egypt for Morocco—
which became the basis of both the Entente Cordiale with England
and the French protectorate in Morocco. During the First World
War—the climax of French colonial expansion—the *parti colonial*
reached the height of its power. The government virtually abdicated
to it the definition of France's imperial war aims.[2]

Colonialism in France was, however, never a mass movement.
French colonialists looked enviously at the 60,000 well-organized
members of the German *Kolonialgesellschaft*. They bemoaned the
lack in France of what they believed to be 'cette conscience "im-

[1] J. Valette, 'L'expédition de Francis Garnier au Tonkin à travers quelques
journaux contemporains', *Revue d'Histoire Moderne et Contemporaine*, XVI (1969);
H. Brunschwig (ed) *Brazza et la fondation du Congo français. II: Les traités Makoko*
(Paris, 1971).

[2] C. M. Andrew and A. S. Kanya-Forstner, 'The French "Colonial Party": Its
Composition, Aims and Influence, 1885–1914', *Historical Journal*, XIV (1971);
idem, 'Gabriel Hanotaux, the Colonial Party, and the Fashoda Strategy', *Journal
of Imperial and Commonwealth History*, III (1974); C. M. Andrew, *Théophile Delcassé
and the Making of the Entente Cordiale* (London, 1968); Andrew and Kanya-Forstner,
'The French Colonial Party and French Colonial War Aims 1914–18', *Historical
Journal*, XVII (1974).

periale" qui, en Angleterre, fait frémir les plus humbles sujets à la seule évocation de la puissance britannique'.[3] The *parti colonial*—the sum of those Frenchmen with a continuing commitment to the Empire—was both small in size and chaotic in organization. Over fifty colonialist societies were founded during the quarter-century before the First World War, most with a particular interest in some area or aspect of French expansion. But their total (overlapping) membership never reached 10,000 and was probably below 5,000 in 1914.[4] Most of these societies went little beyond publishing ephemeral reviews, putting on lectures and organizing banquets. The endless series of colonialist banquets gave the *parti colonial* its nickname 'le parti où l'on dine': to which one colonialist replied that while most French political parties were 'partis où l'on dine', the *parti colonial* was 'le parti où l'on dine *bien*'.[5] Only a handful of colonialist societies—chief among them the Africa, Asian and Moroccan committees, and the colonialist pressure group in parliament—had an important influence on the course of French expansion. The leaders of these societies formed the inner circle which until the First World War dominated the *parti colonial* and determined its policies. At the centre of this inner circle was Eugène Etienne, known to his supporters as 'Notre Dame des coloniaux', the man who as colonial under-secretary (1887; 1889–92) began the unification of France's African Empire. For thirty years until his retirement in 1919 Etienne was the unchallenged leader of the whole colonialist movement.

Most of the colonialist militants led by Etienne were professional men: academics, journalists, politicians, civil servants, diplomats, businessmen and officers in the armed services. All at some stage in their careers, often by accident, sometimes at second hand, had come into contact with the Empire and been fired by the vision of a greater France.[6] Their colonialism apart, the most remarkable thing about them was how unremarkable they were. The colonialists were *un*remarkable in three perhaps surprising ways. First, though their imperial ambitions were notably immoderate, their politics were moderate. Before 1914 most colonialists in parliament were, like Etienne, men of the republican centre. Between the wars four of the five presidents of the colonialist pressure group in the Chamber

[3] *La Dépêche Coloniale*, 4 April 1912; *Bulletin du Comité de l'Afrique Française*, 1913, supplement no. 7.

[4] C. M. Andrew, P. Grupp and A. S. Kanya-Forstner, 'Le parti colonial, 1890–1914: groupements et effectifs', forthcoming in *Revue Française d'Histoire d'Outre-Mer*.

[5] L. Saignes, 'Le parti colonial', *La Politique Coloniale*, 11 July 1906; C. Depincé, 'Une fête coloniale', *Quinzaine Coloniale*, 25 February 1905.

[6] Andrew, Grupp and Kanya-Forstner, 'Le parti colonial'.

of Deputies were radicals, members of the party which by now composed the shifting centre of the Third Republic.[7]

The second perhaps surprising characteristic of the *parti colonial* is that, small though it was, the great majority of its members came from the metropolis rather than the Empire. Most French *colons* were not colonialists. As the colonialists complained, many colonial settlers had a scarcely more enlightened view of the French Empire than most Frenchmen. While they might be passionately attached to the interests of their own particular estate or their own colony, only a minority had any broader vision of the Empire as a whole. The secretary-general of the *Ligue Maritime et Coloniale*, easily the largest colonialist organization between the wars, became increasingly impatient with the narrow-mindedness of most *colons*: 'Que de fois n'ai-je pas été stupéfait, interrogeant les coloniaux sur les régions voisines de leur résidence, de constater qu'ils en ignoraient tout et ne s'étaient jamais demandé ce qui pouvait exister au delà de leur horizon coutumier.'[8] During the long drawn-out debate before the First World War over the reform of the *indigénat*—the system of summary native jurisdiction—most colonialists, at least in parliament, and most *colons*, especially in North Africa, were on opposite sides.[9] When André Malraux went to Indo-China in 1925 to found 'un journal de rapprochement franco-annamite', he was violently opposed by the *colons* in Indo-China but publicly supported by the president of the colonialist group in the Chamber of Deputies.[10] There were, of course, other occasions when the views of *colons* and colonialists coincided. There was also a minority of *colons*—including Etienne himself—who were ardent colonialists. But even Etienne, for all his authority, was never able to impose his views on native policy on the colonialist movement as a whole. The *parti colonial* thus never became simply a *parti colon*.

Nor was it an economic pressure group. There were, of course, many individual colonialists with business interests of various kinds. But the proportion of businessmen among the colonialists in parliament was scarcely higher than among the non-colonialists.[11] As the

[7] Andrew and Kanya-Forstner, 'The *Groupe Colonial* in the French Chamber of Deputies, 1892–1932', *Historical Journal*, XVII (1974).

[8] M. Rondet-Saint', 'Epître aux Coloniaux', *Mer et Colonies*, March 1937; J. Python, 'La politique indigène dans les colonies françaises', *Annales Coloniales*, 22 October 1912.

[9] Andrew and Kanya-Forstner, 'The French "Colonial Party" . . . 1885–1914', p. 126; C-R. Ageron, *Les algériens musulmans et la France, 1871–1919* (Paris, 1968), II, chap. xi.

[10] Interview with Henry Simon, *L'Indochine*, 15 July 1924; W. Langlois, *André Malraux: the Indochina Adventure* (London, 1966).

[11] H. Brunschwig, *French Colonialism, 1871–1914. Myths and Realities* (London, 1964), pp. 109–10; Andrew and Kanya-Forstner, 'The *Groupe Colonial*', p. 843.

colonialists complained, the most characteristic attitude of French business towards colonial expansion was indifference. In 1914 French investment in Russia alone was almost three times that in the whole French Empire. French trade with the Empire, on a percentage basis, was a third of what it had been before the Revolution. Colonialist visions of economic eldorados in such unlikely places as Bahr-el-Ghazal and Lake Chad had little appeal for cautious-minded French businessmen. The *parti colonial* viewed with a recurrent sense of outrage the failure of French business to perceive its imperial mission. That sense of outrage was never greater than during the First World War. The Commission charged with drawing up French colonial war aims called evidence in 1918 from the leaders of industry and commerce, confident that they would produce economic arguments for further French expansion. It was terribly disillusioned: 'Les sociétés industrielles françaises ne désirent pas l'accroissement des colonies. Elles nous l'ont dit'. The commission concluded that French business in general, and French industry in particular, was failing the nation. 'La première chose à faire, c'est de changer la mentalité de nos industriels'.[12]

There were, of course, exceptions to the general apathy of business towards the Empire. But even in those instances where business took an interest in the Empire that interest did not necessarily coincide with the interest of the colonialists. Most French industrialists with colonial interests were anxious to preserve the Empire as private markets for themselves, protected by high tariffs from foreign competition. The colonialists, convinced that protection was damaging colonial development, wanted to lower tariff barriers and give each colony the right to fix its own customs duties. When the colonial tariffs came up for revision in 1910, colonialists and industrialists thus came into open conflict. All the main colonialist societies joined together in the *Fédération Intercoloniale* to campaign for reform.[13] The main employers federation, the *Association de l'Industrie et de l'Agriculture Françaises*, denounced the colonialist campaign and sought to keep the tariffs as they were.[14]

Where economic imperialism did exist, it was as likely to conflict as to co-operate with the *parti colonial*. The internationalism of finance capital ran counter to the nationalism of the colonialists. Those French banks and industries interested in the exploitation of

---

[12] Minutes, Commission d'études des questions coloniales posées par la guerre 18 March, 15 and 29 April, 6 May 1918, Archives Nationales (Section Outre-Mer), 97 Affaires Politiques.

[13] *Quinzaine Coloniale*, 25 December 1910.

[14] Minutes, Assemblée Générale, Association de l'Industrie et de l'Agriculture Françaises, 16 March 1910, Archives Nationales 27 AS 1.

Morocco in the early twentieth century favoured the formation of international consortia. They were opposed by the leaders of the *parti colonial* who wanted an exclusively *French* protectorate in Morocco. The secretary-general of the *Comité du Maroc* insisted: 'Si on veut résister à l'Allemagne au Maroc, il faut commencer par resserrer impitoyablement les cordons de la bourse'.[15] The same conflict between the internationalism of economic imperialism and the nationalism of the *parti colonial* was evident also in French policy towards the Turkish Empire.[16]

The French colonialist movement represents the highest stage, not of French capitalism, but of French nationalism. For its supporters during the first generation of the Third Republic colonial expansion was, first and foremost, the road to national recovery after the traumatic defeat of 1870. During the final years of the Second Empire, Prevost-Paradol had argued that faced with the rapid expansion of Bismarckian Prussia, on her eastern border, France could remain a great power *inside* Europe only by expansion *outside* Europe: in particular by building an African Empire on the southern shores of the Mediterranean.[17] That argument became much more compelling after the humiliation of the Franco-Prussian War. As Gambetta wrote to Ferry after the occupation of Tunisia in 1881: 'Mon cher ami . . . je te félicite du fond du coeur . . . la France reprend son rang de grande puissance'. And it was precisely because colonial expansion seemed to offer France the means of 'becoming a great power again' that both Ferry and Gambetta became colonialists.[18]

A number of French colonialists, not least Ferry himself, offered a more sophisticated explanation for colonial expansion in terms of economic necessity. It is essential, however, to distinguish the imperialist rationale with which Ferry and others sought to justify colonial expansion from the motives which made them colonialists

[15] R. de Caix, 'La question marocaine', *Bulletin du Comité de l'Afrique Française* March 1907. The priorities of most colonialists were summed up by Etienne: 'Il ne s'agit pas pour nous au Maroc, comme nous l'avons fait dans d'autres régions, d'établir notre domination pour y développer nos intérêts économiques. Au Maroc, c'est vraiment l'avenir de la France qui se joue d'une façon irrémédiable', 'Le Banquet du Comité du Maroc', *Bulletin du Comité de l'Afrique Française*, December 1909.

[16] P. Guillen, 'Milieux d'affaires et impérialisme colonial', *Relations Internationales* I (1974).

[17] M. Prévost-Paradol, *La France nouvelle*, 10th edition (Paris, 1869), pp. 373–419.

[18] Brunschwig, *French Colonialism*; C-R. Ageron, 'Gambetta et la reprise de l'expansion coloniale', *Revue Française d'Histoire d'Outre-Mer*, LIX (1972); J. Ganiage, *L'expansion coloniale de la France sous la Troisième République, 1871–1914* (Paris, 1968), chap. III.

in the first place. The same distinction is central to the history of the late nineteenth-century imperialism in the whole of western Europe. It applies equally, for example, to the emergence of *Weltpolitik* and the campaign for a new German navy. Germany needed a new navy, as Bethmann-Hollweg said vaguely but accurately, 'for the general purposes of German greatness'. But having once decided to build a new navy for reasons as vague as that, its supporters then felt bound to produce, as much for their own benefit as for others, a rather more sophisticated rationale. Whatever the rationale, they offered, Jules Ferry and the colonialists of the Third Republic wanted a great French Empire, as Bethmann-Hollweg wanted a great German navy, 'for the general purposes of French greatness', for reasons of national prestige.

The European rivalries born of the African partition strengthened still further the colonialist concern with French prestige. The further the scramble for Africa continued, the more the colonialists became obsessed simply with beating their European rivals in the race for what remained, and the less attention they paid to the value—if any —of the territory they claimed. It was this preoccupation with a race against European rivals which led in 1890 to the founding of the *Comité de l'Afrique Française*, the first important colonialist pressure group. Arenberg, the *Comité's* first president, summed up its aim as follows: 'Il fallait avant tout arriver les premiers partout où des territoires africains étaient encore sans maître'.[19] This too described the aims of those French soldiers engaged in the scramble for Africa who looked further than their own careers. Galliéni, the most famous colonial soldier of his generation, wrote to the secretary-general of the *Comité* in 1890: 'Nous autres militaires, nous n'entendons pas grand' chose à la question économique. . . . Nous savons seulement qu'il y a des territoires en Afrique qui devraient nous appartenir et que les Anglais et les Allemands sont en train de nous "souffler". Et nous essayons de les en empêcher'.[20]

The *parti colonial* founded in the early 1890s represented, and knew itself to represent, only a tiny minority of the French people: a movement a few thousand strong in a nation of forty million. Yet that tiny minority was a striking example of the *minorité agissante*, a group which for a generation possessed an influence spectacularly disproportionate to its size. The main explanation for that influence does not, however, lie with the colonialists themselves. It lies instead with those attitudes in French society and

[19] Speech by Arenberg on his retirement, *Bulletin du Comité de l'Afrique Française*, January 1913; *cf.* Arenberg to Alis, 13 April 1891, Bibliothèque de l'Institut de France, Terrier MS 5891.

[20] Galliéni to Alis, 30 June 1890, Terrier MS 5892.

those weaknesses in the structure of the French government which the colonialists were able to exploit.

The nationalism of French society made it vulnerable to a colonialism with which it was fundamentally out of sympathy.[21] For France, unlike her main European rivals, the nineteenth century was a period of relative decline. Perhaps as a result of that decline, public opinion, especially in Paris where it had most influence on government, was peculiarly sensitive to any slight to French prestige. This sensitivity was noted by acute observers at both ends of the political spectrum. Tocqueville predicted in 1839 that the failure of the July Monarchy to protect national prestige would be more fatal to it than 'the loss of twenty battles'.[22] In 1848, according to Marx 'a series of mortifications to French national sentiment' was among those forces which 'worked like an electric shock on the paralysed masses of the people and awoke their great revolutionary memories and passions'.[23]Half a century later the colonialists developed a remarkably effective electric shock system to rouse the paralysed masses in the colonialist cause.

The *parti colonial* could not make public opinion colonialist. But at moments of crisis it could nonetheless enlist public support for colonialist expansion by presenting *colonial* issues as questions of *national* prestige. Though there had been isolated occasions before —such as the Pritchard affair and the Makoko treaty—when nationalist passions had been roused by colonial issues, the sustained exploitation of French nationalism in the colonialist cause was a new phenomenon. That the colonialists could enlist this support which had hitherto been lacking was due to the reconciliation during the scramble for Africa of French nationalism with French imperialism. Though all colonialists were nationalists before the scramble for Africa, most nationalists were still opposed to colonialism. For a minority of French nationalists during the 1880s, as for Ferry and Gambetta, colonial expansion *outside* Europe was the road to greatness *inside* Europe. But for most nationalists, ranging from Clémenceau on the left to Déroulède on the right, colonial expansion, by diverting French troops and French resources *from* Europe, actually diminished French power *in* Europe.

What resolved the conflict between the two opposing strands of

---

[21] Etienne once acknowledged: 'Si nous avons pu constituer toutes nos colonies africaines, on peut dire que c'est contre l'opinion publique', *Dépêche Coloniale*, 5 July 1910.

[22] D. W. Johnson, *Guizot: Aspects of French History, 1787–1874* (London, 1963), p. 265. Tocqueville told J. S. Mill in 1840, 'L'orgueil national est le plus grand sentiment qui nous reste'. Mill replied that it often gave 'an impression of angry weakness'.

[23] Marx, *Class Struggles in France, 1848–50*.

French nationalism in the 1880s was the fusion during the early 1890s of colonial expansion *outside* Europe with national rivalries *inside* Europe. The more the scramble for Africa, the more the scramble for South East Asia proceeded the more they became a scramble between European powers. For that reason the French public increasingly saw *colonial* expansion in *nationalist* terms: during the 1890s in terms of rivalry with the old enemy, England; during the Moroccan crises of the early twentieth century as a conflict with the new enemy, Germany.

This extension of European rivalries onto an extra-European plane brought about a remarkable change in public attitudes. In the 1880s, when French opinion was not simply indifferent to colonial expansion, it usually appeared actively hostile to it. That hostility reached its peak in March 1885 after a very minor military reverse in Tonkin. The Tonkin episode, trivial though it was, brought down Jules Ferry's government and wrecked his political career. At the general election later in the year the most damaging description the opposition could devise for Ferry was the label 'tonkinois'. By the time of the next Far-Eastern crisis—over Siam in 1893—there had been a remarkable reversal of roles. In 1893 it was the French *government*, not, as in 1885, the French public, which showed itself reluctant to continue a forward policy in South East Asia. And in 1893 the government's decision to occupy a Siamese port was actually a response to public pressure.

Yet this remarkable shift in public attitudes had, at root, a very simple explanation. The Tonkin crisis of 1885 had concerned no other European power than France. The Siam crisis of 1893 was seen in France less as a struggle with Siam than a struggle with *England*, for influence in Siam. In the words of Théophile Delcassé, colonial under-secretary and a prominent member of the *parti colonial*: 'Ce qui émeut l'opinion publique, ce n'est pas le Siam, mais l'Angleterre dont on ne veut pas être le jouet'. The colonialists found it easy to turn this nationalism to the service of colonialism. During the Siamese crisis of 1893 Delcassé threatened to resign unless the government accepted his forward policy in Siam. The non-colonialist majority in the cabinet dared not accept his resignation because, as Delcassé told his wife: 'Comme ils savent que, dans l'opinion je passe pour l'homme qui n'admet pas qu'on baisse pavillon devant John Bull, ils devinent le tollé de la presse en apprenant ma retraite qu'elle attribuera justement à mon refus de consentir à une capitulation'.[24]

The colonialists found John Bull, better known as *Perfide Albion*, a

[24] Delcassé to his wife, 18 and 27 July 1893, Archives du Ministère des Affaires Etrangères, Delcassé, MS 1.

convenient scapegoat throughout the 1890s. During the debate on
the conquest of Madagascar in November 1894, despite the absence
of present British opposition, even the memory of past British
opposition was sufficient to win the *parti colonial* a huge majority in
parliament. Some colonialists were taken aback by the ease with
which Anglophobia could be exploited. Jean de Lanessan, later
vice-president of the colonialist group in the Chamber of Deputies,
declared: 'Si les anticoloniaux eux-mêmes se prononcèrent presque
unanimement en faveur de la campagne . . . si les millions furent
votés sans compter et sans que personne songeât à demander s'ils ne
pourraient pas être employés plus utilement qu'en opérations
militaires, n'est-ce pas encore parce qu'on était dominé par le désir
de "donner une leçon a l'Angleterre"?'[25]

The emergence of what looked like popular imperialism in France
during the 1890s was only part of a much wider European phenomenon. In England the Diamond Jubilee of 1897 was an imperial
as much as a national celebration. *Weltpolitik* in Germany and the
Kaiser's confident assertion that 'the German Empire has become a
World Empire' came at almost the same moment. Yet in France at
least the new popular imperialism was simply old popular nationalism in a new disguise. The imperial crises of the 1890s mattered to
the French public not because of colonial expansion, about which it
cared very little, but because of rivalry with England, about which
it cared a great deal. The Moroccan crises of 1905 to 1911 aroused
so much passion not because of the conquest of Morocco but because of the conflict with Germany. As soon as Egypt, Siam and
tropical Africa ceased to be the foci of disputes with England, as
soon as Morocco ceased to be the cause of a quarrel with Germany,
they also ceased to attract either the interest or the attention of the
great mass of the French people.[26] The bulletin of the main colonialist propaganda organization gloomily concluded on the eve of
war: 'L'éducation coloniale des Français reste entièrement à faire'.[27]

Though it could not convert the public to colonialism, however,
the *parti colonial* was remarkably confident, especially in the 1890s,
of its ability at moments of crisis to whip up public support for
colonial policies by playing on its pre-colonial nationalism. It was
so confident in fact that in 1896 it issued a remarkable public chal-

[25] *La Politique Coloniale*, 12 September 1895. Lanessan was one of those colonialists
opposed to what they considered the unnecessary use of military force in the Mada-
gascan and other expeditions.
[26] Etienne himself acknowledged: 'En France l'attention du grand public ne
s'attache à une question que lorsqu'elle est arrivée à l'état aigu . . . C'est ce qui
est arrivé pour le Maroc comme pour toutes les questions coloniales', *Dépêche
Coloniale*, 5 July 1910.
[27] 'Bulletin de la Ligue Coloniale Française', *Dépêche Coloniale*, 2 February 1914.

lenge to *The Times*. *The Times* correspondent in Paris had correctly observed in an article on Anglo-French rivalry in Egypt that the French public knew nothing about the Egyptian question. He proceeded to draw the logical but false conclusion that the French public *cared* nothing about the Egyptian question. This so enraged the colonialists that their parliamentary spokesman on Egypt, François Deloncle, challenged *The Times* correspondent to put his assertion to the test: 'You say that beyond the boulevards the Egyptian question does not exist. Very well. Choose whatever place in France you wish. Do me the honour of accompanying me thither, and you will have a fresh proof that there is not a hamlet where the Egyptiae question is not known, and where its settlement is not ardently desired'.[28] Tragically for the history of French public opinion, *The Times* failed to rise to the challenge.

French society suffered from a Middle Kingdom complex which played into the colonialists' hands. In its original Chinese version there are, it is said, two principal aspects of the Middle Kingdom complex: first, a general indifference to the doings of the barbarians in the outside world, combined with, secondly, an acute sense of the superiority of the Middle Kingdom and an acute sensitivity to any slight to its prestige. This combination of attitudes was characteristic also of the Third Republic, particularly before 1914. Except at moments of international crisis the French people and their parliaments, despite their sensitivity to French prestige, were largely apathetic to the affairs of the outside world. The foreign policy issue most frequently discussed in parliament during the last twenty years of the nineteenth century was the trivial one of diplomatic relations with the Vatican: an issue far more closely related to the domestic controversy between Church and State than to the broader issues of France's external relations. The fact that French nationalism was thus an ignorant nationalism made it, however, all the easier to exploit. Like Lord Salisbury, Frenchmen 'knew as much about Fashoda and the Upper Nile as about the other side of the moon'. But as Marchand, the leader of the Fashoda expedition, discovered in 1896, all that parliament needed to be convinced of its importance was to be told that it was necessary, in Marchand's words, to 'revendiquer hautement nos droits sur le Nil en face des Anglais'. Despite, or rather because of, its elemental simplicity, that argument won the credits for the Marchand expedition a parliamentary majority of 471 votes to 18. Even more remarkably, that enormous majority was achieved without debate. What opposition there was was led not by a socialist but by Camille Bazille, a dissident colo-

[28] *The Times*, 27 January, 3 February 1896.

nialist who approved the expedition's aims but was rightly convinced of its futility. Bazille, however, was silenced by a patriotic outburst from none other than the socialist leader, Jean Jaurès: 'Ce n'est pas un vote politique que nous émettrons, c'est un vote national'.[29]

The confusion of European rivalries with extra-European expansion remained crucial in winning public support for the two final stages in the construction of the French Empire: the establishment of the Moroccan protectorate in 1912 and the partition of the enemy empires after the First World War. The *Comité du Maroc* itself acknowledged: 'Combien n'ont été convertis à l'idée marocaine que par la réclame inespérée, paradoxale mais formidable, que lui a faite chez nous l'irritante opposition de l'Allemagne!'[30] Just as rivalry with Germany reconciled the French people to a protectorate in Morocco which it did not want, so renewed rivalry with Britain won them over to the unwelcome mandates in Lebanon and Syria. The great majority of the French people had no positive desire for a Middle Eastern Empire, but was easily persuaded that if Britain was to have one France must have one too. Even Clémenceau, the strongest prime minister of the Third Republic, felt the force of this simplistic argument. He viewed the prospect of French mandates in the Middle East with some dismay, but once the war was over, found himself unable 'to still the clamour of the colonial party'. He was, he told the Council of Four, 'le moins colonialiste de tous les Français', but public opinion would not allow him to surrender his claim for Syria. François Georges-Picot summed up the colonialists' ability to exploit the nationalism of public opinion as follows: 'Dans notre vie politique ordinaire, le parti colonial reste au second plan, mais il est des questions où il interprète véritablement la volonté nationale. Qu'une de ces questions, comme celle de la Syrie, vienne à se poser, il passe soudain au premier plan ct il a tout le pays derrière lui'.[31]

Though the colonialists were few, their opponents during the final phase of French expansion were fewer still and far less determined. Even the socialists, for all their theoretical opposition to imperialism, launched no coherent campaign against it. The internal contradictions of a socialist movement which was internationalist in theory but sometimes nationalist in practice went back

---

[29] *Journal Officiel, Débats Parlementaires, Chambre*, 8 December 1896; Andrew and Kanya-Forstner, 'Fashoda Strategy', pp. 76–77.

[30] *Bulletin du Comité de l'Afrique Française*, April 1912.

[31] H. Nicolson, *Peacemaking 1919* (London, 1933), p. 142; P. Mantoux (ed.), *Les délibérations du Conseil des Quatre, 24 mars–28 juin 1919* (Paris, 1955), II, p. 139; Picot to Sykes, 11 September 1918, Public Record Office, Sykes MS FO 800/221.

to the July Monarchy, to the days when Blanc and Blanqui, though preaching that the workers of all nations were brothers, also insisted that Paris was the *ville lumière*, the capital of civilisation. The French, said Louis Blanc, were 'an inspired nation'; the British, on the other hand, were not: 'Le principe de l'égoisme s'est incarné dans le peuple anglais: le principe de dévouement dans le peuple français. L'Angleterre n'a mis pied dans aucune contrée sans y établir des comptoirs. La France n'a passé nulle part sans y laisser le parfum de son spiritualisme'. The *mission civilisatrice*, in Blanc's view, was not limited to Europe but extended to the backward nations beyond. The Mediterranean was destined to become a French lake around which the decadent civilization of Islam would give way to the superior culture of France.[32] Without ever descending to the crude chauvinism of Blanc and Blanqui, even Jean Jaurès felt a continuing fascination for the nationalism of the civilizing mission; he told parliament in 1903: 'Je suis convaincu que la France a, au Maroc, des intérêts de premier ordre; je suis convaincu que ces intérêts mêmes lui créent une sorte de droit. . . . Oui, il est à desirer, dans l'intérêt même des indigènes du Maroc comme dans l'intérêt de la France, que l'action économique et morale de notre pays s'y prolonge et s'y établisse'. Periodic socialist outbursts against the evils of financial and military imperialism were neither sustained nor very effective. Even during the last years before the First World War, the appeals of Algerian socialists for support from French socialists against the Algerian administration went almost unanswered.[33] During the final phase of French expansion, the voice of anti-colonialism was neither as well orchestrated nor remotely as effective as the voice of the *parti colonial*.

Like the ignorant nationalism of public opinion, the incoherent structure of French government played into the hands of the colonialists. The leaders of the *parti colonial* were, in the words of *The Times* Paris correspondent, 'men who know definitely what they are about as well as what they want'.[34] This was more than could be said for the French government. The official machinery of colonial administration was deficient in at least three ways. It was confused, it was often incompetent, and it was usually outside cabinet control. Until almost the end of the nineteenth century France possessed no independent ministry of colonies. The *sous-secrétariat des colonies*, created by Gambetta in 1881, led an underprivileged existence for

[32] A. Loubère, 'Les idées de Louis Blanc sur le nationalisme, le colonialisme et la guerre', *Revue d'Histoire Moderne et Contemporaine*, IV (1957), pp. 50 ff.

[33] *Journal Officiel, Débats Parlementaires, Chambre*, 20 November 1903; C-R. Ageron, *Les algériens musulmans*, II, pp. 1103–04.

[34] *The Times*, 27 January 1896.

the next decade, being shuttled back and forth between the ministries of commerce and the marine, on two occasions disappearing *en route*. The creation of the colonial ministry in 1894 was the result of a colonialist campaign.[35] The official mind of French colonialism, in so far as it existed, was thus a creation of the unofficial mind. At least until the 1920s, however, the colonial ministry remained, along with the ministry of public works, posts and telegraphs, one of the least sought-after cabinet posts.[36] The colonial administration enjoyed a correspondingly low prestige. Except for a minority of committed colonialists, it attracted the least able of French administrators, those who found it difficult to make a career in France itself. According to their files, a third of French colonial administrators before the First World War were considered patently incompetent even by governors whose own competence was often suspect.[37] The main ambition of most colonial governors was to spend as little time as possible in the colonies they governed. As a result until 1920 French colonies changed governors, on average, once a year.[38]

The colonial ministry itself achieved a level of confused incompetence rivalled by no other government department. A parliamentary report concluded in 1920:

> 'La constitution actuelle du ministère des colonies se caractérise par l'éparpillement des attributions et des responsabilités, le chevauchement des services, la multiplication des organismes parasitaires, inutiles et coûteux, et par l'impuissance de tous à concevoir des vues d'ensemble aussi bien qu'à réaliser des efforts coordonnés. . . . Alors que tous les autres ministères ont groupé leurs divers services en quatre ou cinq directions fortement constituées, le ministère des colonies comprend seize services indépendants. . . . Le seul énoncé de ces services serait de nature à provoquer, suivant le tempérament de l'auditeur, ou l'indignation ou l'hilarité.'

There were sinecures at every level of the ministry. More than two-thirds of the shorthand typists (most of whom did not in any case

[35] F. Berge, *Le sous-secrétariat et les sous-secrétaires d'état aux colonies*, (Paris, 1962).

[36] Candace, vice-president of the *groupe colonial* in the Chamber, described the colonial ministry in 1920 as 'au dernier ou à l'avant-dernier rang dans la hiérarchie conventionnelle du conseil des ministres'. Another deputy in the same debate called it 'la cendrillon des ministères'. *Journal Officiel, Débats Parlementaires, Chambre*, 29 June 1920.

[37] W. B. Cohen, *Rulers of Empire: the French Colonial Service in Africa* (Stanford, 1971), pp. 34 ff. By the interwar years the *Ecole Coloniale* had produced a distinct improvement in the quality of the colonial administration.

[38] Report by Paul Laffont, *Journal Officiel, Documents Parlementaires, Chambre*, 1920, no. 807, p. 1106: 'A l'heure actuelle un gouverneur qui prend un congé est à peu près sur de ne jamais rejoindre le poste qu'il vient de quitter'.

know shorthand) had no real job to do. The department responsible for liaison with the ministry of war, a department with no power of decision or real responsibility, yet contained over a hundred officials.[39] No colonial minister before Albert Sarraut had both the time and the energy to attempt any significant reform of his ramshackle ministry. The colonial ministry did not, however, administer all French colonies. Algeria came under the ministry of the interior; the rest of North Africa and later the Middle Eastern mandates were the responsibility of the Quai d'Orsay. A rational constitution for the whole Empire had been promised in 1854; it did not materialize until 1946.

The incompetent and incoherent official structure of colonial policy-making did less than the colonialists to determine the final objectives of French expansion. The *parti colonial* was not, of course, able to decide most of the details of colonial policy. Indeed it was itself divided on important issues of colonial administration. But during the final phase of European expansion its leaders were able to impose their main territorial ambitions on a series of transient governments only dimly aware of the policies to which they had become committed. The *parti colonial* owed its success as a pressure group to its ability to work *inside* as well as outside the official structure of government. Those within the official structure who played any significant part in determining the strategy of French expansion during its final phase were remarkably few in number: a dozen or so soldiers and proconsuls at the outposts of the Empire, perhaps two dozen permanent officials at the colonial and foreign ministries, sometimes—but by no means always—the colonial and foreign ministers themselves. Most of these policy-makers were associated in some way with the colonialist movement. Those officials at the colonial ministry with the greatest influence on African expansion during the 1890s were either members or supporters of the *Comité de l'Afrique Française*.[40] One of the key members of the small Moroccan pressure group which founded the *Comité du Maroc* in 1904 was Delcassé's chief adviser on Moroccan affairs, Paul Révoil. During the First World War all those officials at the Quai d'Orsay responsible for the formulation of Middle Eastern policy were members of the *Comité de l'Asie Française*.[41]

[39] *Ibid.*, p. 1103.

[40] Haussmann, Archinard, and Binger were members during the 1890s; Lagarde and Roume were elected later; J-L Deloncle, though never formally a member of the *Comité*, was closely associated with it (see the correspondence between Deloncle and Alis in Bibliothèque de l'Institut de France, Terrier MS 5891).

[41] Berthelot, de Caix, François Georges-Picot, Gout, and de Margerie. Divergences of view inevitably occurred between those colonialists within the Quai

Most of the leading generals and proconsuls at the outposts of Empire also belonged to the colonialist movement.[42] Their support, especially on the Algerian–Moroccan border, gave the colonialists in Paris a further means of leverage on government policy. Though the handful of diplomats concerned with Moroccan policy during the decade before the French protectorate were converts to the cause of a French Morocco,[43] Etienne and his lieutenants were frequently unhappy with the pace of French advance. Their links with the generals in Algeria gave them the means from time to time to force the pace. From its foundation in 1904, the *Comité du Maroc* secretly supplied General Lyautey, the French commander on the Moroccan border, with funds to assist by bribery the 'discreet penetration' of Morocco which he pursued in defiance of his orders from Paris.[44] General Toutée, who succeeded to Lyautey's command in December 1910 (and was, like Lyautey, a member of the *Comité de l'Afrique Française*) was even readier than his predecessor to force the pace of French penetration.[45] The climax to the collusion between the colonialist leadership and the Algerian generals was the scheme for an expedition to Fez with the ostensible purpose of providing temporary protection for French nationals but with the real aim of precipitating a French protectorate in Morocco.[46] That expedition, approved by a rump cabinet in April 1911, marked a

---

d'Orsay, who had to take daily account of the constraints imposed by the international situation, and the colonialists outside, who did not. But there remained a general identity of aims between them.

[42] Archinard, Brazza, Doumer, Galliéni, Gouraud, Jonnart, Lanessan, Lyautey, René Millet, Révoil and Roume belonged to an average of seven colonialist societies each.

[43] During Pichon's five-year term as foreign minister (1906–11) only six diplomats (Billy, Jules Cambon, Guiot, Marcilly, Regnault and Saint-Aulaire) had any significant influence on the formulation of Moroccan policy. J-C Allain, 'Joseph Caillaux et la seconde crise marocaine', unpublished dissertation (Paris, 1974), pp. 1767 ff.

[44] Andrew and Kanya-Forstner, 'The French "Colonial Party"' . . . 1885–1914', p. 116.

[45] Allain, 'Joseph Caillaux', p. 1676. Allain does not, however, discuss Toutée's longstanding links with the leaders of the *parti colonial*. These links dated back at least to 1894 when the *Comité de l'Afrique Française* had financed Toutée's expedition in West Africa; Toutée to Terrier, 25 September 1895, Bibliothèque de l'Institut de France, Terrier MS 5908.

[46] The details of this collusion were, unsurprisingly, not committed to paper. But that there was collusion seems clear from a number of sources. De Caix (joint secretary-general of the *Comité du Maroc* and secretary-general of the *Comité de l'Asie Française*) wrote to Terrier (joint secretary-general of the *Comité du Maroc* and secretary-general of the *Comité de l'Afrique Française*) on 23 January 1911: 'Samedi 21 déjeuner Etienne. Toutée a exposé son programme . . .' (Bibliothèque de l'Institut de France, Terrier MS 5896).

decisive victory for Etienne and his lieutenants over the more cautious policies of the Quai d'Orsay.[47] Within the cabinet, the leaders of the *parti colonial* could usually count on the sympathy, if not the active support, of the foreign minister. Delcassé and Pichon, who together occupied the Quai d'Orsay for eighteen years, were prominent members of the colonialist movement. Though both as foreign ministers had policy differences with Etienne, both also shared Etienne's main objectives. Before the First World War Delcassé and Pichon were convinced supporters of a French Morocco; during the War and Peace Conference Pichon was a committed advocate of a French Empire in the Middle East. Hanotaux, the only other foreign minister during the final phase of French expansion to serve for as long as four years, was won over to the Fashoda strategy while at the Quai d'Orsay, and became thereafter an active member of the *parti colonial*.[48]

Colonial ministers, though more transient than foreign ministers, were even more dependable supporters of the colonialist cause. Because of the lack of prestige attaching to their ministries, colonial ministers tended to fall into one of two categories. Either they were committed colonialists who, unlike most of their contemporaries, actually wanted to be minister of colonies. Or they were men who had not wanted to be colonial ministers at all, whose startling ignorance of colonial affairs often made them equally susceptible to colonialist pressure. When Emile Chautemps became minister in 1895, for example, he is said to have confused Gabon with the Sudan and Gibraltar with Madagascar.[49] Yet the colonialists inside and outside his ministry quickly converted him to the Fashoda strategy.[50]

[47] During his final months in office Pichon was increasingly fearful of colonialist schemes to precipitate a French protectorate. He wrote to Jules Cambon, his ambassador in Berlin, in January 1911: 'Je trouve notre situation au Maroc aussi bonne que possible. Ne donnons pas aux militaires et au parti colonial trop de prétextes à tronquer le mouvement et à nous lancer dans des aventures'. (I am grateful for this information to Mr David Miller, at present preparing a thesis on Pichon.) Jules Cambon was equally concerned by 'la politique des déjeuners' being hatched by Etienne and the Algerian generals; *Documents Diplomatiques Français*, 2e série, XIII, no. 248. *Cf.* Andrew and Kanya-Forstner, 'The French "Colonial Party" ' . . . 1885–1914', pp. 122–24.

[48] On Delcassé's relations with the *parti colonial*, see Andrew, *Théophile Delcassé*; Pichon was president of the *Comité de l'Orient* 1911–12 and a member of seven other colonialist groups; Hanotaux was elected to the *Comité de l'Afrique Française* in 1902 and to the *Comité de l'Asie Française* in 1914, as well as belonging to several less important organizations.

[49] *Politique Coloniale*, 22 June 1895, citing comments on Chautemps in much of the Paris press.

[50] Andrew and Kanya-Forstner, 'Fashoda Strategy', pp. 69–70.

Clémenceau's two ministers of colonies provide striking examples of the same genre. It was widely believed that Milliès-Lacroix, colonial minister in Clémenceau's first government (1906–09), had been deliberately chosen by Clémenceau to indicate his disdain for colonial affairs. Soon after taking office, Milliès-Lacroix threatened to dismiss his chef de cabinet for failing to inform him of a revolt in a French colony. When asked which colony he had in mind, the minister replied, 'Haiti': only to be informed that Haiti had ceased to be part of the French Empire a century before.[51] For all his ignorance, however, Milliès-Lacroix was quick to assure the colonialists of his devotion to their cause. 'Soyez persuadés, Messieurs', he told a colonialist banquet soon after taking office, 'que je saurai suivre les conseils de mon éminent ami, Monsieur Etienne'.[52] Henry Simon, minister of colonies in Clémenceau's second government, provides an even more astonishing example of deference to the *parti colonial*. In February 1918 the cabinet made him chairman of a commission to draw up France's colonial war aims. At the first meeting of the commission, however, Simon modestly told its members that they knew far more about colonial questions than he did, and took no further part in its discussions. Instead the commission elected as joint vice-presidents (and effective presidents) the two leading colonialists in the Chamber and the Senate, Etienne and Doumergue. The commission became in effect a colonialist pressure group. Its war aims, once decided, became the war aims of the French Government.[53]

As the history of the commission suggests, the main way in which the structure of French government played into the hands of the colonialists, was by its abdication of cabinet control for foreign and colonial policy. During the era of colonial expansion the transient governments of the Third Republic had no tradition of collective cabinet responsibility for colonial policy. Some prime ministers were reluctant to discuss even European policy in cabinet at all. Emile Combes (prime minister, 1902–05) was accustomed to remark on the rare occasions when a minister referred to foreign affairs, 'Laissons cela, Messieurs, c'est l'affaire du Président de la République et du ministre des affaires étrangères'. [54] Few cabinet ministers before the First World War ever discovered the terms of the alliance

51 O. Homberg, *Les coulisses de l'histoire: souvenirs 1898–1928* (Paris, 1938), p. 94; A. Messimy, *Mes souvenirs* (Paris, 1937), p. 39.
52 *Bulletin du Comité de l'Afrique Française*, November 1906.
53 Andrew and Kanya-Forstner, 'War Aims', pp. 96–100. Simon, like Chautemps, Milliès-Lacroix and others of his predecessors, left the colonial ministry a committed colonialist. In 1924 he became president of the *groupe colonial* in the Chamber of Deputies.
54 J. Caillaux, *Mes mémoires*, I (Paris, 1942), p. 221.

with Russia which was the cornerstone of French foreign policy. Indeed even the existence of the treaty was not admitted to parliament until it was eighteen months old.

Each of the three great turning points in the final phase of European expansion which most concerned both France and England—the Fashoda crisis of 1898, the Entente Cordiale of 1904, and the Sykes-Picot agreement of 1916—points the contrast between the dominance of the official mind in Britain and of the unofficial mind in France. The policy agreed by the British cabinet during the Fashoda crisis in 1898 was the logical conclusion to an old policy of imperial defence. There was no such logic behind the development of French government policy on the Upper Nile. The Fashoda strategy to force the British out of Egypt emerged not from the French government or even from the foreign ministry, but from the *Comité de l'Afrique Française*. The first unsuccessful attempt by Delcassé to send an expedition to Fashoda in 1893 was made without the knowledge of the cabinet. Delcassé relied instead on the support of the *Comité de l'Afrique Française* and a sympathetic President. The foreign minister, Develle, learned of the expedition from the newspapers. The Marchand expedition was approved in 1896 by a cabinet under pressure from the *parti colonial* which gave little heed to the consequences of its decision. Once Marchand had left, the cabinet did not discuss the expedition again until it found itself two years later, as a consequence of Marchand's arrival, on the brink of war with England. President Faure's final comment in his diary on the Fashoda strategy seems in retrospect a fair one: 'Nous avons été comme des fous en Afrique, entraînés par des gens irresponsables qu'on appelle les coloniaux'. The real irresponsibility, however, belonged not to the colonialists but to the cabinet which capitulated to them.[55]

The French cabinet's part in the negotiation of the Entente Cordiale was scarcely more impressive. In England, approval of the Entente was in every sense a collective decision by the cabinet as a whole. As soon as negotiations with France began in July 1903, Lansdowne asked for the views of other government departments. Throughout the course of negotiations the cabinet was regularly consulted and its approval sought. In France, however, the cabinet did not discover the outline of the proposed agreement until negotiations had been in progress for six months. While Lansdowne referred throughout the negotiations to the views of the British cabinet, the French ambassador referred simply to the views of

[55] Andrew and Kanya-Forstner, 'The French "Colonial Party" ... 1885–1914', pp. 111–13; *idem*, 'Fashoda Strategy'.

TRANS. 5TH S.—VOL. 26—F*

'Monsieur Delcassé'. And the bargain which formed the basis of the Entente—the barter of Egypt for Morocco—was urged on Delcassé not by his colleagues in the cabinet, but by Eugène Etienne and the leaders of the *parti colonial*.[56]

The same contrast in French and British methods was evident throughout the negotiation of the Sykes-Picot agreement on the Middle East in the winter of 1915–16. The British team of negotiators originally consisted of representatives of the Foreign Office, the War Office and the India Office. The French team from the outset was a single diplomat, François Georges-Picot. Even when Sir Mark Sykes was appointed to negotiate alone with Picot, the progress of the negotiations was continuously monitored by the British cabinet. But Briand, the French prime minister, did not outline the proposed partition of the Middle East to his cabinet until Sykes and Picot had already initialed their agreement, and he did so then with what President Poincaré described in his diary as 'une spirituelle imprécision'. Picot himself has come down to posterity as a curiously anonymous figure. He appears with unfailing regularity in both scholarly monographs on the Middle East and outline histories of the twentieth century, but is never identified except as a member of the French diplomatic corps. He was, in fact, a prominent member of a famous colonialist dynasty. His father was one of the founders of the *Comité de l'Afrique Française*; his elder brother, Charles, was treasurer of the *Comité de l'Asie Française*, of which François was also a member. The Middle Eastern Empire which Picot set out to obtain represented the aspirations not of the government but of the *Comité de l'Asie Française* and its sympathizers within the Quai d'Orsay. Picot was told to draft his own instructions which were then signed without amendment by Briand, whose mind was fixed on Salonika and the Western Front. Throughout the negotiations, as he himself acknowledged, Picot was allowed virtually a free hand.[57] At the Paris Peace Conference the secretary-general of the *Comité de l'Asie Française*, Robert de Caix, drafted into the Quai d'Orsay during the war, emerged as the main influence on the formulation of French policy in the Middle East. In October 1919 he was appointed secretary-general of the new French High Commis-

56 Andrew, *Théophile Delcassé*. Etienne later gained Pichon's support for a scheme to gain German consent for a French Morocco in return for French participation in the Baghdad railway. With Pichon's approval, Etienne put this proposition to the Kaiser in 1907, but without success. Memorandum by Goût, 24 June 1907, Archives du Ministère des Affaires Etrangères, Goût MS 9.

57 Andrew and Kanya-Forstner, 'War Aims', pp. 81–86; Picot to Defrance, 24 December 1915, 17 March 1916, Archives du Ministère des Affaires Etrangères, Defrance MS 2.

sion in Syria.[58] The High Commissioner himself, General Gouraud, better known but less influential than de Caix, was also a prominent member of the *Comité de l'Asie Française.*

During the First World War the *parti colonial* thus succeeded to a remarkable degree in dictating government policy. It also believed itself for the first time within sight of its other great objective, the conquest of public opinion. 'Du parti colonial', Etienne had written in 1912, 'nous voulons faire la France coloniale'.[59] At the end of the Great War the French Empire appeared genuinely popular for the first time in its history. The colonies had provided almost a million soldiers and factory workers whose contribution had been more and more appreciated as the metropolitan armies became ever more exhausted. The bitter German complaints against the use of black troops, on the Western Front during the war, in the Rhineland after the war, made those troops more popular still.[60]

Even more important than the Empire's actual contribution to victory, however, was its potential contribution to post-war recovery. The colonies, claimed Etienne, would become 'la pierre angulaire de notre renaissance économique'.[61] Colonialists insisted that as well as being a reservoir of men, the Empire was also a reservoir of raw materials which would free France from dependence on foreign suppliers. That these resources had still to be exploited was blamed on scandalous neglect by government and business. Colonialists made great play with the 'oeuvre impie' of pre-war investors who had invested three times as much in Russia as in the whole French Empire, only to lose their life savings to the Bolsheviks.[62]

Once again, as after the Franco-Prussian War, so after the First World War, colonialists saw the Empire essentially in metropolitan terms, as the key to *metropolitan* recovery. Initially at least, the colonialist campaign for the *mise en valeur* of the Empire as the road to national prosperity attracted a good deal of support. The *groupe colonial* in the Chamber of Deputies, with the support of almost a

[58] De Caix's role in the peace negotiations will be studied in detail in a monograph on French Colonial War Aims 1914–20 in preparation by myself and Professor Kanya-Forstner.

[59] *Dépêche Coloniale*, 4 April 1912.

[60] On the origins of the idea of the Empire as a reservoir of soldiers see M. Michel, 'Un mythe: la force noire avant 1914', *Relations Internationales*, I (1974).

[61] Preface by Etienne to M. Rondet-Saint, *Dans notre Empire jaune* (Paris, 1917), p. v.

[62] Candace, vice-president of the post-war *groupe colonial*, spoke for many other colonialists: 'J'ai montré quelle oeuvre mauvaise, quelle oeuvre impie avaient faite les grands établissements de crédit contre l'intérêt supérieur de la France . . . Au lieu de drainer pour l'étranger notre épargne, ils auraient dû depuis longtemps orienter cette épargne vers nos colonies'. *Journal Officiel, Debats Parlementaires, Chambre*, 29 June 1920.

third of the deputies elected in 1919, became both larger than ever before and the largest group in parliament. Many deputies who joined the group had, however, only the vaguest idea of the colonial resources they were so anxious to exploit. Désiré Bouteille, the self styled 'député des agriculteurs', replied disarmingly to a questionnaire on the *mise en valeur* from the *Dépêche Coloniale*: 'Votre expérience des affaires coloniales est supérieure à celle de beaucoup des membres du groupe, qui n'ont qu'un désir et ne poursuivent qu'un but: mettre en valeur notre admirable domaine colonial, éviter ainsi des achats si onéreux à l'étranger'. For most deputies, as for most Frenchmen, the *mise en valeur* of an Empire of whose resources they knew little was, like reparations, a way of taking refuge from the appalling economic realities of post-war France.[63]

And the *mise en valeur* of the Empire proved almost as illusory as reparations. In some cases the vast imperial resources on which colonialists pinned their hopes did not exist.[64] In others these resources did exist but required vast amounts of capital to develop, capital which was usually not forthcoming. The *parti colonial* found it far easier to commit the French government to a huge extension of the Empire before and during the Great War than to the development of that Empire, once acquired. By the mid-1920s French opinion was almost as indifferent to the Empire as before the war. 'L'opinion', said Albert Lebrun in 1927, 'ne consent guère à s'intéresser aux colonies que lorsqu'il s'y mêle quelque apparence de scandale'.[65] The largest colonialist organization during the interwar years, the *Ligue Maritime et Coloniale*, increasingly despaired of French adults and concentrated its propaganda in the schools with slogans such as 'Jeunes gens, faites adhérer vos parents'.[66]

For a return to popular favour the Empire had to await the return of war. On the eve of the Second World War the French people once again began to attach the same importance to the Empire as after the First. The sudden change in public attitudes is clearly shown in the first opinion polls privately conducted by the *Institut*

[63] *Dépêche Coloniale*, 26 February 1920; Andrew and Kanya-Forstner, 'The *groupe colonial*', pp. 843-44.

[64] One example is provided by the banner headlines in *Dépêche Coloniale*, 8 October 1924: 'Une découverte sensationnelle. L'invention du pétrole synthétique rendra à la France, grâce à ses colonies, son indépendance économique'.

[65] A. Lebrun, 'Nos colonies au travail', *L'Afrique Française*, November 1927.

[66] 'En dépit des efforts intensifs faits depuis tant d'années et de tant de côtés pour donner aux Français une opinion maritime et coloniale, on est à chaque instant péniblement impressionné de la somme d'ignorance à laquelle on se heurte même dans les milieux les plus cultivés touchant ces matières'; *Mer et Colonies* (the official journal of the *Ligue Maritime et Coloniale*), December 1931. Although the Ligue then claimed a membership of 700,000, almost all were schoolchildren.

Français de l'Opinion Publique after its foundation in 1938. In October 1938, at the moment of Munich, *IFOP* asked the question: 'Pensez-vous qu'il faut donner des colonies à l'Allemagne?'. 59% said yes, only 33% said no. Four months later, in February 1939, only 28% said yes, and 67% said no.[67]

Once again, the *parti colonial* declared that the Empire would make good the weakness of the metropolis. Just as faith in the resources of the Empire had earlier been a refuge from the economic weakness of post-war France, so the manpower of the Empire was now used to disguise France's chronic military inferiority to Germany. Greater Germany in 1939 had a population of over 80 million, twice the size of France. But, insisted the colonialists, the population of Greater France was actually greater than that of Greater Germany. 'La plus grande France'—that is France and her Empire—had 110 million people. The Third Republic's two wartime prime ministers, Daladier and Reynaud, eagerly seized on the *parti colonial's* propaganda. Both adopted the colonialist slogan, 'La France de 110 millions d'habitants fait face à l'Allemagne'. And both insisted too that the resources of Greater France were greater even than those of Greater Germany: 'Elles sont infinies, ces ressources de l'Empire'. Georges Mandel, once an anti-colonialist, now minister of colonies, boasted that the Empire would provide two million soldiers and 500,000 factory workers. Imperial France would conquer continental Germany.[68] That myth was brutally destroyed in the six week blitzkrieg of 1940.

For the small number of its enthusiasts and for the larger number of Frenchmen who took an occasional interest in it, the Empire thus fulfilled throughout the Third Republic a largely mythical function. France's possessions *outside* Europe were to compensate for her weakness *inside* Europe. After the Franco-Prussian War colonial expansion was in some mysterious way to make France, in Gambetta's words, 'a great power once again'; after the First World War colonial development became a road to economic recovery almost as illusory as reparations; at the beginning of the Second World War the Empire was to make France a match for Germany. Yet the undoubted decline of France during the Third Republic was due to a failure to develop not the Empire but her own resources. In

---

[67] P. Henry, 'L'opinion publique française et le problème colonial', *Sondages*, August 1939 (duplicated copy in the Bibliothèque Nationale, 40Jo 924). The questions asked in October 1938 and February 1939, though not identical, were, in Henry's view, sufficiently similar to allow 'une comparaison exacte'.

[68] *France Outre-Mer*, 29 September 1939; 'Main d'oeuvre colonial', Archives Nationales (Section Outre-Mer), Affaires Politiques 853; J. M. Sherwood, *Georges Mandel and the Third Republic* (Stanford, 1971), pp. 217–21.

1870 France had been a match for Germany if not in military skill at least in numbers of men and in the size of her economic production. During the next seventy years Germany's population grew rapidly while France's hardly grew at all. Germany's national income increased five-fold while France's failed to double. No colonial empire could make good that gap in continental power.[69]

[69] This paper is based on research conducted jointly with Professor A. S. Kanga-Forstner, directed towards a history of the French colonialist movement.

Corpus Christi College, Cambridge.

COLONIES—
AN ATTEMPT AT A TYPOLOGY*

By Professor M. I. Finley, Litt.D., F.B.A., F.R.Hist.S.

READ AT THE SOCIETY'S CONFERENCE
19 SEPTEMBER 1975

I

IN her recently published diary of her first visit to Africa, in 1929, Margery Perham reported a conversation with seven degree-course men at the newly established college at Fort Hare. When, inevitably, talk got round to conditions in South Africa, they asked 'terrible questions'. 'Can England do *nothing* then?' 'But South Africa is the possession of England.' 'But the *King*! He is King of South Africa. What does he think? Will *he* do nothing?'[1]

One cannot resist a smile at such a simpleminded view of 'possession'. The seven young men fresh from the bush were of course not wrong to use the word and to link it with the king. They were constitutionally correct, at least: the Interpretation Act of 1889, for example, defined 'British possession' as 'any part of Her Majesty's dominions exclusive of the United Kingdom. . . .'[2] Along with 'possession', it is to be noticed, there is a second, etymologically even stronger term of property, 'dominion'. Both, furthermore, are interchangeable with 'colony' in constitutional documents. Two acts of Parliament a quarter of a century apart will serve to exemplify: the Colonial Laws Validity Act of 1865 defined a 'colony' for purposes of that act as 'all of Her Majesty's Possessions abroad in which there shall exist a legislature' (with exceptions irrelevant in my context), replaced in the Interpretation Act by 'dominions exclusive of the British Isles'.[3]

The mistake Miss Perham's interlocutors made was to take a metaphor literally, and so we smile. But is it so self-evident that 'possessions' and 'dominions' were always just metaphors? And why these particular words? Metaphors do not arise arbitrarily or capriciously. I go further. I am confident, though I cannot demonstrate,

---

* This is a slightly longer version of the paper read at the Conference. I am grateful to John Dunn for his advice and patient criticism.

[1] M. Perham, *African Apprenticeship* (London, 1974), p. 50.

[2] 52 & 53 Vict., c. 63, sect. 18 (2).

[3] 28 & 29 Vict., c. 63, sect. 1, and 52 & 53 Vict., c. 63, sect. 18 (3), respectively.

that the property connotation was never far from men's minds, at home and abroad, virtually until our own day. Seeley's jeremiad on the word 'possession'—'the expression almost seems to imply slavery'[4]—though housed in his chapter on the 'old colonial system', was obviously directed to public opinion at the time he was lecturing, in 1881 and 1882. I cannot *demonstrate* the property-tone, however, because, to my knowledge, the semantics of colonial terminology have not been systematically investigated (unlike 'empire' and its cognates), a situation which I find astonishing.

Only the administrative semantics are fairly clear—some of the time. Administrators have to draw distinctions in more complex governmental situations. The classical Greeks, for example, differentiated an *apoikia* from a *klērouchia*, the Romans of the Republic a Latin *colonia* from a Roman *colonia*, according to whether the migrants did or did not retain citizenship in the mother-city. That was a neat and meaningful dichotomy, more so than the Victorian one based on whether or not a foreign possession had its own legislature. Since Victorian times there has been a riot of terminology and administrative distinction, to the point that Lord Hailey dismissed all the 'labels' in the British Empire as 'immaterial'.[5] When the Colonial Office List of 1946 carries thirty-six main headings, which do not include all the colonies but do include protectorates and trust territories inhabited by more people than lived in the colonies,[6] the historian (and sociologist) had best abandon the lot and establish his own classification.

For the present I shall assume, without trying to defend, that there is value in a typology. That requires converting 'colony' into a technical term (irrespective of administrative usage), which it is not in ordinary speech. There the latitude is boundless. One honourable member rose in the Commons debate over the Corn Laws to argue that free trade was the principle by which 'foreign nations would become valuable Colonies to us, without imposing on us the responsibility of governing them'.[7] No one misunderstood him, any more than we misunderstand when we read that 'colonial territories' occupied about one third of the earth's surface at the end of the Second World War. We understand—most of the time—'decolonization', 'semi-colonial countries' and the rest, though the shifts in

[4] J. R. Seeley, *The Expansion of England*, ed. John Gross (Chicago and London, 1971), p. 55.
[5] Lord Hailey, *An African Survey*, rev. 1956 (London and New York, 1957), p. 146.
[6] See Martin Wight, *British Colonial Constitutions 1947* (Oxford, 1952), pp. 1–5.
[7] Quoted from B. Semmel, *The Rise of Free Trade Imperialism* (Cambridge, 1970), p. 8.

meaning that are implied may be considerable and are not always uncontroversial.

When I now suggest the need for converting 'colony' into a technical term, I am not embarking on the absurd enterprise of trying to change the world's speech habits, or even my own. I shall continue to speak of 'semi-colonial countries' and 'decolonization' when the context supplies the necessary shading; I do not mind such metaphors as the 'English colony in Florence' or the 'German colony in Milwaukee', any more than I mind a 'nudist colony' or a 'colony of bees'. What I am seeking, however, is a way to overcome some of the difficulties and errors in which historians have embroiled themselves by their retention of loose usage in many complicated contexts—historians of ancient Greece, of the twentieth century, and of any and all the centuries in between. Twenty-five years ago two American historians, Merril Jensen and Robert L. Reynolds, published a plea (their word) for comparative study of the 'European colonial experience'.[8] If they have gone largely unheeded, it must be said that their approach was not very encouraging: their stress was on the 'unbroken' 'continuity of European experience in organizing colonial societies' for a thousand years, and their proposed categories of analysis are too incoherent and shifting. Yet a start had been made on the continent in the nineteenth century, not by historians but by economists, lawyers and publicists, in Germany and especially in France. The language of the latter—*comptoirs* or *colonies de commerce, colonies d'exploitation, colonies de plantation, colonies de peuplement*—has found some echo among continental historians, but only as language.[9]

These men required a typology because they were closely involved with policymaking—they were almost all vigorous advocates of colonial expansion—and with the government, and therefore drew

[8] 'European Colonial Experience. A Plea for Comparative Studies', in *Studi in onore di Gino Luzzatto*, iv (Milan, 1950), pp. 75–90.

[9] As an illustration, note how Robert Lopez unnecessarily explains why the medieval Genoese *comptoires* in the Levant could not have become 'colonie di popolamento': *Storia delle colonie genovesi* (Bologna, 1938), p. 457. The two most important works I have in mind are W. Roscher, *Kolonien, Kolonialpolitik und Auswanderung*, originally published in 1848 and much enlarged in a 3rd edn, with K. Jannasch (Leipzig, 1885), by the addition of a new section, 'Deutsche Aufgaben in der Gegenwart'; and Paul Leroy-Beaulieu, *De la colonisation chez les peuples modèrnes* (1874; 3rd edn, Paris, 1886). In view of the repute of R. Maunier, *Sociologie coloniale* (2 vols, Paris, 1932–36), it is worth noting that among the many remarkable things to be found there is the claim that the only attempt before his own to 'define colonization systematically' is Georges Hardy, 'Colonisation', *Revue de synthèse*, i (1931), pp. 61–80. Hardy's sole concern was the French policy of colonization after the Restoration, and his article consists largely of long quotations from the *Grand Larousse*, Leroy-Beaulieu, Girault and others.

distinctions in order to recommend one policy and reject another. It is symbolic that the abridged sixth edition of the popular manual by Arthur Girault was published in Paris by the well-known law publisher Sirey in 1943 and prepared by Maurice Besson, sous-directeur in the Ministère des Colonies and directeur of the Agence Economique des Colonies Françaises.[10] The fact that historians are not normally enmeshed in policy-making does not seem sufficient ground for abdicating the role of analyst. In what follows, I shall argue that it is important to retain the narrower sense of 'colony' which prevailed until it became, in the late nineteenth century, a loosely used synonym for the genus 'dependency' rather than a species of the genus. I hold, in other words, that for most of its history the term had its own specific denotation which the historian, at least, needs to hold on to conceptually, whatever his linguistic habits, a denotation encompassing specific, intrinsic elements that can be enumerated and examined over a range wide enough to take in, say, ancient Bologna or Narbonne and modern Australia or Mozambique.

II

My starting-point is yet another, once common English synonym for 'colony', namely, 'plantation'. Today the dominant sense of 'plantation' is that of a large estate, often with monoculture and usually located in tropical or semi-tropical regions—cotton plantation, sugar plantation, tea plantation. That is the etymologically strict sense. But from at least the sixteenth century into the nineteenth, in English the word 'plantation' took a turn that was very rare in ancient and medieval Latin and effectively unknown in modern Romance languages: people, not crops, were the objects of the 'planting' and the 'transplanting'.[11] That is the theme of Francis Bacon's thirty-second essay, entitled 'Of Plantations'; it is the meaning of the term in the act of the Privy Council of 1 December 1660

[10] The 'title' is worth reproducing in full: *Principes de colonisation et de législation coloniale. Les Colonies françaises avant et depuis 1815. Notions historiques, administratives, juridiques, économiques et financières.* The first edn appeared in 1895; the 5th (1926–29) required five vols.

[11] Thus, I could find only 'colonie', never 'plantation', in this sense in the documents, beginning as early as 1635, quoted in Emilien Petit, *Droit public ou Gouvernment des colonies françaises* (1771; ed. A. Girault, Paris, 1911); or in V. P. Malouet, *Collection de mémoires et correspondances officielles sur l'administration des colonies* (5 vols, Paris, 1802), whereas the latter occasionally uses 'plantation' in the tropical sense' *e.g.* 'plantatiou de café' (i, 71). Among modern French writers, 'colonie de plantation' or 'système de plantation' is of course restricted to the latter type; see *e.g.* Leroy-Beaulieu, *Colonisation*, p. 155; H. Brunschwig, *Mythes et réalités de l'impérialisme colonial français 1871–1914* (Paris, 1960), pp. 1–2.

establishing a Council for Foreign Plantations, a document in which 'dominions' and 'colonies' both occur as synonyms for 'plantations';[12] it is the language of the bitter seventeenth-century controversies over the settlements and resettlements in Ireland.[13] Late in the next century, Burke's speech on American taxation, 19 April 1774, was directed against the Act 'for granting certain duties in the British colonies and plantations in America' (in which 'dominions' again appears as another synonym). The following year, his resolution for reconciliation began with these words, 'That the colonies and plantations of Great Britain in North America, consisting of fourteen separate governments. . . .' The year after that, Adam Smith, in the opening pages of his chapter 'On Colonies', wrote: 'The Latin word (*Colonia*) signifies simply a plantation'—a definition naturally not now to be found in the *Oxford Latin Dictionary*.

I need not go on: the available documentation is infinite, showing that, for more than three hundred years, however much disagreement there may have been about the objectives of colonization or about the ways of governing colonies, there was complete agreement that a colony was a plantation of men, a place to which men emigrated and settled. *Colon* in French, *Siedler* in German, make the same point. That qualification effectively rules out British India, which needs no discussion, but, in my view, it also rules out the so-called Genoese colonies in the Middle Ages, and it implies that the late nineteenth-century struggle for Africa was largely not a struggle for colonies. We shall return to both Genoa and Africa a bit later.

There was also, in those three hundred years, complete agreement that a colony was not only a plantation but also a dependency of the country from which the emigration was initiated.[14] But now there is a tendency, among historians at least, to equate 'colonization' with any 'emigration', which I believe to be as objectionable as the equation, colony = any dependency. As with the latter, there are contexts in which 'colony = any emigration' may not be objectionable. When Edward Gibbon Wakefield wrote explicitly in 1833 that he would use the term 'colony' to express 'the idea of a society at once immigrating and emigrating, such as the United States of America and the English settlements in Canada, South Africa and

[12] See G. L. Beer, *The Old Colonial System* (2 vols, 1913; repr. Gloucester, Mass., 1958), i, 231–34.

[13] See *e.g.* T. W. Moody, *The Londonderry Plantation 1609–41* (Belfast, 1939); T. C. Barnard 'Planters and Policies in Cromwellian Ireland', *Past and Present*, no. 61 (1973), pp. 31–69.

[14] The participation of migrants from other countries is a complication which I cannot discuss, except for a brief mention below.

Australia',[15] he was advocating a policy designed to deal with what he saw to be overpopulation and difficulties in capitalist production in England. He was writing as a political economist, not as a historian,[16] and he was consciously twisting the word 'colony' into a new sense. He was, in fact, in the mainstream of the debate over free trade imperialism, the context which made it reasonable, as it could not have been earlier, for the M.P. I have already quoted to say, even metaphorically, that 'foreign nations would become valuable Colonies to us'.

That need give us no trouble, though it troubled Seeley, curiously, and I cannot resist quoting him on the subject. 'There would be no question at all about the value of colonies,' he wrote, '. . . if it were not for the existence of the United States. But the United States are to us almost as good as a colony; our people can emigrate thither without sacrificing their language or chief institutions or habits. . . . In estimating the value of colonies in the abstract, we shall only confuse ourselves by recollecting this unique case; we ought to put the United States entirely out of view.[17] I do not understand why Seeley floundered so badly, even granted his excessive confidence in the powers of kith and kin and his lack of sophistication in both demography and political economy. Certainly his French contemporaries and counterparts, Leroy-Beaulieu for example, would have known how to dismiss the United States alternative more brutally and more effectively than 'we shall only confuse ourselves by recollecting this unique case'.

There are greater sources of confusion, to which I now turn. Koebner's famous opening chapter of the *Cambridge Economic History of Europe* is entitled 'The Settlement and Colonization of Europe', and throughout he uses the two words, 'settlement' and 'colonization', as synonyms. The only justification I can find in the chapter consists of a short phrase at the end of the second page: 'The use which Roman rule and Roman or Romanized society made of the provinces *implied colonization in the strict economic sense of the term*' (my italics). Koebner does not say what the 'strict economic sense' of the term is, and I am compelled to believe that by 'economic' he means 'etymological': every writer on the subject since the sixteenth

[15] *England and America* (2 vols, London, 1833), ii, 74 (from the 200-page 'note' entitled 'The Art of Colonization'). It is perhaps worth reporting that the 'plantation' synonym for 'colony' was still a current term for Wakefield: 'In the case of every plantation in North America, whether English, French, or Dutch, the settlers had to contend. . . .': *Letter from Sydney* (Everyman's Library edn, London, 1929), p. 36.

[16] On Wakefield's place in the economic debates of the time, see Semmel, *Free Trade Imperialism*, and Donald Winch, *Classical Political Economy and Colonies* (London, 1965), both via the index.   [17] *Expansion of England*, p. 50.

century knew, and most said, that the Latin word *colonia* stems from the verb *colere*, to cultivate, to farm. For a more recent, more extreme and explicit deployment of that linguistic fact I refer to Herbert Lüthy's monograph-long essay, 'Die Epoche der Kolonisation', which begins by noting that 'culture' and 'colonization' have the same etymology and then proceeds, not to write about colonization as promised in the title, but to offer a 'philosophical' *Kulturgeschichte* differentiating Oriental society from Western, and so on.[18] This may be a caricature, but the basic fallacy of etymological arguments remains in more sober treatments. What the Romans meant by *colonia* has no binding force on later ages, but it is perhaps worth noting nonetheless, first, that the *colere*-root conceals the military aspect of Roman *coloniae*; second, that from the beginning of the Empire, *colonia* lost its Republican meaning and became something not only different but etymologically unrelated, namely, the highest status to which a *civitas* could aspire in the municipal administrative structure of the empire, regardless of its origin and early history.

Man's conquest of the earth's surface is a most important theme. Colonization is a part of it, not the whole of it. It is not unrevealing that Koebner writes 'colonization' and 'colonist' on every page, but not 'colony'. There can be no colonization without colonies. I therefore rule out all manifestations of what is often called 'internal colonization'. No one speaks of the colonization of the midwest and west of the United States, and I am unable to find any more justification for that term when it is applied to settlements within the Roman empire or within Charlemagne's empire, or to enforced transplantations by tyrants or conquerors.

The proposition that a colony must be a dependency also rules out all migrations to foreign territory in which from the outset the migrants established independent communities or converted existing organizations into independent states. It is irrelevant whether there was conquest or peaceful settlement by agreement: an early legal distinction in this country between ceded and conquered territories was abandoned because the two overlapped much of the time.[19] More recent attempts to retain the distinction have to rely on such trivialities as Reunion Island, Tahiti or the purchase of Manhattan from the Red Indians.[20] The so-called Greek and

[18] 'Die Epoche der Kolonisation und die Erschliessung der Erde: Versuch einer Interpretation des europäischen Zeitalters', in his *In Gegenwart der Geschichte* (Köln and Berlin, 1967), pp. 179–270.
[19] See Wight, *Colonial Constitutions*, p. 5.
[20] That is the mouse produced by Maunier, *Sociologie coloniale*, in his thunderous assault in the opening chapter on the 'conventional conception' that 'colonization is only one form of conquest', against which, he says, it is 'a contact of peoples'.

Phoenician colonies of the eighth, seventh and sixth centuries B.C., extending from the coasts of the Black Sea to Marseilles and Carthage, were more peaceful enterprises in some instances, less in others, but what is essential is that they were all, from the start, independent city-states, not colonies (apart from a small number of unimportant exceptions). The extensive Macedonian and Greek migration into the territories of the Persian empire conquered by Alexander the Great, which led to the establishment a generation after his death of the Hellenistic kingdoms of Egypt, Syria and the rest, was not a colonizing movement. Neither were the barbarian invasions of the Roman empire, nor the Normans in England and Sicily.

These are the easy cases, and one may wonder why I am insistent on the labels. There are two reasons. The first comes under the heading of abatement of a nuisance, perhaps most understandable to an ancient historian. The nuisance is word magic: words unavoidably carry their semantic clusters with them, and, once a settlement is labelled a colony, that word's cluster becomes attached. Anyone familiar with the literature about the early Greek and Phoenician settlements will immediately recognize the symptoms. Commercial domination, monopoly, even export drives occur and recur in the literature, not because the evidence suggests these things but simply because we have acquired the unfortunate habit of calling the settlements 'colonies'.

My second reason is more substantial. A typology cannot be correct or incorrect; it is only more or less useful for the purposes for which it is designed. Obviously there are contexts in which the fact of emigration is so weighty that the destination (geographical or political) of the migrants may be reduced to a minor variable or ignored altogether—the demographic history of a country or region, for instance. However, the history of colonies is surely the history of the ways in which the power, prestige and profits of some countries were enhanced (or so they hoped) by external dependencies of migrant settlers. Dependency is then a significant variable, which is understressed, when not wholly lost sight of, by a bad system of classification. As Fieldhouse insisted, in a different context, ' "formal" empire' gave a 'power to determine the character of economic development to a degree inconceivable in "informal" dependencies'.[21] I am of course not suggesting that the establishment of the Hellenistic monarchies, say, had no impact other than demographic on old Greece. My point is that, unless one is satisfied with an infinite series of discrete units, a useful classification will

[21] D. K. Fieldhouse in *France and Britain in Africa*, ed. P. Gifford and W. R. Louis (New Haven and London, 1971), pp. 600-01.

inevitably have 'floating' variables that appear in more than one class. Some emigrants are colonists, some are not colonists. Nothing could be more elementary or obvious, yet I find it essential to say the obvious in forthright language.

Now let us look at four less easily agreed cases, all of them medieval—the Crusader states in Palestine, the German expansion east of the Elbe, the Venetian Romania and the Genoese trading 'colonies'. That the first of these, the Crusader states, should be bracketed with the Hellenistic monarchies or the Normans in England as migratory conquests resulting in new, independent states seems self-evident. That is how Roscher, for example, took them.[22] Now, however, a quarter-century of persistent publication by Verlinden and Prawer has separated them off from antiquity and converted them into the first modern colonization movement. Verlinden calls them, together with the Genoese 'colonies' of the Levant, 'entirely comparable' to the New World, with 'no essential differences' in the 'colonial techniques'.[23] The Pilgrim Fathers would have been astonished to know that. Prawer, a pupil of Koebner's,[24] has made a more overt attempt to justify the position, notably in the final chapter of his recent book, *The Latin Kingdom of Jerusalem*, with a subtitle which states his theme, 'European Colonialism in the Middle Ages'. There he begins with a definition: '. . . migration and colonization must not be confused. . . . Only when the migrating element becomes the dominant factor in a newly created polity can one speak of colonization.'[25] But his thesis then requires him to get rid of Greek, Phoenician and Roman 'colonizing movements' in antiquity, the Germanic migrations into the Roman empire and the Normans in Sicily, which he attempts by *ad hoc* arguments.

I cannot go into the arguments, none of which impresses me.[26] I cannot, for example, see the relevance (or even the import) of the statement that the ancient movements were merely Mediterranean whereas the Crusaders were 'bearers of the common heritage of European culture'.[27] Two points seem to me decisive, both of which

---

[22] *Kolonien*, pp. 3–4.
[23] C. Verlinden, *The Beginnings of Modern Colonization* (Ithaca, N.Y., 1970), pp. xiii, xviii. This volume is a collection in English translation of articles published over a considerable time-span.
[24] The relevance of that relationship is particularly clear in Prawer's 'Colonization Activities in the Latin Kingdom of Jerusalem', *Revue belge de philologie et d'histoire*, xxix (1951), pp. 1063–1118.
[25] *The Latin Kingdom of Jerusalem* (London, 1972), p. 469.
[26] Nor did they impress the one review in a scholarly journal I have seen, J. A. Brundage in *Speculum*, l (1975), pp. 145–47, though he concludes that the wrongheaded notion was worth pursuing.
[27] *Latin Kingdom*, p. 470.

Prawer concedes and then pays no attention to. The first is that 'there was no actual colonizing centre or homeland with political or economic claims to future conquests',[28] or, I believe more tellingly, no homeland with claims of any kind. When, in 1100, Baldwin I had himself crowned 'King of the Kingdom of Jerusalem', he was, on this score, doing precisely what Ptolemy I did in Egypt in 304 B.C. (a precedent Prawer neglects to consider). Either both were manifestations of colonization, or neither. To call the Crusaders 'rather unique' and 'a particular case' in colonial history,[29] is to concede that the phenomenon is classified badly.

The other decisive point is that the system which the Crusaders established was a feudal one.[30] Feudalism and colonialism, I would argue, are essentially incompatible. Feudal relations of dominance and subordination are personal, not state relations, and it does not matter whether they fall within or outside what we should call a 'nationality'. Anyway, the feudal relationships of Crusader Palestine existed solely within Palestine: there was no allegiance to kings or barons in Europe. Precisely the same is true of the great medieval German expansion eastwards, a complex movement in many ways unlike the Crusader activities but identical in the respect that the new kingdoms and principalities were never, not even in inception, subordinate to anyone in the territories from which the migrants came.[31] This topic is a minefield, even today, but, no matter what stance one adopts about Germans and Slavs, about conquest or peaceful amalgamation, the basic conclusion that we are concerned with feudal organizations not subject to, or dependent on, a 'motherland' cannot be challenged.[32]

The Venetian Romania, in contrast, was under total control from the motherland. The archives of the Consiglio and other state organs of Venice reveal day-to-day regulation, down to minutiae, of the Romania, which included at its peak Corfu, Crete, Euboea, various Aegean islands and a toehold or two on the mainland of Greece. Again our major authority speaks in his subtitle of the 'domain

[28] *Latin Kingdom*, p. 478.

[29] *Ibid.*, pp. 478, 480.

[30] For an analysis unhampered by the self-imposed chains of 'colonialism', see J. Riley-Smith, *The Feudal Nobility and the Kingdom of Jerusalem* (London, 1973).

[31] The best short account known to me is G. Barraclough, *The Origins of Modern Germany* (2nd edn, Oxford, 1947), chap. 10.

[32] A prime example of the political overtones in present-day accounts is W. Schlesinger, 'Die geschichtliche Stellung der mittelalterlichen deutschen Ostbewegung', *Historische Zeitschrift*, clxxxiii (1957), pp. 517–42. He finds the 'colonization' label 'nicht völlig gerecht' because eastern neighbours do not like it, and because the movement resulted in a 'Wohn- und Wirtschaftsgemeinschaft' that grew into a 'Schicksalsgemeinschaft'.

colonial vénitien'.[33] I note, however, that in the thousands of extant documents the Venetians did not use the term *colonia* (any more than did the Crusaders in Palestine or the Genoese of their 'colonies'). That is not decisive, but it is suggestive. The original Venetian interest was in trade and trade routes. Later, the breakdown of Byzantine authority compelled Venice to intensify her control, and in the thirteenth century she even sent a small number of military settlers (called *feudatorii* and *cavalerie*) to Crete to back up her administrators, merchants and artisans in the cities. She also came to rely heavily on compulsory grain imports from the Romania to meet her own food needs, and, after the Black Death in particular, when shortage of labour on the land became a major worry, Venice imported Armenians and transplanted Aegean islanders to Crete and Euboea. The key element in all this is that agriculture remained exclusively in Greek hands, organized along Byzantine feudal lines, and that there was never any significant Venetian emigration. In my language, therefore, the Romania was not colonial and the Venetians were right not to speak of *coloniae*.

So were the Genoese. Their trading-stations or *comptoirs*, for which there are precedents going back to the Assyrians early in the second millennium B.C., were urban complexes established by treaty. They were granted certain extra-territorial privileges, and they were valuable enough to be fought over constantly by Genoese, Venetians and Pisans. But on no account were they political entities subject to the mother-city. Nor were there many Genoese emigrants. The occasional exception, such as the island of Chios (where the agricultural land was retained by Greeks),[34] does not warrant the colonial identification any more than does the fact, stressed by Verlinden and others, that individual Genoese seamen and adventurers entered the employ of the Portuguese and Spanish monarchs, climaxed of course by Christopher Columbus. More important than their nationality was their invariable practice of occupying newly found territory in the name of the monarch who employed them. That practice by itself breaks the continuity which is claimed by historians. The continuum within which these *comptoirs* are correctly to be located is that of the system later known as Capitulations, traceable from at least the time of Haroun al Rashid in the ninth century and familiar to the ancient world as well.[35]

---

[33] F. Thiret, 'La Romanie vénitienne au moyen-âge' (*Bibl. des Ecoles françaises d'Athènes et de Rome*, no. 193, 1959).

[34] See P. P. Argenti, *The Occupation of Chios by the Genoese . . . 1346–1566* (3 vols, Cambridge, 1958), i, chap. 12.

[35] That is where the 11th edn of the *Encyclopaedia Britannica* located them.

III

'Agriculture is the proper business of all new colonies', wrote Adam Smith, and earlier in the chapter he began the section entitled 'Causes of Prosperity of New Colonies' with these words: 'The colony of a civilized nation which takes possession of a waste country, or of one so thinly inhabited that the natives easily give place to the new settlers, advances more rapidly to wealth and greatness, than any other human society.'[36]

Even when we put aside the large issues of political economy which lay behind this pronouncement, it remains correct, I believe, that land is the element round which to construct a typology of colonies. That is not the customary approach among historians, or even among publicists and theorists contemporary with events, but I suggest that is because they habitually view the issues from the metropolis, rather than from the colonies. When one looks inside the latter, in Africa for example, a first fundamental distinction becomes inescapable, that 'between those in which agriculture came to be based upon an expatriate farming class, and those in which African peasant producers were dominant.'[37]

Territory to be colonized was normally, perhaps always, thinly inhabited, but it was waste land only in the sense that it was inadequately or incompletely exploited.[38] More important, it was invariably someone else's land that was taken away through one device or another. Conquest and confiscation do not necessarily lead to colonization: Roman senatorial occupation of large tracts of *ager publicus* was not colonization, nor, to point to another kind of development, did the imposition of the zamindari and ryotwari land systems in British India benefit colonists, ruinous though it was to the native peasantry. It is the reverse which concerns me: colonization implies expropriation and settlement of land. Both contemporary observers and modern historians tend to concentrate too much on initial motives—glory, trade, overpopulation—which are usually disentangled only artificially and which were never binding on successive generations. Whatever Columbus or Cortez or La Salle may have had in mind, or their backers, they would have

[36] *Wealth of Nations*, ed. E. Cannan (Univ. Paperbacks edn, London, 1961), ii, pp. 124, 75.

[37] E. A. Brett, *Colonialism and Underdevelopment in East Africa* (London, 1973), p. 44.

[38] For 'waste land' as a euphemism, see the documents in the unsuccessful attempt, between 1885–1900, to take the land in the Gold Coast into the Crown's possession, quoted extensively by D. Kimble, *A Political History of Ghana* (Oxford, 1963), chap. 9.

marked the end of the history of the New World, not its beginning, had they not been followed by settlers.

Conquest, colonization, expropriation require justification. Although it is not my intention to consider the theory or ideology of colonization, one digression may be useful at this point, because it takes us to the beginning of modern colonization and places the land issue squarely in the centre. In the second book of *Utopia*, Thomas More wrote the following:

> And if the population throughout the island should happen to swell above the fixed quotas, they enroll citizens out of every city and, on the mainland nearest them, wherever the natives have much unoccupied and uncultivated land, they found a colony (*colonia*) under their own laws. They join with themselves the natives if they are willing to dwell with them. When such a union takes place, the two parties gradually and easily merge and together absorb the same way of life and the same customs, much to the great advantage of both peoples. By their procedures they make the land sufficient for both, which previously seemed poor and barren to the natives. The inhabitants who refuse to live according to their laws, they drive from the territory which they carve out for themselves. If they resist, they wage war against them. They consider it a most just cause for war when a people which does not use its soil but keeps it idle and waste nevertheless forbids the use and possession of it to others who by the rule of nature ought to be maintained by it.
>
> If ever any misfortune so diminishes the number in any of their cities that it cannot be made up out of other parts of the island without bringing other cities below their proper strength (this has happened, they say, only twice in all the ages on account of the raging of a fierce pestilence), they are filled up by citizens returning from colonial territory. They would rather that the colonies should perish than that any of the cities of the island should be enfeebled.[39]

1516 seems an early date for an Englishman to involve himself in this particular debate, and the passage is regularly overlooked in work on colonies.[40] Yet More could not have been unaware of the notorious papal bull of 1492, *Inter Caetera*, granting Ferdinand and Isabella dominion of all lands in the New World not already pos-

[39] *Utopia*, ed. E. Surtz and J. H. Hexter (New Haven and London, 1965), p. 137.

[40] I must thank Quentin Skinner for directing my attention to the passage. The brief commentary on it by the Yale editors is almost wholly irrelevant, but at least they avoid the higher nonsense of others, briefly reported by Russell Ames, *Citizen Thomas More and His Utopia* (Princeton, 1949), pp. 163–67.

sessed by a Christian king or prince; of Henry VII's letters patent,
of 1496, granting John Cabot the right to conquer and possess for
the king any territory previously unknown to Christians; or of how
the issue promptly became enmeshed in the older controversy over
spiritual and temporal authority, which had, at least since Wyclif's
day, been extended to certain questions of the rights to possessions.
In 1510, six years before *Utopia* was published, the Scottish theologian and teacher John Major (or Mair), the first modern writer,
so far as we know, to apply Aristotle's theory of natural slavery to
the Amerindians, nevertheless acknowledged the 'proprietary rights
of the infidel in his own land'.[41] I cannot say whether or not More
knew Major's publication, but the Spanish theologian Vitoria certainly did when he published his *De India noviter inventis* in 1532.[42]
Vitoria was the fountainhead of a line of theorists who fought a
losing battle against the 'law of conquest'. Somehow the proponents
of confiscation could always manage to find an ideological justification for their 'fell and butcherly stratagems', as the *Gold Coast
Methodist Times* called them.[43] Witness the charade about 'tribal
ownership' which surrounded the expropriation, in favour of the
colons, of all the best land in Algeria following the suppression of the
Moqrani revolt of 1871, eventually of more than one-third of the
total.[44]

Putting ideology aside, we must consider in turn the variables
from which a typology of colonies, based on land, can be constructed. The first would obviously be the natural resources: some
land was best suited to agricultural and pastoral products also
available in the homeland, some to such products as cane sugar,
cotton, tobacco or coffee, for which Europe had to rely on foreign
imports. No demonstration is required that both the relationship of
the colony with mother country and other communities and the
internal development of a colony diverged sharply according to this
basic distinction in natural resources. It is, of course, the distinction
underlying the French classification into *colonie de peuplement* and
colonie de plantation.

However, soil suitability was not the sole difference between the
two. The *colonie de plantation* was most often found in tropical or

[41] J. H. Parry, *The Spanish Theory of Empire in the Sixteenth Century* (Cambridge, 1940), p. 20.
[42] A translation will be found in J. B. Scott, *The Spanish Origin of International Law* (Oxford, 1934).
[43] Quoted in Kimble, *History of Ghana*, p. 339.
[44] C.-R. Ageron, *Les Algériens musulmans et la France (1871–1919)* (2 vols., Paris, 1968), i, chap. 4–5; ii, chap. 27–28. On Rhodesia, see W. Roder, 'The Division of Land Resources in Southern Rhodesia', *Annals of the Assn. of American Geographers*, liv (1964), pp. 41–52, at pp. 45–46.

semi-tropical regions, and there was a tendency to monoculture with slaves or some other form of compulsory labour. The tie is so close that there is an impulse to think of these various aspects of land utilization as a unit. Europeans could not or would not work the land under tropical conditions—the standard explanation starts from there. There is truth in that, of course. 'The mosquitoes saved the West Africans' from having much of their land confiscated, said one commentator, 'not the eloquence of the intellectuals.'[45] But the simple explanation is not a sufficient one. It will not explain the radical difference between East and West Africa, between Kenya and Uganda, between Algeria and the rest of the Maghreb, or between the development of the absentee-owned plantations of Asia and the settler-plantations, often with the same tropical crops, of East Africa.[46] Climate, preference for monoculture or mixed farming as the case may be, absenteeism or settlement, the number and nature of the labour force are each either independent variables or functions of independent variables.

Two New World developments will illustrate. In Mexico, where very large holdings quickly emerged after the conquest, where there were silver mines and where the tropical climate was suitable for such products as sugar-cane, the dominant activity on the large estates to the end of the sixteenth century was cattle-ranching and sheep-farming. The decisive variable, in the persuasive argument of François Chevalier, was the desperate shortage of labour.[47] One is reminded of Wakefield's concern over the availability of cheap land and the unavailability of labour in Australia. It was not until the Europeans and Creoles in Mexico, who numbered no more than 100,000, having won their long struggle with the Spanish authorities, were able to reduce the Indians to peonage that crop-raising progressed significantly and the 'mixed hacienda type' (Chevalier's phrase) emerged.

To the north—and this is my second example—Josiah Child complained as early as 1668 that 'New England is the most prejudicial plantation to the kingdom of England' chiefly, though not solely, because 'all our American plantations, except that of New England, produce commodities of different natures from those of this kingdom, as sugar, tobacco, cocoa, wool, ginger, sundry sorts of dyeing woods etc., whereas New England produces generally the

---

[45] George Padmore, quoted in Kimble, *History of Ghana*, p. 354.

[46] On Kenya and Uganda, see Brett, *Colonialism*, part III, who also gives a brief analysis of the difference between settlement and absentee plantations, pp. 173–75.

[47] *Land and Society in Colonial Mexico*, translated by Alvin Eustis (Berkeley and Los Angeles, 1963).

same as we have here, viz. corn and cattle.'[48] When Child wrote that, the southernmost of the continental colonies were Maryland, Virginia and the Carolinas, and, though there were marked climatic and ecological differences between them and New England, they were neither tropical nor sub-tropical, nor was there a significant disparity in the numbers of whites. In 1670, there were 36,913 whites, 225 blacks in Maine, New Hampshire, Vermont and Massachusetts together; 48,215 whites, 4,370 blacks in Maryland, Virginia and the Carolinas. A century later, shortly before the outbreak of the Revolution, the corresponding figures were 333,053 whites, 5,908 blacks for the northern group; 574,858 whites, 396,201 blacks in the southern group. The difference with respect to slaves had become spectacular, but my present concern is with the whites, who, furthermore, were as English–Scotch–Irish in the south as in the north.[49] That last fact is of little significance to me; I mention it because it has mattered to others. Roscher spoke of the 'weak gift of the French' for colonization, and he rather unfairly called on Leroy-Beaulieu as a witness.[50] The latter, in turn, worried about the ratio of Frenchmen among the *colons* in Algeria, only 58 per cent in 1861, but consoled himself with the statistics showing that the French net increase was becoming progressively higher than that of Spaniards, Maltese and Germans in the colony.[51] But no one ever doubted the British 'gift'.

The temptation to play numbers games is powerful. One could say, for example, that in 1965 there were *only* 219,500 whites in Southern Rhodesia, the majority of them urban, against 4,070,000 Africans, or in Mozambique *only* 97,300 whites, 6,431,000 Africans. Virginia alone had almost as many white inhabitants in 1770— 259,411—as the two large African colonies in our day.[52] There are contexts in the study of European history in which 'only' has a denigratory connotation, when the trifling numbers are compared, for example, with the tens of millions of Europeans who migrated to post-colonial North and South America in the nineteenth and

[48] *A New Discourse of Trade* (2nd edn, London, 1694), p. 213.
[49] I have compiled these figures from *Historical Statistics of the United States, Colonial Times to 1957*, published by the U.S. Bureau of the Census (Washington, 1960), p. 756.
[50] *Kolonien*, p. 20 and n. 2.
[51] *Colonisation*, pp. 326–27. Mixed settlers could create difficulties: see J. Poncet, *La colonisation et l'agriculture européennes en Tunisie depuis 1881* (The Hague, 1962), pp. 341–47.
[52] These figures are taken from Clare Palley, *The Constitutional History and Law of Southern Rhodesia 1888–1965* (Oxford, 1966), p. xvii, n. 2; eds. D. M. Abshire and M. A. Samuels, *Portuguese Africa: A Handbook* (London, 1969), p. 82; the U.S. Bureau of the Census volume cited above, n. 49.

twentieth centuries. But there are other contexts, within colonial history in particular, when 'only' has very different overtones, in comparing the settlers in Rhodesia with the far more numerous *colons* of Algeria or Australia. The raw land figures offer one such context—35·7 millions acres set aside for whites, 44·4 millions for Africans in Southern Rhodesia; more than four million and some seven million, respectively, in Mozambique.[53] I say 'raw figures' because they grossly underrate the relative productivity, access to railways, and other considerations in the two land categories, as with the slightly more than one-third of the total in Algeria I mentioned earlier.[54] And all other major aspects of the economy and the political organization provide further contexts within which to assess and compare population figures.

The complaint Leroy-Beaulieu actually made about the French was wholly unrelated to Roscher's 'gift' for colonization. The fatal flaw in early French attempts to colonize North America, he said, following Adam Smith and de Tocqueville, was the 'feudal property regime', both at home and in the colonies.[55] And that brings me to my next variable: the economic, social and political structure of the imperial country. Neither the official Spanish resistance to emigration, nor the mercantilist policy of successive English governments, nor the willingness or unwillingness of Europeans to migrate or to take to the land and work on it, nor the decision on any other fundamental policy was a matter of different royal preferences, national qualities or caprice. I would apologize once again for saying anything so obvious were it not for the way this variable is ignored in so much contemporary historical discussion. What I may call the Verlinden doctrine, with its belief in a thousand-year continuum beginning with the Latin kingdom of Jerusalem and the Genoese *comptoirs*, collapses on this count alone.

'Structure' should in fact be in the plural: they change, and so do the colonies. To illustrate, it is sufficient to consider the numbers of men available for emigration and settlement. Into the nineteenth century there was a chronic shortage, even where the whole process was not discouraged, as in France and Spain (again for structural reasons). Then came the nineteenth-century flood, and a new complication: why should Englishmen assume the burdens and risks of settling in Kenya when they could go to the United States, Australia or South Africa? Seeley could 'put the United States entirely out of view', but Whitehall could not. Only a complex and expensive 'development' programme in Kenya could put the United States

[53] Palley, *op. cit.*, p. 265 n. 4; Abshire and Samuels, *op. cit.*, p. 268.
[54] On Rhodesia, see especially Roder, 'Land Resource'.
[55] *Colonisation*, pp. 150–52.

out of view,[56] and the British government's willingness and ability
to do that for Kenya, but not for Uganda or the Gold Coast, is an
essential, if not the only, key to the eventual differences among these
three dependencies, differences so great that, in my categorization,
Kenya was a colony, Uganda and the Gold Coast were not. Nor
were the Congo, Senegal and the Ivory Coast, and perhaps it is
now more clear why I said earlier that the struggle for Africa was
not, or at least not in large part, a struggle for colonies.

Finally, there are the indigenous populations to add to the list of
variables. Except in Asia, they were technically backward, small-
scale in their political organization, incapable of concerted action,
as compared with their European conquerors. Above all, they were,
the Asiatics included, hopelessly outclassed in their ability to apply
force. That they differed considerably in their capacity for incorporation into a colonial system, which means essentially as a labour
force, hardly needs demonstration, nor that the great heterogeneity
which existed, and exists, arises from varied social structures, not
from 'racial' differences. Furthermore, their adaptability and use-
fulness have not been a fixed quality, even when we look at any
single population alone. The changes and the differences, in this
respect, among the natives of Angola as between the slave-trade
period and the era of Portuguese settlement in the twentieth century, offer a fair example of the dynamic interrelationship between
changing colony and changing metropolis.[57] Nor could Kenya have
been colonized in the days of mercantilism, before, that is, the
emergence of advanced industrial capitalism.

IV

Taking a long view, and narrowing the variables to three, land,
labour and the socio-economic structure of the metropolis, I suggest
the following crude three-stage model. In constructing it, I have
ignored such temporary phenomena as indentured or convict labour,
not because they were not important in one place or another at one
time or another, but because, in my judgment, they were always
marginal devices. To incorporate them into a simple model would
introduce more confusion than clarification.

In antiquity, there were the following possibilities when territory
was encroached upon or subjugated:

   1. it could be left largely autonomous on payment of a regular
tribute, as in the Persian satrapal system;

[56] See Brett, *Colonialism*, pp. 167–71.
[57] See W. Rodney, 'European Activity and African Reaction in Angola', in
Aspects of African History, ed. T. O. Ranger (London, 1968), chap. 3.

2. it could be incorporated into the state, as in the provinces of the Roman empire, usually with a substantial amount of settlement, a complication I shall return to;

3. it could be colonized by military settlements on confiscated land, as in the *coloniae* of the Roman Republic, but that, it should be stressed, was an untypical practice in the ancient world; or

4. it could be peopled by the newcomers, migrating in small numbers to found a new city-state, as among the archaic Phoenicians and Greeks; or migrating as a ruling elite to a new, or newly recreated, independent state, as in the eastern Hellenistic monarchies.

In so far as the newcomers either brought their own labour system with them or adopted the indigenous one, labour was an inert variable, so to speak. Slave labour was a metropolitan institution, not a colonial (or pseudo-colonial) one. That is to say, slaves were imported, at times in large numbers, usually from more backward societies, to meet the labour needs of the metropolis. When the practice was then carried over to newly acquired or conquered territories, that was merely a continuation of the metropolitan practice in another place but under the same socio-political conditions. The one exception to all this was a restricted one: Greeks who founded new settlements—not colonies, I repeat once more—on the margins of the old Greek world in the archaic period not infrequently reduced some of the indigenous people to a semi-servile condition roughly akin to Spartan helotage.[58]

In the early modern period, there were further instances of the difficult Roman imperial syndrome, conquest–incorporation–settlement, but the major development was of course overseas colonization, in which the settlers had the following possibilities:

1. work the land themselves with or without hired labour, chiefly European;

2. work the land with native compulsory labour, peonage; or

3. work the land with imported slave labour.

These were not mutually exclusive possibilities. Size of holding was obviously a factor, so that smallholdings with little or no additional labour coexisted with large estates worked by peons or slaves, as in Mexico or the southern colonies of the United States. There was also some absentee land ownership, that is, non-settler ownership, but

---

[58] The most important study is restricted to the Black Sea area: D. M. Pippidi, 'Le problème de la main-d'oeuvre agricole dans les colonies grecques de la mer Noire', in *Problèmes de la terre en Grèce ancienne*, ed. M. I. Finley (Paris and The Hague, 1973), pp. 63–82, reprinted in his *Scythica Minora* (Bucharest and Amsterdam, 1975), pp. 65–80.

that was not quantitatively or otherwise significant except in the earliest days of some of the colonies.

In the third phase, finally, the nineteenth and twentieth centuries, peonage and slave labour were largely displaced in the genuine colonies by wage labour, while the small family-farm also continued in existence. That a sufficient wage-labour supply was created by a variety of compulsions, such as large-scale expropriation of land and calculated tax devices, is certainly true,[59] but the big distinction between more or less unwilling wage labour and slave labour is not to be brushed aside. The third phase saw a second new and important development, namely, the establishment in dependent territories of large holdings worked by local labour, more or less free, without the settler element. The metropolis provides managers, overseers, clerks, but they, like the army, the police, the civil servants and the mercantile employees, consider themselves sojourners, not migrants, and so they are in the overwhelming percentage of cases. Although both these developments of the third phase can be illustrated in embryo in earlier times, they are pre-eminently the consequence of the transformations that have occurred in the metropolitan economy, of the same structural changes which made it increasingly difficult to stimulate genuine colonization except by sophisticated and massive governmental effort.

On the political level, the paramount distinction which follows centres round the extent to which the settlers have both reasons and the power to determine policy, not only against the indigenous population but, even more important, against the metropolis. This is not a matter of mere numbers, absolute or relative, as South Africa, Rhodesia and Algeria demonstrate. Nor is it the same distinction as the commonly adduced ones of kith-and-kin or the emergence of nationalism, which even Engels was seduced by. Replying to an enquiry from Kautsky in 1892, Engels wrote: 'In my opinion, the colonies proper, that is, the countries occupied by a European population—Canada, the Cape, Australia—will all become independent; on the other hand, the countries inhabited by a native population, which are simply subjugated—India, Algeria, the Dutch, Portuguese and Spanish possessions—must be taken over for the time being by the proletariat and led as rapidly as possible to independence.'[60] That he was not a very good forecaster here is

---

[59] See e.g. W. L. Barber, The Economy of British Central Africa (London, 1971), pp. 29–39, and the alternative analysis by G. Arrighi in chaps. 5 and 7 of Arrighi and J. S. Saul, Essays on the Political Economy of Africa (New York and London, 1973).

[60] Quoted from Karl Marx on Colonialism and Modernization, ed. S. Avineri (Garden City, N.Y., 1969), p. 473. For the original, see the edition of the Engels–Kautsky correspondence by B. Kautsky (Vienna, 1955), p. 63.

self-evident, but the two-way classification he employed was (and is) widely shared, and we must ask why, in the event, the achievement of independence did not divide in that neat way. I can phrase my answer in two rhetorical questions. A central aim of the Algerians in their war for independence was the physical expulsion of the *colons*, and most of them, some 800,000 in fact, left within six months of the end of the war. Whom did the Canadians or Australians wish to expel, or the thirteen American colonies in 1775? And who were the *colons* of India, Nigeria or Ghana? My two rhetorical questions point to two wholly different situations—that is obvious—and I believe my crude model elucidates basic elements of the difference.

Lest I appear to be claiming too much, I turn briefly to a situation about which I confess to being uncertain, namely, what I have called the 'Roman imperial syndrome', to which I should attach the English in Ireland and Wales. In all three, conquest was followed by immediate and formal incorporation into the metropolitan organization, and by confiscation of substantial tracts of land for settlement by migrants from the conquering nation. Administratively the Roman provinces, Wales and Ireland were distinct from colonies. William Molyneux in 1698 protested bitterly any suggestion that Ireland was a 'colony from England' like the Roman *coloniae*. Speaking for the Protestant interest, he wrote: 'Of all the objections raised against us, I take this to be the most extravagant; it seems not to have the least foundation or colour from reason or record.' Ireland, he continued, is 'a complete kingdom in itself. Is this agreeable to the nature of a colony? Do they use the title of Kings of Virginia, New-England or Maryland?'[61] Whatever the merits of this argument in debate, we saw at the start that administrative definitions are essentially unhelpful. Algeria was a fully incorporated department of metropolitan France, yet it was indubitably a colony. In every respect other than the administrative, Algerians in the overwhelming majority still considered themselves, more than a century after the conquest, to be the exploited subjects, not so much of the metropolis as of the settlers backed by the coercive power of the metropolis. This was not the case in the Roman provinces. There the empire rapidly 'ceased to be an alien dominion imposed on unwilling subjects by force. . . . Discontent of the subjects with foreign

---

[61] *The Case of Ireland's Being Bound by Acts of Parliament* . . . (Dublin, 1698), p. 148. This is the notorious book in which Molyneux openly and without permission employed, in a 'subversive' way, the arguments which his friend John Locke had propounded anonymously in the *Second Treatise* against a conqueror's general right to the possessions of the subjugated people; see John Dunn, 'The Politics of Locke in England and America in the Eighteenth Century', in *John Locke; Problems and Perspectives*, ed. J. W. Yolton (Cambridge, 1969), pp. 45–80, at pp. 65–67.

rule was not . . . the cause of disruption, if only because the rule was not foreign.'[62] That there are men in Ireland and Wales who would not subscribe to these generalizations about Rome as an accurate reflection of their views and circumstances is certainly true. It is equally true, I believe, that few Irishmen or Welshmen would, if given the required information, think themselves in a similar position to the Algerians. And so I hesitate and waver.

If I have managed not to mention Irish and Welsh nationalism, that was by design. Of course nationalism (or national liberation) has been an emotive and ideological component in some colonial situations, particularly in colonial revolts. It was not, however, in the North American colonies in the eighteenth century. Nor, in the twentieth, is the concept of nationalism of any use in explaining the complex differences between Algeria and Tunisia, creating divergence both in their colonial history and in their decolonization.[63] Nor does it explain anything about Rhodesia, and on the colony of Rhodesia I rest my case.

Jesus College, Cambridge.

[62] P. A. Brunt, 'Reflections on British and Roman Imperialism', *Comparative Studies in Society and History*, vii (1965), pp. 267–84, at pp. 274, 276.

[63] The distinctions are brought out in detail and sharp clarity by Poncet, *Tunisie*, implicitly throughout and sometimes explicitly.

THE EIGHTEENTH-CENTURY DEBATE ON THE SOVEREIGNTY OF PARLIAMENT

By H. T. Dickinson, M.A., Ph.D., F.R.Hist.S.

READ 17 OCTOBER 1975

I hope to show in this paper that the national debate in the press and in parliament about the doctrine of the sovereignty of parliament is of crucial importance to a proper understanding of the politics and, still more, of the political ideology of eighteenth-century Britain. The significance that this doctrine had come to assume by the later eighteenth century becomes clearly apparent from any study of the dispute between Britain and the American colonies. In the final analysis the most serious point at issue between the mother country and her colonies rested on a fundamental disagreement over the nature and location of sovereignty. The majority of the ruling oligarchy in Britain saw parliament as the creator and interpreter of law and superior to any other rights or powers in the state. To the American colonists it appeared that the arbitrary and absolute power which Hobbes and Filmer had put in the hands of a king had been transferred to the whole legislature of King, Lords and Commons. In rejecting what they regarded as tyranny in another form, the colonists moved towards the concept of divided sovereignty with the people as the ultimate source of authority.[1]

That the concept of a sovereign parliament was hardening into an orthodoxy by the later eighteenth century can be seen most readily by examining William Blackstone's *Commentaries on the Laws of England*, published between 1765 and 1769, and by studying the numerous parliamentary debates on the American problem. Blackstone maintained that there must be a supreme, irresistible, absolute, uncontrolled authority in every orderly state and that in Britain this sovereign power was lodged in parliament, in the combined authority of King, Lords and Commons, whose actions no power on earth could undo except a subsequent parliament.[2] This

[1] Bernard Bailyn, *The Ideological Origins of the American Revolution* (Cambridge, Mass., 1967), pp. 198–229; and John V. Jezierski, 'Parliament or People: James Wilson and Blackstone on the Nature and Location of Sovereignty', *Journal of the History of Ideas*, xxxii (1971), pp. 95–106.

[2] *Commentaries on the Laws of England*, i (18th edn, London, 1829), pp. 46, 48–52, 146, 159–60.

opinion was to be echoed many times in both houses of parliament during the debates on America in the 1760s and the 1770s. It did not come only from the mouths of conservative lawyers[3] and staunch supporters of government policy,[4] but also from the lips of men who sympathized with the American colonists and feared the consequences of ministerial policy.[5] Beyond the confines of parliament many attempts were made to convince the electorate that it was essential to defend the doctrine of parliamentary sovereignty in order to save the empire and preserve the constitution.[6] There was of course some opposition to this claim. While this resistance was never strong enough to persuade parliament to renounce the doctrine, it did ensure that, as far as Britain herself was concerned, parliamentary sovereignty would not be pushed so hard as to override the principle of government by consent. This, in fact, will be the subject of the second part of this paper. First, however, it is necessary to explain why the doctrine of parliamentary sovereignty had become so powerful, indeed irresistible, by the later eighteenth century.

I

A century before the American Revolution, in the two decades before the Glorious Revolution, the prevailing constitutional doctrine placed sovereign authority not in the whole legislature but in the hands of the king. The earlier political disputes of the seventeenth century had convinced almost all educated men that in order to preserve stability in the state it was essential to have an authority

[3] See the speeches of Lord Chancellor Northington and Lord Mansfield, February 1766, in T. C. Hansard, *The Parliamentary History of England* (London, 1806–20) (hereafter cited as *Parl. Hist.*) xvi, pp. 170, 173–75; and the speech of Charles Yorke, 3 February 1766, in 'Parliamentary Diaries of Nathaniel Ryder, 1764–7', ed. P. D. G. Thomas, *Camden Miscellany XXIII* (Camden Society, 4th series, no. 7, 1969), pp. 264–67.

[4] See the speeches of Charles Jenkinson, 6 February 1772 and Lord Lyttelton, 20 January 1775, in *Parl. Hist.*, xvii, p. 269 and xviii, p. 163.

[5] See the speeches of Governor Pownall, April 1769, *ibid*, xvi, p. 612; Edmund Burke, 6 February 1772 and 19 April 1774, *ibid*, xvii, pp. 276, 1266; Mr Cruger, 16 December 1774, *ibid*, xviii, p. 66; and the Earl of Coventry, 18 November 1777, *ibid*, xix, pp. 358–59. The Rockingham Whigs, who regarded themselves as the friends of America, passed the Declaratory Act of 1766 which endorsed the doctrine of parliamentary sovereignty. Even the Earl of Chatham never entirely rejected the doctrine. *Ibid*, xvi, p. 99.

[6] See, *e.g.* Samuel Johnson, *Taxation no Tyranny* (London, 1775); Josiah Tucker, *The Respective Pleas and Arguments of the Mother Country, and of the Colonies, distinctly set forth* (London, 1776); and Edmund Burke, *A Letter to the Sheriffs of Bristol on the Affairs of America* (1777), in *Works*, ii (Bohn ed.; 8 vols, London, 1854–57), pp. 25–27.

whose actions were unquestionable and irresistible. The majority of the gentry and virtually all of the clergy of the Church of England were convinced that such power could only be exercised by the crown. Sir Robert Filmer, whose most famous work, *Patriarcha*, was published posthumously in 1680, maintained that God had granted absolute power to kings and not to the people or their representatives. Bodin, who had so much influenced royalists earlier in the seventeenth century, had claimed that kings were supreme, but not arbitrary. Filmer rejected such restrictions on sovereignty and claimed that God had granted kings absolute and arbitrary power. While they might consult advisers or even parliaments before making laws, it was not essential for them to do so. The authority of the king could not be challenged by the common law, the decisions of the two houses of parliament or the will of the people.[7] These arguments were immensely influential and many political theorists and propagandists repeated Filmer's defence of the absolute power of kings. His doctrine of the divine right of kings was also reinforced from two other directions. The Church of England buttressed the absolute authority of the king by preaching the doctrines of nonresistance and passive obedience, while the historical researches of Robert Brady showed that parliament had only recently become politically significant. Parliament's authority rested on the will of the king, who called it into existence and who could ignore it at his pleasure. The laws and liberties of England therefore owed their existence solely to the royal will.[8]

The doctrine of royal absolutism did not of course go unchallenged. The seventeenth century had already witnessed a long campaign to justify the rights of parliament and to prove that the sovereign authority in the state was the whole legislature of King, Lords and Commons.[9] In the 1680s the publication of the works of Filmer, Brady and their disciples met considerable resistance. Algernon Sidney and Henry Neville, in rejecting the divine right of kings, claimed that the legislature was supreme and that the two houses of parliament alone had the authority to limit the power of the king

[7] *Patriarcha and other Political Works of Sir Robert Filmer*, ed. Peter Laslett (Oxford, 1949), pp. 93–118.

[8] For Brady, see his *Preface* to *The Complete History of England* (London, 1685); C. C. Weston, 'Legal Sovereignty in the Brady Controversy', *Historical Journal*, xv (1972), pp. 409–31; J. G. A. Pocock, 'Robert Brady, 1627–1700', *Cambridge Historical Journal*, x (1951), pp. 186–204; and *idem*, *The Ancient Constitution and the Feudal Law* (Cambridge, 1957), pp. 194–225.

[9] See, *e.g.*, J. W. Allen, *Political Thought in England 1603–1660: Volume One, 1603–1644* (London, 1938); Margaret A. Judson, *The Crisis of the Constitution* (New Brunswick, 1949); and George L. Mosse, *The Struggle for Sovereignty in England* (East Lansing, Michigan, 1950).

and even to decide who had the right to wear the crown.[10] William Petyt, in opposition to Brady, stressed the antiquity of parliament, which he traced back to the Anglo-Saxons. In his view statute law was superior not only to common law, but to the decisions of kings or judges.[11]

The debate against Filmer and Brady might never have been won if the Glorious Revolution had not dealt such a serious blow to the defenders of the divine right of kings. The success of the Revolution owed far more to the political mistakes of James II and to the determination of William of Orange than to the propaganda campaign being waged against the doctrine of royal absolutism, but it undoubtedly gave the initiative to the defenders of parliamentary sovereignty. A stream of books, sermons and pamphlets justifying the Revolution poured from the presses. Most of these were primarily, even exclusively, concerned with asserting the right of subjects to preserve their liberties by resisting a tyrannical king. A number of writers, however, took the opportunity to proclaim the sovereignty of parliament in no uncertain terms. Both George Petyt and Robert Atkyns, for example, argued that not only was statute law superior to the royal prerogative, but that no parliament could be bound by any laws passed by previous parliaments.[12] John Locke did not go so far, but in his *Second Treatise of Government*, published in 1690, he presented the most sophisticated and coherent case for the sovereignty of the legislature. Locke maintained that civil societies arose out of social contracts. These contracts were made in order to set up an authority for the better preservation of the life, liberty and property of all men than could be achieved by individual men in the state of nature. This authority, to be effective, must be sovereign and the true test of sovereignty was the ability to make laws which must be obeyed by all members of society.[13] Though he never explicitly referred to England, there can be no doubt that Locke regarded the legislative authority in his own

[10] Algernon Sidney, *Discourses concerning Government* (published posthumously 1698; 3rd edn, London, 1751), pp. 375–84 and Henry Neville, *Plato Redivivus* (London, 1681) in *Two English Republican Tracts*, ed. Caroline Robbins (Cambridge, 1969), pp. 114, 119–20.

[11] William Petyt, *The Antient Right of the Commons of England Asserted* (London, 1680). See also *idem, Jus Parliamentarium: Or, the Ancient Power, Jurisdiction, Rights and Liberties, of the most High Court of Parliament, revived and asserted* (London, 1739). This was probably written in the 1680s. Petyt died in 1707.

[12] Robert Atkyns, *The Power, Jurisdiction and Privilege of Parliament; and the Antiquity of the House of Commons asserted* (London, 1689), p. 60; and George Petyt, *Lex Parliamentaria: Or, A Treatise of the Laws and Custom of the Parliaments of England* (London, 1690), pp. 22, 29.

[13] *Second Treatise*, paras. 131, 132, 134, 143, 150.

country as being the combined institutions of King, Lords and Commons.

The eventual stability of the Revolution settlement and the subsequent fame of Locke's *Second Treatise* can give the misleading impression that the doctrine of parliamentary sovereignty won almost universal approval in the 1690s and went virtually unchallenged in the eighteenth century. The recognition of the succession of William and Mary and the passing of the Bill of Rights can certainly be seen as important indications of the sovereignty of parliament and there is no doubt that some members of the Convention Parliament fully recognized this.[14] Many others, however, argued that William and Mary were simply filling the vacancy left by James II's abdication and that the Bill of Rights merely restored the ancient constitution and the fundamental liberties of the subject. They were not prepared to accept the contract theory as the explanation of the origin of civil society and they were horrified at the notion that subjects might legitimately resist their lawful king. Their acceptance of the Revolution was therefore reluctant and conditional. There was no mass conversion to the Whig doctrine of parliamentary sovereignty.[15] Indeed, several thousand Anglican clergymen were not prepared to take the new oaths of allegiance and supremacy to William and Mary and, until well into the eighteenth century, there existed a Jacobite movement that was determined to undo the Revolution settlement. The doctrine of parliamentary sovereignty won increasing support from Whig propagandists in the 1690s,[16] but it took much longer to convince most of the Anglican clergy and Tory gentry of the wisdom and legitimacy of granting sovereign authority to the legislature.

The conservative elements in the political nation did not easily or readily abandon their traditional support for the doctrines of divine right, indefeasible hereditary succession and non-resistance. These political convictions had been sincerely held and deeply felt. They waned only after considerable heart-searching and much argument. This revolution in conservative ideology was far from sudden. The Whigs continued their efforts to promote the doctrine of parliamentary sovereignty,[17] but this propaganda campaign was not

[14] George L. Cherry, 'The Role of the Convention Parliament (1688–89) in Parliamentary Supremacy', *Journal of the History of Ideas*, xvii (1956), pp. 390–406; and the Bishop of Ely's speech, 6 February 1689, in *Parl. Hist.*, v, p. 75.

[15] J. P. Kenyon, 'The Revolution of 1688: Resistance and Contract', in *Historical Perspectives*, ed. Neil McKendrick (London, 1974), pp. 53–69.

[16] See, *e.g.*, James Tyrrell, *Bibliotheca Politica: Or an Enquiry into the Ancient Constitution of the English Government* (London, 1694), pp. 307–72.

[17] See, *e.g.*, Henry Care, *English Liberties: Or, the Free Born Subject's Inheritance* (London, 1700), p. 59; Humphrey Mackworth, *A Vindication of the Rights of the*

enough to convert the Tories. Much more successful in promoting
this conversion was the unwillingness of most Whigs to push their
political principles to their logical conclusion. The Whig doctrines
that were most unacceptable to the Tories were the notions that
the people established civil society by contract and that, in order
to protect their life, liberty and property, they could rebel against
those in authority. This right of resistance was regarded as the first
dangerous step to anarchy and mob rule. To combat this fear, which
was undoubtedly genuine, many Whigs began to equivocate about
the right of resistance. Locke himself had not expected that subjects
would lightly or frequently rebel.[18] Other Whig propagandists
stressed this point repeatedly. They made it clear that resistance
was only justified in dire emergencies where the lives, liberties and
property of the whole community were threatened.[19] At the famous
trial of Dr Henry Sacheverell, who was impeached in 1710 for
casting doubts on the legitimacy of the Revolution, the Whig
managers took great care to argue that the Revolution was an
exceptional response to a unique situation.[20] This retreat from the
radical implications of the right of resistance eventually led some
Whig theorists to abandon the doctrine altogether.[21]

To maintain political stability and to restrict political influence
to the men of wealth, the Whigs became increasingly conservative.
The Tories, meanwhile, came to realize that they were more fearful
that the licentious multitude would reduce society to a state of
anarchy than they were attached to the prerogatives of the crown.
They concluded that the doctrine of non-resistance was still a firm

---

Commons of England (London, 1701), p. 3; Peter Paxton, Civil Polity. A Treatise
Concerning the Nature of Government (London, 1703), pp. 155–73; The Original
Institution, Power and Jurisdiction of Parliament (London, 1707), passim; An Introduc-
tion to a Treatise concerning the Legislative Power (London, 1708), passim; and [William
Hay], An Essay on Civil Government (London, 1728), pp. 29–31.

[18] Second Treatise, paras. 208, 225, 230.

[19] An Essay upon the Original and Designe of Magistracie (London, 1689), pp. 6–7;
The New Oath of Allegiance Justified, from the Original Constitution of the English
Monarchy (London, 1689), p. 21; James Tyrrell, Bibliotheca Politica, pp. 177, 779–
81, 808; Benjamin Hoadly, The Measures of Submission to the Civil Magistrate con-
sidered (London, 1706), pp. 171–74; and idem, The Original and Institution of Civil
Government Discuss'd (London, 1710), pp. 125–27, 150–56.

[20] See Robert Walpole's speech in The Tryal of Dr Henry Sacheverell (London,
1710), p. 92.

[21] E.g., William Blackstone, Commentaries on the Laws of England, i, pp. 160–61;
Josiah Tucker, A Treatise Concerning Civil Government (London, 1781), pp. 3–96;
Robert Nares, Principles of Government deduced from Reason, supported by English Ex-
perience, and opposed to French Errors (London, 1792), pp. 139–40: [John Reeves],
Thoughts on the English Government (London, 1795), pp. 38–43; and [George Chal-
mers], A Vindication of the Privilege of the People, in respect of the Constitutional Right of
Free Discussion (London, 1796), pp. 65–67.

buttress to law and order, whereas the doctrine of the divine right of kings could only lead them to Jacobitism and civil war. Thus, their desire for order convinced men of conservative sentiments that it was better to have any government to which men were prepared to submit than a legitimate government which men were determined to resist. Some argued that the surprising success of the Revolution was a sign of God's intervention in the political affairs of England. They must therefore submit to the inscrutable workings of Divine Providence.[22] It seems likely that a larger number surrendered to the commands of sheer political necessity. Sir John Bramston voiced the opinions of many Tories when he gave his reasons for reluctantly accepting the Revolution settlement:

> By his [James II's] absence it became necessary that Governement should be by some body, to avoid confusion. There can be no Governement without submission to it, that can, whether by one or more, have no assurance of submission but by a religious tye and obligation; the constant practice in all states is by oath to obleige obedience. When the Governement is fixed, obedience becomes necessarie to it, and conscience obleiges privat persons to yeild obedience, as well as prudence and safety to prevent anarchy, and the rable from spoilinge and robbinge the noble and wealthy. These assertions and reasons seem to me to arise out of pure necessity.[23]

The government that appeared to have been fixed by the Revolution was based on the combined authority of King, Lords and Commons. The Tories were therefore driven to the task of instructing subjects in their moral and religious duty to obey the powers that be; in other words, to submit to the authority of the legislature. As they came to abandon the divine right of kings, they began to substitute the divine right of the legislature. A clear sign of this new interpretation of the doctrine of non-resistance can be found in the famous sermon that John Sharp, the Tory Archbishop of York, delivered to the House of Lords on 30 January 1700. In pleading the right of the clergy to preach the traditional doctrine of non-resistance, he made it clear that the authority that must be obeyed was statute law and not the royal prerogative:

> To speak this as plainly as I can. As the laws of the land are the measures of our active obedience; so are also the same laws the

---

[22] Gerald M. Straka, *Anglican Reaction to the Glorious Revolution* (Madison, Wisconsin, 1962), pp. 65–79 and 'The Final Phase of Divine Right Theory in England 1688–1702', *EHR*, lxxvii (1962), pp. 638–58.

[23] *The Autobiography of Sir John Bramston*, ed. P. Braybrooke (Camden Society, old series, xxxii, 1845), p. 355.

measure of our submission. And as we are not bound to obey but where the laws and constitution require our obedience; so neither are we bound to submit but as the laws and constitution do require our submission.[24]

This first tentative attempt at reconciling the most important Tory doctrine to the Revolution settlement was soon supported by the efforts of many other Anglican divines. Offspring Blackall, Bishop of Exeter in Anne's reign, explicitly recognized that the legislature was the sovereign authority in the state and that it was this power that could never be resisted. Blackall's whole thesis is of crucial importance in understanding the way in which moderate Tories came to accept some of the political doctrines of conservative Whigs. He stressed that government was ordained by God and so was the submission of subjects; but he denied that God had decreed that only absolute monarchies were legitimate forms of government. God had in fact allowed a variety of forms of government to develop in different societies. By arguing this thesis Blackall was able to jettison the doctrine of the divine right of kings, while still preaching the doctrine of non-resistance to the powers that be. An absolute ruler, who had voluntarily agreed to share his sovereignty with a representative assembly, could not subsequently recover his previous unlimited authority without the express consent of that assembly. Conversely, if a government had been set up by a social contract, then the people could never reclaim their original authority but must render unqualified obedience to the sovereign power that they themselves had created.[25] With these arguments Blackall could reject the claims of both Jacobites and radical Whigs. While accepting one aspect of Whig ideology, namely that sovereignty lay with King, Lords and Commons, he was able to remain loyal to the traditional Tory and Anglican doctrine of non-resistance.

Blackall's thesis was invaluable to those Tories who were anxious to dissociate themselves from Jacobitism. Jonathan Swift, for example, was an Anglican divine who sympathized with much Tory ideology; but, as an Irish Protestant, he was alarmed at the prospect of a Catholic monarch sitting once more on the throne. It is therefore not surprising to find him advocating non-resistance to the sovereign legislature.[26] The Whigs were certainly taken aback, how-

[24] John Sharp, *A Sermon preached before the House of Lords, 30 January 1700* (London, 1700), pp. 20–21.
[25] Offspring Blackall, *The Subject's Duty* (London, 1705) and idem., *The Divine Institution of Magistracy* (London, 1709).
[26] *The Sentiments of a Church-of-England Man, with respect to Religion and Government* (London, 1708) in *The Prose Works of Jonathan Swift*, ed. Herbert Davis, ii (Oxford,

ever, when they discovered that the managers of Dr Sacheverell's defence in 1710 were prepared to develop the same argument. The impeachment of Sacheverell had been designed for the purpose of making party capital for the Whigs by convicting a Tory divine of preaching against the Revolution. The Tory managers for the defence could not deny that Sacheverell had preached the utter illegality of resistance, but they hoped to confound the Whigs by asserting that the Doctor had meant the whole legislature and not merely James II when he referred to the supreme authority in the state. Samuel Dodd, one of the managers for the defence, claimed:

> The supreme power is the Queen and Parliament, and to this supreme power the Doctor has prest the utter unlawfulness of resistance; and I have not heard it said by any that it is lawful to resist the Queen in Parliament. Here is the strength of the nation, and here there ought to be a standing obedience, otherwise it is setting up the people to be judges, and not the collective body of the people assembled in Parliament.[27]

It is extremely doubtful whether Sacheverell had preached any such doctrine, but it is highly significant that more moderate Tories were prepared to accept this doctrine in order to reconcile their principles to the established fact of the Revolution settlement.

This change in ideology depended heavily on the Tory belief in the divine origin of political authority, but it also owed much to the powerful appeal of legal customs and traditions. Men of property and the defenders of order had long understood politics in legal as well as in religious terms. They knew that much English law was based on custom, precedent and prescription rather than on the deliberate, conscious decisions of an absolute monarch or a sovereign legislature. They also knew that many property rights were based on possession and long prescriptive right rather than on legal documents. Thus, in both the field of common law and the sphere of property rights, it was recognized that an appeal to prescription could make good a lack of documentary legal evidence. Conservative upholders of order, both Whig and Tory, were able to use this respectable doctrine of prescriptive right as a means to reconcile themselves to the sovereign authority of parliament. They recognized that it was dangerous to claim that the legislature had a right

---

1939), p. 16; and *The Examiner*, no. 33 (22 March 1710/11) in *ibid.*, iii (Oxford, 1940), pp. 110–16.

[27] *The Tryal of Dr Henry Sacheverell*, p. 203. Sir Simon Harcourt, the principal manager of Sacheverell's defence, was the first to introduce this argument. *Ibid.*, p. 179.

to the exercise of sovereign authority merely because parliament was in fact exercising such power. In other words, it would not satisfy them to maintain unequivocally that might was right. The doctrine of prescription, however, enabled them to defend parliamentary sovereignty as legitimate. The fact of power was, by means of prescription, made to coincide with a right to exercise it.[28]

The first champion of William III's prescriptive right to power was William Sherlock, a former defender of the divine right of kings. In coming to terms with the Revolution he justified his action by claiming that the canons of the Church of England recognized the legitimacy and sanctity of any thoroughly-settled government. Canon XXVIII in Bishop Overall's *Convocation Book*, written in 1606 but first published in 1690, stated that any new form of government, once firmly established, even though begun by rebellion or usurpation, received its authority from God.[29] Sherlock's thesis was rejected by the non-jurors, but his use of prescriptive right was imitated by others who applied it not merely to William's claim to the throne, but to the sovereign authority of parliament. Offspring Blackall maintained:

'Tis most reasonable that in every place that should be taken to be the most rightful government which is established; the powers that be are ordained by God; and the best title to government is that which has prevailed by prescription.[30]

And Blackall, as we have seen, claimed that sovereign authority was exercised by the legislature. William Higden, another non-juror who eventually came to terms with the Revolution in 1709, borrowed from both Sherlock and Blackall. He maintained that a monarch who had taken possession of a throne and a parliament that exercised sovereign authority both gained the prescriptive right to do so once they were firmly established.[31]

Throughout the eighteenth century the conservative defenders of order made constant use of prescriptive right to justify the sovereignty of parliament. David Hume maintained that almost all governments originated in usurpation or conquest, but, once firmly

[28] For evidence on the political use made of prescription immediately after the Glorious Revolution I am indebted to Jeffrey M. Nelson of Harvard University, who let me see his unpublished paper, 'The Presumption of Power: Law and Ideology in the Glorious Revolution'.

[29] *Bishop Overall's Convocation Book*, MCDVI (1690), pp. 55–59. Sherlock's arguments were presented in *Their Present Majesties Government proved to be th[o]roughly settled* (London, 1691) and *The Case of Allegiance due to Sovereign Powers* (London, 1691).

[30] Offspring Blackall, *The Divine Institution of Magistracy*, pp. 2–3.

[31] William Higden, *A View of the English Constitution* (London, 1709), pp. 22–48.

established, they were rarely challenged and they had the right to demand obedience.[32] Edmund Burke was even less concerned than most defenders of prescription with the original good title to authority. It was the passage of time that created a right to exercise power. Prescription 'through long usage, mellows into legality governments that were violent in their commencement.'[33] The British constitution itself was, in Burke's view, the best example of right established by custom: 'Our constitution is a prescriptive constitution; it is a constitution whose sole authority is that it has existed time out of mind.'[34] For William Paley the authority of parliament and the willingness of subjects to obey it rested heavily on prejudice, while prejudice itself was founded on prescription:

> They who obey from prejudice, are determined by an opinion of right in their governors; which opinion is founded upon *prescription.* . . . Nor is it to be wondered at, that mankind should reverence authority founded in prescription, when they observe that it is prescription which confers the title to almost every thing else. The whole course, and all the habits of civil life, favour this prejudice. Upon what other foundation stands any man's right to his estate? . . . It is natural to transfer the same principles to the affairs of government, and to regard those exertions of power which have been long exercised and acquiesced in, as so many *rights.* . . .[35]

Fear of anarchy and dread of civil war made the acceptance of parliamentary sovereignty appear to be a political necessity. The concepts of the divine right of the legislature and of prescriptive right provided this necessity with the respectable cloak of religious and legal justification. Finally, the utility of parliament convinced most men of wealth and power that they should protect the legislature's claim to sovereign authority. During the eighteenth century they increasingly realized that the sovereignty of parliament could

[32] David Hume, 'Of the Original Contract', in *Three Essays, Moral and Political* (London, 1748), pp. 29–54.

[33] Edmund Burke, *Reflections on the Revolution in France* (London, 1790), in *Works* ii, p. 435. See also *ibid.*, ii, pp. 331, 442–43.

[34] 'Speech on the Reform of the Representation of the House of Commons', in *Works*, vi, p. 146. See also Russell Kirk, 'Burke and the Philosophy of Prescription' *Journal of the History of Ideas*, xiv (1953), pp. 365–80; J. G. A. Pocock, 'Burke and the Ancient Constitution—A Problem in the History of Ideas', *Historical Journal*, iii (1960), pp. 125–43; and Paul Lucas, 'On Edmund Burke's Doctrine of Prescription; Or, An Appeal from the New to the Old Lawyers', *ibid.*, xi (1968), pp. 35–63.

[35] William Paley, *Principles of Moral and Political Philosophy* (London, 1785), pp. 407–08. Paley's italics.

both limit the power of the crown and protect the propertied élite from any threat from the lower orders of society. The legislature's ultimate control over the raising of revenue ensured that the king would not be able to exercise arbitrary or absolute power. The electoral system, with rotten boroughs, a propertied franchise and with substantial property qualifications for M.P.s, meant that parliament was dominated by the aristocracy, gentry and wealthy merchants. To prevent the voters bringing pressure to bear upon them, the majority of M.P.s strove to keep their behaviour in the house secret and insisted that they must be the independent representatives not the instructed delegates of the people.[36]

It was soon realized that parliament was not restricted to the negative role of limiting the royal prerogative and keeping power out of the hands of the people; it could serve men of property in more positive ways. Soon after annual sessions of parliament became accepted as normal practice members began to promote private and local bills to protect and benefit sectional interests. While it is true that no eighteenth-century administration saw its priorities in terms of a legislative programme, every session of parliament passed numerous bills on such matters as turnpikes, enclosures and river navigation that were designed to benefit men of property and influence.[37] Parliament was also used to increase the protection given to property. Between 1688 and 1820 the number of offences against property that could be punished by the death sentence increased from about fifty to over two hundred. Parliament also passed a mass of legislation about crimes involving grain, wood, trees, fruit, dogs, cattle, horses, hedges and game—crimes that affected the gentry in particular—which allowed these cases to be tried by summary proceedings. Thus, men of property did not have to worry about the problems of drawing up formal legal indictments or about acquittals being granted by tender-minded juries. As J.P.s they could deal summarily with those who dared to attack their property.[38]

The Revolution settlement made it clear that the doctrine of parliamentary sovereignty had the enthusiastic support of many Whigs. The willingness of many Tories to vote for the Act of Settlement of 1701 and the Regency Act of 1706 were clear indications

[36] Lucy S. Sutherland, 'Edmund Burke and the Relations between Members of Parliament and their Constituents', *Studies in Burke and his Time*, x (London, 1968), pp. 1005–21.

[37] Between 1711 and 1811 the annual legislative output increased from 74 acts, public and private, to 128 public and 295 local or private acts. Sheila Lambert, *Bills and Acts* (Cambridge, 1971), p. 52.

[38] Douglas Hay, 'Property, Authority and the Criminal Law', in *Albion's Fatal Tree*, ed. Douglas Hay, Peter Linebaugh and E. P. Thompson (London, 1975), pp. 17–63.

that they too were coming to recognize the authority of the legislature to settle the succession to the crown. It is possible, however, that the full implications of parliamentary sovereignty were not yet appreciated by many Whigs and Tories. It was not until 1716 that the full extent of parliament's sovereign authority was made quite explicit. In that year the Septennial Act prolonged the life of a parliament, which had originally been elected for three years. The majority who passed this act clearly accepted that no power or right could limit the exercise of parliament's authority. It was decided that parliament's power could not be curbed by the wishes of an electorate which had chosen representatives for three years only or by the authority of previous statutes defining the length of parliament. This interpretation of the extent of parliament's sovereignty was to be the prevailing one throughout the eighteenth century and beyond. The considerable opposition to the Septennial Act, however, shows that some men were convinced that there were limits to parliament's authority. It is to the debates on the nature of these limitations that I will now turn.

II

The doctrine of parliamentary sovereignty prevailed against its critics not just because it was supported by the men of greatest influence, but because these critics were never united among themselves. They differed about the location and nature of political sovereignty. On the extreme wing of the forces of conservatism a few Jacobites still clung to their traditional support for the divine right of kings. On the fringes of the Whig party a radical element propagated the doctrine of the sovereignty of the people. Between these two extremes was a much larger and, in parliamentary terms, far more significant body of opinion. Unfortunately for its chances of success, this body was sometimes confused in its views on the nature and location of sovereignty and was rarely united in action. While it was prepared to concede that there was no institution in the state that had greater power than parliament, it was not ready to accord the legislature absolute sovereign authority. In trying to restrict the sphere of parliament's authority, appeals were sometimes made to the law of nature and sometimes to the constitution or to fundamental law. Very few men followed the example of the American colonists and devised new ways of dealing with the dangers inherent in the doctrine of parliamentary sovereignty.

The Jacobites were of course the first opponents of parliamentary sovereignty. Relying heavily on the work of Sir Robert Filmer, they asserted the doctrines of the divine right of kings and of non-resistance to the Lord's anointed, despite the success of the Glorious Revolution. Resting their moral case on an appeal to Holy Scripture, their historical case on the absolute power of William the Conqueror and their political case on the need to preserve order at all costs, they concluded that the king must have absolute and arbitrary authority in the state. While parliaments might be summoned and consulted, their power was entirely subordinate to the will of the king. Parliament had no more right than the most humble subject to resist the royal commands. Such were the authoritarian concepts still being propagated by Charles Leslie, Luke Milbourne, Matthias Earbery and others until the virtual collapse of Jacobitism after the abortive rebellion of 1715.[39]

The supporters of absolute monarchy were on the defensive after 1688 and barely visible after 1715. Those Whigs, on the other hand, who claimed that the people were sovereign were in evidence throughout the eighteenth century. The ideological position built up by Sidney, Locke, Tyrrell and others in the late seventeenth century rested on the fundamental doctrine that political authority was based on the social contract. This compact involved either the express or tacit consent of the people. Since political authority originated with the people, then this power should be exercised for the benefit of the people. The people therefore only granted power to those in authority on condition that they did not abuse their trust. Whenever the supreme authority broke its trust by attacking the fundamental rights of the whole community, then the people had the right to resist such a breach of the terms of the original contract.

This Whig concept of government by consent was essential to combat the doctrine of the divine right of kings, but it had radical implications that could endanger the privileged position of the men of property. If the people were encouraged to regard themselves as the ultimate source of authority, then perhaps the impoverished and

---

[39] For the propagation of divine right arguments after the Revolution see, *e.g.*, *The Debates in Deposing Kings; and of the Royal Succession of Great Britain* (London, 1688); William Sherlock, *The Case of Resistance of the Supreme Powers stated and resolved, according to the Doctrines of the Holy Scriptures* (London, 1690); J. Kettlewell, *The Duty of Allegiance settled upon its true grounds, according to Scripture, reason, and the Opinion of the Church* (London, 1691); George Dawson, *Origo Legum: Or a Treatise of the Origin of Laws, and their Obliging Power* (London, 1694); Luke Milbourne, *The People not the Original of Civil Power, proved from God's word, the doctrine and liturgy of the establish'd church, and from the laws of England* (London, 1707); [Charles Leslie], *The Best Answer Ever was Made and to which No Answer Will be Made* (London, 1709); [*idem*] *The Finishing Stroke* (London, 1711); *Jura Regiae Majestatis in Anglia: Or, the Rights of the English Monarchy* (London, 1711); [George Harbin] *The Hereditary Right of the Crown of England Asserted* (London, 1713); [Charles Leslie], *The Old English Constitution* (London, 1714); and [Matthias Earbery], *The Old English Constitution vindicated* (London, 1717).

licentious multitude would refuse to obey their masters and would seek wealth and power for themselves. The Whigs of the late seventeenth century had no desire to see such an exercise of popular sovereignty. They therefore took care to deny the people any effective power. John Locke, for example, while granting that the people had created the legislative power and were therefore in a sense superior to it, nevertheless limited the further practical exercise of popular sovereignty. Once the political community had been established, then the legislature was sovereign. Locke did not allow the people to recover their original authority unless the social contract was clearly broken and civil society was dissolved. Such a total breakdown of order was regarded as a very rare event. While the civil society remained in being, then the people had little active power. Locke assumed that explicit consent to the acts of the sovereign legislature would be given by a representative body that in fact shared the legislative function with the king. He also implied that this assembly, as in the England of his day, would represent the interests of the men of property.[40] Other Whig theorists were even more explicit in restricting political power to men of substance. Both Algernon Sidney and James Tyrrell restricted political rights to masters of families who owned enough property to make themselves economically independent.[41] Daniel Defoe was even more explicit. While he acknowledged that all political power originated with the people and could be regained by them, his definition of 'the people' was limited to the owners of land:

I do not place this right upon the inhabitants, but upon the Freeholders; the *Freeholders* are the proper owners of the Country: It is their own, and the other inhabitants are but sojourners, like lodgers in a house, and ought to be subject to such laws as the Freeholders impose upon them, or else they must remove, because the Freeholders having a right to the land, the other have no right to live there but upon sufferance. . . . And I make no question but that property of land is the best title to government in the world; and if the King was universal landlord, he ought to be universal governour of right, and the people so living on his lands ought to obey him, or go off of his premises.[42]

[40] J. W. Gough, *John Locke's Political Philosophy* (Oxford, 1950), pp. 64–92 and John Dunn, *The Political Thought of John Locke* (Cambridge, 1969), pp. 120–47.

[41] Algernon Sidney, *Discourses concerning Government* (3rd edn, London 1751), pp. 74–75, 423, 450; James Tyrrell, *Patriarcha Non Monarcha* (London, 1681), pp. 83–84 and *idem*, *Bibliotheca Politica*, *advertisement* and p. 808.

[42] [Daniel Defoe], *The Original Power of the Collective Body of the People of England, Examined and Asserted* (London, 1702), p. 18.

Since even the Real Whigs or Commonwealthmen did not regard all men as having political rights,[43] the Whig notion of popular sovereignty was not in fact a direct or immediately-perceived threat to the doctrine of parliamentary sovereignty. The limited definition of 'the people' corresponded closely to the actual electorate and there was little evidence to suggest that the voters believed that they had the right to reject the authority of parliament. Until the later eighteenth century the electorate and those who respected the rights of the voters were less concerned with challenging the sovereignty of parliament and more preoccupied with increasing the influence of the electors on parliament. They therefore concentrated their attacks on the corruption of the House of Commons by the executive. Attempts were made to force M.P.s to be more responsive to their constituents, but this was done to give the opposition more power within parliament, not to take authority away from parliament in order to make the people sovereign.[44]

By the later eighteenth century the concept of the sovereign people came to pose a much more serious threat to the doctrine of parliamentary sovereignty. Perhaps inspired by the American argument of 'no taxation without representation' a new generation of radicals began to claim that all those who paid taxes should have the right to vote. The next step was to maintain that those who paid indirect taxes contributed as much or more revenue to the national exchequer and therefore had as much right to be represented. It was then but a short step to the claim that all men had the right to vote.[45] This campaign for electoral reform was accompanied by renewed claims that M.P.s were merely the delegates of the people and that the legislature derived its authority from the people. The sovereign people therefore could withdraw this power if parliament betrayed its trust. The pure doctrine of popular sovereignty was now being put for the first time in the eighteenth century. Richard Price, along

[43] See, e.g., [John Toland], *The Militia Reform'd* (London, 1698), pp. 18–23; Henry Neville, *Discourses concerning Government* (London, 1698), pp. 68–69; John Trenchard and Thomas Gordon, *Cato's Letters* (5th edn, London, 1748), no. 85 (14 June 1722) and no. 133 (15 June 1723); and *The Works of Sallust*, ed. Thomas Gordon (London 1744), p. 83.

[44] Lucy S. Sutherland, 'Edmund Burke and the Relations between Members of Parliament and their Constituents', *Studies in Burke and his Time*, x (1968), 1005–08.

[45] The debate on extending the franchise from men of property to taxpayers and finally to all men can be followed in *Reflexions on Representation in Parliament* (London, 1766), pp. 9–15; *London Magazine* (November, 1770), pp. 553–59; [John Cartwright], *Take Your Choice!* (London, 1776), pp. 19–23; [David Williams], *Letters on Political Liberty* (London, 1782), pp. 79–80; and *An Authentic Copy of the Duke of Richmond's Bill for a Parliamentary Reform* (London, 1783), pp. 6–9.

with many others, rejected parliamentary sovereignty in favour of the sovereign rights of the people:

Nothing, therefore, can be more absurd than the doctrine which some have taught, with respect to the omnipotence of parliaments. They possess no power beyond the limits of the trust for the execution of which they were formed. If they contradict this trust, they betray their constituents, and dissolve themselves. All delegated power must be subordinated and limited.—If omnipotence can, with any sense, be ascribed to a legislature, it must be lodged where all legislative authority originates; that is, in the PEOPLE. For their sakes government is instituted; and their's is the only real omnipotence.[46]

The radicals, despite the volume of their propaganda, had few supporters among men of political influence. Edmund Burke spoke for the overwhelming majority of the ruling oligarchy in and out of parliament when he condemned the doctrine of the sovereignty of the people. He argued that the original contract, the ancient constitution and the Revolution settlement all testified to the fact that the people had no power distinct from the legislature that represented them. Sovereignty had been given explicitly and inviolably to King, Lords and Commons.[47] In the 1790s, when Burke was restating the doctrine of parliamentary sovereignty, he could count on overwhelming support from the men of property who feared that revolution might spread from France to Britain. For most of the eighteenth century, however, it was possible to find considerable opposition from even conservative men of property to the concept of an absolutely sovereign legislature. All men of political influence were not hypocrites who only paid lip-service to the notion of government by consent. The genuine pride taken in the constitution and in the liberties of Englishmen, and the traditional hostility to arbitrary, absolute power, made many men doubt the wisdom of giving parliament unfettered authority.

[46] Richard Price, *Observations on the Nature of Civil Liberty* (7th edn, London, 1776), pp. 15–16. Similar statements can be found in [Obadiah Hulme], *An Historical Essay on the English Constitution* (London, 1771), pp. 4–7; *Resistance no Rebellion* (London, 1775), pp. 12–13; Richard Watson, *The Principles of the Revolution vindicated* (Cambridge, 1776), p. 11; Richard Price, *A Discourse on the Love of Our Country* (London, 1790), pp. 26–35; Thomas Paine, *Rights of Man* (1791–92), ed. Henry Collins (Harmondsworth, 1969), pp. 111, 142, 146, 150–52, 165–66, 213; James Mackintosh, *Vindiciae Gallicae* (London, 1791), p. 294; *The Birthright of Britons* (London, 1792), pp. 120–23; and John Thelwall, *The Natural and Constitutional Rights of Britons to Annual Parliaments, Universal Suffrage, and the Freedom of Popular Association* (London, 1795), *passim*.

[47] Edmund Burke, *Reflections on the Revolution in France*, in *Works*, ii, pp. 287–308 and *An Appeal from the New to the Old Whigs* (London, 1791), in *ibid.*, iii, pp. 25–86.

These doubts were expressed in a variety of arguments. Indeed, the variety of the arguments may have blunted their effectiveness at the time and may account for their subsequent neglect by historians. One popular argument took a moral line. It was maintained that the law of God, derived either explicitly from the Scriptures or indirectly from the law of nature, was superior to that of any human agency.[48] The Church of England continued to teach the doctrine of passive obedience: where the command of any secular authority ran counter to the commands of God, then subjects must refuse to obey though they must passively submit to any punishment inflicted upon them for their disobedience. Both John Locke and William Blackstone, who were among the staunchest defenders of the doctrine of legislative sovereignty, stressed that no human power could command what was against the law of nature.[49] Locke defined those rights given to all men by the law of nature as the right to life, liberty and property; with the emphasis clearly on property. Blackstone too was most concerned to protect the rights of property,[50] though he never clearly defined what he meant by the law of nature. Nevertheless, he was quite convinced of its authority: 'This law of nature, being coeval with mankind, and dictated by God himself, is of course superior in obligation to any other. It is binding over all the globe, in all countries, and at all times: no humane laws are of any validity if contrary to this. . . .'[51]

Eighteenth-century parliaments were careful not to provoke the hostility of the Church of England and they were usually concerned to protect rather than to infringe the rights to property. Nevertheless, there were numerous occasions when a minority in parliament believed that the legislature was clearly exceeding its authority. In these cases the most usual line of attack was not to invoke the law of God or the law of nature, but to appeal to the fundamental laws of the constitution.[52] Sometimes it was claimed that specific constitutional decisions were inviolable and could not be altered or repealed by subsequent acts of parliament. The examples most fre-

[48] See, e.g. [George Ridpath], Parliamentary Right maintain'd or the Hanover Succession justify'd (London, 1714), p. 165; Lord Camden's speech, 10 February 1766, in Parl. Hist., xvi, p. 168; [Granville Sharp], A Declaration of the People's Right to a Share in the Legislature (London, 1774), p. 11; and H. Goodricke, Observations on Dr Price's Theory and Principles of Civil Liberty and Government (York, 1776), pp. 43–44 n.

[49] Locke, Second Treatise, paras. 135–42 and Blackstone, Commentaries, i, pp. 40, 42.

[50] See Daniel Boorstin, The Mysterious Science of the Law (Boston, Mass., 1941), esp. chap. ix.

[51] Commentaries, i, p. 40. At times Blackstone appeared to believe that the crown was sovereign. Ibid., i, 250–52. See also Ernest Barker, Essays on Government (Oxford, 1945), pp. 121–54.

[52] For a fuller treatment of the debate on fundamental law, see J. W. Gough, Fundamental Law in English Constitutional History (Oxford, 1955), pp. 160–202.

quently cited were Magna Carta, the Triennial Act and the Act of Union with Scotland.[53] The Scots protested on several occasions that parliament was acting unconstitutionally in seeking to amend the terms of the Union,[54] while the passing of the Septennial Act in 1716 was accompanied by one of the most determined onslaughts on the doctrine of parliamentary sovereignty.[55] The government's success in passing the Septennial Act was the clearest demonstration of the *fact* of parliamentary sovereignty, but it did not convince the opposition to it of parliament's *right* to this authority. Throughout the rest of the eighteenth-century efforts were made to repeal this act, which was widely regarded as unconstitutional, and to restore triennial parliaments. More frequent still were complaints by opposition elements in parliament that ministers were introducing legislation that was contrary to the spirit of the constitution. The critics of Sir Robert Walpole's policies, for example, and the later opposition to government policy towards the American colonies invariably raised the charge that parliament was undermining the principles of the constitution. Obadiah Hulme was voicing the fears of a significant body of opinion when he declared:

> There is not a more dangerous doctrine can be adopted in our state, than to admit that the legislative authority hath any right to alter, the first principles of our constitution, by acts of parliament. Upon this foundation, they may mould it into what shape they please; and, in the end, make us slaves, by law.[56]

[53] See, *e.g.*, Daniel Defoe's *Review*, iii, no. 151 (19 December 1706); iv, no. 49 (3 June 1707), no. 51 (7 June 1707), no. 69 (22 July 1707), no. 72 (29 July 1707); v, no. 106 (30 November 1708); vi, no. 20 (19 May 1709), no. 53 (4 August 1709), no. 128 (31 January 1710); ix, no. 19 (4 October 1712), no. 20 (7 October 1712); Richard Steele, 18 December 1719, in *Parl. Hist.*, vii, pp. 611–12; Ald. Sawbridge, April 1771, *ibid.*, xvii, p. 176; Sir Roger Newdigate, 6 February 1772, *ibid.*, xvii, p. 256; and Granville Sharp, *A Declaration of the People's Natural Right to a Share in the Legislature* (London, 1774), pp. 197–238.

[54] Some Scots claimed that the Treason Act of 1709, the Patronage Act of 1712, the Malt Tax of 1713 and the Heritable Jurisdictions Act of 1747 were contrary to the terms of the Act of Union and hence unconstitutional.

[55] *Parl. Hist.*, vii, pp. 304–57.

[56] [Obadiah Hulme], *An Historical Essay on the English Constitution* (London, 1771) p. 141. See also Bolingbroke, *A Dissertation upon Parties* (1733–34) in *Works*, ii (London, 1844), pp. 150-51; Lord Polwarth, 3 February 1738, in *Parl. Hist.*, x, p. 456; *Common Sense*, no. 140 (6 October 1739); Admiral Vernon, 27 November 1753, in *Parl. Hist.*, xv, pp. 160–61; [William Jones], *The Constitutional Crisis* (London 1768), pp. 12–14; Granville Sharp, *A Declaration of the People's Natural Right to a Share in the Legislature* (London, 1774), pp. 16–17; Willoughby Bertie, Earl of Abingdon, *Thoughts on the Letter of Edmund Burke, Esq., to the Sheriffs of Bristol, on the Affairs of America* (Oxford, 1777), p. 43; John Wilkes, 10 December 1777, in *Parl. Hist.*, xix, p. 570; and [Capel Lofft], *An Argument on the Nature of Party and Faction* (London, 1780), p. 13.

The opponents of the doctrine of parliamentary sovereignty were numerous and vocal, but appeals to such vague, ill-defined notions as natural rights, natural law, fundamental law or the spirit of the constitution proved to be ineffective. The American colonists were much more successful not only in actually rejecting parliament's claims to sovereign authority, but in devising means to limit sovereignty in their new state. They divided sovereignty between executive, legislative and judiciary, and between federal and state governments. They also defined the people's rights in a written constitution and established a system of judicial review to defend this constitution. Furthermore, in the last analysis, they acknowledged the sovereignty of the people. The critics of parliamentary sovereignty in eighteenth-century Britain never developed, and only rarely suggested, such effective restraints. The major exception was Thomas Paine. A devoted admirer of the American experiment, he was convinced that the natural rights of man could only be safeguarded if a written constitution clearly restricted the authority of both the legislature and the executive. In his opinion, it was essential that such a written constitution should be the act of the whole people and that it should not confine itself to general principles. It must lay down detailed restrictions on the authority of those in power. If such a constitution had been in existence in the reign of George I, then parliament could never have passed the Septennial Act.[57]

Paine's constitutional proposals were never put to the test. Attempts to frame a written constitution and to endorse popular sovereignty through the calling of huge, representative National Conventions foundered.[58] Other, more modest, schemes for curbing the sovereignty of parliament were even less popular and were certainly no more successful. The doctrine of the separation of powers was rejected in favour of the concept of a balanced constitution of King, Lords and Commons, though occasional references were made to the possibility of divided sovereignty.[59] Major Cartwright once

[57] *Rights of Man*, Part Two, chap. 4.

[58] James Burgh first suggested that a National Convention should be called so that the people could resume their sovereign rights and regain their constitutional liberties. *Political Disquisitions*, iii (London, 1774), pp. 428–34. John Jebb hoped that the Association movement of 1779 might set up a national delegation which could dictate to parliament, but this suggestion alarmed the more moderate reformers of the County Movement. See Ian R. Christie, *Wilkes, Wyvill and Reform* (London, 1962), pp. 78–81. The scheme for a National Convention was revived in Joseph Gerrald, *A Convention the Only Means of Saving us from Ruin* (London, 1793), but, when a Convention met that year in Edinburgh, the authorities ruthlessly prosecuted the organizers. G. S. Veitch, *The Genesis of Parliamentary Reform* (London, 1913), pp. 275–98.

[59] Bolingbroke's discussion of the balanced constitution was sometimes ambiguous and this has led to suggestions that he advocated a separation of powers

wrote in favour of the system of judicial review, by which a court could decide whether acts of parliament were unconstitutional or not, but this scheme found little favour with other reformers.[60] In his *Fragment on Government*, Jeremy Bentham considered the notion of judicial review, but was not convinced of the merits of such a scheme because it gave too much power to judges, who were not representative of the nation as a whole. In a later work he admitted that the supreme legislature might be limited by a written constitution, as in the case of Germany, Switzerland and the United Provinces. If the legislature wished subsequently to change the terms of the constitution, then it could seek the consent of the people, perhaps through some form of plebiscite or referendum. Bentham clearly showed little enthusiasm for such a constitutional arrangement. In general he approved of the sovereignty of parliament, though it is not clear whether he regarded attempts to limit the supreme legislature as impossible or merely dangerous. He certainly concluded that the most effective limitation on the sovereignty of parliament was the recognition by those in authority that the people might not obey, and might even forcibly resist, acts of parliament.[61]

It should now have become evident that while the doctrine of parliamentary sovereignty developed in the eighteenth century to become one of the most distinctive features of Britain's unwritten constitution, this development did not go unchallenged. The critics of the doctrine may not have succeeded in having it rejected, but they almost certainly convinced even its strongest supporters that the doctrine was a *legal fiction*. Its value and utility lay in preserving order while allowing for prompt action. These benefits would have

---

between King, Lords and Commons. He certainly wished these three institutions to retain their independent rights and privileges, but he never intended that there should be three absolutely distinct sovereign powers. For a fuller discussion see H. T. Dickinson, *Bolingbroke* (London, 1970), pp. 202–04 and the authorities referred to on these pages. Governor Johnstone, in a parliamentary speech, 26 October 1775, referred to the divided sovereignty to be observed in Germany and the United Provinces. *Parl. Hist.*, xviii, pp. 748–50. David Hume commented on the two independent legislatures of Ancient Rome, but he did not advocate the adoption of the practice in Britain. 'Of Some Remarkable Customs' (1752), in *Essays, Moral, Political and Literary* (London, 1758), pp. 205–07.

[60] [John Cartwright], *American Independence the Interest and Glory of Great Britain* (1774) in *English Defenders of American Freedoms 1774–1778*, ed. Paul H. Smith (Washington D.C., 1972), p. 156.

[61] Jeremy Bentham, *A Fragment on Government and an Introduction to Principles of Morals and Legislation*, ed. Wilfred Harrison (Oxford, 1948), pp. 96–102 and 434–435. These two works were originally published in 1776 and 1789 respectively. For a recent discussion, see H. L. A. Hart, 'Bentham on Sovereignty', in *Jeremy Bentham: Ten Critical Essays*, ed. Bhikhu Parekh (London, 1974), pp. 145–53.

been jeopardized by any rash attempts to trample on the rights and liberties of the people. Even the staunchest advocates of a sovereign parliament were well aware of the strength of the general commitment to government by consent and to the rights of the subject. We have already seen that Locke, Blackstone and Bentham, while generally in favour of parliament's sovereign authority, were conscious of the fact that in practice there were things that parliament should not or could not do. The same mental reservations can be detected in other upholders of the doctrine of parliamentary sovereignty. Burke acknowledged the supreme authority of parliament, but he stressed the dangerous consequences that might ensue if the legislature lost sight of the need to carry public opinion along with it.[62] George III, the most stubborn defender of the sovereign authority of parliament during the dispute with the American colonies, was at times a little uncertain about the full implications of the doctrine he upheld. He believed that parliament might not be free to pass laws for the relief of Roman Catholics because such laws would conflict with the terms of such earlier acts of parliament as the Act of Supremacy and the Act of Uniformity.[63] Finally, some of the acts passed by parliament itself disregarded the implications of the legislature's claim to unfettered sovereign authority. When parliament passed the Act of Union with Ireland in 1800 it claimed that the established Church of Ireland was 'an essential and fundamental part of the union' and it asserted that the union would last 'for ever.'[64] Yet, in 1869, parliament disestablished the Church of Ireland without dissolving the union and eventually the union itself was set aside by parliamentary legislation. Clearly, the survival of the doctrine of parliamentary sovereignty owes a great deal to its general value and utility, but not a little to the awareness that it would not be wise for any parliament to test the full extent of its authority. These valuable political lessons were first learned during the debates on the sovereignty of parliament in the eighteenth century.[65]

University of Edinburgh.

[62] *A Letter to the Sheriffs of Bristol on the Affairs of America* (1777) in *Works*, ii, pp. 27, 35. Even in his most conservative phase Burke could write: 'We have never dreamt that parliaments have any right whatever to violate property, to overrule prescription.' *Reflections on the Revolution in France*, in *Works*, iik p. 423.

[63] George III to Lord Chancellor Kenyon, 7 March 1795. *H.M.C.*, *Lord Kenyon*, pp. 542–43. Lord Kenyon tried hard to explain the doctrine of parliamentary sovereignty to the king, but George was not convinced. G. T. Kenyon, *The Life of Lloyd, First Lord Kenyon* (London, 1873), pp. 305–20.

[64] Articles 1 and 5 of the Act of Union. *Statutes at Large*, xviii (London, 1800), pp. 359, 361.

[65] I am indebted to my colleague F. D. Dow for her helpful comments on an earlier draft of this paper.

PRESIDENTIAL ADDRESS

By Professor G. R. Elton, M.A., Ph.D., Litt.D., F.B.A.

TUDOR GOVERNMENT:
THE POINTS OF CONTACT

III. THE COURT

READ 21 NOVEMBER 1975

WHEN on the previous two occasions I discussed Parliament and Council as political centres, as institutions capable of assisting or undermining stability in the nation, I had to draw attention to quite a few unanswered questions. However, I also found a large amount of well established knowledge on which to rely. Now, in considering the role of the King's or Queen's Court, I stand more baffled than ever, more deserted. We all know that there was a Court, and we all use the term with frequent ease, but we seem to have taken it so much for granted that we have done almost nothing to investigate it seriously. Lavish descriptions abound of lavish occasions, both in the journalism of the sixteenth century and in the history books, but the sort of study which could really tell us what it was, what part it played in affairs, and even how things went there for this or that person, seems to be confined to a few important articles. At times it has all the appearance of a fully fledged institution; at others it seems to be no more than a convenient conceptual piece of shorthand, covering certain people, certain behaviour, certain attitudes. As so often, the shadows of the seventeenth century stretch back into the sixteenth, to obscure our vision. Analysts of the reigns of the first two Stuarts, endeavouring to explain the political troubles of that age, increasingly concentrate upon an alleged conflict between the Court and the Country; and so we are tempted, once again, to seek the prehistory of the ever interesting topic in the age of Elizabeth or even Henry VIII. This may do some good, but only if we know something reasonably precise about the entities we deal in. And here our mentors tend to let us down: for the historians of the early seventeenth century have not yet managed to define their terms. What is the Court? Those whom the Country dislikes. What is the Country? Those whom the Court despises. If we follow Professor Zagorin, we read the Court as embracing all office-holders, including some men in the shires who may never have set eyes on their sovereign.[1] But if we follow him, we must apparently leave out non-officed frequenters of St James's and Whitehall. I do not find this helpful.

There is often virtue in beginning at the beginning: when can we find the sort of Court that Elizabeth queened it in, that stage of all public life, social and cultural and political? I seem to sense a general conviction that its age is coeval with kingship, but I do not think this is true. Perhaps we might heed the intuition of the poet. In *Henry V*, Shakespeare takes us to the Court of France, of Charles VI, but the King of England is shown in Council, camp and battle—never in anything resembling a true Court. Is a Court such as we find under the Tudors conceivable under Henry VI? Dr Ross has suggested that there was some real novelty about Edward IV's Court, with its ceremonial detail and lavish life,[2] and it is apparent that both ceremony and display were imports from Burgundy and France whose example continued to direct the development of the Tudor Court at least down to Henry VIII's death. At present we do not know much about the Court of Henry VII except for the occasional—very occasional—feasts and celebrations that occurred there; and though this ignorance may reflect only the deficiencies of the evidence, I think it really springs from the fact that there is little to know. The Tudor Court as a centre of social and political life springs suddenly into existence with the accession of Henry VIII, and there are reasons why it should have done so.

The true Court of our imagining could not exist until the Crown had destroyed all alternative centres of political loyalty or (to emphasize another function of the Court) all alternative sources of worldly advancement. While there were magnates, their patronage and standing took away from the King's patronage and sovereignty, and their residences from the uniqueness of his Court. The work of raising the King upon an unattainably high platform above all his subjects was not completed until the second Tudor added the visible enjoyment of that position to the reality created by the first. Even in the sixteenth century, mini-alternatives occasionally appeared, carrying with them the phenomena of Court-like centres; Buckingham and possibly Leicester come to mind, as does that pitiful Sheffield-plate copy of the reality, the second earl of Essex. The jealousy of Tudor monarchs, who took care to sterilize such out of date endeavours, was really very well advised: their rule, their power, depended on their uniqueness, and it was their Courts that gave continuous expression to that solitary eminence. Thus the

---

[1] P. Zagorin, *The Court and the Country: the Beginning of the English Revolution* (London, 1969), p. 41.
[2] C. D. Ross, *Edward IV* (London, 1974), p. 312.

politics of the sixteenth century—personal or national, principled or merely ambitious—of necessity 'happened' in the confines of the Court. Most commonly, but not exclusively, of course: let us not forget the politics of Parliament and Council which by no means always coincided with those of the Court. But these latter were the most omnipresent, possibly the most intense, certainly the most confusing and obscure. The contrast between Court and Country ('rusticity') is in this age always one between involvement in and withdrawal from public life, never a posing of alternative public attitudes and activities. Literary convention dictated that the second should be preferred on moral and indeed on medical grounds, as in a charming and unusually lively little book by Bishop Guevara, councillor to Charles V, which that inveterate courtier Sir Francis Bryan translated a year or two before his death when old age had caused even him to tire of the Court.[3] But whether they were sincere or not in their professed preference for the happy life and untroubled sleep of rural retirement, both Guevara and Bryan, like everybody else, took it for granted that politics equals the Court.

Thus in our search for stability-creating institutions we need to look at the people who composed the Court, no easy task because their demography has not been written, and even their population (in the natural-science sense of the term) has not been defined. There is relatively little trouble about the one formal, almost professional, component of the Court, the royal Household in its departments—the lord steward's and lord chamberlain's departments to which under the early Tudors we must now add the Privy Chamber as a separate sector.[4] Here we find bureaucratic organization— specific offices filled by knowable persons who in the sixteenth century were nearly all still personally discharging their duties, so that we only rarely need to look for obscure deputies to sinecurists. However, though this part of the Court may be accessible we still lack studies of it to compare with the work done on its Stuart successor by Professor Aylmer. The Household provided the largest single establishment of salaried and fee-earning posts in the realm, and therefore the most concentrated area for the seekers after patronage. The satisfaction of legitimate ambition ought to be readily traceable here, but this again is work that has not yet been done at all systematically. The problem is not simple or single. Take the lord steward's department. Clerks of the Kitchen and serjeants of the Pantry were men of some standing and reasonable expectation

[3] Antonio de Guevara, *A Dispraise of the Life of a Courtier and a Commendation of the Life of a Labouring Man*, trs. F. Bryan (London, 1548).
[4] *Cf.* D. R. Starkey, 'The King's Privy Chamber 1485–1547,' unpublished Ph.D. dissertation (Cambridge, 1973).

of profit: was there competition for such appointments, and could bestowal of office be influenced by the political standing of patrons? What happens as we penetrate lower down, to grooms, pages, cooks and scullions? The patronage structure of that quite teeming world needs unravelling, though a word of warning against excessive subtlety exists in the well attested fact that certain offices came to be the property, for several generations, of family dynasties like the Thynnes (exceptional only in that they rose to high eminence in the end). My general impression is that the purposes of social stability within the governing order were little affected by success or failure of job-hunting at this level, but our state of ignorance is such that I could be as readily wrong as right.

For obvious reasons one would expect to get more interesting results from a study of the Chamber where employment was offered to the offspring of the political nation, to the sons and daughters of gentlemen, esquires, and (at the top) noblemen. As Dr Starkey has begun to show, the history of the monarch's immedi- ate entourage reflects nothing so much as the power politics of an elite. This is clearly true for the staff of Henry VIII's Privy Chamber and there are modest indications of a similar state of affairs under Henry VII; what, however, was the situation after 1547 and in particular, what was the significance of Elizabeth's changing group of attendants? One thing is clear enough: competition for appoint- ments was at this level fierce, and the supply of places inadequate. The Privy Chamber repeatedly expanded beyond the size laid down, sometimes because the monarch might transfer his favour to new companions without wishing to cast out the old, sometimes simply because these places of honour and potential profit attracted men whose importunity was backed by influence. Any new opportunities in the Chamber establishment produced phenomena familiar, in another way, from the disposal of the confiscated property of the Church—strident appeals for the satisfaction of a share, channelled through the top agents of the Royal patronage. When Henry VIII proposed in 1538 to revive the corps of gentlemen-pensioners, candi- dates for admission (usually on behalf of their sons) lined up in throngs that recall scenes on the mornings of rights issues in the happier days of capitalism. A pensioner's place was bound to be quite expensive to the occupier, while immediate rewards were small; but the fathers who in their dozens wrote to Thomas Crom- well rightly viewed these jobs as investments, and fairly safe invest- ments at that. With power as well as the horn of patronage plenty now firmly monopolized by the Crown, a place at Court was the thing for anyone with ambitions to better himself. Even if a man's affairs or tastes kept him in the country he was well advised to

attend the Court by proxy, that is to say, by placing a son or a
nephew in a strategic position there.[5] Not that the ultimate ambition could be satisfied merely by presence at Court: membership
of the Council, influence on the making of policy, power in its
political guise, continued to depend only in small part on the
function or place of the courtier. The statesmen of the age were no
strangers to the Court, but neither were they its creatures: Christopher Hatton's career, which appeared to be an exception to that
rule, caused significantly raised eyebrows. The one area of public
life of which Cromwell had had no experience before he embarked
on his career in the King's service was the Court, and I do not think
that he ever fully penetrated its essence, any more than did Sir
Thomas Smith.

Nevertheless, these men and their like spent a good deal of their
time in the Court, wherever it might be, and they form a group
about whose role in that setting obscurity gathers most discourag-
ingly. Some of them occupied an ambiguous place halfway between
the Household officer and the politician or bureaucrat definitely
not of the Household, an ambiguity which has continued to be-
wilder historians. The fact that, as the warrant of April 1540 puts it,
the two principal secretaries were to have 'an ordinary chamber or
lodging within the gates of his grace's house, in all places where the
same may be', with bouge of court, has apparently persuaded a
good many scholars (especially but not only those who can see no
reason for accepting that major administrative changes occurred in
the reign of Henry VIII) that the Elizabethan secretaries of state
were still in a real sense Household officers, just like their Yorkist
predecessors. Yet that same warrant clearly makes them much more
specifically attendants upon the Lord Privy Seal than the King,
and no one has yet supposed that they were really members of
Cromwell's household.[6] The truth is both simpler and subtler: they
were part of the general machinery of the reformed state, outside the
royal Household but of necessity often compelled to come to Court,
a contingency for which administrative provision had to be made.
But were they courtiers?

I wish we were able to confine the term courtier to its strict
meaning, to the holders of specifically Court offices; but that is
manifestly insufficient. There can be no sense in any interpretation
which allocates Lord Treasurer Burghley to a political sphere
separate and distinguishable from that in which the earl of Leicester,

[5] Wallace T. MacCaffrey, 'Place and Patronage in Elizabethan Politics',
Elizabethan Government and Society, ed. S. T. Bindoff, J. Hurstfield, C. H. Williams
(London, 1961), pp. 100–10.
[6] G. R. Elton, *The Tudor Constitution* (Cambridge, 1960), p. 122.

master of the Horse, had his being. Sir Walter Raleigh was a great figure at Court—the quintessential courtier—from 1582, but he had to wait a full seven years for an actual Court office, the captaincy of the Guard.[7] As I have suggested, the identification of offices and holders has its uses at a lower level of eminence, but it ceases to help once we come to look at the people at Court whose functions and ambitions extended to the political sphere. Here influence, even if sometimes reflected in office, really depended on personal standing with the prince; that standing might or might not be embodied in office, nor need that office be Court office, nor can standing necessarily be measured by the relative importance of offices held.

Few moments in English public life carried more significance than those occupied by the monarch in signing papers—despatches, legislative proposals, the approval of private petitions: especially the last. Despite the very considerable area of activities which in England came under delegated authority—where King or Queen neither acted nor necessarily knew of the action—a greater sector of public life depended upon the ruler's personal participation, usually supplied by such signatures. In particular, this was true of the dispensing of patronage, the one thing all of them reserved to themselves so long as they were of age and *compos mentis*, and far and away the thing most frequently demanded of them by their subjects. Thus, as is well enough known, the person who acted as channel between petitioner and sovereign occupied a place of singular influence and attraction. King or Queen could sign only what was offered up to them, and the flow was regulated by others. Conventional doctrine holds that those others were the secretaries of state, a view shared by themselves. Robert Beale's instructions on the office of principal secretary assume without question that her highness will sign only in the presence of that officer who will do well to ease the royal labours during that painful time with 'some relation or speech whereat she may take some pleasure' (and which might distract her attention from what she was giving away?).[8] He does not forget that other people could be involved, like the various civil servants whose countersignatures, obtained in advance, will assure the Queen that she could properly approve those petitions and pardons, but with respect to her immediate attendants he feels that their function is only to prepare the perspiring secretary for the reception he is likely to get: 'Learn before your access her majesty's disposition by some of her privy chamber.'[9] He is quite

[7] W. M. Wallace, *Sir Walter Raleigh* (London, 1959), pp. 25, 29.

[8] Conyers Read, *Mr Secretary Walsingham and the Policy of Queen Elizabeth* i, (Oxford, 1925), p. 438.

[9] *Ibid.*, 437.

explicit that even the suits of those close and favoured persons must pass through the secretary's hands. Perhaps this is really what happened in Elizabeth's reign; perhaps by then the secretary had truly monopolized this vital weapon of power. But it was not always so: Cromwell faced the rivalry which ready access to the King's person gave to gentlemen of the Privy Chamber and solved the problem by staffing that department with men of his choosing, while late in Henry VIII's reign the Privy Chamber virtually drove the secretaries from that field. Once again, it is clear that in the conduct of politically meaningful business distinctions between courtiers (holders of Court office) and administrators, real enough in terms of appointment, tenure, function and often also life-style, are less significant than the distinction between Crown officers above and below the line that divided politicians from mere civil servants.

Thus the only definition of the Court which makes sense in the sixteenth century is that it comprised all those who at any given time were within 'his grace's house'; and all those with a right to be there were courtiers to whom the fact, and the problems, of the Court constituted a central preoccupation in their official lives and in the search for personal satisfaction.

All those who had access: but how was that controlled? The Chamber bureaucracy was so organized as to ensure that sufficient gentlemen, gentlemen ushers, grooms and pages attended at Court to provide the personal services required, but this was a strictly administrative arrangement which it would be wrong to investigate for political significance reflected in presence or absence. Formal reorganization, of course, carried deeper meaning: the clean-up of the Privy Chamber in 1519, for instance, or the holocaust which struck it in the Boleyn disaster of 1536, signified upheavals which need to be read in the context of political power struggles. No such major blow seems to have fallen in the reign of Elizabeth, but the occasional removals from Court of the Queen's maids of dishonour should be investigated to see whether really nothing more was involved than the Queen's virginal wrath.

For the non-officed courtiers, on the other hand, the right to come to Court formed the clearest visible barometer of politics and was so used by those assiduous observers, foreign ambassadors. The test was less applicable during Wolsey's heyday when Henry several times complained about the dearth of attendants around him, a dearth which put such extra burdens on the shoulders of that reluctant courtier, Sir Thomas More, compelled to stay long into the night so that the King might be amused.[10] As Skelton pointed

[10] *Two Early Tudor Lives*, ed. R. S. Sylvester and D. P. Harding (New Haven, Conn., 1962), p. 202.

out, people did not come to Court because there was better profit in attending the Cardinal's rival court; and the people who stayed away included, strikingly enough, Wolsey himself whose visits to Court grew increasingly rarer and more ceremonious as time went on. Part-time courtiers like Cromwell made the effort, but Cromwell found it necessary, once his power was established, to be present by deputy, the function discharged especially by Ralph Sadler throughout the later 1530s. At least Cromwell grasped the need to keep others away; both Norfolk and Gardiner, his chief rivals, discovered the difficulty of getting permission to come during the years of the Lord Privy Seal's ascendancy. At the height of the Boleyn crisis of 1536 he even stopped Cranmer from coming to Court, apparently on the King's orders.[11] It seems that such matters were handled with relative delicacy: people were advised that there was no occasion to come or that their service might be better discharged elsewhere, rather than brutally ejected. Elizabeth on occasion practised more direct methods, publicly denying her presence to those who had fallen from grace, like her leading councillors after the execution of the Queen of Scots, Essex after his mudstained return from Ireland, or Raleigh after his shotgun-marriage to Bess Throckmorton. We may suppose that this experience helped to persuade Raleigh that the Court glowed like rotten wood.

Access and exclusion mattered so much because the game of politics, unlike the government of the realm, remained so firmly fixed upon the monarch's person. It was the sight of the royal face that people needed who wished to advance their causes, a striking case of interest overcoming natural feelings as both Henry VIII and Elizabeth grew older and uglier. (It is hard to believe that anyone ever really liked looking upon Queen Mary.) And I am not sure that even now we have got these highly personal situations absolutely correct: I think we may have consistently overestimated the formality of behaviour and therefore of access. True, people knelt uncovered in the royal presence, a rule which offered well-taken opportunities for calculated graciousness. True, ceremony dominated even the mealtimes of royalty. Yet there are odd indications here and there that our imaginations, nourished by accounts of the great occasions and views of the set-piece portraits, may have endowed life at the Tudor Court with a degree of coldly distant order that did not exist. I am not so much thinking of the well attested squalor of filthy kitchen-boys, accumulated garbage, stinking throngs of beggars and sight-seers—all those features, inadequately covered in cloth of gold and

11 *Letters and Papers of Henry VIII* [hereafter *LP*], x. 792.

precious stones, which regularly forced the Court to move after a few weeks from quarters which its humanity had polluted beyond bearing. Rather I have in mind the behaviour of the monarchs themselves and those who spoke to them. Of course, we know all about the uses of affability, and we have heard enough about the Tudor skill in preserving a necessary dignity without losing some sort of common touch, a task easier for that potential bar-room bore, King Henry, than for his daughter whose occasional escape into the aggressive masculinity of bad language and bad manners so shocked nineteenth-century historians. What I have in mind are hints that behaviour in the royal presence could be far less governed by formal respect and monarch-worshipping dread than one might suppose from reading Tudor courtiers' precepts on the subject. And if these doubts are justified, it follows that we should also have to adjust our estimate of monarchs' and courtiers' relative position in the making of careers and policy.

What looks like the surprising reality is well indicated by some of the interviews which Robert Carey, youngest son of Lord Hunsdon, had with his sovereign. When he was in disgrace for having married without the Queen's approval, his father acted as intermediary and kept his courtier's laurels reasonably green. That fits the common notions of Elizabeth. When finally he managed to get access again he used very plain language to her that fits less well, replying to her reproaches for his apparent desertion of the presence that he had seen no profit in staying: 'if she had graced me with the least of her favours, I had never left her nor her court'. And some years later, when in effect he committed Essex's offence by leaving his post at Berwick without licence to rush to Theobalds for a word with Elizabeth, he was warned off, with every sign of apprehension and solicitude, by Robert Cecil, principal secretary, and by his own eldest brother, the lord chamberlain, only to find that William Killigrew, a gentleman of the Privy Chamber, could get him access and forgiveness with no trouble at all.[12] Perhaps Cecil and the second Lord Hunsdon were on that occasion acting as back-friends, but to me it looks more as though everything was so haphazard and uncertain about this business of seeing the Queen that highly placed courtiers could completely misread the signs. The majesty of majesty? Rather, what a way to run a railroad.

More striking still are the improbabilities we encounter in the reign of Henry VIII. Two stories about him, neither totally unfamiliar, will bear retelling for the strange light they throw on the manners of Court life and the relations between King and courtiers.

[12] *The Memoirs of Robert Carey*, ed. F. H. Mares (Oxford, 1972), pp. 29, 30–31, 43–44.

Do we not suppose that people went in fear of the King's wrath, which is death? That they had cause to expect physical blows if they did not watch their step? Surely they would not speak to him in ways that even lesser humans would find insufferably offensive. What then are we to make of the scene, some time around 1533, when Sir George Throckmorton, a knight of the Reformation Parliament who had consistently opposed the Crown's bills touching religion and the Church, was summoned to the royal presence to explain himself?[13] Being told, mildly enough, that the King was sorely troubled about his marriage to his brother's widow, Sir George riposted that marriage to Anne Boleyn would come to trouble him similarly, 'for it is thought you have meddled both with the mother and the sister'—relations which created the same canonical impediment as that alleged to exist in the Aragon marriage. Here was a man of neither standing nor significance, with a record of opposition, accusing the King to his face of multiple adultery as well as hypocrisy: surely the royal wrath struck him dead? What Henry VIII actually said, in some embarrassment, was only 'never with the mother', a reply so naively revealing as to infuriate Cromwell who, standing by, interjected, 'nor never with the sister either, and therefore put that out of your mind'. I have some difficulty in accommodating this scene to the vision of the majestic lord who broke all those bonds of man and God.

Perhaps even more significant of the realities of Court life is an occasion observed by Eustace Chapuys in April 1536.[14] Chapuys and Cromwell had for some time been negotiating over ways to reduce the Anglo-Imperial tension, and the time had come (so Cromwell thought) to bring the King into the business. Thus the ambassador went to Court where he was received with cordial kindness all round. However, either (it seems) Cromwell had miscalculated, or Henry changed his mind: he turned very cool towards the proposals worked out by ambassador and minister, and after a while withdrew into a window with Cromwell and Lord Chancellor Audley. Chapuys, who could see but not hear what was going on, noticed a dispute growing in acrimony, and after this had gone on for quite some time Cromwell came away from the window, grumbling to himself and complaining of thirst. He went out of the King's sight to sit down on a coffer and sent for a drink. Shortly after this Henry broke off his conversation and returned to the centre of the chamber; Chapuys, who first thought that the King wished to speak to him once more, then found that he was merely looking to see what had become of Cromwell. There is nothing at all

13 *LP*, xii. II. 952.   14 *LP*, x, pp. 291–92.

odd about the core of this scene, about the display of disagreement or the failure of diplomacy. But should we really have expected that Cromwell would so publicly argue with the King, would so unceremoniously leave the royal presence (making his fury plain to all), would sit down for a drink (even if out of sight), and that Henry's only reaction would be to come looking for his minister? Is that the Henry VIII of our imaginings?

The point of these doubts is relevant to the theme under discussion. If we have got the actuality of being in the royal presence out of true, if we have to think of these monarchs as far more relaxed and bewildered in their public behaviour than usually we do, it becomes difficult to maintain that Court life consisted predominantly of currying favour, of flattering or worshipping a godlike dominant person. Courtiers may have written poems to Astraea, but they talked to Queen Elizabeth and wove their webs around her. Not even she or her father, possibly the two most royal monarchs in our history, answered to the superhuman stereotype of rulers which, for instance, we find described by their latest biographers who, taking their stand with the throne, assume that everything happened as and because the monarch wished it to happen.[15] The real Henry VIII and Elizabeth lived in a setting composed of powerful people and resounding to clashing ambitions in which they had to behave with frequent circumspection if they were not (as Henry VIII and Mary frequently did) to make the most appalling mistakes under the influence of others who exploited the pretended omnipotence of royalty. But if the battle for promotion and survival did not consist simply in gaining the King's ear or catching the Queen's eye and then dealing directly with the fountain of honour as supplicants to an all-powerful being, we need to know how those to whom Court air was the vital ingredient of political life really carried on their business.

Courtiers, in fact, did not constitute a gathering of individuals all individually looking towards the throne, but identifiable—and often surprisingly enduring—groupings around one or more leaders upon whom the way to the throne depended. We need to investigate faction, and perhaps this is obvious: but I would suggest that an element which we all recognize in the politics of the fifteenth century or the Stuart age has usually been left out under the Tudors, on the erroneous grounds that those monarchs governed personally, by which is meant a rule embodying direct personal action based upon personal initiative and judgment. On the contrary, like all monarchical rule that of the Tudors was both *regale* and *politicum*, but

[15] L. Baldwin Smith, *Henry VIII: the Mask of Royalty* (London, 1971); P. Johnson, *Elizabeth I: a Study in Power and Intellect* (London, 1974).

politicum in a sense different from Fortescue's: they were managed at worst, manœuvred at best, by the purposeful groupings of interests that articulated the nation's politics. The idea of faction is familiar enough in Parliament, where in the sixteenth century it occurred with some regularity though only a minority of the House of Commons ever adhered to such alliances, and in the Council where it existed (so far as the evidence goes) far less commonly than is usually supposed; its presence at the Court, however often asserted, has hardly been investigated at all because its vital importance has been outshone by the supposed free domination of the monarch.

The crises of Henry VIII's reign, for instance, were really all crises at Court; even the Pilgrimage of Grace fits that description when it is remembered that it was the work of noblemen who either resented exclusion from the Court (Northumberland, Hussey) or wished to transform the Court (Darcy). In particular it is true of the King's matrimonial history which so deeply influenced affairs. His last five wives were produced by Court factions in their struggles for power, but the matter has been investigated from this point of view for only one case, the fall of Anne Boleyn.[16] It is, admittedly, the clearest and most revealing episode, with an unusual number of factions interacting. There were the Boleyns themselves, with their strong hold on the Privy Chamber and their weakening hold on the King. There was the Norfolk–Suffolk group, uneasily poised for flight from alliance with the Boleyns. We can discern at least two so-to-speak conservative groupings. The remnant of the Aragonese faction, also powerful in the Privy Chamber, now concentrated on promoting the interests of the Princess Mary; while what one might call an old-nobility faction (Exeter, Pole, Darcy) adopted its anti-Boleyn stance more from resentment at innovation and centralization in general. The decline of Anne brought polarization into this melée, though it took the intervention of Cromwell, building up his own Court faction while neatly utilizing the jealousies of the rest, to precipitate the actual crisis and its solution. In the outcome, the kaleidoscope rearranged itself. The old-nobility faction remained identifiable, to be destroyed in the Pilgrimage and its aftermath in 1538; Cromwell took over the Court interest of the fallen favourite; Norfolk and Suffolk began to drift in the direction of his enemies without, however, going so far as to amalgamate with them, so that they escaped the disaster of

---

[16] E. W. Ives, 'Faction at the Court of Henry VIII: the Fall of Anne Boleyn', *History*, 47 (1972), pp. 169 ff. In a still unpublished paper, written before Dr Ives' article appeared, Dr D. R. Starkey offers a slightly different and rather more penetrating interpretation which rightly stresses the role of the Privy Chamber in the story. I am obliged to Dr Starkey for letting me see his essay.

1538. It must be remembered that the noble leadership of the Pilgrimage had had hopes of winning Norfolk to their side. In 1538-39 Cromwell dangerously dominated the Court, as he dominated everything else, a position he used to tie Henry to Anne of Cleves and the north-European anti-papal alliance; his fall was the work of the Court faction vanquished in 1538 but enabled to revive by the fiasco of the Cleves marriage and Norfolk's change of sides. The stories of Katherine Howard and Katherine Parr similarly need to be seen less as examples of capricious despotism on the king's part and more as the effect of such factional manœuvrings upon his supposed freedom of action.

We usually ascribe the rise of Edward Seymour to his military performances in the 1540s, and it would certainly be hard to see him as a power at Court before the last two years of the reign. Yet it was only his sister's early death that prevented the creation of a Seymour faction which could have been as troublesome to Cromwell as the Boleyns had become by 1536. And Seymour's final jump to prominence was once again a purely Court affair, the achievement of the faction war which overthrew the Howards and, at the critical moment of Henry's effective withdrawal from rule left Hertford and Paget in command of Court, Privy Chamber and the King's dry stamp, the instrument of power. Edward VI's reign may seem a less promising age in which to study Court faction because the purpose of such groupings was, of course, to gain influence (or more) over an active King, one whose word (properly influenced) would on any given occasion generate the action desired. It is thus no wonder that the politics of the reign have usually been studied with reference to the Council rather than the Court. Yet even Northumberland's Council, enlarged (as we have seen)[17] to make room for more members of his faction, did not involve numbers large enough to show what was really going on; here, too, Court appointments and replacements should be looked at to get the politics of the age clear. This holds true even for the reign of Mary when the combination of an ecclesiastical Chancellor, a foreign King, and the probably biased reporting of an imperial ambassador has firmly directed attention again to the Privy Council rather than the Court, leaving the impression that the factions were strictly conciliar. The study of the Court is here complicated by the intrusion of Philip's entourage, but that makes a deeper investigation of Mary's Court only the more necessary.

One thing is clear about the situation between 1509 and 1558: factions at Court were trying to get exclusive control but never succeeded in doing so. Wolsey came nearest to triumph; or rather

[17] *Ante*, 25 (1975) 205.

he may look to have been in that position because we still do not know enough about the inner history of the Court in the 1520s. The rise of Anne Boleyn assuredly demonstrated the prevalence and significance of Court factions even during the Cardinal's ascendancy: again, we need more work, though Dr Starkey's study of the Henrician Privy Chamber has covered the central ground satisfactorily. Cromwell for a brief period nearly eliminated rival factions, but partly because the role of courtier sat uneasily upon him, partly because he contented himself with keeping Gardiner and Norfolk away from Court rather than rid himself of them for good on the several occasions when with a little more Machiavellian juggling he could readily have done so, he never transmuted ascendancy into secure dominance. The chief cause of the continued faction strife lay, however, elsewhere—in the King himself. If faction enabled the politicians to use him (as it did), he also found in it the obvious means for preventing any one of them from imprisoning him. This appears to have been entirely deliberate. Unlike his father (so far as I can tell) and his elder daughter, Henry VIII purposely kept his Court divided. He had his favourites, and thanks to the existence of the Privy Chamber they played important roles in the national politics of the day; but Henry saved himself by so frequently swapping favourites that no faction ever won outright—or none, at least, until in his last decline the Seymour faction took the sceptre from his failing hands.

Notoriously this was a lesson that Elizabeth also learned, whether from him or from her own experience cannot be judged. We have grown so familiar with the notion of faction in her age that we forget how little the structure of those groupings has been studied. Even Professor MacCaffrey, for whom the first dozen years of the reign rightly revolve around the partified alliances of politicians, never specifically analyses their members or tracks the tendrils emanating from the Court.[18] Let me quote a casual aside in which Dr Neville Williams sums up the common opinion: 'Factions—the ancestors of political parties—developed round leading courtiers, and Elizabeth sought to maintain a nice balance to keep the peace.'[18a] I do not quarrel with this statement; I merely cannot tell whether it is really adequate. Did factions 'develop', and were their leaders always courtiers in any precise sense of the word? Did family traditions and local allegiances play a part as well as personality? Was Elizabeth really able to keep that famous balance by her own willed action; was she so much more in control of everybody than

[18] Wallace T. MacCaffrey, *The Shaping of the Elizabethan Regime* (Princeton, N.J., 1968).
[18a] N. J. Williams, *All the Queen's Men* (London, 1972), p. 14.

PRESIDENTIAL ADDRESS 225

her father would seem to have been? And that parenthesis about political parties—perceptive though it is—also points to the cause of my uncertainties. The only attempts to identify factions and see them at work have concentrated on affairs, on strains in the Council, on rival advice and policy. Though everyone who looks at Raleigh or Essex is forced to consider the life of the Court, no one has yet made a proper study of Elizabeth's Court as a political centre; and the biographer of Burghley and Walsingham was able to write five large volumes without seemingly becoming aware that Court faction differed from political party, even if (possibly) one fathered the other.[19] The disastrous disappearance of Leicester's papers, together with the better survival of the *Acts of the Privy Council*, has helped to create this distortion; and I think that when Professor Hurstfield's work on Robert Cecil is before us we shall see some redressing of the balance. But so long as we are guided to regard the Court of Elizabeth as mainly a cultural centre for the English Renaissance (with Philip Sidney our paradigmatic courtier), or as merely the organization which permitted the percolation of patronage; so long as we fail to treat it as the centre of political power struggles; so long as it is held that in the affairs that mattered the Queen ruled all with an even hand and a subtle mind; in short, so long as Gloriana continues to occupy that throne, I doubt whether we shall ever really get to the roots of political life in her reign. We need no more reveries on accession tilts and symbolism, no more pretty pictures of gallants and galliards; could we instead have painful studies of Acatry and Pantry, of vicechamberlains and ladies of the Privy Chamber?

At any rate, the vital political role of the Court, and the deep significance of Court factions, are recognizable facts of Tudor life. It remains to consider their meaning—in which there also lies some sort of an answer to the question which I have tried to pose throughout this series of lectures, the question of stability. Let us return to Dr Williams's definition. It is certainly true that faction gathered round leading political personalities, though before 1558 few of them were strictly one-man bands. Wolsey and Cromwell—more especially Wolsey—conducted themselves almost like modern party leaders, but the Boleyn or old-nobility factions were at the top alliances of equals. Northumberland certainly, and possibly Somerset too, were not singlehanded faction leaders; they shared temporary alliances with others to build up a following. Whether we are right to speak as plainly as we do of Burghley's faction or Leicester's, of Norfolk's or Essex's, must remain uncertain until we

[19] Conyers Read, *Mr Secretary Walsingham* (three volumes); *Mr Secretary Cecil and Queen Elizabeth* (London, 1955); *Lord Burghley and Queen Elizabeth* (London, 1960).

have been told more about them; but even at this date we should not forget men like Arundel, Sussex and Sidney early in the reign, like Raleigh, Cobham or Nottingham in the last twenty years of the century. However, the problem of leadership apart, it is evident that faction existed for the purpose of promoting individual fortunes, those of both leaders and led: it was the mechanism which, at Court, organized the satisfaction of personal ambition for wealth and power. And, though by no means everyone received what he regarded as his due and some indeed suffered total eclipse, it appears that faction sufficiently delivered the goods to prevent the build-up of resentments that could have destroyed stability. Essex alone took his resentment further than impotent grumbling—and we all know what became of Essex.

What, then, about faction being the ancestor of political party? Dr Ives would seem to think that this was indeed true of Elizabethan factions, engaged in the advocacy of rival policies and partly at least structured by religious affiliations, but he did not think that such purposes informed any of the Henrician factions except the old-nobility group of Exeter, Pole and perhaps Darcy.[20] In this I think he was too sceptical. The outward appearance of Henry's Court factions was governed by the personal rivalries which the events of the day, and the King, encouraged; and attitudes were obviously coloured by a situation in which political opposition could so easily be made to look like disloyalty or even treason. Yet nevertheless every one of the factions that one can identify cherished and promoted political ends that had nothing to do with mere personal advancement or the exploitation of patronage. Cromwell manifestly needed the backing of a faction to establish his hold on monarch and machine; as manifestly he used that control to carry out a very positive political programme. The factions that rivalled his influence unquestionably found part of their *raison d'être* in hatred of the minister, but the hatred drew more strength from opposition to his policies than from contempt for the upstart. The note thus sounded in the 1530s never died away entirely, even if at times purely personal ambition is markedly more evident than the possession of larger political purposes. (Of course, this is equally true of real political parties on frequent occasions). Nor is the reason for this continuance of a genuine principled division between the factions at all obscure. From the moment that Henry VIII entered upon his breach with the papacy and thus opened the door to the Reformation, all political debate—all issues of domestic and foreign policy—acquired an ideological component in addition to its normal

---

[20] Ives, *op. cit.*, pp. 177–78.

character as conflicts for power. Especially the Henrician factions subsisted on the religious split: you could no more follow Cromwell if you were a convinced papist than you could attach yourself to Norfolk and Gardiner if you thought that there had been no true religion before Luther. Of course, there were moderate men and time-servers who threaded their way between the factions, or more commonly from one to the other, but even for them every alignment and attachment to a given leader had notable political overtones. Even that supposedly most powerful faction-cement of the age, kinship, could crumble under the pressure of politics, as the vagaries of the various members of the Howard clan demonstrate throughout the century. The third duke of Norfolk remains, I think, the only uncle in our history who presided over two tribunals that condemned two nieces to death for treasonable adultery. I am not trying to make out that politics was everything—only that it always contributed, was usually ideological, and gave a purposeful backbone to those groupings of generally very self-seeking men (and women).

There are things about the Elizabethan factions which make me wonder whether the power of ideological politics was then quite as strong as it had been in the 1530s. After all, both Burghley's and Leicester's factions wished to advance the cause of the reformed religion though they differed over methods. When the debate becomes one of means rather than ends, mere personality— ambition, hatred, also affection—can prevail more easily. Still, all the Court factions of the century rested on more than personal purpose and personal attachment; they were indeed truly political groupings, though I myself would not care to try tracing their long-distance paternity to the emergence of party. And here we touch on what I suggest was the vital characteristic of Tudor Court faction. The Tudor Court was the centre of politics not only in the sense that those seeking power needed to pursue it there, but more significantly still in the sense that the battle of politics was there fought out. None of the main solutions to the problems of the day lacked advocates within the very heart of the Court itself—not even peace with Rome in the 1540s, or the puritan programme in the 1570s. Whether Elizabeth took care to maintain the factions simply to prevent herself being overwhelmed by any one of them must remain a matter for doubt; the effect, however, of her refusal to allow total victory to this or that group was to provide all political ambition with a platform at the very centre of affairs. In her reign, and in her father's too, conflict took place within the Court. When Stuart policy, whether from preference or blindness, permitted the monopolizing of the Court by single favourites and exclusive faction, conflict was forced out of Court into a public arena: but this was new. The concepts of Court and Country have their place in an analysis of Tudor politics; but in contradistinction to what happened in the seventeenth century they do not represent rival poles around which faction, or party, might gather. The factions in the Country linked to members of the Court; Court faction spread its net over the shires. The realm was one and had one centre; and the situation prevailing at Court made sure that the many political divisions within that one realm and one centre should work themselves out in the ordinary context and contests of political life, without ever threatening to divide the political nation into ins and outs. The age of Buckingham has no Tudor prehistory.

Sixteenth-century England experienced much trouble, unrest and upheaval. It was an age when true disruption and even chaos were never far away. Disaster was held off by usually strong government and the successful creation of a national selfconsciousness around the visible symbolism of a divinely appointed monarchy. These things have taken the eye, as the Tudors intended they should, but the machinery of rulership is by no means the whole story. In reality Tudor stability depended on the sharing of power, right through the structure, from monarchs to village elders; at all points there existed institutional mechanisms to give reality to the principle of participation, defined by custom and law but articulated by political awareness. At the level of national affairs, Parliament offered means of advancement, the fulfilment of personal and family requirements, and a chance to the voice of both advocacy and criticism. The Privy Council, if it had not been reformed for the purpose of efficient administration, might have become a similar instrument for political stability through participation; instead its contribution lay on the side of control rather than co-operation (and a very necessary contribution it was, too). But above all, the Court—the true seat of power, profit and policy—preserved peace in the midst of strife by making certain that the strife should take place within the official centre of political life itself. No one who subscribed to a few basic loyalties needed to feel left out, and there was no occasion for a political opposition.

THE ROYAL HISTORICAL SOCIETY

REPORT OF COUNCIL, SESSION 1974–75

THE Council of the Royal Historical Society has the honour to present the following report to the Anniversary Meeting.

A conference on 'Britain and Europe' was held at Lopes Hall, University of Exeter from 19 to 21 September 1974. The papers read were:

'England, Scotland and Europe: The Problem of the Frontier', by Professor Denys Hay.

'Industrial Britain and Europe in the Late Eighteenth Century', by Professor Peter Mathias.

'England and Europe: *Utopia* and its Aftermath', by Dr. D. B. Fenlon.

'Idealists and Realists: British Views of Germany, 1864–1939', by Dr. P. M. Kennedy.

'War and Peace in the Early Middle Ages', by Professor J. M. Wallace-Hadrill.

Fifty-six members of the Society and ten guests attended. The University held a reception for them on 20 September. It was decided to hold the sixth annual conference at the University of Liverpool from 18 to 20 September 1975, on the topic 'Colonies'.

An evening party was held for Fellows and guests at University College London on 2 July 1974 for which 135 acceptances were received.

At the Anniversary Meeting in November 1974, Dr. G. R. C. Davis retired from being Treasurer of the Society, a position he had held for seven years. Mr. K. V. Thomas and Professor G. W. S. Barrow retired at the same time from being Literary Directors after respectively four and ten years in office. Council wishes to record its gratitude to all three for the substantial services they have given to the Society. Mr. M. Roper was elected Treasurer, and Dr. Valerie Pearl was elected Literary Director with Dr. C. T. Allmand as Assistant Literary Director.

The representation of the Society upon various bodies was as follows: Professor G. E. Aylmer and Mr. A. T. Milne on the Joint Anglo-American Committee exercising a general supervision over the production of the *Bibliographies of British History*; the President, Professor C. N. L. Brooke, Professor Sir Goronwy Edwards and Professor J. C. Holt on the Advisory Committee of the new edition of Gross, *Sources and Literature of English History*; Professor G. W. S.

Barrow, Dr. P. Chaplais and Professor P. H. Sawyer on the Joint
Committee of the Society and the British Academy established to
prepare an edition of Anglo-Saxon charters; Dr. E. B. Fryde on a
committee to regulate British co-operation in the preparation of a
new repertory of medieval sources to replace Potthast's *Bibliotheca
Historica Medii Aevi*; Professor P. Grierson on a committee to promote the publication of photographic records of the more significant collections of British coins; Professor A. G. Dickens on the
Advisory Council on the Export of Works of Art; the President and
Professor C. H. Wilson on the British National Committee of the
International Historical Congress; Professor G. H. Martin on the
Council of the British Records Association; Professor A. M. Everitt
on the Standing Conference for Local History; Mr. M. R. D. Foot
on the Committee to advise the publishers of *The Annual Register*;
Dr. P. D. A. Harvey on the Ordnance Survey Archaeological
Advisory Committee, and Miss K. Major on the Lincolnshire
Archaeological Trust. Council received reports from these repre-
sentatives.

The President is *ex officio* a Trustee of the *Spectator*. Professor
Medlicott represents the Society on the Court of the University of
Exeter.

The Honorary Secretary represented the Society at the fiftieth
anniversary meetings of the Mediaeval Academy of America held in
Cambridge, Massachusetts, from 17 to 18 April 1975.

The Vice-Presidents retiring under By-law XVI were Professor
C. N. L. Brooke and Professor A. Goodwin. Professor J. C. Holt and
Professor J. Hurstfield were elected to replace them. The members
of Council retiring under By-law XIX were Professor I. R. Christie,
Mr. M. R. D. Foot, Professor A. R. Myers and Mrs. A. E. B. Owen.
Dr. J. M. Roberts, Mr. K. V. Thomas, Professor W. L. Warren and
Professor Joyce A. Youings were elected to fill the vacancies.
Messrs. Beeby, Harmar & Co. were appointed auditors for the year
1974-75 under By-law XXXVIII.

On numerous occasions during the year Council has been asked
to comment on matters which are of concern to historians generally.
To the Advisory Council on Public Records Council has expressed
its concern over the new charges imposed at the Public Record
Office for filming. Council has been consulted about the deposit of
parochial ecclesiastical records of the Church in Wales, a draft of a
Parochial Register and Records Measure to be considered by the
General Synod of the Church of England and has joined in the
representations about the proposal to move the Registrar-General's
Records from London to Southport. Council supported the request
of the Slade School of Fine Art for a grant from the Department

of Education and Science to finance the work of the Slade School Film Archive. The trustees of the British Museum consulted Council about the extension of the Law of Treasure Trove and Council has also considered the question of the siting of the British Library. Most recently, Council has made a submission to the Committee of Privy Counsellors on Ministerial Memoirs.

Publications, and Papers Read

This year Council has made an agreement with the Harvester Press to produce the *Annual Bibliography of British and Irish History* which was referred to in the last Report. Council has also decided in principle to explore the possibilities of producing a Bibliography of British History from 1914, thus completing the series of bibliographies of British History. The financing of this project remains yet to be settled, but Council is pleased to announce that Professor K. G. Robbins has accepted an invitation to edit the volume.

The following works were published during the session: *Transactions*, Fifth Series, volume 25; *Camden Miscellany XXVI* (Fourth Series, volume 14) and *Sidney Ironworks Accounts, 1541–1573* (Camden, Fourth Series, volume 15).

At the ordinary meetings of the Society the following papers were read:

'Domesday Book and Anglo-Norman Governance', by Dr. Sally P. J. Harvey. (18 October 1974.)

'François Chabot and his Plot', by Professor Norman Hampson. (7 February 1975.)

*'Catholics and the Poor in Early Modern Europe', by Professor B. S. Pullan. (7 March 1975.)

'Imperial Facade: Some constraints upon and constrictions in the British position in India, 1919–35', by Dr. Judith M. Brown. (9 May 1975.)

'Why did the Dutch Revolt last Eighty Years?' by Dr. Geoffrey Parker. (20 June 1975.)

* Professor Pullan was unable through illness to read his paper but this will be published in *Transactions*. On the day the President stepped into the breach and gave an address on 'The sixteenth century as an age of reform'.

At the Anniversary Meeting on 22 November 1974 the President, Professor G. R. Elton, delivered an address on 'Tudor Politics— Points of Contact. 2. Privy Council'.

The Alexander Prize was not awarded for 1974.

Membership

Council records with regret the death of 2 Corresponding Fellows, 21 Fellows and 2 Associates since 30 June 1974. Among these Council would mention especially Professor E. M. J. Perroy and

Professor L. Santifaller, Corresponding Fellows; Professor the Rev. M. D. Knowles, a former President, Sir James Butler, M.V.O., O.B.E. and Mr. H. G. Richardson, former members of Council; Professor H. P. R. Finberg, F.S.A., Mr. J. Saltmarsh, F.S.A. and Professor A. S. Whitfield. The resignation of 13 Fellows and 9 Libraries was received. 3 Libraries were removed from the roll.

53 Fellows and 10 Associates were elected, 27 Libraries were admitted and 2 Libraries re-admitted. Professor Henri Michel was elected a Corresponding Fellow. The membership of the Society on 30 June 1975 comprised 1271 Fellows (including 108 Life Fellows and 39 Retired Fellows), 31 Corresponding Fellows, 161 Associates and 768 Subscribing Libraries (1252, 32, 153 and 751 respectively on 30 June 1974). The Society exchanged publications with 15 Societies, British and foreign.

Finance

Despite an increase in net expenditure of almost 20% the Society finished its financial year with a substantial surplus of £7,333 on the Income and Expenditure Account. The increase in income which made this possible was principally attributable to the raising of Library subscriptions from 1 July 1974, the recovery of a large proportion of the subscriptions reported as outstanding last year, the inclusion for the first time of a full year's income from the Browning Fund and the generally improved yield from the Society's investments, especially from money on 7-day deposit. The doubling of the proceeds from sales of publications, due partly to the good initial sale of *A Guide to the Papers of British Cabinet Ministers, 1900–1951* and partly to increases in the prices of *Transactions* and the *Camden Series* by 50p a volume, also contributed to the surplus for the year.

There are, however, no grounds for complacency. Whereas income is expected to rise little if at all in 1975–76, it is certain that expenditure will continue to increase at about the same rate as in 1974–75, if not at an even higher one. Substantial rises in both staff and publications costs are certain to occur. To mitigate the recent huge increases in postal charges, the bulk delivery of publications to Fellows, Associates and Libraries in U. K. universities and institutions has been introduced and Council will continue to seek further ways of holding increases in expenditure in check.

The Society's investments have increased in market value over the year, making good some of the fall in value during 1973–74.

The final annual instalment of the sum due on the surrender of the lease of 96 Cheyne Walk was received during the year and this item is, therefore, making its last appearance on the Balance Sheet.

THE ROYAL HISTORICAL SOCIETY
BALANCE SHEET AS AT 30 JUNE 1975

30.6.74
£

ACCUMULATED FUNDS

GENERAL FUND

45,297 (see note 2)	As at 1 July 1974		47,323
1,469	Royalties from reprints of the Society's publications received in the year and treated as capital . .	822	
7	Royalties from *Essays in Medieval and Modern History* (Macmillan, 1968)	—	
43	Donations from Life Members included in Income 1975	—	
1,519			822
46,816			48,145
608	*Add* Profit on Sale of Investments in year . .		—
			48,145
(101) deficit	*Add* Excess of Income over Expenditure and Provisions for year		7,333
47,323			55,478

SIR GEORGE W. PROTHERO BEQUEST

13,852	As at 1 July 1974	13,852	
—	Surplus on sale of Investment	857	
			14,709

REDDAWAY FUND

5,000	As at 1 July 1974		5,000

ANDREW BROWNING FUND

76,225	As at 1 July 1974	73,776	
—	*Add* Sale of Stamp Collection (part) . . .	156	
(5,041) loss	Profit on sale of Investments	497	
2,592	Income from Investments and tax recovered (included in General Income 1975)	—	
73,776			74,429
£139,951			**£149,616**

REPRESENTED BY:

INVESTMENTS

121,684	Quoted Securities—at cost	125,696	
	Market Value £133,571 (1974: £109,471)		
14,500	MONEY ON 7-DAY DEPOSIT	13,500	
71	DUE FROM STOCKBROKERS	128	
136,255			139,324

SUM DUE ON SURRENDER OF LEASE of 96 Cheyne Walk

2,500	As at 1 July 1974	1,250	
1,250	Paid in year	1,250	
	(Payable in annual instalments of £1,250)		
1,250			—

CURRENT ASSETS

Balances at Bank:

1,425	Current Accounts	2,975	
10,654	Deposit Accounts	14,127	
16	Cash in Hand.	68	
—	Income Tax repayment due	1,419	
139	Payments in Advance	195	
—	Stock of paper in hand	2,311	
12,234			21,095

Less CURRENT LIABILITIES

1,305	Subscriptions received in advance .	1,430	
187	Conference Fees received in advance .	103	
996	Sundry Creditors	975	
7,300	Provision for Publications in Hand .	8,295	
9,788			10,803
2,446			10,292
£139,951			**£149,616**

NOTES: 1. The cost of the Society's Library, Furniture and Office Equipment, and the Stock of its own publications, has been written off to Income and Expenditure Account as and when acquired.

2. The General Fund balance as at 1 July 1973 was incorrectly shown as £44,297 in the printed accounts for 1973-74. It is correctly shown as £45,297 in this year's accounts.

THE ROYAL HISTORICAL SOCIETY
Income & Expenditure Account for the Year Ended 30 June 1975

30.6.74 £

INCOME

30.6.74			30.6.75
	INCOME		
357	Subscriptions for 1974/75: Associates	410	
2,849	Libraries	4,801	
6,960	Fellows	7,362	
10,166			12,573
	(The Society also had 108 Life Fellows at 30 June 1975)		
639	Tax recovered on Covenanted Subscriptions . .		909
599	Arrears of Subscriptions recovered in year . . .		1,650
4,701	Interest and Dividends received and Income Tax recovered (including the Andrew Browning Fund) . .		10,033
279	Prothero Royalties and Reproduction Fees . .		161
66	Donations and Sundry Receipts		355
£16,450			£25,681

EXPENDITURE

30.6.74				30.6.75
	SECRETARIAL & ADMINISTRATIVE EXPENSES			
5,184	Salaries, Pension Contributions and National Insurance		7,666	
701	General Printing and Stationery		844	
556	Postage, Telephone and Sundries		484	
291	Accountancy and Audit		405	
48	Office Equipment		70	
136	Insurance		118	
377	Meeting and Conference Expenses		311	
7,293				9,898
	PUBLICATIONS			
200	Directors' Expenses		225	
	Publishing Costs in the year:			
	Transactions, Fifth Series, Vol. 24 (total cost)	3,250		
	Camden, Fourth Series, Vol. 13 (total cost)	3,296		
	Camden, Fourth Series, Vol. 14 (total cost)	3,410		
		9,956		
	Less Provision made 30 June 1974 .	7,300		
2,431			2,656	
	Provision for Publications in Progress:			
	Transactions, Fifth Series, Vol. 25 . .	4,295		
	Camden, Fourth Series, Vol. 15 . .	4,000		
7,300			8,295	
63	Purchase of *Essays in Medieval History* . . .		—	
135	Preparation expenses *Annual Bibliography* . .		71	
12	Carriage of Stock		—	
10,141			11,247	
1,775	*Less* Sales of Publications		3,528	
8,366				7,719
£15,659	*Carried forward*			£17,61

EXPENDITURE (contd.)   £

	Brought forward		17,617

LIBRARY AND ARCHIVES

212	Purchase of Books and Publications	327	
535	Library Assistance and Equipment	344	
747			671

OTHER CHARGES

19	Alexander Prize and expenses	17	
18	Subscriptions to other bodies	18	
108	Prothero Lecture fee and expenses	25	
145			60

16,551	TOTAL EXPENDITURE	18,348
16,450	INCOME AS ABOVE	25,681

(£101) deficit	EXCESS OF INCOME OVER EXPENDITURE AND PROVISIONS FOR THE YEAR	£7,333

G. R. ELTON, *President.*

M. ROPER, *Treasurer.*

We have examined the foregoing Balance Sheet and Income and Expenditure Account with the books and vouchers of the Society. We have verified the Investments and Bank Balances appearing in the Balance Sheet. In our opinion the above Balance Sheet and annexed Income and Expenditure Account are properly drawn up so as to exhibit a true and fair view of the state of the affairs of the Society according to the best of our information and the explanations given to us and as shown by the Books of the Society.

BEEBY, HARMAR & CO.,
Chartered Accountants, Auditors

FINSBURY COURT,
FINSBURY PAVEMENT,
LONDON EC2A 1HH
13th August 1975

THE DAVID BERRY TRUST

Receipts and Payments Account for the Year Ended 30 June 1975

30.6.74	£	Receipts	£	
		BALANCE IN HAND 1 July 1974:		
		Cash at Bank:		
	6	Current Account	14	
	115	Deposit Account	66	
	530	483.63 Shares Charities Official Investment Fund . .	530	
651				610
76		DIVIDEND ON INVESTMENT per Charity Commissioners .		78
11		INTEREST RECEIVED ON DEPOSIT ACCOUNT . . .		8
£738				£696

Payments

	48	DAVID BERRY PRIZE	—	
	50	DAVID BERRY MEDAL	—	
	30	EXAMINERS' FEES	—	
128				
		MEETINGS AND SUNDRY EXPENSES		10
		ADVERTISING—*The Times*	37	
		The Scotsman	13	
				50
		BALANCE IN HAND 30 June 1975:		
		Cash at Bank:		
	14	Current Account	3	
	66	Deposit Account	103	
		483.63 Shares Charities Official Investment		
610	530	Fund (Market Value 30.6.75 £471)	530	636
£738				£696

We have examined the above account with the books and vouchers of the Trust and find it to be in accordance therewith.

BEEBY, HARMAR & CO.,
Chartered Accountants, Auditors

FINSBURY COURT,
FINSBURY PAVEMENT,
LONDON EC2A 1HH
13th August 1975

The late David Berry, by his Will dated 23rd day of April, 1926, left £1,000 to provide in every three years a gold medal and prize money for the best essay on the Earl of Bothwell or, at the discretion of the Trustees, on Scottish History of the James Stuarts I to VI in memory of his father, the late Rev. David Berry.

The Trust is regulated by a scheme sanctioned by the Chancery Division of the High Court of Justice dated 23rd day of January, 1930, and made in an action 1927 A.1233 David Anderson Berry Deceased, Hunter and another v. Robertson and another.

The Royal Historical Society is now the Trustee. The Investment held on Capital Account consists of 634 Charities Official Investment Fund Shares (Market Value £618).

The Trustee will in every second year of the three year period advertise in *The Times* and elsewhere inviting essays.

ALEXANDER PRIZE

The Alexander Prize was established in 1897 by L. C. Alexander, F.R.Hist.S. It consists of a silver medal awarded annually for an essay upon some historical subject. Candidates may select their own subject provided such subject has been previously submitted to and approved by the Literary Director. The essay must be a genuine work of original research, not hitherto published, and one which has not been awarded any other prize. It must not exceed 6,000 words in length and must be sent in on or before 1 November 1976. The detailed regulations should be obtained in advance from the Secretary.

LIST OF ALEXANDER PRIZE ESSAYISTS (1898–1974)[1]

1898. F. Hermia Durham ('The relations of the Crown to trade under James I').
1899. W. F. Lord, B.A. ('The development of political parties in the reign of Queen Anne').
1901. Laura M. Roberts ('The Peace of Lunéville').
1902. V. B. Redstone ('The social condition of England during the Wars of the Roses').
1903. Rose Graham ('The intellectual influence of English monasticism between the tenth and twelfth centuries').
1904. Enid W. G. Routh ('The balance of power in the seventeenth century').
1905. W. A. P. Mason, M.A. ('The beginnings of the Cistercian Order').
1906. Rachel R. Reid, M.A. ('The Rebellion of the Earls, 1569').
1908. Kate Hotblack ('The Peace of Paris, 1763').
1909. Nellie Nield, M.A. ('The social and economic condition of the unfree classes in England in the twelfth and thirteenth centuries').
1912. H. G. Richardson ('The parish clergy of the thirteenth and fourteenth centuries').
1917. Isobel D. Thornley, B.A. ('The treason legislation of 1531–1534').
1918. T. F. T. Plucknett, B.A. ('The place of the Council in the fifteenth century').
1919. Edna F. White, M.A. ('The jurisdiction of the Privy Council under the Tudors').
1920. J. E. Neale, M.A. ('The Commons Journals of the Tudor Period')
1922. Eveline C. Martin ('The English establishments on the Gold Coast in the second half of the eighteenth century').
1923. E. W. Hensman, M.A. ('The Civil War of 1648 in the east midlands').
1924. Grace Stretton, B.A. ('Some aspects of mediæval travel').
1925. F. A. Mace, M.A. ('Devonshire ports in the fourteenth and fifteenth centuries').
1926. Marian J. Tooley, M.A. ('The authorship of the *Defensor Pacis*').

[1] No award was made in 1900, 1907, 1910, 1911, 1913, 1914, 1921, 1946, 1948, 1956, 1969 and 1975. The prize Essays for 1909 and 1919 were not published in the *Transactions*. No Essays were submitted in 1915, 1916 and 1943.

1927. W. A. Pantin, B.A. ('Chapters of the English Black Monks, 1215–1540').
1928. Gladys A. Thornton, B.A., Ph.D. ('A study in the history of Clare, Suffolk, with special reference to its development as a borough').
1929. F. S. Rodkey, A.M., Ph.D. ('Lord Palmerston's policy for the rejuvenation of Turkey, 1839–47').
1930. A. A. Ettinger, D.Phil. ('The proposed Anglo-Franco-American Treaty of 1852 to guarantee Cuba to Spain').
1931. Kathleen A. Walpole, M.A. ('The humanitarian movement of the early nineteenth century to remedy abuses on emigrant vessels to America').
1932. Dorothy M. Brodie, B.A. ('Edmund Dudley, minister of Henry VII').
1933. R. W. Southern, B.A. ('Ranulf Flambard and early Anglo-Norman administration').
1934. S. B. Chrimes, M.A., Ph.D. ('Sir John Fortescue and his theory of dominion').
1935. S. T. Bindoff, M.A. ('The unreformed diplomatic service, 1812–60').
1936. Rosamund J. Mitchell, M.A., B.Litt. ('English students at Padua, 1460–1475').
1937. C. H. Philips, B.A. ('The East India Company "Interest", and the English Government, 1783–4').
1938. H. E. I. Phillips, B.A. ('The last years of the Court of Star Chamber, 1630–41').
1939. Hilda P. Grieve, B.A. ('The deprived married clergy in Essex, 1553–61').
1940. R. Somerville, M.A. ('The Duchy of Lancaster Council and Court of Duchy Chamber').
1941. R. A. L. Smith, M.A., Ph.D. ('The *Regimen Scaccarii* in English monasteries').
1942. F. L. Carsten, D.Phil. ('Medieval democracy in the Brandenburg towns and its defeat in the fifteenth century').
1944. Rev. E. W. Kemp, B.D. ('Pope Alexander III and the canonization of saints').
1945. Helen Suggett, B.Litt. ('The use of French in England in the later middle ages').
1947. June Milne, B.A. ('The diplomacy of Dr John Robinson at the court of Charles XII of Sweden, 1697–1709').
1949. Ethel Drus, M.A. ('The attitude of the Colonial Office to the annexation of Fiji').
1950. Doreen J. Milne, M.A., Ph.D. ('The results of the Rye House Plot, and their influence upon the Revolution of 1688').
1951. K. G. Davies, B.A. ('The origins of the commission system in the West India trade').
1952. G. W. S. Barrow, B.Litt. ('Scottish rulers and the religious orders, 1070–1153').
1953. W. E. Minchinton, B.Sc.(Econ.) ('Bristol—metropolis of the west in the eighteenth century').
1954. Rev. L. Boyle, O.P. ('The *Oculus Sacerdotis* and some other works of William of Pagula').
1955. G. F. E. Rudé, M.A., Ph.D. ('The Gordon riots: a study of the rioters and their victims').
1957. R. F. Hunnisett, M.A., D.Phil. ('The origins of the office of Coroner').
1958. Thomas G. Barnes, A.B., D.Phil. ('County politics and a puritan *cause célèbre*: Somerset churchales, 1633').

1959. Alan Harding, B.Litt. ('The origins and early history of the Keeper of the Peace').
1960. Gwyn A. Williams, M.A., Ph.D. ('London and Edward I').
1961. M. H. Keen, B.A. ('Treason trials under the law of arms').
1962. G. W. Monger, M.A., Ph.D. ('The end of isolation: Britain, Germany and Japan, 1900–1902').
1963. J. S. Moore, B.A. ('The Domesday teamland: a reconsideration').
1964. M. Kelly, Ph.D. ('The submission of the clergy').
1965. J. J. N. Palmer, B.Litt. ('Anglo-French negotiations, 1390–1396').
1966. M. T. Clanchy, M.A., Ph.D. ('The Franchise of Return of Writs').
1967. R. Lovatt, M.A., D.Phil., Ph.D. ('The *Imitation of Christ* in late medieval England').
1968. M. G. A. Vale, M.A., D.Phil. ('The last years of English Gascony, 1451–1453').
1970. Mrs Margaret Bowker, M.A., B.Litt. ('The Commons Supplication against the Ordinaries in the light of some Archidiaconal Acta').
1971. C. Thompson, M.A. ('The origins of the politics of the Parliamentary middle group 1625–1629').
1972. I. d'Alton, B.A., ('Southern Irish Unionism: A study of Cork City and County Unionists, 1884–1914').
1973. C. J. Kitching, B.A., Ph.D. ('The quest for concealed lands in the reign of Elizabeth I').
1974. H. Tomlinson, B.A. ('Place and Profit: an Examination of the Ordnance Office, 1660–1714').

DAVID BERRY PRIZE

The David Berry Prize was established in 1929 by David Anderson-Berry in memory of his father, the Reverend David Berry. It consists of a gold medal and money prize awarded every three years for Scottish history. Candidates may select any subject dealing with Scottish history within the reigns of James I to James VI inclusive, provided such subject has been previously submitted to and approved by the Council of the Royal Historical Society. The essay must be a genuine work of original research not hitherto published, and one which has not been awarded any other prize. The essay must not exceed 50,000 words. It must be sent in on or before 31 October 1976.

LIST OF DAVID BERRY PRIZE ESSAYISTS (1937–73)[1]

1937. G. Donaldson, M.A. ('The polity of the Scottish Reformed Church *c.* 1560–1580, and the rise of the Presbyterian movement').

1943. Rev. Prof. A. F. Scott Pearson, D.Th., D.Litt. ('Anglo-Scottish religious relations, 1400–1600').

1949. T. Bedford Franklin, M.A., F.R.S.E. ('Monastic agriculture in Scotland, 1440–1600').

1955. W. A. McNeill, M.A. (' "Estaytt" of the king's rents and pensions, 1621').

1958 Prof. Maurice Lee, Ph.D. ('Maitland of Thirlestane and the foundation of the Stewart despotism in Scotland').

1964. M. H. Merriman ('Scottish collaborators with England during the Anglo-Scottish war, 1543–1550').

1967. Miss M. H. B. Sanderson ('Catholic recusancy in Scotland in the sixteenth century').

1970. Dr Athol Murray, M.A., LL.B., Ph.D. ('The Comptroller, 1425–1610').

1973. Dr J. Kirk ('Who were the Melvillians: A study in the Personnel and Background of the Presbyterian Movement in late Sixteenth-century Scotland').

[1] No Essays were submitted in 1940. No award was made in 1946, 1952 and 1961.

THE ROYAL HISTORICAL SOCIETY
(INCORPORATED BY ROYAL CHARTER)
OFFICERS AND COUNCIL—1975

Patron
HER MAJESTY THE QUEEN

President
PROFESSOR G. R. ELTON, MA, PhD, LittD, FBA

Honorary Vice-Presidents
PROFESSOR SIR HERBERT BUTTERFIELD, MA, LLD, DLitt, DLit, LittD, FBA.
PROFESSOR C. R. CHENEY, MA, DLitt, FBA.
SIR CHARLES CLAY, CB, MA, LittD, FBA, FSA.
PROFESSOR SIR GORONWY EDWARDS, MA, DLitt, LittD, FBA, FSA.
PROFESSOR V. H. GALBRAITH, MA, DLitt, LittD, FBA.
PROFESSOR R. A. HUMPHREYS, OBE, MA, PhD, DLitt, LittD, DLitt, DUniv.
THE HON SIR STEVEN RUNCIMAN, MA, DPhil, LLD, LittD, DLitt, LitD, DD, DHL, FBA, FSA.
SIR RICHARD SOUTHERN, MA, DLitt, LittD, DLitt, FBA.
DAME LUCY SUTHERLAND, DBE, MA, DLitt, LittD, DCL, FBA.

Vice-Presidents
P. CHAPLAIS, PhD, FBA, FSA.
PROFESSOR D. HAY, MA, DLitt, FBA.
Professor J. M. WALLACE-HADRILL, MA, DLitt, FBA
PROFESSOR G. E. AYLMER, MA, DPhil.
PROFESSOR R. H. C. DAVIS, MA, FSA.
PROFESSOR F. J. FISHER, MA.
PROFESSOR J. C. HOLT, MA, DPhil, FSA.
PROFESSOR J. HURSTFIELD, DLit.

STANDING COMMITTEES—1975

Finance Committee
PROFESSOR T. C. BARKER.
C. E. BLUNT, OBE, FBA, FSA.
R. F. HUNNISETT.
N. J. WILLIAMS, MA, DPhil, FSA.
PROFESSOR C. H. WILSON, MA, FBA.
And the Officers.

Publications Committee
PROFESSOR G. E. AYLMER.
P. CHAPLAIS.
PROFESSOR F. J. FISHER.
B. H. HARRISON.
PROFESSOR D. W. J. JOHNSON.
MRS A. E. B. OWEN.
PROFESSOR P. H. SAWYER.
K. V. THOMAS.
PROFESSOR D. C. WATT.
And the Officers.

Library Committee
T. H. ASTON.
PROFESSOR G. E. AYLMER.
PROFESSOR F. J. FISHER.
J. M. ROBERTS.
And the Officers.

243

LIST OF FELLOWS OF THE
ROYAL HISTORICAL SOCIETY

(CORRECTED TO 31 DECEMBER 1975)

Names of Officers and Honorary Vice-Presidents are printed in capitals.
Those marked* have compounded for their annual subscriptions.

Abbott, A. W., CMG, CBE, Frithys Orchard, West Clandon, Surrey.
Adair, J. E., MA, PhD, 1 Crockford Park Road, Addlestone, Surrey.
Adam, R. J., MA, Cromalt, Lade Braes, St Andrews, Fife.
*Addleshaw, G. W. O., The Very Rev. the Dean of Chester, MA, BD, FSA, The Deanery, Chester CH1 2JF.
Ainsworth, Sir John, Bt, MA, c/o National Library, Kildare Street, Dublin 2, Eire.
Akrigg, Professor G. P. V., BA, PhD, Dept of English, University of British Columbia, Vancouver 8, B.C., Canada.
Alcock, L., MA, FSA, 29 Hamilton Drive, Glasgow G12 8DN.
Alder, Professor G. J., PhD, Dept of History, The University, Whiteknights, Reading RG6 2AA.
Alderman, G., BA, MA, DPhil, 172 Colindeep Lane, London NW9 6EA.
Allan, D. G. C., MSc(Econ), FSA, Hambalt Road, London SW4 9EQ.
Allen, D. H., BA, PhD, 105 Tuddenham Avenue, Ipswich, Suffolk IP4 2HG.
Allen, Professor, H. C., MC, MA, School of English and American Studies, University of East Anglia, University Plain, Norwich NOR 88C.
ALLMAND, C. T., MA, DPhil, *(Assistant Literary Director)*, 59 Menlove Avenue, Liverpool L18 2EH.
Altholz, Professor J., PhD, Dept of History, University of Minnesota, 614 Social Sciences Building, Minneapolis, Minn. 55455, USA.
Altschul, Professor M., PhD, Case Western Reserve University, Cleveland, Ohio 44106, USA.
Anderson, Professor M. S., MA, PhD, London School of Economics, Houghton Street, WC2 2AE.
Anderson, Mrs O. R., MA, BLitt, Westfield College, NW3.
*Anderson, R. C., MA, LittD, FSA, 9 Grove Place, Lymington, Hants.
Andrew, C. M., MA, PhD, Director of Studies, Corpus Christi College, Cambridge.
Andrews, K. R., BA, PhD, Dept of History, University of Hull, Cottingham Road, Hull HU6 7RX.
Anglesey, The Most Hon., The Marquess of, FSA, FRSL, Plas-Newydd, Llanfairpwll, Anglesey.
Anglo, S., BA, PhD, FSA, Dept of History of Ideas, University College, Swansea.
Annan, Lord, OBE, MA, DLitt, DUniv, University College, Gower Street, WC1E 6BT.
Annis, P. G. W., BA, 70 Northcote Road, Sidcup, Kent DA14 6PW.
Appleby, J. S., Little Pitchbury, Brick Kiln Lane, Great Horkseley, Colchester, Essex CO6 4EU.
Armstrong, Miss A. M., BA, 7 Vale Court, Mallord Street, SW3.

Armstrong, C. A. J., MA, FSA, Hertford College, Oxford.
Armstrong Professor F. H., PhD, University of Western Ontario, London 72, Ontario.
Armstrong, W. A., BA, PhD, Eliot College, The University, Canterbury, Kent.
Arnstein, Professor W. L., PhD, Dept of History, University of Illinois at Urbana–Champaign, 309 Gregory Hall, Urbana, Ill. 61801, U.S.A.
Ashton, Professor R., PhD, The Manor House, Brundall, near Norwich NOR 86Z
Ashworth, Professor W., BSc(Econ), PhD, Dept of Econ. and Soc. History, The University, Bristol.
Aston, Mrs M. E., MA, DPhil, Castle House, Chipping Ongar, Essex.
Aston, T. H., MA, FSA, Corpus Christi College, Oxford, OX1 4JF.
Auchmuty, Professor J. J., CBE, MA, PhD, DLitt, LLD, FAHA, MRIA, 9 Glynn Street, Hughes, ACT 2605, Australia.
Austin, M. R., BD, MA, PhD, The Glead, 2a Louvain Road, Derby DE3 6BZ.
Avery, D. J., MA, BLitt, 6 St James's Square, London, SW1.
Axelson, Professor E. V., DLitt, University of Cape Town, Rondebosch, S. Africa.
*Aydelotte, Professor W. O., PhD, State University of Iowa, Iowa City, Iowa, U.S.A.
Aylmer, Professor G. E. MA, DPhill, University of York, Heslington, York YO1 5DD.

Bagley, J. J., MA, 10 Beach Priory Gardens, Southport, Lancs.
Bagshawe, T. W., FSA, c/o Luton Museum, Wardown Park, Luton. Bedfordshire.
Bahlman, Dudley W. R., PhD, Dept of History, Williams College, Williamstown, Mass., U.S.A.
Baillie, H. M. G., MBE, MA, FSA, 12B Stanford Road, W8 3QJ.
Baily, L. W. A., The Granary, New Parks, Shipton-by-Beningbrough, York YO6 1BD.
Bailyn, Professor B., MA, PhD, LittD, LHD, Widener J. Harvard University, Cambridge, Mass. 02138, U.S.A.
Baker, L. G. D., MA, BLitt, Dept of Medieval Hist., The University, Edinburgh.
Baker, T. F. T., BA, Camden Lodge, 50 Hastings Road, Pembury, Kent.
Balfour, Professor M. L. G., CBE, MA, Waine's Cottage, Swan Lane, Burford, Oxon.
Ballhatchet, Professor K. A., MA, PhD, 35 Rudall Crescent, Hampstead, London, NW3 6UE.
Banks, Professor J. A., MA, Dept of Sociology, The University, Leicester LE1 7RH.
Barber, M. C., BA, PhD, Dept of History, The University, Reading, Berks. RG6 2AA.
Barker, E. E., MA, PhD, FSA, 60 Marina Road, Little Altcar, Formby, via Liverpool, Lancs. L37 6BP.
Barker, Professor T. C., MA, PhD, Minsen Dane, Brogdale Road, Faversham, Kent.
Barkley, Professor the Rev. J. M. MA, DD 2 College Park, Belfast, N. Ireland.
*Barlow, Professor F. MA, DPhil, FBA, Middle Court Hall, Kenton, Exeter.

Barnes, Miss P. M., PhD, Public Record Office, Chancery Lane, WC2.
Barnes, Professor T. G. AB, DPhil, University of California, Berkeley, Calif., 94720, U.S.A.
*Barnes, Professor Viola F., MA, PhD, LLD, 16 North Sycamore Street, South Hadley, Mass. 01075, U.S.A.
Barratt, Miss D. M., DPhil, The Corner House, Hampton Poyle, Kidlington, Oxford.
Barron, Mrs C. M., MA, PhD, 35 Rochester Road, NW1.
Barrow, Professor G. W. S., MA, DLitt, The Old Manse, 19 Westfield Road, Cupar, Fife KY15 5AP.
Bartlett, C. J., PhD, 5 Strathspey Place, West Ferry, Dundee DD5 1QB.
Batho, G. R., MA, Dept of Education, The University, 48 Old Elvet, Durham DH1 3JH.
Baugh, Professor Daniel A., PhD, Dept of History, McGraw Hall, Cornell University, Ithaca, N.Y. 14850, U.S.A.
Baxter, Professor S. B., PhD, 608 Morgan Creek Road, Chapel Hill, N.C. 27514 U.S.A.
Baylen, Professor J. O., MA, PhD, Georgia State University, 33 Gilmer Street S.E., Atlanta, Georgia 30303, U.S.A.
Beales, D. E. D. MA, PhD, Sidney Sussex College, Cambridge.
Beales, H. L., DLitt, 16 Denman Drive, London, NW.11
Bealey, Professor F., BSc(Econ), Dept of Politics, Taylor Building, Old Aberdeen AB9 2UB.
Bean, Professor J. M. W., MA, DPhil, 622 Fayerweather Hall, Columbia University, New York, N.Y. 10027, U.S.A.
Beardwood, Miss Alice, BA, BLitt, DPhil, 415 Miller's Lane, Wynnewood, Pa. U.S.A.
Beasley, Professor W. G. PhD, FBA, 172 Hampton Road, Twickenham, Middlesex TW2 5NJ.
Beattie, Professor J. M., PhD Dept of History, University of Toronto, Toronto M5S 1A1, Canada.
Beaumont, H., MA, Silverdale, Severn Bank, Shrewsbury.
Beckett, Professor J. C., MA, 19 Wellington Park Terrace, Belfast 9, N. Ireland.
Beckingsale, B. W., MA, 8 Highbury, Newcastle upon Tyne NE2 3DX.
Beddard, R. A., MA, DPhil, Oriel College, Oxford.
Beeler, Professor J. H., PhD, 1302 New Garden Road, Greensboro, N.C. 27410, U.S.A.
*Beer, E. S. de, CBE, MA, DLitt, FBA, FSA, 31 Brompton Square, SW3 2AE.
Beer, Professor Samuel H., PhD, Faculty of Arts & Sciences, Harvard University, Littauer Center G-15, Cambridge, Mass, 02138, U.S.A.
Begley, W. W., 17 St Mary's Gardens, SE11.
Behrens, Miss C. B. A., MA, Dales Barn, Barton, Cambridge.
Bell, P. M. H., BA, BLitt, The School of History, The University, P.O. Box 147, Liverpool L69 3BX.
Beller, E. A., DPhil, Dept of History, Princeton University, N.J., 08540, U.S.A.
Beloff, Professor M., MA, BLitt, The Univ. College at Buckingham, Hunter Street, Buckingham MK18 1EG.
Bennett, Capt. G. M., RN(ret.), DSC, Stage Coach Cottage, 57 Broad Street, Ludlow, Salop, SY8 1NH.
Bennett, Rev. Canon G. V., MA, DPhil, FSA, New College, Oxford.
Bennett, R. F., MA, Magdalene College, Cambridge.

Bethell, D. L. T., MA, Dept of Medieval History, University College, Belfield, Dublin 4, Ireland.

Bethell, L. M., PhD, University College, Gower Street, WC1 E6BT.

Biddiss, M. D., MA, PhD, The University, Leicester LE1 7RH.

Biddle, M, MA, FSA, Winchester Research Unit, 13 Parchment Street, Winchester.

Bidwell, Brig. R. G. S., OBE, Royal United Services Institute, Whitehall, SW1A 2ET.

Bindoff, Professor S. T., MA, 2 Sylvan Gardens, Woodlands Road, Surbiton, Surrey.

*Bing, H. F., MA, 45 Rempstone Road, East Leake, nr Loughborough, Leics.

Binney, J. E. D., DPhil, 6 Pageant Drive, Sherborne, Dorset.

Birch, A., MA, PhD, University of Hong Kong, Hong Kong.

Bishop, A. S., BA, PhD, 254 Leigham Court Road, Streatham, SW16 2RP.

Bishop, T. A. M., MA, The Annexe, Manor House, Hemingford Grey, Hunts.

Black, Professor Eugene C., PhD, Dept of History, Brandeis University, Waltham, Mass. 02154 U.S.A.

Blair, P. Hunter, MA, LittD, Emmanuel College, Cambridge CB2 3AP.

Blake, E. O., MA, PhD, Roselands, Moorhill Road, Westend, Southampton SO3 3AW.

Blake, Professor J. W., CBE, MA, DLitt, Willow Cottage, Mynoe, Limavady, Co. Londonderry, N. Ireland.

Blake, Lord, MA, FBA, The Provost's Lodgings, The Queen's College, Oxford OX1 4AW.

Blakemore, H., PhD, 43 Fitzjohn Avenue, Barnet, Herts.

*Blakey, Professor R. G., PhD, c/o Mr Raymond Shove, Order Dept, Library, University of Minnesota, Minneapolis, Minn., U.S.A.

Blakiston, H. N., BA, 6 Markham Square, SW3.

Blaxland, Major W. G., Lower Heppington, Street End, Canterbury, Kent, CT4 7AN.

Blomfield, Mrs K., 8 Elmdene Court, Constitution Hill, Woking, Surrey GU22 7SA.

Blunt, C. E., OBE, FBA, FSA, Ramsbury Hill, Ramsbury, Marlborough, Wilts.

*Bolsover, G. H., OBE, MA, PhD, 7 Devonshire Road, Hatch End, Middlesex.

Bolton, Miss Brenda, BA, Dept. of History, Westfield College, NW3 7ST.

Bolton, Professor G. C., MA, DPhil, 6 Melvista Avenue, Claremont, Western Australia.

Bolton, Professor W. F., AM, PhD, FSA, Douglass College, Rutgers University, New Brunswick, N.J. 08903, U.S.A.

Bond, M. F., OBE, MA, FSA, 19 Bolton Crescent, Windsor, Berks.

Borrie, M. A. F., BA, 14 Lancaster Gate, W2.

Bossy, J. A., MA, PhD, The Queen's University, Belfast B17 1NN, N. Ireland.

Bottigheimer, Professor Karl S., Dept of History, State University of New York at Stony Brook, Long Island, N.Y., U.S.A.

Boulton, Professor J. T., BLitt, PhD, School of English Studies, The University, Nottingham.

Bowker, Mrs M., MA, BLitt, 5 Spens Avenue, Cambridge.

Bowyer, M. J. F., 32, Netherhall Way, Cambridge.

*Boxer, Professor C. R., DLitt, FBA, Ringshall End, Little Gaddesden, Berkhamsted, Herts.
Boyce, D. G., BA, PhD, Dept of Political Theory and Government, University College, Swansea, SA2 8PP.
Boyle, Professor the Rev. L. E., DPhil, STL, Pontifical Institute of Mediaeval Studies, 59 Queen's Park, Toronto 181, Canada.
Boynton, L. O. J., MA, DPhil, FSA, Westfield College, NW3.
Bramsted, E. K., PhD, DPhil, Woodpeckers, Brooklands Lane, Weybridge, Surrey KT13 8UX.
Breck, Professor A. D., MA, PhD, LittD, DLitt, University of Denver, Denver, Colorado 80210, U.S.A.
Brentano, Professor R., DPhil, University of California, Berkeley, Calif., U.S.A.
Brett-James, E. A., MA, Royal Military Academy, Sandhurst, Camberley, Surrey.
Bridge, F. R., PhD, The Poplars, Radley Lane, Radley, Leeds.
Briers, Miss P. M., BLitt, 58 Fassett Road, Kingston-on-Thames, Surrey.
Briggs, Professor A., BSc(Econ), MA, DLitt, University of Sussex, Stanmer House, Stanmer, Brighton.
Briggs, J. H. Y., University of Keele, Staffs ST5 5BG.
Briggs, R., MA, All Souls College, Oxford OX1 4AL.
Brock, M. G., MA, 31 Linton Road, Oxford OX1 6UL.
Brock, Professor W. R., MA, PhD, Department of History, University of Glasgow, Glasgow 2.
Brodie, Miss D. M., PhD, 137 Roberts Road, Pietermaritzburg, Natal, South Africa.
Brogan, D. H. V., MA, St John's College, Cambridge.
*Bromley, Professor J. S., MA, Merrow, Dene Close, Upper Bassett, Southampton.
Brooke, Professor C. N. L., MA, LittD, FBA, FSA, Westfield College, London NW3 7ST.
Brooke, J., BA, 63 Hurst Avenue, Chingford, London E4 8DL.
Brooke, Mrs R. B., MA, PhD, c/o Westfield College, London NW3 7ST.
Brooks, F. W., MA, FSA, The University, Hull.
Brooks, N. P., MA, DPhil, The University, St Andrews, Fife.
Brown, Professor A. L., MA, DPhil, The University, Glasgow G12 8QQ.
Brown, G. S., PhD, 1720 Hanover Road, Ann Arbor, Mich., 48103, U.S.A.
Brown, Judith M., MA, PhD, Dept of History, The University, Manchester M13 9PL.
Brown, Miss L. M., MA, PhD, 93 Church Road, Hanwell, W7.
Brown, Professor M. J., MA, PhD, 333 South Candler Street, Decatur, Georgia 30030, U.S.A.
Brown, P. R. Lamont, MA, FBA, Hillslope, Pullen's Lane, Oxford.
Brown, R. A., MA, DPhil, FSA, King's College, Strand, WC2.
Bruce, J. M., MA, 6 Albany Close, Bushey Heath, Herts, WD2 3SG.
Bryant, Sir Arthur W. M., CH, CBE, LLD, 18 Rutland Gate, SW7.
Bryson, Professor W. Hamilton, School of Law, University of Richmond, Richmond, Va. 23173, U.S.A.
Buckland, P. J., MA, PhD, 6 Rosefield Road, Liverpool L25 8TF.
Bueno de Mesquita, D. M., MA, PhD, Christ Church, Oxford.
Bullock, Sir Alan (L.C.), MA, DLitt, FBA, St Catherine's College, Oxford.
Bullough, Professor D. A., MA, FSA, Dept of Mediaeval History, 71 South Street, St Andrews, Fife.

Burke, U. P., MA, 15 Lower Market Street, Hove, Sussex, BN3 1AT.
Burleigh, The Rev. Professor J. H.S., BD, 21 Kingsmuir Drive, Peebles, EH45 9AA.
Burns, Professor J. H., MA, PhD, 39 Amherst Road, W.13.
Burroughs, P., Ph D, Dalhousie University, Halifax, Nova Scotia, Canada.
Burrow, J. W., MA, PhD, Sussex University, Falmer, Brighton.
Bury, J. P. T., MA, LittD, Corpus Christi College, Cambridge.
Butler, Professor L. H., MA, DPhil, Principal, Royal Holloway College, Englefield Green, Surrey.
Butler, R. D'O, CMG, MA, All Souls College, Oxford.
BUTTERFIELD, Professor Sir Herbert, MA, LLD, DLitt, DLit, LittD, FBA, 28 High Street, Sawston, Cambridge CB2 4BG.
Bythell, D., MA, DPhil, 23–26 Old Elvet, The University, Durham DH1 3HY.

Cabaniss, Professor J. A., PhD, University of Mississippi, Box No. 153, University, Mississippi, U.S.A.
Calvert, Brig. J. M. (ret.) MA, Flat 9, Station Parade, East Horsley, Sussex.
Calvert, P. A. R., MA, PhD, AM, Dept of Politics, University of Southampton, Highfield, Southampton SO9 5NH.
Cameron, Professor K., PhD, The University, Nottingham.
Campbell, Professor A. E., MA, PhD, School of History, University of Birmingham, P.O. Box 363, Birmingham B15 2TT.
*Campbell, Miss A. M., AM, PhD, 190 George Street, Brunswick, N.J., U.S.A.
Campbell, Major D. A., FSAScot, An Cladach, Achnacree Bay, Connel, Argyll PA37 1RD.
Campbell, J., MA, FSA, Worcester College, Oxford.
*Campbell, Professor Mildred L., PhD, Vassar College, Poughkeepsie, N.Y., U.S.A.
Campbell, Professor R. H., MA, PhD, University of Stirling, Scotland.
Campbell, Miss Sybil, OBE, MA, Drim-na-Vulun, Lochgilphead, Argyll.
Cant, R. G., MA, 2 Kilburn Place, St Andrews, Fife.
Cantor, Professor Norman F., PhD, Dept of History, State University of New York at Binghampton, N.Y. 13901, U.S.A.
Capp, B. S., MA, DPhil, Dept of History, University of Warwick, Coventry, Warwickshire CV4 7AL.
Cargill-Thompson, W. D. J., MA, PhD, Dept of Ecclesiastical History, King's College, Strand, WC2.
*Carlson, Leland H., PhD, 255 S. Avenue 50, Los Angeles, Cal. 90042, U.S.A.
Carlton, Professor Charles, Dept of History, North Carolina State University, Raleigh, N.C. 27607, U.S.A.
Carman, W. Y., FSA, 94 Mulgrave Road, Sutton, Surrey.
Carr, A. R. M., MA, St Antony's College, Oxford.
Carr, W., PhD, 16 Old Hay Close, Dore, Sheffield S17 3GQ.
Carrington, Miss Dorothy, 3 Rue Emmanuel Arene, 20 Ajaccio, Corsica.
Carter, Mrs A. C., MA, 12 Garbrand Walk, Ewell, Epsom, Surrey.
Cartlidge, Rev. J. E. G., Sunnyside House, Snowhill, St George's, Oakengates, Salop.
*Carus-Wilson, Professor E. M., MA, FBA, FSA, 14 Lansdowne Road, W11.

Catto, R. J. A. I., MA, Oriel College, Oxford.
Chadwick, Professor W. O., DD, DLitt, FBA, Selwyn Lodge, Cambridge.
Challis, C. E., MA, PhD, 14 Ashwood Villas, Headingley, Leeds 6.
Chambers, D. S., MA, DPhil, Warburg Institute, Woburn Square, WC1.
Chandaman, Professor C. D., BA, PhD, St David's University College, Lampeter, Cardiganshire.
Chandler, D. G., MA, Hindford, Monteagle Lane, Yately, Camberley, Surrey.
Chaplais, P., PhD, FBA, FSA, Wintles Farm House, 36 Mill Street, Eynsham, Oxford OX8 1JS.
Charles-Edwards, T. M., DPhil, Corpus Christi College, Oxford.
*CHENEY, Professor C. R., MA, DLitt, FBA, 236 Hills Road, Cambridge CB2 2QE.
Chew, Miss H. M., MA, PhD, Seven Hills Nursing Home, St Margaret's Road, St Marychurch, Torquay.
Chibnall, Mrs Marjorie, MA, DPhil, 6 Millington Road, Cambridge CB3 9HP.
Child, C. J., OBE, MA, PhM, 94 Westhall Road, Warlingham, Surrey CR3 9HB.
Chorley, The Hon. G. P. H., BA, 40 Castelnau Mansions, London SW13.
Chrimes, Professor S. B., MA, PhD, LittD, 24 Cwrt-y-Vil Road, Penarth, Glam. CF6 2HP.
Christie, Professor I. R., MA, 10 Green Lane, Croxley Green, Herts., WD3 3HR.
Church, Professor R. A., BA, PhD, School of Social Studies, University of East Anglia, Norwich NOR 88C.
Cirket, A. F., 71 Curlew Crescent, Bedford.
Clanchy, M. T., PhD, FSA, The University, Glasgow G12 8QQ.
Clark, A. E., MA, 32 Durham Avenue, Thornton Cleveleys, Blackpool.
Clark, Professor Dora Mae, PhD, 134 Pennsylvania Ave., Chambersburg, Pa. 17201, U.S.A.
Clarke, P. F., MA, PhD, Dept of History, University College, Gower Street, WC1E 6BT.
*CLAY, Sir Charles (T.), CB, MA, LittD, FBA, FSA, 30 Queen's Gate Gardens, SW7.
Clementi, Miss D., MA, DPhil, Flat 7, 43 Rutland Gate, SW7 PB1.
Clemoes, Professor P. A. M., BA, PhD, Emmanuel College, Cambridge.
Cliffe, J. T., BA, PhD, 263 Staines Road, Twickenham, Middx.
Clive, Professor J. L., PhD, 38 Fernald Drive, Cambridge, Mass. 02138, U.S.A.
Clough, C. H., MA, DPhil, School of History, The University, 8 Abercromby Square, Liverpool 7.
Cobb, H. S., MA, FSA, 1 Child's Way, Hampstead Garden Suburb, NW11.
Cobb, Professor R. C., MA, FBA, Worcester College, Oxford.
Cobban, A. B., MA, PhD, School of History, The University, 8 Abercromby Square, Liverpool 7.
Cockburn, J. S., LLB, LIM, PhD, c/o Public Record Office, Chancery Lane, London WC2A 1LR.
Cocks, E. J., MA, Middle Lodge, Ardingly, Haywards Heath, Sussex.
*Code, Rt Rev. Monsignor Joseph B., MA, STB, ScHistD, DLitt, The Executive House 21E, 4466 West Pine Blvd., St Louis, MO 63108, U.S.A.

Cohn, H. J., MA, DPhil, University of Warwick, Coventry CV4 7AL.
Cohn, Professor N., MA, DLitt, 61 New End, NW3.
Cole, Lieut-Colonel H. N., OBE, TD, DL, FRSA, 4 Summer Cottages, Guildford Road, Ash, nr Aldershot, Hants.
Coleman, B. I., MA, PhD, Dept of History, The University, Exeter.
Coleman, Professor D. C., BSc, PhD, FBA, Over Hall, Cavendish, Sudbury, Suffolk.
Collier, W. O., MA, FSA, 34 Berwyn Road, Richmond, Surrey.
Collins, Mrs I., MA, BLitt, School of History, 8 Abercromby Square, Liverpool 7.
Collinson, Professor P., MA, PhD, Department of History, University of Sydney, N.S.W. 2006 Australia.
Colvin, H. M., CBE, MA, FBA, St John's College, Oxford.
Conacher, Professor J. B., MA, PhD, 151 Welland Avenue, Toronto 290, Ontario, Canada.
Congreve, A. L., MA, FSA, Orchard Cottage, Cranbrook, Kent TN17 3NW.
Connell-Smith, Professor G. E., PhD, 7 Braids Walk, Kirkella, Hull, Yorks. HU10 7PA.
Constable, G., PhD, 25 Mount Pleasant Street, Cambridge, Mass, U.S.A.
Conway, Professor A. A., MA, University of Canterbury, Christchurch 1, New Zealand.
Cook, A. E., MA, PhD, 20 Nicholas Road, Hunter's Ride, Henley-on-Thames, Oxon.
Cooke, Professor J. J., PhD, Dept of History, College of Liberal Arts, University of Mississippi, University, Miss. 38677, U.S.A.
Coolidge, Professor R. T., MA, BLitt, 27 Rosemount Avenue, Westmount, Quebec, Canada.
Cooper, J. P., MA, Trinity College, Oxford.
Cope, Professor Esther S., PhD, Dept of History, Univ. of Nebraska, Lincoln, Neb. 68508, U.S.A.
Copeland, Professor T. W., PhD, Dept. of English, Univ. of Massachusetts, Amherst, Mass. 01002, U.S.A.
Cornford, Professor J. P., Dept of Politics, University of Edinburgh, William Robertson Bldg., George Sq., Edinburgh EH8 9JY.
Cornwall, J. C. K., MA, 1 Orchard Close, Copford Green, Colchester, Essex.
Corson, J. C., MA, PhD, Mossrig, Lilliesleaf, Melrose, Roxburghshire.
Costeloe, M. P., BA, PhD, Hispanic and Latin American Studies, The University, Bristol, 83 Woodland Road, Bristol.
Cowan, I. B., MA, PhD, University of Glasgow, Glasgow, G12 8QH.
Cowdrey, Rev. H. E. J., MA, St Edmund Hall, Oxford OX1 4AR.
Cowie, Rev. L. W., MA, PhD, 38 Stratton Road, Merton Park, S.W.19.
Cowley, F. G., PhD, 17 Brookvale Road, West Cross, Swansea.
Cragg, Professor G. R., PhD, Vancouver School of Theology, 6000 Iona Drive, Vancouver, B.C., V6T 1L4, Canada.
Craig, R. S., BSc(Econ), 99 Muswell Avenue, N10.
Cramp, Professor Rosemary, MA, BLitt, FSA, Department of Archaeology, The Old Fulling Mill, The Banks, Durham.
Cranfield, L. R., 31a Clara Street, South Yarra, Victoria, Australia.
*Crawley, C. W., MA, 1 Madingley Road, Cambridge.
Cremona, The Hon. Mr Justice Professor J. J., DLitt, PhD, LLD, 5 Victoria Gardens, Sliema, Malta.

Crittall, Miss E., MA, FSA, 16 Downside Crescent, NW3.
Crombie, A. C., BSc, MA, PhD, Trinity College, Oxford OX1 3BH.
Cromwell, Miss V., MA, University of Sussex, Falmer, Brighton, Sussex.
Cross, Miss M. C., MA, PhD, University of York, York YO1 5DD.
Crowder, C. M. D., MA, DPhil, Queen's University, Kingston, Ontario, Canada.
Crowe, Miss S. E., MA, PhD, St Hilda's College, Oxford.
Cruickshank, C. G., MA, DPhil, 15 McKay Road, Wimbledon Common, SW20.
Cumming, Professor I., MEd, PhD, The University, Auckland, New Zealand.
Cummins, Professor J. S., PhD, University College, Gower Street, WC1E 6BT.
Cumpston, Miss I. M., MA, DPhil, Birkbeck College, Malet Street, WC1.
Cunliffe, Professor M. F., MA, BLitt, Dept of American Studies, University of Sussex, Falmer, Brighton BN1 9QN.
Cunningham, Professor A. B., MA, PhD, Simon Fraser University, Burnaby 2, B.C., Canada.
Curtis, Professor L. Perry, PhD, Dept of History, Brown University, Providence, R.I. 02912, U.S.A.
Curtis, M. H., PhD, Scripps College, Claremont, Calif., U.S.A.
Cushner, Rev. N. P., SJ, MA, Canisius College, Buffalo, New York 14208, U.S.A.
*Cuttino, Professor G. P., DPhil, Department of History, Emory University, Atlanta, Ga., U.S.A.

Dakin, D., MA, PhD, 7 Langside Avenue, SW15.
Darlington, Professor R. R., BA, PhD, FBA, FSA, Warrenhurst, Twyford, Reading.
Davies, Professor Alun, MA, 46 Eaton Crescent, Swansea.
Davies, C. S. L., MA, DPhil, Wadham College, Oxford.
Davies, I. N. R., MA, DPhil, 22 Rowland Close, Wolvercote, Oxford.
Davies, P. N., MA, PhD, Cmar, Croft Drive, Caldy, Wirral, Merseyside.
Davies, R. R., DPhil, University College, Gower Street, WC1E 6BT.
*Davis, G. R. C., MA, DPhil, FSA 214 Somerset Road, SW19 5JE.
Davis, Professor R. H. C., MA, FSA, 56 Fitzroy Avenue, Harborne, Birmingham B17 8RJ.
*Dawe, D. A., 46 Green Lane, Purley, Surrey.
*Day, P. W., MA, 2 Rectory Terrace, Gosforth, Newcastle upon Tyne.
Deane, Miss Phyllis M., MA, Newnhan College, Cambridge.
*Deanesly, Professor Margaret, MA, FSA, 196 Clarence Gate Gardens, NW1.
*Deeley, Miss A. P., MA, 41 Linden Road, Bicester, Oxford.
de la Mare, Miss A. C., MA, PhD, Bodleian Library, Oxford.
Denham, E. W., MA, 27 The Drive, Northwood, Middx, HA6 1HW.
Dennis, Professor P. J., MA, PhD, Dept of History, The Royal Military College of Canada, Kingston, Ont. K7L 2W3. Canada.
Denton, J. H., BA, PhD, The University Manchester M13 9PL.
Dickens, Professor A. G., CMG, MA, DLit, FBA, FSA, Institute of Historical Research, University of London, Senate House, WC1E 7HU.
Dickinson, H. T., MA, PhD, Dept of Modern History, The University, Edinburgh.

Dickinson, Rev. J. C., MA, FSA, The University, Birmingham 15.
Dickson, P. G. M., MA, DPhil, St Catherine's College, Oxford.
Diké, Professor K. O., MA, PhD, Dept of History, Harvard University, Cambridge, Mass, 02138, U.S.A.
Dilks, Professor D. N., BA, Dept of International History, The University, Leeds.
Dilworth, Rev. G. M., MA, OSB, PhD, The Abbey, Fort Augustus, Inverness-shire PH32 4DB, Scotland.
Dobson, R. B., MA, DPhil, Department of History, The University, Heslington, York YO1 5DD.
*Dodwell, Miss B., MA, The University, Reading.
Dodwell, Professor C. R., MA, PhD, FSA, History of Art Department, The University, Manchester M13 9PL.
Dolley, Professor R. H. M., BA, MRIA, FSA, The Queen's University, Belfast BT7 1NN, N. Ireland.
Don Peter, The Right Rev. Monsignor, Archbishop's House, Colombo 8, Sri Lanka.
Donald, Professor M. B., MSc, Rabbit Shaw, 6 Stagbury Avenue, Chipstead, Surrey CR3 3TA.
*Donaldson, Professor G., MA, PhD, DLitt, Preston Tower Nursery Cottage, Prestonpans, East Lothian EH32 9EN.
*Donaldson-Hudson, Miss R., BA, (address unknown).
Donoughue, B., MA, DPhil, 7 Brookfield Park, London NW5 1ES.
Dore, R. N., MA, Holmrook, 19 Chapel Lane, Hale Barns, Altrincham, Cheshire WA15 0AB.
Douglas, Professor D. C., MA, DLitt, FBA, 4 Henleaze Gardens, Bristol.
Douie, Miss D. L., BA, PhD, FSA, Flat A, 2 Charlbury Road, Oxford.
Downer, L. J., MA, LLB, Mediaeval Studies, Australian National University, Canberra.
Doyle, A. I., MA, PhD, University College, The Castle, Durham.
Driver, J. T., MA, BLitt, 25 Abbot's Grange, Off Liverpool Road, Chester CH2 1AJ.
*Drus, Miss E., MA, The University, Southampton.
Du Boulay, Professor F. R. H., MA, Broadmead, Riverhead, Sevenoaks, Kent.
Duckham, B. F., MA, Hillhead Cottage, Balfron, Stirlingshire G63 0PH.
Duggan, C., PhD, King's College, Strand, WC2.
Dugmore, The Rev. Professor C. W., DD, King's College, Strand, WC2.
Duke, A. C., MA, Dept of History, The University, Southampton SO9 5NH.
Duly, Professor L. C., PhD, Dept of History, University of Nebraska, Lincoln, Neb. 68508, U.S.A.
Dunbabin, J. P. D., MA, St Edmund Hall, Oxford.
Duncan, Professor A. A. M., MA, University of Glasgow, 9 University Gardens, Glasgow G12 8QH.
Dunham, Professor W. H., PhD, 200 Everit Street, New Haven, Conn. 06511, U.S.A.
Dunn, Professor R. S., PhD, Dept of History, The College, University of Pennsylvania, Philadelphia 19104, U.S.A.
Dunning, Rev. P. J., CM, MA, PhD, St. Vincent's, 293 Waldegrave Road, Strawberry Hill, Twickenham, Middx. TW1 4SO.
Dunning, R. W., BA, PhD, FSA, 16 Comeytrowe Rise, Taunton, Somerset.
Durack, Mrs I. A., MA, PhD, University of Western Australia, Crawley, Western Australia.

Dykes, D. W., MA, Cherry Grove, Welsh St Donats, nr Cowbridge, Glam. CF7 7SS.

Dyos, Professor H. J., BSc(Econ), PhD, 16 Kingsway Road, Leicester.

Eastwood, Rev. C. C., PhD, Heathview, Monks Lane, Audlem, Cheshire.

Eckles, Professor R. B., PhD, P.O. Box 3035, West Lafayette, Indiana, 47906, U.S.A.

Ede, J. R., MA, Public Record Office, Chancery Lane, WC2A 1LR.

Edmonds, Professor E. L., MA, PhD, Dean of Education, Univ. of Prince Edward Island, Charlottetown, Prince Edward Island, Canada.

Edwards, F. O., SJ, BA, FSA, 114 Mount Street, W1Y 6AH.

EDWARDS, Professor Sir (J.) Goronwy, MA, DLitt, LittD, FBA, FSA, 35 Westmorland Road, SW13.

Edwards, Miss K., MA, PhD, FSA, Dunbar Cottage, 10 Dunbar Street, Old Aberdeen.

Edwards, Professor R. W. D., MA, PhD, DLitt, 21 Brendan Road, Donnybrook, Dublin 4.

Ehrman, J. P. W., MA, FBA, FSA, Sloane House, 149 Old Church Street, SW3 6EB.

Elliott, Professor J. H., MA, PhD, FBA, King's College, Strand, WC2.

Ellis, R. H., MA, FSA, Cloth Hill, 6 The Mount, NW3.

Ellul, M., BArch, DipArch, 'Pauline', 55 Old Railway Road, Birkirkara, Malta.

Elrington, C. R., MA, FSA, Institute of Historical Research, Senate House, WC1E 7HU.

ELTON, Professor G. R., MA, PhD, LittD, FBA (President), 30 Millington Road, Cambridge CB3 9HP.

Elvin, L., 10 Almond Avenue, Swanpool, Lincoln.

*Emmison, F. G., MBE, PhD, DUniv, FSA, Bibury, Links Drive, Chelmsford.

d'Entrèves, Professor A. P., DPhil, Strada Ai Ronchi 48, Cavoretto, Torino, Italy.

Erickson, Charlotte J., PhD, London School of Economics, Houghton Street, WC2.

*Erith, E. J., Shurlock House, Shurlock Row, Berkshire.

Erskine, Mrs A. M., MA, BLitt, FSA, 44 Birchy Barton Hill, Exeter EX1 3EX.

Evans, Mrs A. K. B., PhD, FSA, White Lodge, 25 Knighton Grange Road, Leicester LE2 2LF.

Evans, Sir David (L.), OBE, BA, DLitt, 2 Bay Court, Doctors Commons Road, Berkhamsted, Herts.

Evans, Miss Joan, DLitt, DLit, LLD, LittD, FSA, Thousand Acres, Wootton-under-Edge, Glos.

Evans, R. J. W., MA, PhD, Brasenose College, Oxford.

Evans, The Very Rev. S. J. A., CBE, MA, FSA, The Old Manor, Fulbourne, Cambs.

Everitt, Professor A. M., MA, PhD, The University, Leicester.

Eyck, Professor U. F. J., MA, BLitt, Dept of History, University of Calgary, Alberta T2N IN4, Canada.

Fage, Professor J. D., MA, PhD, Centre of West African Studies, The University, Birmingham B15 2TT.

Fagg, J. E., MA, 47 The Avenue, Durham DH1 4ED.

Farmer, D. F. H., BLitt, FSA, The University, Reading.

Farr, M. W., MA, FSA, 12 Emscote Road, Warwick.
Fearn, Rev. H., MA, PhD, Holy Trinity Vicarage, 6 Wildwood, North-wood, Middlesex.
Fenlon, D. B., BA, PhD, Gonville and Caius College, Cambridge.
Fenn, Rev. R. W. D., The Rectory, Staunton-on-Wye, Hereford.
Ferguson, Professor A. B., PhD, Dept of History, 6727 College Station, Duke University, Durham, N.C. 27708, U.S.A.
Feuchtwanger, E., MA, PhD, Highfield House, Dean, Sparsholt, nr Winchester, Hants.
Fieldhouse, D. K., MA, Nuffield College, Oxford.
Finer, Professor S. E., MA, Dept of Government and Public Administration, All Souls College, Oxford OX1 4AL.
Fink, Professor Z. S., PhD, 6880 Hawthorne Circle, Tucson, Arizona 85710, U.S.A.
Finlayson, G. B. A. M., MA, BLitt, 11 Burnhead Road, Glasgow G43 2SU.
Finley, Professor M. I., MA, PhD, DLitt, FBA, 12 Adams Road, Cambridge CB3 9AD.
Fisher, D. J. V., MA, Jesus College, Cambridge CB3 9AD.
Fisher, Professor F. J., MA, London School of Economics, Houghton Street, WC2.
Fisher, F. N., Duckpool, Ashleyhay, Wirksworth, Derby DE4 4AJ.
Fisher, J. R., BA, MPhil, PhD, 6 Meadway, Upton, Wirral, Merseyside L49 6JG.
Fisher, Professor S. N., PhD, Box 162, Worthington, Ohio 43085, U.S.A.
Fitch, Dr M. F. B., FSA, 37 Avenue de Montoie, 1007 Lausanne, Switzerland.
*Fletcher, The Rt Hon The Lord, PC, BA, LLD, FSA, The Barn, The Green, Sarratt, Rickmansworth, Herts. WD3 6BP.
Flint, Professor J. E., MA, PhD, Dalhousie University, Halifax, Nova Scotia, B3H 3J5, Canada.
Flint, Valerie I. J., MA, DPhil, Dept of History, The University, Private Bag, Auckland, New Zealand.
Fogel, Professor R. W., PhD, Dept of Economics, University of Chicago, Chicago, Ill., U.S.A.
Foot, M. R. D., MA, BLitt, 88 Heath View, London N2 0QB.
Forbes, D., MA, 89, Gilbert Road, Cambridge.
Ford, W. K., 48 Harlands Road, Haywards Heath, West Sussex RH16 1LS.
Forster, G. C. F., BA, FSA, The University, Leeds 2.
Foster, Professor Elizabeth R., AM, PhD, 205 Stafford Avenue, Wayne, Pa. 19087, U.S.A.
Fowler, Professor K. A., BA, PhD, 2 Nelson Street, Edinburgh 3.
Fox, L., OBE, DL, LHD, MA, FSA, FRSL, Silver Birches, 27 Welcombe Road, Stratford-upon-Avon.
Fox, R., MA, DPhil, The University, Bailrigg, Lancaster LA1 4YG.
Francis, A. D., CBE, MVO, MA, 21 Cadogan Street, SW3.
Franklin, R. M., BA, Baldwins End, Eton College, Windsor, Berks.
*Fraser, Miss C. M., PhD, 39 King Edward Road, Tynemouth, Tyne and Wear NE30 2RW.
Fraser, Miss Maxwell, MA, Crowthorne, 21 Dolphin Road, Slough, Berks SL1 1TF.
Fraser, P., BA, PhD, Dept of History, Dalhousie University, Halifax, 8 Nova Scotia, Canada.

Frend, Professor W. H. C., TD, MA, DPhil, DD, FSA, Marbrae, Balmaha, Stirlingshire.

Fryde, Professor E. B., DPhil, Preswylfa, Trinity Road, Aberystwyth, Dyfed.

*Fryer, Professor C. E., MA, PhD, (address unknown).

Fryer, Professor W. R., BLitt, MA, 68 Grove Avenue, Chilwell, Beeston, Notts.

Frykenberg, Professor R. E., MA, PhD, 1840 Chadbourne Avenue, Madison, Wis. 53705, U.S.A.

*Furber, Professor H., MA, PhD, History Department, University of Pennsylvania, Philadelphia, Pa., U.S.A.

Fussell, G. E., DLitt, 55 York Road, Sudbury, Suffolk, CO10 6NF.

Fyrth, H., BSc(Econ.), Dept of Extra Mural Studies, University of London, 7 Ridgemount Street, WC1.

Gabriel, Professor A. L., PhD, FMAA, CFIF, CFBA, Box 578, University of Notre Dame, Notre Dame, Indiana 46556, U.S.A.

*Galbraith, Professor J. S., BS, MA, PhD, University of California, Los Angeles, Calif. 90024, U.S.A.

GALBRAITH, Professor V. H., MA, DLitt, LittD, FBA, 20A Bradmore Road, Oxford.

Gale, Professor H. P. P., OBE, PhD, 6 Nassau Road, London SW13 9QE.

Gale, W. K. V., 19 Ednam Road, Goldthorn Park, Wolverhampton WV4 5BL.

Gann, L. H., MA, BLitt, DPhil, Hoover Institution, Stanford University, Stanford, Calif. 94305, U.S.A.

Ganshof, Professor F. L., 12 Rue Jacques Jordaens, Brussels, Belgium.

Gash, Professor N., MA, BLitt, FBA, Gowrie Cottage, 73 Hepburn Gardens, St Andrews.

Gee, E. A., MA, DPhil, FSA, 28 Trentholme Drive, The Mount, York YO2 2DG.

Gerlach, Professor D. R., MA, PhD, University of Akron, Akron, Ohio 44325, U.S.A.

Gibbs, G. C., MA, Birkbeck College, Malet Street, WC1.

Gibbs, Professor N. H., MA, DPhil, All Souls College, Oxford.

Gibson, Margaret T., MA, DPhil, School of History, The University, Liverpool L69 3BX.

Gifford, Miss D. H., PhD, FSA, Public Record Office, Chancery Lane, WC2.

Gilbert, Professor Bentley B., PhD, Dept of History, University of Ill. at Chicago Circle, Box 4348, Chicago, Ill. 60680, U.S.A.

Gilbert, M., MA, The Map House, Harcourt Hill, Oxford.

Gilley, S., BA, DPhil, Dept of Ecclesiastical History, St Mary's College, University of St Andrew's, St Andrew's, Fife.

Ginter, D. E., AM, PhD, Dept of History, Sir George Williams University, Montreal 107, Canada.

Girtin, T., MA, Butter Field House, Church Street, Old Isleworth, Mddx.

Gleave, Group Capt. T. P., CBE, RAF(Ret.), Willow Bank, River Gardens, Bray-on-Thames, Berks.

*Glover, Professor R. G., MA, PhD, Carleton University, Ottawa 1, Canada.

*Godber, Miss A. J., MA, FSA, Mill Lane Cottage, Willington, Bedford.

Godfrey, Professor J. L., MA, PhD, 231 Hillcrest Circle, Chapel Hill, N.C., U.S.A.
Goldthorp, L. M., MA, Wilcroft House, Pecket Well, Hebden Bridge, Yorks.
Gollancz, Miss M., MA, 41 Crescent Court, Surbiton, Surrey, KT6 4BW.
Gooch, John, BA, PhD, Dept of History, The University, Bailrigg, Lancaster LA1 4YG.
Goodman, A. E., MA, BLitt, Dept of Medieval History, The University, Edinburgh.
Goodspeed, Professor D. J., BA, 164 Victoria Street, Niagara-on-the-Lake, Ontario, Canada.
*Gopal, S., MA, DPhil, 30 Edward Elliot Road, Mylapore, Madras, India.
Gordon, Professor D. J., MA, PhD, Wantage Hall, Upper Redlands Road, Reading.
Gordon-Brown, A., Velden, Alexandra Road, Wynberg, C.P., South Africa.
Goring, J. J., MA, PhD, Little Iwood, Rushlake Green, Heathfield, East Sussex TN21 9QS.
Gorton, L. J., MA, 41 West Hill Avenue, Epsom, Surrey.
Gosden, P. H. J. H., MA, PhD, The University, Leeds.
Gough, J. W., MA, DLitt, Oriel College, Oxford.
Gowing, Professor Margaret M., BSc(Econ), Linacre College, Oxford.
*Graham, Professor G. S., MA, PhD, Hobbs Cottage, Beckley, Rye, Sussex.
Gransden, Mrs A., MA, PhD, FSA, The University, Nottingham NG7 2RD.
Grassby, R. B., MA, Jesus College, Oxford.
Grattan-Kane, P., 12 St John's Close, Helston, Cornwall.
Graves, Professor Edgar B., PhD, LLD, 318 College Hill Road, Clinton, New York 13323, U.S.A.
Gray, J. W., MA, Dept of Modern History, The Queens University of Belfast, Belfast BT7 1NN.
Gray, Miss M., MA, BLitt, 10 Clod Lane, Haslingden, Rossendale, Lancs. BB4 6LR.
Greaves, Mrs R. L., PhD, 1920 Hillview Road, Lawrence, Kansas, U.S.A.
Greaves, Professor R. W., MA, DPhil, 1920 Hillview Road, Lawrence, Kansas, U.S.A.
Green, H., BA, 16 Brands Hill Avenue, High Wycombe, Bucks HP13 5QA.
Green, Rev. V. H. H., MA, DD, Lincoln College, Oxford.
Greene, Professor Jack P., Dept of History, Johns Hopkins University, Baltimore, Md. 21218, U.S.A.
Greenhill, B. J., CMG, BA, FSA, National Maritime Museum, Greenwich, SE10 9FN.
Greenleaf, Professor W. H., BSc(Econ), PhD, University College, Singleton Park, Swansea, Glam.
Grenville, Professor J. A. S., PhD, University of Birmingham, P.O. Box 363, Birmingham 15.
Gresham, C. A., BA, DLitt, FSA, Bryn-y-deryn, Criccieth, Caerns. LL5 0HR.
Grierson, Professor P., MA, LittD, FBA, FSA, Gonville and Caius College, Cambridge.
Grieve, Miss H. E. P., BA, 153, New London Road, Chelmsford, Essex.
Griffiths, J., MA, Springwood, Stanley Road, New Ferry, Wirral, Cheshire L62 5AS.
Griffiths, R. A., PhD, University College, Singleton Park, Swansea.

Grimble, I., PhD, 13 Saville Road, Twickenham, Mddx.
Grimm, Professor H. J., PhD, Department of History, 216 North Oval Drive, The Ohio State University, Columbus, Ohio, U.S.A.
Grisbrooke, W. J., MA, 1 Whetstone Close, Farquhar Road, Birmingham B15 2QL.
*Griscom, Rev. Acton, MA, (address unknown).
Gum, Professor E. J., PhD, 5116 Grant Street, Omaha, Nebraska 68104. U.S.A.
Gundersheimer, Professor W. L., MA, PhD, 507 Roumfort Road, Philadelphia, Pa. 19119, U.S.A.

Habakkuk, H. J., MA, FBA, Jesus College, Oxford OX1 3DW.
Haber, Professor F. C., PhD, 3026 2R Street NW, Washington, DC 20007, U.S.A.
*Hadcock, R. N., DLitt, FSA, Winchcombe Farm, Briff Lane, Bucklebury, Reading.
Haffenden, P. S., PhD, 36 The Parkway, Bassett, Southampton.
Haigh, C. A., BA, PhD, Dept of History, The University, Manchester M13 9PL.
Haight, Mrs M. Jackson, PhD, 8 Chemin des Clochettes, Geneva, Switzerland.
Haines, Professor R. M., MA, MLitt, DPhil, FSA, Dalhousie University, Halifax, N.S., Canada.
Hair, P. E. H, MA, DPhil, The School of History, The University, P.O. Box 147, Liverpool LS9 3BX.
Halcrow, Miss E. M., MA, BLitt, Achimota School, Achimota, P.B.11, Ghana, West Africa.
Hale, Professor, J. R., MA, FSA, University College, Gower Street, WC1E 6BT.
Haley, Professor K. H. D., MA, BLitt, 15 Haugh Lane, Sheffield 11.
Hall, Professor A. R., MA, PhD, 23 Chiswick Staithe, London W4 3TP.
Hall, Professor B., MA, PhD, FSA, St John's College, Cambridge CB2 1TP.
Hall, Professor D. G. E., MA, DLit, 4 Chiltern Road, Hitchin, Herts.
Hallam, Professor H. E., MA, PhD, University of Western Australia, Nedlands 6009, Western Australia.
Haller, Professor W., PhD, Rte 2, Southbridge, Holland, Mass. 01550, U.S.A.
Hamer, Professor D., MA, DPhil, History Dept, Victoria University of Wellington, P.O. Box 196, Wellington, New Zealand.
Hamilton, B., BA, PhD, The University, Nottingham NG7 2RD.
Hammersley, G. F., BA, PhD, University of Edinburgh, William Robertson Building, George Square, Edinburgh EH8 9JY.
Hampson, Professor N., MA, Ddel'U, 305 Hull Road, York YO1 3LB.
Hand, G. J., MA, DPhil, Woodburn, Sydney Avenue, Blackrock, Co. Dublin, Ireland.
Hanham, H. J., MA, PhD, The Dean, School of Humanities and Social Science, Massachusetts Institute of Technology, Cambridge, Mass. 02139, USA.
Hanke, Professor L. U., PhD, University of Massachusetts, Amherst, Mass. 01002, U.S.A.
Harding, A., MA, BLitt, 3 Tantallon Place, Edinburgh.
Harding, F. J. W., MA, BLitt, FSA, Brynrhos, 187 Mayals Road, Swansea SA3 5HQ.
Harding, H. W., BA, LLD, 39 Annunciation Street, Sliema, Malta.

Hargreaves, Professor J. D., MA, 146 Hamilton Place, Aberdeen.
Hargreaves-Mawdsley, Professor W. N., MA, DPhil, FSA, The University, Brandon, Manitoba, Canada.
Harman, L. W., 20 Brooksby Street, London N1.
Harris, Mrs J. F., BA, PhD, Dept of Social Science and Administration, London School of Economics, London WC2.
Harris, Professor J. R., MA, PhD, The University, P.O. Box 363, Birmingham.
Harrison, B. H., MA, DPhil, Corpus Christi College, Oxford OX1 4JF.
Harrison, C. J., BA, PhD, The University, Keele, Staffs. ST5 5BG.
Harrison, Professor Royden, MA, DPhil, 4 Wilton Place, Sheffield S10 2BT.
Harriss, G. L., MA, DPhil, Magdalen College, Oxford.
Hart, C. J. R., MA, MB, DLitt, Goldthorns, Stilton, Peterborough, Northants PE7 3RH.
Hart, Mrs J. M., MA, St Anne's College, Oxford.
Harte, N. B., BSc(Econ), University College, Gower Street, London WC1E 6BT.
Hartwell, R. M., MA, DPhil, Nuffield College, Oxford OX1 1NF.
Harvey, Miss B. F., MA, BLitt, Somerville College, Oxford OX2 6HD.
Harvey, Margaret M., MA, DPhil, St Aidan's College, Durham DH1 3LJ.
Harvey, P. D. A., MA, DPhil, FSA, 9 Glen Eyre Close, Bassett, Southampton SO2 3GB.
Harvey, Sally P. J., MA, PhD, School of History, The University, Leeds LS2 9JT.
Haskell, Professor F. J., MA, FBA, Trinity College, Oxford.
Haskins, Professor G. L., AB, LLB, JD, MA, University of Pennsylvania, The Law School, 3400 Chestnut Street, Philadelphia, Pa. 19104 U.S.A.
Haslam, E. B., MA, 5 Pymers Mead, Dulwich SE21 8NQ.
Hassall, W. O., MA, DPhil, FSA, The Manor House, 26 High Street, Wheatley, Oxford OX9 1XX.
Hastings, Professor Margaret, PhD, 9 Silverwood Terrace, South Hadley, Mass. 01075, U.S.A.
Hatcher, M. J., BSc(Econ), PhD, Eliot College, The University, Canterbury, Kent.
Hattersley, Professor A. F., MA, DLitt, 1 Sanders Road, Pietermaritzburg, S. Africa.
Hatton, Professor Ragnhild M., PhD, London School of Economics, Houghton Street, WC2.
Havighurst, Professor A. F., MA, PhD, Blake Field, Amherst, Mass. 01002, U.S.A.
Havran, Professor M. J., PhD, Corcoran Dept of History, Randall Hall, University of Virginia, Charlottesville, Va. 22903, U.S.A.
Hay, Professor D., MA, DLitt, FBA, Dept of History, The University, Edinburgh EH8 9JY.
Hayes, P. M., PhD, Keble College, Oxford OX1 3PG.
Hazlehurst, G. C. L., BA, DPhil, FRSL, Inst. of Advanced Studies, R.S.S.S., Australian National University, Box 4, P.O. Canberra, ACT, Australia.
Headlam-Morley, Miss A., BLitt, MA, 29 St Mary's Road, Wimbledon SW19.
Hearder, Professor H., PhD, University College, Cathays Park, Cardiff.
Hembry, Mrs P. M., PhD, Flat 24, Thorncliffe, Lansdown Road, Cheltenham GL51 6PZ.
Hemleben, S. J., MA, DPhil, (address unknown).

260

Henderson, A. J., AM, PhD, 247 North Webster, Jacksonville, Ill. 62650, U.S.A.

Hendy, M. F., MA, The Barber Institute of Fine Arts, The University, Birmingham B15 2TS.

Henning, Professor B. D., PhD, Saybrook College, Yale University, New Haven, Conn., U.S.A.

Hennock, P., MA, PhD, School of Cultural and Community Studies, University of Sussex, Falmer, Brighton, Sussex BN1 9QN.

Hexter, Professor J. H., PhD, Dept of History, 237 Hall of Graduate Studies, Yale University, New Haven, Conn. 06520, U.S.A.

Highfield, J. R. L., MA, DPhil, Merton College, Oxford.

Hill, Sir (J. W.) Francis, CBE, MA, LLD, LittD, FSA, The Priory, Lincoln.

Hill, J. E. C., MA, DLitt, FBA, The Master's Lodgings, Balliol College, Oxford.

Hill, Professor L. M., MA, PhD, 5066 Berean Lane, Irvine, Calif. 92664, U.S.A.

*Hill, Miss M. C., MA, Crab End, Brevel Terrace, Charlton Kings, Cheltenham, Glos.

*Hill, Professor Rosalind M. T., MA, BLitt, FSA, Westfield College, Hampstead NW3.

Hilton, Professor R. H., DPhil, University of Birmingham, P.O. Box 363, Birmingham 15.

Himmelfarb, Professor Gertrude, PhD, The City University of New York Graduate Center, 33 West 42 St, New York, N.Y. 10036.

*Hinsley, Professor F. H., MA, St John's College, Cambridge.

Hockey, The Rev. S. F., BA, Quarr Abbey, Ryde, Isle of Wight PO33 4ES.

*Hodgett, G. A. J., MA, FSA, King's College, Strand, WC2.

*Hogg, Brigadier O. F. G., CBE, FSA, 1 Hardy Road, Blackheath SE3.

HOLDSWORTH, C. J. (Hon. Secretary), West End House, 56 Totteridge Common, London N20 8LZ.

Hollaender, A. E. J., PhD, FSA, 110 Narbonne Avenue, South Side, Clapham Common SW4 9LQ.

*Hollingsworth, L. W., PhD, Flat 27, Mayfair, 74 Westcliff Road, Bournemouth BH4 8BG.

Hollis, Patricia, MA, DPhil, 30 Park Lane, Norwich NOR 47F.

Hollister, Professor C. Warren, MA, PhD, University of California, Santa Barbara, Calif. 93106, U.S.A.

Holmes, G. A., MA, PhD, 431 Banbury Road, Oxford.

Holmes, Professor G. S., MA, BLitt, Tatham House, Burton-in-Lonsdale, Carnforth, Lancs.

Holt, Miss A. D., Fasga-na-Coille, Nethy Bridge, Inverness-shire.

Holt, Professor J. C., MA, DPhil, FSA, University of Reading, Whiteknights Park, Reading, Berks RG6 2AA.

Holt, Professor P. M., MA, DLitt, FBA, School of Oriental and African Studies, Malet Street, London WC1E 7HP.

Hook, Mrs Judith, MA, PhD, Dept of History, Taylor Building, King's College, Old Aberdeen AB9 2UB.

Hope, R. S. H., 25 Hengistbury Road, Bournemouth, Hants BH6 4DQ.

Hopkins, E., MA, PhD, 77 Stevens Road, Stourbridge, West Midlands DY9 0XW.

Horwitz, Professor H. G., BA, DPhil, Dept of History, University of Iowa, Iowa City, Iowa 52240, U.S.A.

*Howard, C. H. D., MA, 15 Sunnydale Gardens, NW7.

*Howard, M. E., MC, MA, FBA, The Homestead, Eastbury, Newbury, Berks.
Howarth, Mrs J. H., MA, St Hilda's College, Oxford.
Howat, G. M. D., MA, BLitt, Old School House, North Moreton, Berks.
Howell, Miss M. E., MA, PhD, 10 Highland Road, Charlton Kings, Cheltenham, Glos. GL53 9LT.
Howell, Professor R., MA, DPhil, Bowdoin College, Brunswick, Maine 04011, U.S.A.
Huehns, Miss G., PhD, 35A Sterling Avenue, Edgware, Mddx. HA8 8BP.
Hufton, Professor Olwen H., PhD, 40 Shinfield Road, Reading, Berks.
Hughes, Professor, J. Q., BArch. PhD, Loma Linda, Criccieth, Caerns., North Wales.
Hughes, Miss K. W., MA, PhD, LittD, FSA, Newnham College, Cambridge.
Hull, F., BA, PhD, Roundwell Cottage, Bearsted, Maidstone, Kent ME14 4EU.
Hulton, P. H., BA, FSA, 46 St Paul's Road, N1.
HUMPHREYS, Professor R. A., OBE, MA, PhD, LittD, DLitt, DUniv, 13 St Paul's Place, Canonbury N1 2QE.
Hunnisett, R. F., MA, DPhil, 54 Longdon Wood, Keston, Kent BR2 6EW.
Hurst, M. C., MA, St John's College, Oxford.
Hurstfield, Professor J., DLit, 7 Glenilla Road, NW3.
Hurt, J. S., BA, BSc(Econ), PhD, 66 Oxford Road, Moseley, Birmingham B13 9SQ.
*Hussey, Professor Joan M., MA, BLitt, PhD, FSA, Royal Holloway College, Englefield Green, Surrey.
Hyams, P. R., MA, DPhil, Pembroke College, Oxford.
Hyde, Professor F. E., MA, PhD, Heather Cottage, 41 Village Road, West Kirby, Wirral, Cheshire.
*Hyde, H. Montgomery, MA, DLit, Westwell, Tenterden, Kent.
Hyde, J. K., MA, PhD, The University, Manchester.

Ingham, Professor K., MA, DPhil, The Woodlands, 94 West Town Lane, Bristol BS4 5DZ.
Ives, E. W., PhD, 214 Myton Road, Warwick.

Jack, Professor R. I., MA, PhD, University of Sydney, Sydney, N.S.W., Australia.
Jack, Mrs Sybil M., MA, BLitt, University of Sydney, N.S.W., Australia.
Jackman, Professor S. W., PhD, FSA, 1065 Deal Street, Victoria, British Columbia, Canada.
Jackson, E. D. C., FSA, (address unknown).
Jaffar, Professor S. M., BA, Khudadad Street, Peshawar City, N.W.F. Province, W. Pakistan.
James, M. E., MA, University of Durham, 43–45 North Bailey, Durham.
James, Professor Robert R., MA, FRSL, United Nations, N.Y. 10017, U.S.A.
Jarvis, R. C., ISO, FSA, Shelley, Station Road, Hockley, Essex.
Jasper, The Very Rev. R. C. D., DD, The Deanery, York YO1 2JD.
Jeffs, R. M., MA, DPhil, 25 Lawson Road, Sheffield S10 5BU.
Jenkins, D., MA, LLM, LittD, Dept of Law, Hugh Owen Building, Univ. College of Wales, Aberystwyth, Cards. SY23 2DB.

Jeremy, D. J., BA, MLitt, 16 Britannia Gardens, Westcliff-on-Sea, Essex
SS0 8BN.
John, Professor A. H., BSc(Econ), PhD, London School of Economics,
Houghton Street, WC2.
John, E., MA, The University, Manchester M13 9PL.
Johnson, D. J., BA, 41 Cranes Park Avenue, Surbiton, Surrey.
Johnson, Professor D. W. J., BA, BLitt, University College, Gower Street,
WC1E 6BT.
*Johnson, J. H., MA, Whitehorns, Cedar Avenue, Chelmsford.
Johnson, W. Branch, FSA, Hope Cottage, 22 Mimram Road, Welwyn,
Herts.
Johnston, Professor Edith M., MA, PhD, Dept of History, Maquarie Univ.
North Ryde, N.S.W. 2113, Australia.
Johnston, Professor S. H. F., MA, Fronhyfryd, Llanbadarn Road, Aber-
ystwyth.
Jones, Dwyryd W., MA, DPhil, The University, Heslington, York YO1
5DD.
Jones, G. A., MA, PhD, Dept of History, Faculty of Letters, University
of Reading, Whiteknights, Reading, Berks.
Jones, Professor G. Hilton, PhD, Dept of History, Eastern Ill. University,
Charleston, Ill. 61920, U.S.A.
Jones, G. J., The Croft, Litchard Bungalows, Bridgend, Glam.
Jones, H. W., MA, PhD, 32 Leylands Terrace, Bradford BD9 5QR.
Jones, Professor I. G., MA, 12 Laura Place, Aberystwyth, Cards.
Jones, Professor J. R., MA, PhD, School of English and American Studies
University Plain, Norwich.
Jones, Professor M. A., MA, DPhil, Dept of History, University College,
Gower Street, WC1E 6BT.
Jones, M. C. E., MA, DPhil, The University, Nottingham NG7 2RD.
Jones, The Rev. Canon O. W., MA, The Vicarage, Builth Wells LD2 3BS,
Powys.
Jones, P. J., DPhil, Brasenose College, Oxford.
Jones, Professor W. J., PhD, Dept of History, The University of Alberta,
Edmonton T6G 2E1, Canada.
Jordan, Professor P. D., PhD, LLD, 26 Cascade Terrace, Burlington,
Iowa 52601, U.S.A.
Jordan, Professor W. K., PhD, 3 Conrad Avenue, Cambridge, Mass.
02138, U.S.A.
Judson, Professor Margaret A., PhD, 8 Redcliffe Avenue, Highland Park,
N.J. 08904, U.S.A.
Jukes, Rev. H. A. Ll, MA, The Vicarage, Tilney All Saints, nr King's
Lynn, Norfolk.

Kamen, H. A. F., MA, DPhil, The University, Warwick, Coventry CV4
7AL.
*Kay, H., MA, 16 Bourton Drive, Poynton, Stockport, Cheshire.
Keeler, Mrs Mary F., The Center for Parliamentary History, Yale Uni-
versity, Box 1603A, Yale Station, Conn. 06520, U.S.A.
Keen, L. J., 14 Fairfield's Close, Roe Green, London NW7.
Keen, M. H., MA, Balliol College, Oxford.
Kellaway, C. W., MA, FSA, 2 Grove Terrace, NW5.
Kellett, J. R., MA, PhD, Dept of Economic History, University of Glasgow,
G12 8QQ.

Kelly, Professor T., MA, PhD, FLA, Oak Apple House, Ambleside Road, Keswick, Cumbria CA12 4DL.
Kemp, Miss B., MA, FSA, St Hugh's College, Oxford.
Kemp, B. R., BA, PhD, 12 Redhatch Drive, Earley, Reading, Berks.
Kemp, The Right Rev. E. W., DD, The Lord Bishop of Chichester, The Palace, Chichester, Sussex PO19 1PY.
Kemp, Lt-Commander P. K., RN, Malcolm's, 51 Market Hill, Maldon. Essex.
Kendall, Professor P. M., PhD, 928 Holiday Drive, Lawrence, Kansas 66044, U.S.A.
Kennedy, J., MA, 14 Poolfield Avenue, Newcastle-under-Lyme, Staffs. ST5 2NL.
Kennedy, P. M., BA, DPhil, University of East Anglia, Norwich NOR 88C.
Kent, Rev. J. H. S., MA, PhD, Dept of Theology, University of Bristol, Senate House, Bristol BS8 1TH.
Kenyon, Professor J. P., PhD, Nicholson Hall, Cottingham, Yorks.
Ker, N. R., MA, DLitt, FBA, FSA, Slievemore, Foss, by Pitlochry, Perthshire.
Kerling, Miss N. J. M., PhD, 26 Upper Park Road, NW3.
Kerridge, E. W. J., PhD, Llys Tudur, Myddleton Park, Denbigh LL16 4AL.
Kershaw, Ian, BA, DPhil, 6 Cranston Drive, Sale, Cheshire.
Ketelbey, Miss C. D. M., MA, 18 Queen's Gardens, St Andrews, Fife.
Khan, M. Siddiq, MA, LLB, The Bougainvilleas, No. 64 North Dhanmondi, Kalabagan, Dacca-5, Bangladesh.
Khanna, Kahan Chand, MA, PhD, 3-B Mathura Road, New Delhi 14, India.
Kiernan, Professor V. G., MA, University of Edinburgh, William Robertson Building, George Square, Edinburgh EH8 9JY.
*Kimball, Miss E. G., BLitt, PhD, Drake's Corner Road, Princeton, N.J., U.S.A.
King, E. J., MA, PhD, Dept of History, The University, Sheffield S10 2TN.
King, P. D., BA, PhD, Lancaster View, Bailrigg, Lancaster.
Kinsley, Professor J., MA, PhD, DLitt, FBA, University of Nottingham, Nottingham NG7 2RD.
Kirby, D. P., MA, PhD, Manoraven, Llanon, Cards.
Kirby, J. L., MA, FSA, 209 Covington Way, Streatham, London SW19 3BY.
Kitchen, Professor Martin, BA, PhD, Dept of History, Simon Fraser University, Burnaby, B.C., Canada V5A 1S6.
Klibansky, Professor, R., MA, PhD, DPhil, FRSC, Dept of Philosophy, McGill University, Montreal, Canada.
Knecht, R. J., MA, 22 Warwick New Road, Leamington Spa, Warwickshire.
*Knight, L. Stanley, MA, Little Claregate, 1 The Drive, Malthouse Lane, Tettenhall, Wolverhampton.
Knowles, C. H., PhD, University College, Cathays Park, Cardiff CF1 1XL.
Kochan, L. E., MA, PhD, 237 Woodstock Road, Oxford.
Koenigsberger, Professor H. G., PhD, Dept of History, Kings College, Strand, London WC2.
Koeppler, Professor H., CBE, DPhil, Wilton Park, Wiston House, Steyning, Sussex.

Koss, Professor S. E., c/o The Netherlands Institute for Advanced Study, Meybloomlaan 1, Wassenaar, The Netherlands.
Kossmann, Professor E. H., DLitt, Rijksuniversiteit te Groningen, Groningen, The Netherlands.

Lambert, M. D., MA, 17 Oakwood Road, Henleaze, Bristol BS9 4NP.
Lamont, W. M., PhD, 9 Bramleys, Kingston, Lewes, Sussex.
Lancaster, Miss J. C., MA, FSA, 43 Craigmair Road, Tulse Hill, SW2.
Lander, J. R., MA, MLitt, Middlesex College, University of Western Ontario, London, Ont., Canada.
Landes, Professor D. S., PhD, Widener U, Harvard University, Cambridge, Mass, 02138, U.S.A.
Landon, Professor M. de L., MA, PhD, The University, Mississippi 38677 U.S.A.
La Page, J., FSA, Craig Lea, 44, Bank Crest, Baildon, Yorkshire.
Laprade, Professor W. T., PhD, 1108 Monmouth Avenue, Durham, N. Carolina, U.S.A.
Larkin, Professor the Rev. J. F., CSV, PhD, Univ. College, De Paul University, 2323 N. Seminary Avenue, Chicago, Ill. 60614, U.S.A.
Larner, J. P., MA, The University, Glasgow W2.
Latham, Professor R. C., MA, Magdalene College, Cambridge.
Lawrence, Professor C. H., MA, DPhil, Bedford College, Regent's Park, NW1.
*Laws, Lieut-Colonel M. E. S., OBE, MC, Bank Top Cottage, Seal Chart, Sevenoaks, Kent.
Leddy, J. F., MA, BLitt, DPhil, University of Windsor, Windsor, Ontario, Canada.
Lee, J. M., MA, BLitt, Dept of Politics, Birkbeck College, 7–15 Gresse Street, London W1A 2PA.
Lees, R. McLachlan, MA, Kent Cottage, Harbridge, Ringwood, Hants.
Legge, Professor M. Dominica, MA, DLitt, FBA, 191A Woodstock Road, Oxford OX2 7AB.
Lehmann, Professor J. H., PhD, De Paul University, 25E Jackson Blvd., Chicago, Ill. 60604, U.S.A.
Lehmberg, Professor S. E., PhD, Dept of History, University of Minnesota, Minneapolis, Minn. 55455, U.S.A.
Lenanton, Lady, CBE, MA, FSA, Bride Hall, nr Welwyn, Herts.
Le Patourel, Professor J. H., MA, DPhil, Ddel'U, FBA, Westcote, Hebers Ghyll Drive, Ilkley, West Yorkshire LS29 9QH.
Leslie, Professor R. F., BA, PhD, 23 Grove Park Road, W4.
Levine, Professor Mortimer, PhD, 529 Woodhaven Drive, Morgantown, West Va. 26505, U.S.A.
Levy, Professor F. J., PhD, University of Washington, Seattle, Wash. 98195, U.S.A.
Lewis, Professor A. R., MA, PhD, History Dept, University of Massachusetts, Amherst, Mass, 01003, U.S.A.
Lewis, Professor B., PhD, FBA, Near Eastern Studies Dept, Jones Hall, The University, Princeton, N.J. 08540, U.S.A.
Lewis, C. W., BA, FSA, University College, Cathays Park, Cardiff.
Lewis, P. S., MA, All Souls College, Oxford.
Lewis, R. A., PhD, University College of North Wales, Bangor.
Leyser, K., MA, Magdalen College, Oxford.
Lhoyd-Owen, Commander J. H., RN, 37 Marlings Park Avenue, Chislehurst, Kent.

Liebeschütz, H., MA, DPhil, Dockenhuden, Mariner Road, Liverpool 23.
*Lindsay, Mrs H., MA, PhD (address unknown).
Linehan, P. A., MA, PhD, St John's College, Cambridge.
Lipman, V. D., DPhil, FSA, Flat 14, 33 Kensington Court, W8.
Livermore, Professor H. V., MA, Sandycombe Lodge, Sandycombe Road, St Margarets, Twickenham.
Lloyd, H. A., BA, DPhil, The University, Cottingham Road, Hull HU6 7RX.
Loades, D. M., MA, PhD, Oatlands, Farnley Mount, Durham.
Lobel, Mrs M. D., BA, FSA, 16 Merton Street, Oxford.
Lockhart, L., MA, PhD, LittD, Cedarwood House, West Green, Barrington, Cambridge CB2 5SA.
Lockie, D. McN., MA, Chemin de la Panouche, Saint-Anne, Grasse, Alpes Maritimes, France.
Logan, Rev. F. D., MA, MSD, Emmanuel College, 400 The Fenway, Boston, Mass, 02115, U.S.A.
London, Miss Vera C. M., MA, Underholt, Westwood Road, Bidston, Birkenhead, Cheshire.
Longford, The Right Honble The Countess of, MA, DLitt, Bernhurst, Hurst Green, Sussex.
Longley, D. A., BA, King's College, The University, Old Aberdeen AB9 2UB.
Longrais, Professor F. Joüon des, D-en-droit, LèsL, 4 rue de la Terrasse, Paris XVII, France.
Loomie, Rev. A. J., SJ, MA, PhD, Fordham University, New York, N.Y. 10458, U.S.A.
Lourie, Elena, MA, DPhil, 66 Brandeis Street, Tel-Aviv, Israel.
Lovatt, R. W., MA, DPhil, Peterhouse, Cambridge.
Lovell, J. C., BA, PhD, Eliot College, University of Kent, Canterbury.
Lowe, P. C., BA, PhD, The University, Manchester.
Loyn, Professor H. R., MA, FSA, 196 Fidlas Road, Llanishen, Cardiff.
Lucas, C. R., MA, DPhil, Balliol College, Oxford OX1 3BJ.
Lucas, P. J., MA, PhD, University College, Belfield, Dublin 4, Ireland.
Luft, The Rev. H. M., MA, MLitt, Merchant Taylor's School, Crosby, Liverpool.
Lumb, Miss S. V., MA, Torr-Collin House, 106 Ridgway, Wimbledon, London SW19.
Luscombe, Professor D. E., MA, PhD, 129 Prospect Road, Totley Rise, Sheffield S17 4HX.
Luttrell, A. T., MA, DPhil, Dept of History, The Royal University of Malta, Msida, Malta.
Lyman, Professor R. W., PhD, Office of the President, Stanford University, Stanford, Calif. 94305, U.S.A.
Lynch, Professor J., MA, PhD, University College, Gower Street, London WC1E 6BT.
Lyon, Professor Bryce D., PhD, Dept of History, Brown University Providence, Rhode Island 02912, U.S.A.
Lyons, Professor F. S. L., MA, PhD, LittD, The Provost, Trinity College, Dublin.
Lyttelton, The Hon, N. A. O., BA, St Antony's College, Oxford.

Mabbs, A. W., Public Record Office, Chancery Lane, WC2.
MacCaffrey, Professor W. T., PhD, 745 Hollyoke Center, Harvard University, Cambridge, Mass. 02138, U.S.A.

McCaughan, Professor R. E. M., MA, BArch, DSc., Rowan Bank, Kingsley Green, nr Fernhurst, West Sussex.

McConica, Professor J. K., OSB, MA, DPhil, Pontifical Institute of Medieval Studies, 59 Queen's Park Crescent, Toronto 181, Ont., Canada.

McCord, N., PhD, 7 Hatherton Avenue, Cullercoats, North Shields, Northumberland.

McCracken, Professor J. L., MA, PhD, New University of Ulster, Coleraine, Co. Londonderry, N. Ireland.

McCulloch, Professor S. C., MA, PhD, 2121 Windward Lane, Newport Beach, Calif. 92660, U.S.A.

MacDonagh, Professor O., MA, PhD, RSSS, Australian National University, Box 4 GPO, Canberra, ACT, Australia.

Macdonald, Professor D. F., MA, DPhil, Queen's College, Dundee.

McDonald, Professor T. H., MA, PhD, T. H. McDonald Enterprises, 514 Magnolia Street, Truth or Consequences, New Mexico 87901, U.S.A.

McDowell, Professor R. B., PhD, LittD, Trinity College, Dublin.

Macfarlane, A., MA, DPhil, PhD, King's College, Cambridge CB2 1ST.

Macfarlane, L. J., PhD, FSA, King's College, University of Aberdeen, Aberdeen.

McGrath, P. V., MA, University of Bristol, Bristol.

MacGregor, D. R., BA, FSA, 99 Lonsdale Road, SW13 9DA.

McGregor, Professor O. R., BSc(Econ), MA, Far End, Wyldes Close, London N.W.11.

McGurk, J. J. N., BA, MPhil, Conway House, Stanley Avenue, Birkdale, Southport, Lancs.

McGurk, P. M., PhD, Birkbeck College, Malet Street, London WC1E 7HX.

Machin, G. I. T., MA, DPhil, Dept of Modern History, University of Dundee, DD1 4HN.

MacIntyre, A. D., MA, DPhil, Magdalen College, Oxford.

McKendrick, N., MA, Gonville and Caius College, Cambridge.

McKenna, Professor J. W., MA, PhD, Haverford College, Haverford, Pa. 19041, U.S.A.

Mackesy, P. G., MA, Pembroke College, Oxford.

McKibbin, R. I., MA, DPhil, St John's College, Oxford OX1 3JP.

*Mackie, Professor J. D., CBE, MC, MA, LLD, FSAScot, 67 Dowanside Road, Glasgow W2.

McKinley, R. A., MA, 42 Boyers Walk, Leicester Forest East, Leics.

Mackintosh, Professor J. P., MA, MP, House of Commons, London SW1A 0AA.

McKisack, Professor May, MA, BLitt, FSA, 59 Parktown, Oxford.

Maclagan, M., MA, FSA, Trinity College, Oxford.

Maclean, J. N. M., BLitt, PhD, 21 Drummond Place, Edinburgh EH3 6PN.

MacLeod, R. M., AB, PhD, Dept of History and Social Studies of Science, Physics Bldg, University of Sussex, Falmer, Brighton BN1 9QH.

McManners, Professor J., MA, Christ Church, Oxford OX1 1DP.

MacMichael, N. H., FSA, 2B Little Cloister, Westminster Abbey, SW1.

MacNiocaill, G., PhD, Dept of History, University College, Galway, Ireland.

McNulty, Miss P. A., BA, St George's Hall, Elmhurst Road, Reading.

MacNutt, Professor W. S., MA, University of New Brunswick, Fredericton, N.B., Canada.

Macpherson, C. B., BA, MSc(Econ), DSc(Econ), DLitt, LLD, FRSC, University of Toronto, 100 George Street, Toronto, M55 1A1, Canada.

McRoberts, Rt Rev. Monsignor David, STL, DLitt, FSA, 16 Drummond Place, Edinburgh EH3 6PL.
Madariaga, Miss Isabel de, PhD, 27 Southwood Lawn Road, N6.
Madden, A. F. McC., DPhil, Nuffield College, Oxford.
Maddicott, J. R., MA, DPhil, Exeter College, Oxford.
Maehl, Professor W. H., PhD, Dept of History, 455 W Lindsey Street, Room 406, Univ of Oklahoma, Norman, Oklahoma 73069, U.S.A.
Maffei, Professor Domenico, MLL, Dr Jur, Via delle Cerchia 19, 53100 Sienna, Italy.
Magnus-Allcroft, Sir Phillip, Bt. CBE, FRSL, Stokesay Court, Craven Arms, Shropshire SY7 9BD.
Mahoney, Professor T. H. D., AM, PhD, MPA, Massachusetts Institute of Technology, Cambridge, Mass. 02138, U.S.A.
Major, Miss K., MA, BLitt, LittD, 21 Queensway, Lincoln.
Mallett, M. E., MA, DPhil, University of Warwick, Coventry CV4 7AL.
Malone, Professor J. J., PhD, 629 St James Street, Pittsburgh, Pa. 15232, U.S.A.
Mann, Miss J. de L., MA, The Cottage, Bowerhill, Melksham, Wilts.
Manning, B. S., MA, DPhil, The University, Manchester.
Manning, Professor R. B., PhD, 2848 Coleridge Road, Cleveland Heights, Ohio 44118, U.S.A.
Mansergh, Professor P. N. S., OBE, DPhil, DLitt, LittD, FBA, The Master's Lodge, St John's College, Cambridge.
Marchant, The Rev Canon R. A., PhD, BD, Laxfield Vicarage, Woodbridge, Suffolk IP13 8DT.
Marder, Professor A. J., PhD, University of California, Irvine, Calif. 92664, U.S.A.
Marett, W. P., BSc(Econ), BCom, MA, PhD, 20 Barrington Road, Stoneygate, Leicester LE2 2RA.
Margetts, J., DipEd, DrPhil, 5 Glenluce Road, Liverpool L19 9BX.
Markus, Professor R. A., MA, PhD, The University, Nottingham NG7 2RD.
Marriner, Sheila, MA, PhD, Dept of Economic History, Eleanor Rathbone Building, Myrtle Street, P.O. Box 147, Liverpool L69 3BX.
Marsden, A., BA, PhD, 9 Fort Street, Dundee DD2 1BS.
Marshall, J. D., PhD, 16 Westgate, Morecambe, Lancs.
Marshall, P. J., MA, DPhil, King's College, Strand, WC2.
Martin, E. W., Crossways, 41 West Avenue, Exeter EX4 4SD.
Martin, Professor G. H., MA, DPhil, 21 Central Avenue, Leicester LE2 1TB.
Marwick, Professor, A. J. B., MA, BLitt, Dept of History, The Open University, Walton Hall, Walton, Bletchley, Bucks.
Mason, F. K., 147 London Road, St Albans, Hertfordshire.
Mason, J. F. A., MA, DPhil, FSA, Christ Church, Oxford OX1 1DP.
Mason, T. W., MA, DPhil, St Peter's College, Oxford OX1 2DL.
Mather, F. C., MA, 69 Ethelburg Avenue, Swaythling, Southampton.
*Mathew, The Most Rev. Archbishop D. J., MA, LittD, FSA, Stonor Park, Henley-on-Thames, Oxon.
Mathias, Professor P., MA, All Souls College, Oxford.
*Mathur-Sherry, Tikait Narain, BA, LLB, 3/193-4 Prem-Nagar, Dayalbagh, Agra-282005 (U.P.), India.
Matthew, D. J. A., MA, DPhil, The University, Durham.
Mattingly, Professor H. B., MA, Dept of Ancient History, The University, Leeds LS2 9JT.

Mayr-Harting, H. M. R. E., MA, DPhil, St Peter's College, Oxford.
Medlicott, Professor W. N., MA, DLit, DLitt, 2 Cartref, Ellesmere Road, Weybridge, Surrey.
Meekings, C. A. F., OBE, MA, 42 Chipstead Street, SW6.
Merson, A. L., MA, The University, Southampton.
Mews, Stuart, PhD, Dept of Religious Studies, Cartmel College, Bailrigg, Lancaster.
Micklewright, F. H. A., MA, 228 South Norwood Hill, SE25.
Midgley, Miss L. M., MA, 84 Wolverhampton Road, Stafford ST17 4AW.
Miller, E., MA, LittD, 36 Almoners Avenue, Cambridge CB1 4PA.
Miller, E. J., BA, FSA, 37 Aldbourne Road, W12 0LW.
Miller, Miss H., MA, 32 Abbey Gardens, NW8.
Milne, A. T., MA, 9 Dixon Close, SE21 7BD.
Milne, Miss D. J., MA, PhD, King's College, Aberdeen.
Milsom, Professor S. F. C., MA, FBA, London School of Economics, Houghton Street, WC2.
Milward, Professor A. S., MA, PhD, Inst. of Science and Technology, University of Manchester, PO Box 88, Sackville Street, Manchester M60 1QD.
Minchinton, Professor W. E., BSc(Econ), The University, Exeter EX4 4PU.
Mingay, Professor G. E., PhD, Mill Field House, Selling Court, Selling, nr Faversham, Kent.
Mitchell, C., MA, BLitt, LittD, Woodhouse Farmhouse, Fyfield, Abingdon, Berks.
Mitchell, L. G., MA, DPhil, University College, Oxford.
Mitchison, Mrs R. M., MA, Great Yew, Ormiston, East Lothian EH35 5NJ.
*Moir, Rev. Prebendary A. L., MA, 55 Mill Street, Hereford.
Momigliano, Professor A. D., DLitt, FBA, University College, Gower Street, WC1E 6BT.
Moody, Professor T. W., MA, PhD, Trinity College, Dublin.
Moore, B. J. S., BA, University of Bristol, 67 Woodland Road, Bristol.
Moore, R. I., MA, The University, Sheffield S10 2TN.
*Moorman, Mrs, MA, Bishop Mount, Ripon, Yorks.
Morey, Rev. Dom R. Adrian, OSB, MA, DPhil, LittD, Benet House, Mount Pleasant, Cambridge CB3 0DL.
Morgan, B. G., BArch, PhD, 29 Gerard Road, Wallasey, Wirral, Merseyside L45 6UQ.
Morgan, K. O., MA, DPhil, The Queen's College, Oxford OX1 4BH.
Morgan, Miss P. E., 1A The Cloisters, Hereford, HR1 2NG.
*Morrell, Professor W. P., MA, DPhil, 20 Bedford Street, St Clair, Dunedin SW1, New Zealand.
Morris, The Rev. Professor C., MA, 53 Cobbett Road, Bitterne Park, Southampton SO2 4HJ.
Morris, G. C., MA, King's College, Cambridge.
Morris, J. R., BA, Little Garth, Ashwell, nr Baldock, Herts.
Morris, Professor R. B., PhD, Dept of History, Colombia University in the City of New York, 605 Fayerweather Hall, New York, N.Y. 10552 U.S.A.
Morton, Miss C. E., MA, MLS, FSA, Fairview Cottage, Buckland St. Mary, Chard, Somerset TA20 3LE.
Morton, Professor W. L., MA, BLitt, LLD, DLitt, Champlain College, Trent University, Peterborough, Ont. K9J 7B8, Canada.

Mosse, Professor G. L., PhD, Dept of History, The University of Wisconsin, 3211 Humanities Bldg., 435 N. Park Street, Madison, Wis. 53706 U.S.A.
Mosse, Professor W. E. E., MA, PhD, Dawn Cottage, Ashwellthorpe, Norwich, Norfolk.
MULLINS, E. L. C., OBE, MA (*Librarian*), Institute of Historical Research, University of London, Senate House, WC1E 7HU.
Muntz, Miss I. Hope, FSA, Fairview Cottage, Buckland St. Mary, Chard, Somerset TA20 3LE.
Murray, A., BA, BPhil, The University, Newcastle upon Tyne NE1 7RU.
Murray, Athol L., MA, LLB, PhD, 33 Inverleith Gardens, Edinburgh EH3 5PR.
Myers, Professor A. R., MA, PhD, FSA, Rosemount, 3 Cholmondeley Road, West Kirby, Wirral, Cheshire.
Myres, J. N. L., CBE, MA, LLD, DLitt, DLit, FBA, PSA, The Manor House, Kennington, Oxford OX1 5PH.

Naidis, Professor M., PhD, 10847 Canby Avenue, Northbridge, California 91324.
Nath, Dwarka, MBE, 30 Crowther Road, South Norwood, SE25.
*NEALE, Professor Sir John (E), MA, DLitt, LittD, LHD, FBA, Adare, Penn Road, Beaconsfield, Bucks.
Nef, Professor J. U., PhD, 2726 N Street NW, Washington DC 20007, U.S.A.
New, Professor J. F. H., Dept of History, Waterloo University, Waterloo, Ontario, Canada.
Newman, A. N., MA, DPhil, 33 Stanley Road, Leicester.
Newsome, D. H., MA, Christ's Hospital, Horsham, Sussex.
Newton, K. C., MA, 82 Dorset Road, Maldon, Essex.
Nicholas, Professor H. G., MA, FBA, New College, Oxford.
Nicholl, Professor D., MA, Rosthene, Common Lane, Betley, nr Crewe, Cheshire.
Nicol, Professor D. M., MA, PhD, King's College, London WC2R 2LS.
Noakes, J. D., MA, DPhil, Queen's Bldg, The University, Exeter EX4 4OJ.
Norman, E. R., MA, PhD, Peterhouse, Cambridge.

Obolensky, Prince Dimitri, MA, PhD, FSA, Christ Church, Oxford.
O'Connell, Professor D. P., BA, LLM, PhD, LLD, All Souls College, Oxford.
*Offler, Professor H. S., MA, 28 Old Elvet, Durham.
O'Gorman, F., BA, PhD, The University, Manchester M13 9PL.
Orme, N. I., MA, DPhil, The University, Exeter EX4 4OJ.
*Orr, J. E., MA, ThD, DPhil, 11451 Berwick Street, Los Angeles, Cal. 90049, U.S.A.
Osborn, Professor J. M., DLitt, LHD, FSA, Beinecke Library, 1603A Yale Station, New Haven, Conn. 06520, U.S.A.
Oschinsky, Dorothea, DPhil, PhD, The University, Liverpool L69 3BX.
Otway-Ruthven, Professor A. J., MA, PhD, 7 Trinity College, Dublin, Eire.
Outhwaite, R. B., MA, PhD, Gonville and Caius College, Cambridge CB2 1TA.
Owen, A. E. B., MA, 79 Whitwell Way, Coton, Cambridge CB3 7PW.
Owen, Mrs D. M., MA, FSA, 79 Whitwell Way, Coton, Cambridge CB3 7PW.

Owen, G. D., MA, PhD, Casa Alba, Wray Lane, Reigate, Surrey.
Owen, J. B., BSc, MA, DPhil, The University, Calgary 44, Alberta, Canada.

*Packard, Professor S. R., PhD, DrJur, DHL, 126 Vernon Street, Northampton, Mass., U.S.A.
Pagden, A. R. D., BA, Merton College, Oxford OX1 4JD.
Palliser, D. M., MA, DPhil, 14 Verstone Croft, Birmingham B31 2QE.
Pallister, Miss Anne, BA, PhD, The University, Reading RG6 2AA.
Palmer, J. J. N., BA, BLitt, PhD, 59 Marlborough Avenue, Hull.
Parker, N. G., MA, PhD, Dept of Modern History, St Salvator's College, The University, St Andrew's, Fife.
Parker, R. A. C., MA, DPhil, The Queen's College, Oxford OX1 4BH.
Parker, The Rev. Dr T. M., MA, DD, FSA, 36 Chalfont Road, Oxford OX2 6TH.
*Parkinson, Professor C. N., MA, PhD, Les Caches House, St Martins, Guernsey, C.I.
Parris, H., MA, Civil Service College, Sunningdale Park, Ascot, Berks. SL5 0QE.
Parry, E. Jones, MA, PhD, 3 Sussex Mansions, Old Brompton Road, SW7.
Parry, Professor J. H., MA, PhD, Pinnacle Road, Harvard, Mass. 01451, U.S.A.
Parsloe, C. G., MA, 1 Leopold Avenue, SW19 7ET.
Patterson, Professor A. T., MA, The Sele, Stoughton, Chichester, Sussex.
PEARL, Mrs V. L., MA, DPhil, (*Literary Director*), 11 Church Row, Hampstead, NW3. 6UT
Pearn, B. R., OBE, MA, The White House, Beechwood Avenue, Aylmerton, Norfolk NOR 25Y.
Peaston, Rev. A. E., MA, BLitt, The Manse, Dromore, Co. Down, N. Ireland.
Peek, Miss H. E., MA, FSA, FSAScot, Taintona, Moretonhampstead, Newton Abbot, Devon TQ13 8LG.
Pegues, Professor F. J., PhD, 71 Acton Road, Columbus, Ohio 43214, U.S.A.
Pelham, R. A., MA, PhD, The Court House, West Meon, Hants.
Pennington, D. H., MA, Balliol College, Oxford.
*Percy-Smith, Lt Col H. K., 14 Elmcroft, Fairview Avenue, Woking, Surrey GU22 7NX.
Perkin, Professor H. J., MA, Borwicks, Caton, Lancaster.
Petrie, Sir Charles, Bt, CBE, MA, 190 Coleherne Court, SW5.
Philip, I. G., MA, FSA, 28 Portland Road, Oxford.
Philips, Professor Sir Cyril (H.), MA, PhD, DLitt, 3 Winterstoke Gardens, London NW7.
Phillips, Sir Henry (E. I.), CMG, MBE, MA, 34 Ross Court, Putney Hill, SW15.
Phillips, J. R. S., BA, PhD, Dept of Medieval History, University College, Dublin 4, Ireland.
Pitt, H. G., MA, Worcester College, Oxford.
Platt, C. P. S., MA, PhD, FSA, 24 Oakmount Avenue, Highfield, Southampton.
Platt, Professor D. C. St M., MA, DPhil, St Antony's College, Oxford.
Plumb, Professor J. H., PhD, LittD, FBA, FSA, Christ's College, Cambridge.

Pocock, Professor J. G. A., PhD, Johns Hopkins University, Baltimore, Md. 21218, U.S.A.

Poirer, Professor Philip P., PhD, Dept of History, The Ohio State University, 216 North Oval Drive, Columbus, Ohio 43210, U.S.A.

Pole, J. R., MA, PhD, 6 Cavendish Avenue, Cambridge CB1 4US.

Pollard, Professor S., BSc(Econ), PhD, Dept of Economic History, The University, Sheffield S10 2TN.

Porter, B. E., BSc(Econ), PhD, Dept of International Politics, Uinversity College of Wales, Aberystwyth SY23 3DB.

Porter, H. C., MA, PhD, Selwyn College, Cambridge.

Postan, Professor M. M., MA, FBA, Peterhouse, Cambridge CB2 1RD.

*Potter, Professor G. R., MA, PhD, FSA, Herongate, Derwent Lane, Hathersage, Sheffield S30 1AS.

Powell, W. R., BLitt, MA, FSA, 2 Glanmead, Shenfield Road, Brentwood, Essex.

Powicke, Professor M. R., MA, University of Toronto, Toronto 5, Ont., Canada.

Prest, W. R., MA, DPhil, Dept of History, University of Adelaide, Adelaide, S. Australia 5001.

Preston, Professor A. W., PhD, (address unknown).

*Preston, Professor R. A., MA, PhD, Duke University, Durham, N.C., U.S.A.

Prestwich, J. O., MA, The Queen's College, Oxford.

Prestwich, Mrs M., MA, St Hilda's College, Oxford.

Prestwich, M. C., MA, DPhil, Dept of Medieval History, The University, St Andrews, Fife.

Price, A. W., 19 Bayley Close, Uppingham, Rutland, LE15 9TG.

Price, F. D., MA, BLitt, FSA, Keble College, Oxford.

Price, Professor Jacob, M., AM, PhD, University of Michigan, Ann Arbor, Michigan 48104, U.S.A.

Pritchard, Professor D. G., PhD, 11 Coedmor, Sketty, Swansea, Glam. SA2 8BQ.

Proctor, Miss Evelyn E. S., MA, Little Newland, Eynsham, Oxford.

Pronay, N., BA, School of History, The University, Leeds.

Prothero, I. J., BA, PhD, The University, Manchester.

*Pugh, Professor R. B., MA, DLit, FSA, 67 Southweed Park, N.6

Pugh, T. B., MA, BLit, 28 Bassett Wood Drive, Southampton SO 3PS.

Pullan, Professor B. S., MA, PhD, The University, Manchester M13 9PL.

Pulman, M. B., MA, PhD, University of Denver, Colorado 80210, U.S.A.

Pulzer, P. G. J., MA, PhD, Christ Church, Oxford OX1 1DP.

Quinn, Professor D. B., MA, PhD, DLit, DLitt, 9 Knowsley Road, Cressington Park, Liverpool 19.

Rabb, Professor T. K., MA, PhD, Princeton University, Princeton, N.J. 08540, U.S.A.

Radford, C. A. Ralegh, MA, DLitt, FBA, FSA, Culmcott, Uffculme, Cullompton, Devon EX15 3AT.

*Ramm, Miss A., MA, Somerville College, Oxford OX2 6HD.

*Ramsay, G. D., MA, DPhil, 15 Charlbury Road, Oxford OX2 6UT.

Ramsey, Professor P. H., MA, DPhil, Taylor Building, King's College, Old Aberdeen.

Ranft, Professor B. McL., MA, DPhil, 16 Eliot Vale, SE3.

Ranger, Professor T., MA, DPhil, The University, Manchester M13 9PL.

Ransome, Miss M. E., MA, 16 Downside Crescent, NW3.

Rathbone, Eleanor, PhD, Flat 5, 24 Morden Road, SE3.

Rawley, Professor J. A., PhD, University of Nebraska, Lincoln, Nebraska 68508, U.S.A.

Ray, Professor R. D., BA, BD, PhD, University of Toledo, 2801 W. Bancroft Street, Toledo, Ohio 43606, U.S.A.

Read, Professor D., BLitt, MA, Darwin College, University of Kent at Canterbury, Kent CT2 7NY.

Reader, W. J., BA, PhD, 67 Wood Vale, N10 3DL.

Rees, Professor W., MA, DSc, DLitt, FSA, 2 Park Road, Penarth, Glam. CF6 2BD.

Reese, T. R., PhD, Institute of Commonwealth Studies, 27 Russell Square, WC1B 5DS.

Reeves, Miss M. E., MA, PhD, 38 Norham Road, Oxford.

Reid, Professor L. D., MA, PhD, 200 E. Brandon Road, Columbia, Mo. 65201, U.S.A.

Reid, Professor W. S., MA, PhD, University of Guelph, Guelph, Ontario, Canada.

Renold, Miss P., MA, 6 Forest Side, Worcester Park, Surrey.

Reynolds, Miss S. M. G., MA, 26 Lennox Gardens, SW1.

Richards, Rev. J. M., MA, BLitt, STL, Heythrop College, 11–13 Cavendish Square, W1M 0AN.

*Richards, R., MA, FSA, Gawsworth Hall, Gawsworth, Macclesfield, Cheshire.

Richardson, K. E., MA, PhD, Lanchester Polytechnic, Priory Street, Coventry.

Richardson, R. C., BA, PhD, Thames Polytechnic, London SE18.

Richardson, Professor W. C., MA, PhD, Louisiana State University, Baton Rouge, Louisiana, U.S.A.

Richter, M., DrPhil, Dept of Medieval History, University College, Dublin 4, Ireland.

Rigold, S. E., MA, FSA, 2 Royal Crescent, W11.

Riley, P. W. J., BA, PhD, The University, Manchester.

Riley-Smith, J. S. C., MA, PhD, 53, Hartinton Grove, Cambridge.

Rimmer, Professor, W. G., MA, PhD, University of New South Wales, P.O. Box 1, Kensington, N.S.W. 2033, Australia.

Ritcheson, Professor C. R., DPhil, 47 Chelsea Square, London SW3 6LH.

Roach, Professor J. P. C., MA, PhD, 1 Park Crescent, Sheffield S10 2DY.

Robbins, Professor Caroline, PhD, 815 The Chetwynd, Rosemont, Pa. 19010, U.S.A.

Robbins, Professor K. G., MA, DPhil, University College of North Wales, Bangor, Gwynedd.

Roberts, J. M., MA, DPhil, Merton College, Oxford OX1 4JD.

Roberts, Professor M., MA, DPhil, FilDr, FBA, 38 Somerset Street, Grahamstown, C.P., South Africa.

Roberts, Brig. M. R., DSO, Swallowfield Park, Swallowfield, Reading, Berks. RG7 1TG.

Roberts, P. R., MA, PhD, FSA, Keynes College, The University of Kent at Canterbury, Kent CT2 7NP.

Roberts, Professor R. C., PhD, 284 Blenheim Road, Columbus, Ohio 43214, U.S.A.

Roberts, Professor R. S., PhD, University of Rhodesia, Salisbury, P.B. 167H, Rhodesia.

*Robinson, Professor Howard, MA, PhD, LLD, 75 Elmwood Place, Oberlin, Ohio, U.S.A.

Robinson, K. E., CBE, MA, DLitt, LLD, The Old Rectory, Church Westcote, Kingham, Oxford OX7 6SF.

Robinson, R. A. H., BA, PhD, School of History, The University, Birmingham B15 2TT.

Robinton, Professor Madeline R., MA, PhD, 210 Columbia Heights, Brooklyn, New York, U.S.A.

*Rodkey, F. S., AM, PhD, 152 Bradley Drive, Santa Cruz, Calif., U.S.A.

Rodney, Professor W., MA, PhD, 14 Royal Roads Military College, Victoria, B.C., Canada.

Roe, F. Gordon, FSA, 19 Vallance Road, London N22 4UD.

Rogers, A., MA, PhD, FSA, The Firs, 227 Plains Road, Mapperley, Nottingham.

Rolo, Professor P. J. V., MA, The University, Keele, Staffordshire.

Roots, Professor I. A., MA, FSA, University of Exeter, Exeter EX4 4QH.

ROPER, M., MA (*Hon. Treasurer*), Public Record Office, Chancery Lane, London WC2A 1LR.

ROPER, J. S., MA (*Hon. Solicitor*), Sixland, 133 Tipton Road, Woodsetton, nr. Dudley, West Midlands.

Rose, P. L., MA, D.enHist (Sorbonne), Dept of History, James Cook University, Douglas, Queensland 4811, Australia.

Roseveare, H. G., PhD, King's College, Strand, WC2.

Roskell, Professor J. S., MA, DPhil, FBA, The University, Manchester M13 9PL.

Roskill, Captain S. W., CBE, DSC, RN(ret), Frostlake Cottage, Malting Lane, Cambridge CB3 9HF.

Ross, C. D., MA, DPhil, Wills Memorial Building, Queens Road, Bristol.

Rothney, Professor G. O., PhD, University of Manitoba, Winnipeg R3T 2N2, Canada.

Rothrock, Professor G. A., MA, PhD, University of Alberta, Edmonton, Alberta T6G 2E1, Canada.

Rothwell, Professor H., PhD, Hill House, Knapp, Ampfield, nr Romsey, Hants.

*Rowe, Miss B. J. H., MA, BLitt, St Anne's Cottage, Winkton, Christchurch, Hants.

Rowe, W. J., DPhil, 20 Seaview Avenue, Irby, Wirral, Merseyside L61 3UH.

Rowland, Rev. E. C., 8 Fay Street, Frankston, Victoria 3200, Australia.

Rowse, A. L., MA, DLitt, DCL, FBA, All Souls College, Oxford.

Roy, I., MA, DPhil, Dept of History, King's College, Strand, London WC2.

Roy, Professor R. H., MA, PhD, 2841 Tudor Avenue, Victoria, B.C., Canada.

Rubens, A., FRICS, FSA, 16 Grosvenor Place, SW1.

Rubini, D. A., DPhil, Temple University, Philadelphia, Penn., U.S.A.

Rubinstein, Professor N., PhD, Westfield College, Hampstead, NW3.

Ruddock, Miss A. A., PhD, FSA, Birkbeck College, Malet Street, WC1.

Rudé, Professor G. F. E., MA, PhD, Sir George Williams University, Montreal 107, P.Q., Canada.

*RUNCIMAN, The Hon. Sir Steven, MA, DPhil, LLD, LittD, DLitt, LitD, DD, DHL, FBA, FSA, Elshiesfields, Lockerbie, Dumfriesshire.

Rupp, Professor the Rev. E. G., MA, DD, FBA, 580 Newmarket Road, Cambridge CB5 8LL.

Russell, C. S. R., MA, Bedford College, NW1.
Russell, Mrs J. G., MA DPhil, St Hugh's College, Oxford.
Russell, Professor P. E., MA, 23 Belsyre Court, Woodstock Road, Oxford.
Ryan, A. N., MA, University of Liverpool, 8 Abercromby Square, Liverpool 7.
Ryder, A. F. C., MA, DPhil, University of Ibadan, Nigeria.

Sachse, Professor W. L., PhD, Dept of History, University of Wisconsin, Madison, Wis. 53706 U.S.A.
Sainty, J. S., MA, 22 Kelso Place, W8.
*Salmon, Professor E. T. MA, PhD, McMaster University, Hamilton, Ontario, Canada L85 4L9.
Salmon, Professor J. H. M., MA, MLitt, DLit, Bryn Mawr College, Bryn Mawr, Pa. 19101, U.S.A.
*Saltman, Professor A., MA, PhD, Bar Ilan University, Ramat Gan, Israel.
Samaha, Professor Joel, PhD, Dept of Criminal Justice Studies, University of Minnesota, Minneapolis, U.S.A.
Sammut, E., LLD, 4 Don Rue Street, Sliema, Malta.
Samuel, E. R., 8 Steynings Way, N12 7LN.
Sanders, I. J., MA, DPhil, Ceri, St Davids Road, Aberystwyth.
Sanderson, Professor G. N., MA, PhD, Dept of Modern History, Royal Holloway College, Englefield Green, Surrey.
Saville, Professor J., BSc(Econ), Dept of Economic and Social History, The University, Hull HU6 7RX.
Sawyer, Professor P. H., MA, The University, Leeds LS2 9JT.
Sayers, Miss J. E., MA, BLitt, FSA, 17 Sheffield Terrace, Campden Hill, W8
Scammell, G. V., MA, Pembroke College, Cambridge.
Scammell, Mrs J. M., MA, Clare Hall, Cambridge.
Scarisbrick, Professor J. J., MA, PhD, 35 Kenilworth Road, Leamington Spa, Warwickshire.
Schenck, H. G., MA, DPhil, Dr Jur, University College, Oxford.
Schoeck, Professor R. J., PhD, Folger Shakespeare Library, Washington, D.C. 20003, U.S.A.
Schofield, A. N. E. D., PhD, 15 Westergate, Corfton Road, W5.
Schofield, R. S., MA, PhD, 27 Trumpington Street, Cambridge CB2 1QA.
Scouloudi, Miss I. C., MSc(Econ), FSA, 67 Victoria Road, W8.
Seaborne, M. V. J., MA, Chester College, Cheyney Road, Chester CH1 4BJ.
Seary, Professor E. R., MA, PhD, LittD, DLitt, FSA, Memorial University of Newfoundland, St John's, Newfoundland, Canada.
Semmel, Professor Bernard, PhD, Dept of History, State University of New York at Stony Brook, Stony Brook, N.Y. 11790, U.S.A.
Serjeant, W. R., BA, 51 Derwent Road, Ipswich IP3 0QR.
Seton-Watson, C. I. W., MC, MA, Oriel College, Oxford.
Seton-Watson, Professor G. H. N., MA, FBA, Dept of Russian History, School of Slavonic Studies, London WC1.
Shackleton, R., MA, DLitt, LittD, FBA, FSA, Brasenose College, Oxford,
Shannon, R. T., MA, PhD, 84 Newmarket Road, Norwich, Norfolk.
Sharp, Mrs M., MA, PhD, 59 Southway, NW11 6SB.
Shaw, I. P., MA, 3 Oaks Lane, Shirley, Croydon, Surrey CR0 5HP.
*Shaw, R. C., MSc, FRCS, FSA, Orry's Mount, Kirk Bride, nr Ramsey, Isle of Man.

Shead, N. F., MA, BLitt, 16 Burnside Gardens, Clarkston, Glasgow.
Shennan, Professor J. H., PhD, Glenair, Moorside Road, Brookehouse, Caton, nr Lancaster.
Sheppard, F. H. W., MA, PhD, FSA, 55 New Street, Henley-on-Thames, Oxon RG9 2BP.
Sherborne, J. W., MA, 26 Hanbury Road, Bristol BS8 2EP.
Sigsworth, Professor E. M., BA, PhD, The University, Heslington, York.
Sillery, A., MA, DPhil, 24 Walton Street, Oxford.
Simmons, Professor J., MA, The University, Leicester.
Simpson, G. G., MA, PhD, FSA, Taylor Building, King's College, Old Aberdeen AB9 2UB.
Sinar, Miss J. C., MA, 60 Wellington Street, Matlock, Derbyshire DE4 3GS.
Siney, Professor Marion C., MA, PhD, 2676 Mayfield Road, Cleveland Heights, Ohio 44106, U.S.A.
Singhal, Professor D. P., MA, PhD, University of Queensland, St Lucia, Brisbane, Queensland, Australia 4067.
Skidelsky, Professor R., BA, PhD, Flat 1, 166 Cromwell Road, London SW5 0TJ.
Skinner, Q. R. D., MA, Christ's College, Cambridge.
Slack, P. A., MA, DPhil, Exeter College, Oxford OX1 3DP.
Slade, C. F., PhD, FSA, 28 Holmes Road, Reading, Berks.
Slater, A. W., MSc(Econ), 146 Castelnau, SW13 9ET.
Slatter, Miss M. D., MA, 32 Deanfield Road, Botley, Oxford OX2 9DW.
Slavin, Professor A. J., PhD, University of California, Los Angeles, Calif., U.S.A.
Smail, R. C., MBE, MA, PhD, FSA, Sidney Sussex College, Cambridge.
*Smalley, Miss B., MA, PhD, FBA, 5c Rawlinson Road, Oxford OX2 6UE.
Smith, A. G. R., MA, PhD, 40 Stanley Avenue, Paisley, Renfrewshire.
Smith, A. Hassell, BA, PhD, Inst. of East Anglian Studies, University of East Anglia, University Village, Norwich.
Smith, E. A., MA, Dept of History, Faculty of Letters, The University, Whiteknights, Reading RG6 2AA.
Smith, Professor F. B., MA, PhD, Dept of History, Australian National University, Canberra, A.C.T., Australia 2600.
Smith, Professor Goldwin A., MA, PhD, DLitt, Wayne State University, Detroit, Michigan 48202, U.S.A.
Smith, J. Beverley, M.A., University College, Aberystwyth SY23 2AX.
Smith, Professor L. Baldwin, PhD, Northwestern University, Evanston, Ill. 60201, U.S.A.
Smith, P., MA, DPhil, 81 St. Stephen's Road, West Ealing, London W13 8JA.
Smith, S., BA, PhD, Les Haies, 40 Oatlands Road, Shinfield, Reading, Berks.
Smith, W. J., MA, 5 Gravel Hill, Emmer Green, Reading, Berks.
*Smyth, Rev. Canon C. H. E., MA, 12 Manor Court, Pinehurst, Cambridge.
Snell, L. S., MA, FSA, Newman College, Bartley Green, Birmingham 32.
Snow, Professor V. F., MA, PhD, Dept of History, Syracuse University, 311 Maxwell Hall, Syracuse, New York 13210, U.S.A.
Snyder, Professor H. L., MA, PhD, 1324 Strong Avenue, Lawrence, Kansas 66044, U.S.A.
Soden, G. I., MA, DD, Buck Brigg, Hanworth, Norfolk.

Somers, Rev. H. J., JCB, MA, PhD, St Francis Xavier University, Antigonish, Nova Scotia.

Somerville, Sir Robert, KCVO, MA, FSA, 15 Foxes Dale, Blackheath, London SE3.

Sosin, Professor J. M., PhD, History Dept, University of Nebraska, Lincoln, Nebraska 68508, U.S.A.

SOUTHERN, Sir Richard (W.), MA, DLitt, LittD, DLitt, FBA, The President's Lodgings, St John's College, Oxford OX1 3JP.

Southgate, D. G., BA, DPhil, 40 Camphill Road, Broughty Ferry, Dundee, Scotland.

Speck, W. A., MA, DPhil, The University, Newcastle upon Tyne NE1 7RU.

Spencer, B. W., BA, FSA, 6 Carpenters Wood Drive, Chorleywood, Herts.

Spooner, Professor F. C., MA, PhD, The University, 23 Old Elvet, Durham DH1 3HY.

Spufford, Mrs H. Margaret, MA, PhD, 101 Horwood, The University, Keele, Staffs ST5 5BG.

Spufford, P., MA, PhD, The University, Keele, Staffs ST5 5BG.

Stanley, Professor G. F. G., MA, BLitt, DPhil, Library, Mount Alison University, Sackville, New Brunswick, Canada.

Stansky, Professor Peter, PhD, Dept of History, Stanford University, Stanford, Calif. 94305, U.S.A.

Steefel, Professor L. D., MA, PhD, 3549 Irving Avenue South, Minneapolis, Minn. 55408 U.S.A.

Steele, E. D., MA, PhD, The University, Leeds LS2 9JT.

Steer, F. W., MA, DLitt, FSA, 63 Orchard Street, Chichester, Sussex.

Steinberg, J., MA, PhD, Trinity Hall, Cambridge.

Steiner, Mrs Zara S., MA, PhD, New Hall, Cambridge.

Stéphan, Rev. Dom John, OSB, FSA, St Mary's Abbey, Buckfast, Buckfastleigh, Devon.

Stephens, W. B., MA, PhD, FSA, 37 Batcliffe Drive, Leeds 6.

Steven, Miss M. J. E., PhD, University of Western Australia, Perth, W. Australia 6009.

Stewart, A. T. Q., MA, PhD, The Queen's University, Belfast BT7 1NN.

Stitt, F. B., BA, BLitt, William Salt Library, Stafford.

Stone, E., MA, DPhil, FSA, Keble College, Oxford.

Stone, Professor L., MA, Princeton Univesrity, Princeton, N.J., U.S.A.

*Stones, Professor E. L. G., PhD, FSA, Dept. of History, The University, Glasgow G12 8QH.

Storey, Professor R. L., MA, PhD, 19 Elm Avenue, Beeston, Nottingham NG9 1BU.

*Stoye, J. W., MA, DPhil, Magdalen College, Oxford.

Street, J., MA, PhD, 6 Thulborn Close, Teversham, Cambridge.

Strong, Mrs F., MA, South Cloister, Eton College, Windsor SL4 6DB.

Strong, R., BA, PhD, FSA, Victoria & Albert Museum, London SW7.

Stuart, C. H., MA, Christ Church, Oxford.

Styles, P., MA, FSA, 21 Castle Lane, Warwick.

Supple, Professor B. E., BSc(Econ), PhD, Dept of Econ. and Social History, The University of Sussex, Falmer, Brighton BN1 9QQ.

Surman, Rev. C. E., MA, 352 Myton Road, Leamington Spa CV31 3NY.

Sutherland, Professor D. W., DPhil, State University of Iowa, Iowa City, Iowa 52240, U.S.A.

SUTHERLAND, Dame Lucy, DBE, MA, DLitt, LittD, DCL, FBA, 59 Park Town, Oxford.
Sutherland, N. M., MA, PhD, St John's Hall, Bedford College, NW1.
Swanton, M. J., BA, PhD, FSA, The University, Exeter EX4 4QH.
Swart, Professor K. W., PhD, LittD, University College, Gower Street, London WC1E 6BT.
Sydenham, M. J., PhD, Carleton University, Ottawa 1, Canada.
Sylvester, Professor R. S., PhD, The Yale Edition of the works of St Thomas More, 1986 Yale Station, New Haven, Conn. U.S.A.
Syrett, Professor D., PhD, 46 Hawthorne Terrace, Leonia, N.J. 07605, U.S.A.

Talbot, C. H., PhD, BD, FSA, 47 Hazlewell Road, SW15.
Tanner, J. I., MA, PhD, Flat One, 57 Drayton Gardens, SW10 9RU.
Tanner, L. E., CVO, MA, DLitt, FSA, 32 Westminster Mansions, Great Smith Street, Westminster SW1P 3BP.
Tarling, Professor P. N., MA, PhD, LittD, University of Auckland, Private Bag, Auckland New Zealand.
Taylor, Arnold J., CBE, MA, DLitt, FBA, FSA, Rose Cottage, Lincoln's Hill, Chiddingfold, Surrey GU8 4UN.
Taylor, Professor Arthur J., MA, The University, Leeds LS2 9JT.
Taylor, J., MA, The University, Leeds LS2 9JT.
Taylor, J. W. R., 36 Alexandra Drive, Surbiton, Surrey KT5 9AF.
Taylor, W., MA, PhD, FSAScot, 25 Bingham Terrace, Dundee.
Temple, Nora C., BA, PhD, University College, Cardiff.
Templeman, G., MA, PhD, FSA, 22 Ethelbert Road, Canterbury, Kent.
Thirsk, Mrs I. J., PhD, St Hilda's College, Oxford OX4 1DY.
Thistlethwaite, F., MA, LHD, University of East Anglia, Norwich NR4 7JT.
Thomas, Professor H. S., MA, University of Reading, Reading.
Thomas, Rev. J. A., MA, PhD, 164 Northfield Lane, Brixham, Devon.
Thomas, K. V., MA, St John's College, Oxford OX1 3JP.
Thomas, P. G. D., MA, PhD, University College, Aberystwyth SY23 2AU.
Thomas, W. E. S., MA, Christ Church, Oxford OX1 1DP.
Thomis, M. I., MA, PhD, 28 Keir Street, Bridge of Allan, Stirlingshire.
Thompson, A. F., MA, Wadham College, Oxford OX1 3PN.
Thompson, Mrs D. K. G., MA, School of History, The University, Birmingham.
Thompson, E. P., MA, Warwick University, Coventry.
Thompson, Professor F. M. L., MA, DPhil, Bedford College, Regent's Park NW1 4NS.
Thomson, J. A. F., MA, DPhil, The University, Glasgow W2.
*Thomson, T. R. F., MA, MD, FSA, Cricklade, Wilts.
Thorne, C., BA, School of European Studies, University of Sussex, Brighton.
Thorne, Professor S. E., MA, LLB, FSA, Harvard Law School, Cambridge, Mass., U.S.A.
Thornton, Professor A. P., MA, DPhil, 11 Highbourne Road, Toronto 7, Canada.
Thorpe, Professor Lewis, BA, LèsL, PhD, Ddel'U, FIAL, FSA, FRSA, 26 Parkside, Wollaton Vale, Nottingham NG8 2NN.
*Thrupp, Professor S. L., MA, PhD, University of Michigan, Ann Arbor, Mich., 48104, U.S.A.

Thurlow, The Very Rev. A. G. G., MA, FSA, Dean of Gloucester, The Deanery, Gloucester.
Tibbutt, H. G., FSA, 12 Birchdale Avenue, Kempston, Bedford.
Titterton, Commander G. A., RN(ret), Flat 4, Clarence House, 8 Granville Road, Eastbourne, Sussex.
Tomkeieff, Mrs O. G., MA, LLB, 88 Moorside North, Newcastle upon Tyne NE4 9DU.
Toynbee, Miss M. R., MA, PhD, FSA, 22 Park Town, Oxford OX2 6SH.
Trebilcock, R. C., MA, Pembroke College, Cambridge CB2 1RF.
*Trevor-Roper, Professor H. R., MA, FBA, Oriel College, Oxford.
Trickett, Professor The Rev. A. Stanley, MA, PhD, 236 South Lake Drive, Lehigh Acres, Florida, 33936, U.S.A.
Tyacke, N. R. N., MA, DPhil, 1a Spencer Rise, London NW5.
Tyler, P., BLitt, MA, DPhil, University of Western Australia, Nedlands, Western Australia 6009.

Ugawa, Professor K., BA, MA, PhD, 1008 Ikebukuro, 2 Chome, Toshima, Tokyo 171, Japan.
Ullmann, Professor W., MA, LittD, Trinity College, Cambridge.
Underdown, Professor David, PhD, Dept of History, Brown University, Providence, Rhode Island 02912, U.S.A.
Underhill, C. H., The Lodge, Needwood, Burton-upon-Trent, Staffs DE13 9PQ.
Upton, A. F., MA, 5 West Acres, St Andrews, Fife.
Urry, W. G., PhD, FSA, St Edmund Hall, Oxford.

Vaisey, D. G., MA, FSA, 12 Hernes Road, Oxford.
Vale, M. G. A., MA, DPhil, Dept of History, The University, Heslington, York. YO1 5DD.
Van Caenagem, Professor R. C., LLD, Veurestraat 18, 9821 Afsnee, Belgium.
Van Cleve, Professor T. C., MA, PhD, DLitt, Bowdoin College, Brunswick, Maine, U.S.A.
Vann, Professor Richard T., PhD, Dept of History, Wesleyan University, Middletown, Conn. 06457, U.S.A.
*Varley, Mrs J., MA, FSA, 164 Nettleham Road, Lincoln.
Vaughan, Sir (G.) Edgar, KBE, MA, 27 Birch Grove, West Acton, London W3 9SP.
Veale, Elspeth M., BA, PhD, Goldsmith's College, New Cross, London SE14 6NW.
Véliz, Professor C., BSc, PhD, Dept of Sociology, La Trobe University Melbourne, Victoria, Australia.
Vessey, D. W. T. C., MA, PhD, 10 Uphill Grove, Mill Hill, London NW7.
Villiers, Lady de, MA, BLitt, 4 Church Street, Beckley, Oxford.
Virgoe, R., BA, PhD, University of East Anglia, Norwich.

Waddell, Professor D. A. G., MA, DPhil, University of Stirling, Stirling FK9 4LA.
*Wagner, Sir Anthony R., KCVO, MA, DLitt, FSA, College of Arms, Queen Victoria Street, EC4.
Waites, B. F., MA, FRGS, 6 Chater Road, Oakham, Rutland LE15 6RY.
Walcott, Professor R., MA, PhD, The College of Wooster, Wooster, Ohio 44691 U.S.A.

Waley, D. P., MA, PhD, Dept of Manuscripts, British Museum, WC1B 3DG.
Waford, A. J., MA, PhD, FLA, 45 Parkside Drive, Watford, Herts.
Walker, Rev. Canon D. G., DPhil, FSA, University College, Swansea.
Wallace, Professor W. V., MA, New University of Ulster, Coleraine, N. Ireland.
Wallace-Hadrill, Professor J. M., MA, DLitt, FBA, All Souls College, Oxford OX1 4AL.
Wallis, Miss H. M., MA, DPhil, FSA, 96 Lord's View, St John's Wood Road, NW8 7HG.
Wallis, P. J., MA, 27 Westfield Drive, Newcastle upon Tyne NE3 4XY.
Walne, P., MA, FSA, County Record Office, County Hall, Hertford.
Walsh, T. J., MB, MB, BCh, PhD, MA, LC, 5 Lower George Street, Wexford, Ireland.
Walters, (W.) E., MA, Burrator, 355 Topsham Road, Exeter.
Wangermann, E., MA, DPhil, The University, Leeds LS2 9JT.
*Ward, Mrs G. A., PhD, FSA, Unsted, 51 Hartswood Road, Brentwood, Essex.
Ward, Professor J. T., MA, PhD, Dept of Economic History, McCance Bldg., 16 Richmond Street, Glasgow C1 1XQ.
Ward, Professor W. R., DPhil, University of Durham, 43 North Bailey, Durham.
*Warmington, Professor E. H., MA, 48 Flower Lane, NW7.
Warren, Professor W. L., MA, DPhil, FRSL, The Queen's University, Belfast, N. Ireland BT7 1NN.
*Waterhouse, Professor E. K., CBE, MA, AM, FBA, Overshot, Badger Lane, Hinksey Hill, Oxford.
*Waters, Lt-Commander D. W., RN, FSA, Jolyons, Bury, nr Pulborough, West Sussex.
Watkin, Rev. Dom Aelred, OSB, MA, FSA, St. Benet's, Beccles, Suffolk NR34 9NR.
Watson, A. G., MA, BLitt, FSA, University College, Gower Street, London WC1E 6BT.
Watson, D. R., MA, BPhil, Department of Modern History, The University, Dundee.
Watson, J. S., MA, The University, College Gate, North Street, St Andrews, Fife, Scotland.
Watt, Professor D. C., MA, London School of Economics, Houghton Street, WC2.
Watt, D. E. R., MA, DPhil, Dept of Mediaeval History, St Salvator's College, St Andrews, Fife, Scotland.
Watt, J. A., BA, PhD, The University, Hull HU6 7RX.
Webb, J. G., MA, 11 Blount Road, Pembroke Park, Old Portsmouth, Hampshire PO1 2TD.
Webb, Professor R. K., PhD, 3307 Highland Place N.W., Washington DC 20008, U.S.A.
Webster (A.) Bruce, MA, FSA, 5 The Terrace, St Stephens, Canterbury.
Webster, C., MA, DSc, Corpus Christi College, Oxford.
Wedgwood, Dame Veronica, OM, DBE, MA, LittD, DLitt, LLD, 22 St Ann's Terrace, St John's Wood, NW8.
Weinbaum, Professor M., PhD, 133-33 Sanford Avenue, Flushing, N.Y. 11355, U.S.A.
Weinstock, Miss M. B., MA, 26 Wey View Crescent, Broadway, Weymouth, Dorset.

280 LIST OF FELLOWS

Wernham, Professor R. B., MA, Marine Cottage, 63 Hill Head Road, Hill Head, Fareham, Hants.
*Weske, Mrs Dorothy B., AM, PhD, Oakwood, Sandy Spring, Maryland 20860, U.S.A.
West, Professor F. J., PhD, Dept of History, The University College at Buckingham, Old Bank Building, 2 Bridge Street, Buckingham.
Weston, Professor Corinne C, PhD, 200 Central Park South, New York N.Y. 10019, U.S.A.
*Whatmore, Rev. L. E., MA, St Wilfred's South Road, Hailsham, Sussex.
Whelan, Rev. C. B., OSB, MA, Belmont Abbey, Hereford.
White, Professor B. M. I., MA, DLit, FSA, 3 Upper Duke's Drive, East-bourne, Sussex BN20 7XT.
White, Rev. B. R., MA, DPhil, 55 St Giles', Regent's Park College, Oxford.
*Whitelock, Professor D., CBE, MA, LittD, FBA, FSA, 30 Thornton Close, Cambridge.
Whiteman, Miss E. A. O., MA, DPhil, FSA, Lady Margaret Hall, Oxford OX2 6QA.
Wiener, Professor J. H., BA, PhD, City College of New York, Convent Avenue at 138 Street, New York, 10031 U.S.A.
Wilkinson, Rev. J. T., MA, DD, Brantwood, 3 The Dingle, Farrington Lane, Knighton, Powys LD7 1LD.
Wilks, M. J., MA, PhD, Dept of History, Birkbeck College, Malet Street, London WC1E 7HX.
*Willan, Professor T. S., MA, DPhil, 3 Raynham Avenue, Didsbury, Manchester M20 0BW.
Williams, Professor C. H., MA, 6 Blackfriars, Canterbury.
Williams, D., MA, PhD, DPhil, University of Calgary, Calgary, Alberta T2N 1N4, Canada.
Williams, Sir Edgar (T.), CB, CBE, DSO, MA, Rhodes House, Oxford.
Williams, Professor Glanmor, MA, DLitt, University College, Swansea,
Williams, Glyndwr, BA, PhD, Queen Mary College, Mile End Road, E1.
Williams, Professor G. A., MA, PhD, University of Wales, Cathay's Park, Cardiff CF1 3NS.
Williams, J. A., BSc(Econ), MA, 44 Pearson Park, Hull, E. Yorks HU5 2TG.
Williams, N. J., MA, DPhil, FSA, 57 Rotherwick Road, NW11 7DD.
Williams, P. H., MA, DPhil, New College, Oxford OX1 3BN.
*Williams, T. G., MA, 63 Eardley Crescent, SW5.
*Wilson, Professor A., McC, MA, PhD, 1 Brookside, Norwich, Vermont 05055, U.S.A.
Wilson, Professor C. H., MA, FBA, Jesus College, Cambridge.
Wilson, Professor D. M., MA, FSA, Department of Scandinavian Studies, University College, Gower Street, London WC1E 6BT.
Wilson, H. S., BA, BLitt, The University, Heslington, York YO1 5DD.
Wilson, Professor T., MA, DPhil, Dept of History, University of Adelaide, Adelaide, South Australia.
Winks, Professor R. W. E., MA, PhD, 648 Berkeley College, Yale University, New Haven, Conn. 06520, U.S.A.
Wiswall, F. L., PhD, 55 Du Bois Street, Darien, Conn. 06820, U.S.A.
Withrington, D. J., MA, MEd, Centre for Scottish Studies, King's College, University of Aberdeen, Old Aberdeen AB9 2UB.
Wolffe, B. P., MA, BLitt, DPhil, Highview, 19 Rosebarn Avenue, Exeter EX4 6DY.

*Wood, Rev. A. Skevington, PhD, Ridgeway, Curbar, Sheffield S30 1XD.
Wood, Mrs S. M., MA, BLitt, St Hugh's College, Oxford.
Woodfill, Professor W. L., PhD, University of California, Davis, Calif. 95616, U.S.A.
Wood-Legh, Miss K. L., BLitt, PhD, DLitt, 49 Owlstone Road, Cambridge.
Woods, J. A., MA, PhD, The University, Leeds 2.
Woolf, Professor S. J., MA, DPhil, University of Essex, Wivenhoe Park, Colchester CO4 3SQ.
Woolrych, Professor A. H., BLitt, MA, Patchetts, Caton, nr Lancaster.
Worden, A. B., MA, DPhil, St Edmund Hall, Oxford OX1 4AR.
Wormald, B. H. G., MA, Peterhouse, Cambridge CB2 1RD.
Wortley, The Rev. J. T., MA, PhD, History Dept, University of Manitoba, Winnipeg, Manitoba R3T 2N2, Canada.
Wright, Professor E., MA, Institute of United States Studies, 31 Tavistock Square, London WC1H 9EZ.
Wright, L. B., PhD, 3702 Leland Street, Chevy Chase, Md. 20015, U.S.A.
Wright, Maurice, MA, PhD, Dept of International Politics, University College of Wales, Aberystwyth, Dyfed SY23 2AX.
Wroughton, J. P., MA, 11 Powlett Court, Bath, Avon BA2 6QJ.

Yates, W. N., MA, City Record Office, The Guildhall, Portsmouth PO1 2AL.
Yost, Professor John K., Dept of History, University of Nebraska, Lincoln, Neb. 68508, U.S.A.
Youings, Professor Joyce A., PhD, The University, Exeter EX4 4QH.
Young, Brigadier P., DSO, MC, MA, FSA, Bank House, Ripple, Tewkesbury, Glos. GL20 6EP.

Zagorin, Professor P., PhD, 4927 River Road, Scottsville, N.Y. 14546.
Zeldin, T., MA, DPhil, St Antony's College, Oxford OX2 6JF.

ASSOCIATES OF THE
ROYAL HISTORICAL SOCIETY

Addy, J., MA, PhD, 66 Long Lane, Clayton West, Huddersfield HD8 9PR.
Anderson, Miss S. P., MA, BLitt, 5 Spring Street, London W2 3RA.

Baird, Rev. E. S., BD, The Vicarage, Harrington, Workington, Cumberland.
Begley, M. R., 119 Tennyson Avenue, King's Lynn, Norfolk.
Bird, E. A., 29 King Edward Avenue, Rainham, Essex RNL3 9RH.
Brake, The Rev. G. Thompson, 19, Bethell Avenue, Ilford, Essex.
Bratt, C., 65 Moreton Road, Upton, Wirral, Cheshire.
Brigg, Mrs M., The Hollies, Whalley Road, Wilpshire, Blackburn, Lancs.
Brocklesby, R., BA, The Elms, North Eastern Road, Thorne, nr Doncaster, York.
Bryant, W. N., MA, PhD, College of S. Mark and S. John, Derriford Road, Plymouth, Devon.
Bullivant, C. H., FSA, Sedgemoor House, Warden Road, Minehead, Somerset.
Burton, Commander R. C., RN(ret), Great Streele Oasthouse, Framfield, Sussex.
Butler, Mrs M. C., MA, 4 Castle Street, Warkworth, Morpeth, Northumberland NE65 0UW.

Cairns, Mrs W. N., MA, Alderton House, New Ross, Co. Wexford, Eire.
Carter, F. E. L., CBE, MA, 8 The Leys, London N2 0HE.
Cary, R. H., BA, 23 Bath Road, W4.
Chandra, Shri Suresh, MA, MPhil, 90–36, 155th Street, Jamaica, New York 11432.
Condon, Miss M. M., BA, 56 Bernard Shaw House, Knatchbull Road, London NW10.
Cook, Rev. E. T., 116 Westwood Park, SE23 3QH.
Cooper, Miss J. M., MA, PhD, 203B Woodstock Road, Oxford.
Cox, A. H., Winsley, 11A Bagley Close, West Drayton, Middlesex.
Creighton-Williamson, Lt.-Col D., Foxhills, 25 Salisbury Road, Farnborough, Hants.

d'Alton I, BA, 5 Cosin Court, Peterhouse, Cambridge.
Davies, The Rev. M. R., MA, BD, MTh, The Manse, Nazareth Road, Pontyates, Llanelli, Dyfed, S. Wales.
Dawson, Mrs S. L., 5 Sinclair Street, Nkana/Kitwe, Zambia.
Dowse, Rev. I. R., Y Caplandy (The Cathedral Chaplain's House), Glanrafon, Bangor, Caerns. LL57 1LH.
Draffen of Newington, George, MBE, KLJ, MA, Meadowside, Balmullo, Leuchars, Fife KY16 0AW.
Drew, J. H., MA, FRSA, 19 Forge Road, Kenilworth, Warwickshire.

Emberton, W. J., Firs Lodge, 13 Park Lane, Old Basing, Basingstoke Hants.
Emsden, N., Strathspey, Lansdown, Bourton-on-the-Water. Cheltenham, Glos. GL54 2AR.

Fawcett, Rev. T. J., BD, PhD, 4 The College, Durham DH1 3EH.

Ferguson, J. T., MA, Fayerweather Hall, Columbia University, New York N Y., U.S.A.
Field, C. W., FSG, The Twenty-Sixth House, Robertsbridge, Sussex TN32 5AQ.
Fitzwilliam, B. R., ACP, ThA, Rockhampton Grammar School, Archer Street, Rockhampton, Queensland 4700, Australia.
Fryer, J., BA, Greenfields, Whitemore, nr Congleton, Cheshire.

Gardner, W. M., Chequertree, Wittersham, nr Tenterden, Kent.
Granger, E. R., Bluefield, Blofield, Norfolk.
Greatrex, Mrs J. G., MA, Dept of History, St Patrick's College, Carleton University, Colonel By Drive, Ottawa K1S 1N4, Canada.
Green, P. L., MA, 9 Faulkner Street, Gate Pa, Tauranga, New Zealand.
Griffiths, Rev. G. Ll., MA, BD, Rhiwlas, 10 Brewis Road, Rhos-on-Sea, Colwyn Bay, Denbighs.

Haines, F. D., PhD, Southern Oregon College, Ashland, Oregon, U.S.A.
Hall, P. T., Accrington College of Further Education, Sandy Lane, Accrington, Lancs.
Hanawalt, Mrs B. A., MA, PhD, Indiana University, Bloomington, Ind. 47401, U.S.A.
Hannah, L., MA, DPhil, Emmanuel College, Cambridge.
Harding, Rev. F. A. J., BSc(Econ), 74 Beechwood Avenue, St Albans.
Hardy, Rev. P. E., The Manse, 20 Victoria Road, Hanham, Bristol.
Hawtin, Miss G., BA, PhD, FSAScot, FRSAI, Honey Cottage, 5 Clifton Road, London SW19 4QX.
Heal, Mrs F., PhD, 13 Friar Road, Brighton, Sussex.
Heath, P., MA, Dept of History, The University, Hull HU6 7RX.
Henderson-Howat, Mrs A. M. D., 7 Lansdown Crescent, Edinburgh EH12 5EQ.
Henriques, Miss U. R. Q., BA, BLitt, 4 Campden Hill Square, W11.
Hoare, E. T., 70 Addison Road, Enfield, Middx.
Hodge, Mrs G., 85 Hadlow Road, Tonbridge, Kent.
Hope, R. B., MA, MEd, PhD, 5 Partis Way, Newbridge Hill, Bath, Avon BA1 3QG.
Hopewell, S., MA, Headmaster's House, Royal Russell School, Addington, Croydon, Surrey CR9 5BX.
Hughes, R. G., 'Hafod', 92 Main Road, Smalley, Derby DE7 6DS.
Hunt, J. L., 90 Woodside, Leigh-on-Sea, Essex SS9 4RB.
Hunt, J. W., MA, 123 Park Road, Chiswick W4.

Jarvis, L. D., Middlesex Cottage, 86 Mill Road, Stock, Ingatestone, Essex.
Jermy, K. E., MA, 8 Thelwall New Road, Thelwall, Warrington, Cheshire WA4 2JF.
Jerram-Burrows, Mrs L. E., Parkanaur House, 88 Sutton Road, Rochford, Essex.
Johnston, F. R., MA, 20 Russell Street, Eccles, Manchester.
Johnstone, H. F. V., 96 Wimborne Road, Poole, Dorset.
Joy, E. T., MA, BSc(Econ), The Rotunda, Ickworth, Bury St Edmunds, Suffolk IP29 5QE.

Keir, Mrs G. I., BA, 25 Catton Gardens, Bath, Avon.
Kennedy, M. J., BA, Dept of Medieval History, The University, Glasgow G12 8QQ.

Kirk, J., MA, PhD, Dept of Scottish History, The University, Glasgow G12 8QQ

Kitching, C. J., BA, PhD, Flat 3, 62 Messina Avenue, London NW6.

Knight, G. A., BA, 46 Bold Street, Pemberton, Wigan, Lancs. WN5 9E2.

Knowlson, Rev. G. C. V., St John's Vicarage, Knutsford Road, Wilmslow, Cheshire.

Laws, Captain W. F., MLitt, University of Otago, P.O. Box 56 Dunedin, New Zealand.

Lea, R. S., MA, 29 Crestway, SW15.

Lee, Professor M. duP, PhD, Douglass College, Rutgers University, NB, NJ 08903, U.S.A.

Lewin, Mrs J., MA, 3 Sunnydale Gardens, Mill Hill NW7.

Lewis, J. B., MA, CertEd, FRSA, 11 Hawkesbury Road, Buckley, Clwyd CH7 3HR.

Lewis, Professor N. B., MA, PhD, 8 Westcombe Park Road SE3 7RB.

Loach, Mrs J., MA, Somerville College, Oxford.

McIntyre, Miss S. C., BA, Lady Margaret Hall, Oxford.

McLeod, D. H., BA, PhD, School of History, Warwick University, Coventry CV4 7AL.

Mansfield, Major A. D., 38 Churchfields, West Mersea, Essex.

Mathews, E. F. J., BSc(Econ), PhD, 2 Park Lake Road, Poole, Dorset.

Meatyard, E., BA, DipEd, Guston, Illtyd Avenue, Llantwit Major, Glam. CF6 9TG.

Meek, D. E., MA, Dept of Celtic, The University, Glasgow G12 8QQ.

Metcalf, D. M., MA, DPhil, 40 St. Margaret's Road, Oxford OX2 6LD.

Mills, H. J., BSc, MA, 71 High Street, Billingshurst, West Sussex.

Morgan, D. A. L., MA, Dept of History, University College, Gower Street, London WC1E 6BT.

Nagel, L. C. J., BA, 21 Sussex Mansions, Old Brompton Road, London SW7.

Newman, L. T., LRIC, CEng, MIGasE, AMInstF, 12 Gay Bowers, Hockley, Essex.

Nicholls, R. E., MA, PhD, Glenholm, Hook Road, Surbiton, Surrey.

Obelkevich, J., MA, (address unknown).

O'Day, Mrs M. R., BA, PhD, 77A St Clements Street, Oxford OX4 1AW.

Oggins, R. S., PhD, c/o Dept of History SM, State University of New York, Binghampton 13901, U.S.A.

Oldham, C. R., MA, Te Whare, Walkhampton, Yelverton, Devon PL20 6PD.

Parsons, Mrs M. A., MA, (address unknown).

Partridge, Miss F. L., BA, 17 Spencer Gardens, SW14 7AH.

Pasmore, H. S., MB, BS, 21 Edwardes Square, W8.

Paton, L. R., 49 Lillian Road, Barnes, SW13.

Paulson, E., BSc(Econ), 11 Darley Avenue, Darley Dale, Matlock, Derbys.

Perry, E., FSAScot, 28 Forest Street, Hathershaw, Oldham, OL8 3ER.

Pitt, B. W. E., Flat 4, Red Roofs, Bath Road, Taplow, Maidenhead, Berks.

Priestley, E. J., MA, MPhil, 10 Kent Close, Bromborough, Wirral, Cheshire L63 0EF.

Raban, Mrs S. G., MA, PhD, Homerton College, Cambridge.
Rankin, Col. R. H., 3338 Gunston Road, Alexandria, Va. 22302, U.S.A.
Rendall, Miss J., BA, Alcuin College, University of York, Heslington, York.
Richards, N. F., PhD, 376 Maple Avenue, St Lambert, Prov. of Quebec, Canada.
Richmond, C. F., DPhil, 59 The Covert, The University, Keele, Staffs.
Rosenfield, M. C., AM, PhD, Box 395, Mattapoisett, Mass. 02739, U.S.A.

Sabben-Clare, E. E., MA, c/o The University Registry, Clarendon Building, Broad Street, Oxford.
Sainsbury, F., 16 Crownfield Avenue, Newbury Park, Ilford, Essex.
Saksena, D. N., First Secretary (Education), Embassy of India, Moscow U.S.S.R.
Scannura, C. G., 1/11 St. Dominic Street, Valetta, Malta.
Scott, The Rev. A. R., MA, BD, PhD, Ahorey Manse, Portadown, Co. Armagh, N. Ireland.
Seddon, P. R., BA, PhD, The University, Nottingham.
Sellers, J. M., MA, 9 Vere Road, Pietermaritzburg, Natal, S. Africa.
Sharpe, F., FSA, Derwen, Launton, Bicester, Oxfordshire OX6 0DP.
Shores, C. F., ARICS, 40 St Mary's Crescent, Hendon NW4 4LH.
Sibley, Major R. J., 8 Ways End, Beech Avenue, Camberley, Surrey.
Sloan, K., BEd, MPhil, 6 Netherland Close, Fixby, Huddersfield, Yorks.
Smith, Professor C. D., MA, PhD, 416 Hall of Languages, Syracuse University, Syracuse, N.Y., 13210, U.S.A.
Smith, D. M., Borthwick Institute, St Anthony's Hall, York.
Sorensen, Mrs M. O., MA, 8 Layer Gardens, W3 9PR.
Sparkes, I. G., FLA, 124 Green Hill, High Wycombe, Bucks.
Stafford, D. S., BA, 10 Highfield Close, Wokingham, Berks.

Taylor, R. T., MA, Dept of Political Theory and Government, University College, Swansea SA2 8PP.
Thewlis, J. C., BA, The University, Hull HU6 7RX.
Thomas, Miss E. J. M., 8 Ravenscroft Road, Northfield End, Henley-on-Thames, Oxon.
Thompson, C. L. F., MA, Orchard House, Stanford Road, Orsett, nr. Grays, Essex, RM16 3BX.
Thompson, L. F., Orchard House, Stanford Road, Orsett, nr Grays, Essex RM16 3BX.
Thorold, M. B., 20 Silsoe House, Park Village East, London NW1 4AS.
Tomlinson, H. C., Flat 2, 40 Leverton Street, London NW5.
Tracy, J. N., BA, MPhil, Phd, c/o P. Huth Esq, 6 Chaucer Court, 28 New Dover Road, Canterbury, Kent.
Tristram, B., DipEd, (address unknown).
Tuffs, J. E., 360 Monega Road, Manor Park E12 6TY.

Waldman, T. G., MA, 131 Riverside Drive, New York, N.Y., 10024, U.S.A.
Wall, Rev. J., BD, MA, Ashfield, 45 Middleton Lane, Middleton St George, nr Darlington, Co. Durham.
Wallis, K. W., BA, 48 Berkeley Square, W1.

Warrillow, E. J. D., MBE, FSA, Hill-Cote, Lancaster Road, Newcastle, Staffs.
Whiting, J. R. S., MA, DLitt, 15 Lansdown Parade, Cheltenham, Glos.
Wilkinson, F. J., 40 Great James Street, Holborn, London WC1N 3HB.
Williams, A. R., MA, 5 Swanswell Drive, Granley Fields, Cheltenham, Glos.
Williams, C. L. Sinclair, ISO, Derbies, Well Street, East Malling, Kent.
Williams, H., (address unknown).
Williams, Miss J. M., MA, History Dept, University of Auckland, Private Bag, Auckland, New Zealand.
Windrow, M. C., 40 Zodiac Court, 165 London Road, Croydon, Surrey.
Wood, A. W., 11 Blessington Close, SE13.
Wood, J. O., BA, MEd, Fountains, Monument Gardens, St Peter Port, Guernsey, C.I.
Woodall, R. D., BA, Bethel, 7 Wynthorpe Road, Horbury, nr Wakefield, Yorks WF4 5BB.
Woodfield, R., BD, MTh, 43 Playfield Crescent, SE22.
Worsley, Miss A. V., BA, 17 Essex Street, Forest Gate, London E7 0HL.
Wright, J. B., BA, White Shutters, Braunston, Rutland LE15 8QT.

Zerafa, Rev. M. J., St Dominic's Priory, Valletta, Malta.

CORRESPONDING FELLOWS

Andersson, Ingvar, FilDr, Engelbrektsgatan 6A IV, Stockholm, Sweden.

Bartoš, Professor F. M., PhDr, II, (address unknown).
Bischoff, Professor B., DLitt, 8033 Planegg C. München, Ruffini-Allee 27, Germany.
Braudel, Professor F., École Pratique des Hautes Études, 20 rue de la Baume, Paris VIIIe, France.

Cárcano, M. A., Centeno 3131, Buenos Aires, Argentina.
Coolhaas, Professor W. P., Gezichtslaan 71, Bilthoven, Holland.
Creighton, Professor D. G., MA, DLitt, LLD, Princess Street, Brooklin, Ontario, Canada.

Donoso, R., Presidente de la Sociedad Chilena de Historia y Geografía, Casilla, 1386, Santiago, Chile.

Ganshof, Professor F. L., 12 rue Jacques Jordaens, Brussels, Belgium.
Giusti Rt Rev. Mgr M., JCD, Prefect Archivio Segreto Vaticano, Vatican City, Italy.
Glamann, Professor K., DrPhil, Frederiksberg, Bredegade 13A, 2000 Copenhagen, Denmark.
Gwynn, Professor the Rev. A., SJ, MA, DLitt, Milltown Park, Dublin 6, Eire.

Hancock, Professor Sir Keith, KBE, MA, DLitt, FBA, Australian National University, Box 4, P.O., Canberra, ACT, Australia.
Hanke, Professor L. U., PhD, University of Massachusetts, Amherst, Mass. 01002, U.S.A.
Heimpel, Professor Dr H., DrPhil, Direktor des Max Planck-Instituts für Geschichte, Gottingen, Düstere Eichenweg 28, Germany.

Inalcik, Professor Halil, PhD, The University of Ankara, Ankara, Turkey.

Kuttner, Professor S., MA, JUD, SJD LLD, Institute of Medieval Canon Law, University of California, Berkeley, Calif. 94720, U.S.A.

Langer, Professor W. L., PhD, LLD, DPhil, LIID, LittD, 1 Berkeley Street, Cambridge, Mass. 02138, U.S.A.

Michel, Henri, 32 rue Leningrad, Paris 8e, France.
Morison, Professor S. E., PhD, LittD, Harvard College Library, 417 Cambridge, Mass., U.S.A.

Ostrogorsky, Professor G., The University, Belgrade, Yugoslavia.

Peña y Cámara, J. M. de la, (address unknown).
Perkins, Professor D., MA, PhD, LLD, University of Rochester, Rochester, N.Y., U.S.A.

Renouvin, Professor P., D-ès-L, 2 Boulevard Saint Germain, Paris, France.

Rodrígues, Professor José Honório, Rua Paul Redfern, 23, ap. C.O.1, Rio de Janeiro, Gb. ZC—37, Brasil.

Sapori, Professor A., Università Commerciale Luigi Bocconi, Via Sabbatini 8, Milan, Italy.

Van Houtte, Professor J. A., PhD, FBA, Termunkveld, Groeneweg 51, Egenhoven, Heverlee, Belgium.

Verlinden, Professor C., PhD, 8 Via Omero (Valle Giulia), Rome, Italy.

Zavala, S., LLD, (address unknown).

TRANSACTIONS AND PUBLICATIONS
OF THE
ROYAL HISTORICAL SOCIETY

The annual publications of the Society issued to Fellows and Subscribing Libraries include the *Transactions*, supplemented since 1897 by a continuation of the publications of the Camden Society (1838–97) as the *Camden Series*, and since 1937 by a series of *Guides and handbooks*. The Society also began in 1937 an annual bibliography of *Writings on British History*, for the continuation of which the Institute of Historical Research accepted responsibility in 1965; it publishes, in conjunction with the American Historical Association, a series of *Bibliographies of British History*; and from time to time it issues miscellaneous publications. Additional copies of the *Transactions*, the *Camden Series*, the *Guides and handbooks*, and the 'Miscellaneous publications' may be obtained by Fellows and Subscribing Libraries at the prices stated below. The series of annual bibliographies of *Writings on British History* and the *Bibliographies of British history* are not included among the volumes issued to subscribers, but may be obtained by them at the special prices stated below by ordering from a bookseller or from the publishers. Associates, while receiving only the *Transactions* in return for their subscription, are entitled to purchase at a reduction of 25 per cent one copy of other volumes issued to Fellows and Subscribing Libraries and one copy of each of the volumes of the *Writings on British history* and the *Bibliographies of British history* at the special price.

N.B. Current volumes of the *Transactions* and *Camden Series* (*i.e.* those for the current year and two years preceding) are not sold by the Society to the public, but are available only to members on application to the Society.

In the case of some of these volumes, it is possible for members to buy copies at a special price. Those who wish to take advantage of this arrangement are asked to contact the Society in the first place.

TRANSACTIONS

Additional copies of *Transactions* may be had for £5·00 (Special price to members, who should order from the Society, £3·75).

Volumes out of print in *Transactions, Old, New and Third Series* may be obtained from Kraus-Thomson Organisation Ltd.

Old series, 1872–82. Vols. I to X.
New series, 1884–1906. Vols. I to XX.
Third series, 1907–17. Vols. I to XI.
Fourth series, 1918–50. Vols. I to XXXII.
Fifth series, 1951–   . Vols. I to XXV.

MISCELLANEOUS PUBLICATIONS

Copies of the following, which are still in print, may be obtained from the Society, with the exception of *The Domesday Monachorum of Christ Church, Canterbury* and *The Royal Historical Society, 1868–1968*, which can be ordered from Dawsons of Pall Mall, Cannon House, Folkestone, Kent.

Domesday studies. 2 vols. Edited by P. E. Dove. 1886. £3·50. (Vol. 1 out of print.)

German opinion and German policy before the War. By G. W. Prothero. 1916. 75p.

The *Domesday monachorum* of Christ Church, Canterbury. 1944. £15.

Essays in Medieval History, selected from the Transactions of the Royal Historical Society. Edited by R. W. Southern. 1968. London, Macmillan. *p.b.*, 50p.

The Royal Historical Society, 1868–1968. By R. A. Humphreys. 1969. £1·25.

BIBLIOGRAPHIES ISSUED IN CONJUNCTION WITH THE AMERICAN HISTORICAL ASSOCIATION

Copies of the following cannot be supplied by the Society, but may be ordered through a bookseller. If members have difficulty in obtaining volumes at the special price, reference should be made to the Society.

Bibliography of British history: Stuart period, 1603–1714. 2nd ed. Edited by Mary F. Keeler, 1970. Oxford Univ. Press. £5. (Special price, £3·75.)

Supplement to Bibliography of British history: 1714–89. Edited by S. M. Pargellis and D. J. Medley. Edited by A. T. Milne and A. N. Newman, *in preparation.*

Bibliography of British history: 1789–1851. Edited by Ian R. Christie and Lucy M. Brown, *in preparation.*

Bibliography of British history: 1851–1914. Edited by H. J. Hanham, *in preparation.*

Bibliography of English History to 1485. Based on The Sources and Literature of English History from earliest times by Charles Gross. Revised and expanded by Edgar B. Graves. 1975. Oxford Univ. Press. £20. (Special price, £15.)

ANNUAL BIBLIOGRAPHIES

Copies of the following cannot be supplied by the Society, but may be ordered from a bookseller or the Institute of Historical Research.

Writings on British history, 1901–33 (5 vols. in 7); Vol. 1–3, 1968, Vol. 4, 1969, Vol. 5, 1970. London, Jonathan Cape. Vol. 1, £5·25 (special price £4·58); Vol. 2, £3·15 (special price £2·75); Vol. 3, £5·25 (special price £4·58); Vol. 4 (in two parts), £7·35 (special price £6·40); Vol. 5 (in two parts), £8·40 (special price £7·35).

Writings on British history, 1946–48. Compiled by D. J. Munro. 1973. University of London Inst. of Historical Research, £12·00. (Special price £9·00.)

GUIDES AND HANDBOOKS

Main series

1. Guide to English commercial statistics, 1696–1782. By G. N. Clark, with a catalogue of materials by Barbara M. Franks. 1938. £1·50.
2. Handbook of British chronology. Edited by F. M. Powicke and E. B. Fryde, 1st ed. 1939; 2nd ed. 1961. £4·50.
3. Medieval libraries of Great Britain, a list of surviving books. Edited by N. R. Ker, 1st ed. 1941; 2nd ed. 1964. £4·50.

4. Handbook of dates for students of English history. By C. R. Cheney. 1970. £1·50.
5. Guide to the national and provincial directories of England and Wales, excluding London, published before 1856. By Jane E. Norton. 1950. £2·00. (Out of print.)
6. Handbook of Oriental history. Edited by C. H. Philips. 1963. £2·25.
7. Texts and calendars: an analytical guide to serial publications. Edited by E. L. C. Mullins. 1958. £4·50.
8. Anglo-Saxon charters. An annotated list and bibliography. Edited by P. H. Sawyer. 1968. £5·25.
9. A Centenary Guide to the Publications of the Royal Historical Society, 1868–1968. Edited by A. T. Milne. 1968. £3·50.

Supplementary series

1. A Guide to Cabinet Ministers' papers, 1900–51. Edited by Cameron Hazlehurst and Christine Woodland. 1974. £3·00.

Provisionally accepted for future publication:

A Handbook of British Currency. Edited by P. Grierson and C. E. Blunt.

Texts and calendars: an analytical guide to serial publications. Supplement, 1958–68. By E. L. C. Mullins.

A Guide to the Local Administrative Units of England and Wales. Edited by F. A. Youngs.

A Register of Parliamentary Poll Books, c. 1700–1870. Edited by E. L. C. Mullins.

A Guide to Bishops' Register to 1640. Edited by D. M. Smith.

A Guide to the Records and Archives of Mass Communications. Edited by Nicholas Pronay.

A Guide to the Maps of the British Isles. Edited by Helen Wallis.

The Reports of the U.S. Strategic Bombing Survey. Edited by Gordon Daniels.

THE CAMDEN SERIES

Camdens published before the *Fourth Series* are listed in A. T. Milne's *A Centenary Guide to the Publications of the Royal Historical Society*.

Additional copies of volumes in the *Camden Series* may be had for £5·50 (Special price to members £4·15.)

Volumes out of print in the *Camden Old* and *New Series* may be obtained from Johnson Reprint Co. Ltd. Orders for out-of-print volumes in *Camden Third* and *Fourth Series* should be placed with Wm. Dawson & Sons, Ltd., Cannon House, Folkestone, Kent.

FOURTH SERIES

1. Camden Miscellany, Vol. XXII: 1. Charters of the Earldom of Hereford, 1095–1201. Edited by David Walker. 2. Indentures of Retinue with John of Gaunt, Duke of Lancaster, enrolled in Chancery, 1367–99. Edited by N. B. Lewis. 3. Autobiographical memoir of Joseph Jewell, 1763–1846. Edited by A. W. Slater. 1964.
2. Documents illustrating the rule of Walter de Wenlock, Abbot of Westminster, 1283–1307. Edited by Barbara Harvey. 1965.
3. The early correspondence of Richard Wood, 1831–41. Edited by A. B. Cunningham. 1966. (Out of print.)

4. Letters from the English abbots to the chapter at Cîteaux, 1442–1521. Edited by C. H. Talbot. 1967.
5. Select writings of George Wyatt. Edited by D. M. Loades. 1968.
6. Records of the trial of Walter Langeton. Bishop of Lichfield and Coventry (1307–1312). Edited by Miss A. Beardwood. 1969.
7. Camden Miscellany, Vol. XXIII: 1. The Account Book of John Balsall of Bristol for a trading voyage to Spain, 1480. Edited by T. F. Reddaway and A. A. Ruddock. 2. A parliamentary diary of Queen Anne's reign. Edited by W. A. Speck. 3. Leicester House politics, 1750–60, from the papers of John, second Earl of Egmont. Edited by A. N. Newman. 4. The Parliamentary diary of Nathaniel Ryder, 1764–67. Edited by P. D. G. Thomas. 1969.
8. Documents illustrating the British Conquest of Manila, 1762–63. Edited by Nicholas P. Cushner. 1971.
9. Camden Miscellany, Vol. XXIV: 1. Documents relating to the Breton succession dispute of 1341. Edited by M. Jones. 2. Documents relating to Anglo-French negotiations, 1439. Edited by C. T. Allmand. 3. A 'Fifteenth century chronicle' at Trinity College, Dublin. Edited by G. L. Harriss. 1972.
10. Herefordshire Militia Assessments of 1663. Edited by M. A. Faraday. 1972.
11. The early correspondence of Jabez Bunting, 1820–29. Edited by W. R. Ward. 1972.
12. Wentworth Papers, 1597–1628. Edited by J. P. Cooper. 1973.
13. Camden Miscellany, Vol. XXV: 1. The Letters of William, Lord Paget. Edited by Barrett L. Beer and Sybil Jack. 2. The Parliamentary Diary of John Clementson, 1770–1802. Edited by P. D. G. Thomas. 3. J. B. Pentland's Report on Bolivia, 1827. Edited by J. V. Fifer. 1974.
14. Camden Miscellany, Vol. XXVI: 1. Duchy of Lancaster Ordinances, 1483. Edited by Sir Robert Somerville. 2. A Breviat of the Effectes devised for Wales. Edited by P. R. Roberts. 3. Gervase Markham, The Muster-Master. Edited by Charles L. Hamilton. 4. Lawrence Squibb, A Booke of all the Severall Officers of the Court of the Exchequer (1642). Edited by W. H. Brysom. 5. Letters of Henry St John to Charles, Earl of Orrery, 1709–11. Edited by H. T. Dickinson. 1975.
15. Sidney Ironworks Accounts, 1541–73. Edited by D. W. Crossley. 1975.
16. The Account Book of Beaulieu Abbey. Edited by S. F. Hockey. 1975.
17. A calendar of Western Circuit Assize Orders, 1629–49. Edited by J. S. Cockburn (*in the press*).

Provisionally accepted for future publication:

Select documents illustrating the internal crisis of 1296–98 in England. Edited by Michael Prestwich.
The *Acta* of Archbishop Hugh of Rouen (1130–64). Edited by T. Waldman.
Cartularies of Reading Abbey. Edited by B. R. Kemp.
The Letter Book of Thomas Bentham, Bishop of Coventry and Lichfield. Edited by M. Rosemary O'Day and J. A. Berlatsky.
Correspondence of Henry Cromwell, 1655–59. Edited by Clyve Jones.
Correspondence of William Camden. Edited by Richard DeMolen.
Four English Political Tracts of the later Middle Ages. Edited by J.-Ph. Genet.
Heresy Trials in the Diocese of Norwich, 1428–31. Edited by N. P. Tanner.

Proceedings of the Short Parliament of 1640. Edited by Esther S. Cope in collaboration with Willson H. Coates.

George Rainsford's *Ritratto d'Ingliterra*, 1556. Edited by Peter S. Donaldson.

Early Paget Correspondence. Edited by C. J. Harrison and A. C. Jones.

The Letters of the Third Viscount Palmerston, 1804–63. Edited by Kenneth Bourne.

Edmund Ludlow's Memoir 1660–74: A Voyce from the Watch Tower. Edited by A. B. Worden.